Woodrow Wilson and the Roots of Modern Liberalism

D0947624

American Intellectual Culture
Series Editors: Jean Bethke Elshtain, University of Chicago;
Ted V. McAllister, Pepperdine University; and
Wilfred M. McClay, University of Tennessee at Chattanooga

Woodrow Wilson and the Roots of Modern Liberalism

Ronald J. Pestritto

ROWMAN & LITTLEFIELD PUBLISHERS, INC.
Lanham • Boulder • New York • Toronto • Oxford

ROWMAN & LITTLEFIELD PUBLISHERS, INC.

Published in the United States of America
by Rowman & Littlefield Publishers, Inc.
A wholly owned subsidary of The Rowman & Littlefield Publishing Group, Inc.
4501 Forbes Boulevard, Suite 200, Lanham, Maryland 20706
www.rowmanlittlefield.com

PO Box 317
Oxford
OX2 9RU, UK

Copyright © 2005 by Rowman & Littlefield Publishers, Inc.

British Library Cataloguing in Publication Information Available

Library of Congress Cataloging-in-Publication Data

Pestritto, Ronald J.
　　Woodrow Wilson and the roots of modern liberalism / Ronald J. Pestritto.
　　　　p. cm. — (American intellectual culture)
　　Includes bibliographical references and index.
　　ISBN 0-7425-1516-8 (cloth : alk. paper) — ISBN 0-7425-1517-6 (pbk. : alk.
paper)
　　　　1. Political science—United States. 2. Democracy—United States. 3.
Liberalism—United States. 4. Wilson, Woodrow, 1856–1924—Views on the
Constitution. 5. Wilson, Woodrow, 1856–1924—Political and social views. I.
Title. II. Series.

　　JA84.U5P47 2004
　　320.51'3'092—dc22　　　　　　　　　　　　　　　　　　2004014106

Printed in the United States of America

♾️™ The paper used in this publication meets the minimum requirements of American
National Standard for Information Sciences—Permanence of Paper for Printed Library
Materials, ANSI/NISO Z39.48-1992.

To my children,
Anthony, Carmelina, Sebastian, Angelo, and Dominic

Contents

Acknowledgments

I have received a great deal of assistance in producing this book. I acknowledge a debt of gratitude here, while accepting sole responsibility for the work's deficiencies. Most important, a substantial intellectual debt is owed to my teacher and friend, Charles R. Kesler, who first showed me the importance of Wilson to the American political tradition, and whose articles on the topic have substantially influenced my own research.

Work on the book was made possible primarily through the support of two organizations. The Claremont Institute for the Study of Statesmanship and Political Philosophy provided a generous research fellowship that allowed me to complete work on the manuscript. I am particularly grateful for the assistance and encouragement provided by the institute's president, Brian Kennedy, and the institute's former director of research, Glenn Ellmers. Initial work on the book was made possible by a yearlong sabbatical, which was generously provided by the John M. Olin Foundation. I thank the foundation and also Bradford P. Wilson, who facilitated the grant through the National Association of Scholars.

Several earlier projects led up to my work on the book, and I am especially grateful to the Earhart Foundation for making these possible. My home institution—the University of Dallas—also provided much appreciated support.

I am grateful for the comments of many individuals who read all or part of the manuscript. I would like to thank, in particular, James Stoner and Joseph Bessette for their time and assistance. I also profited from the comments and advice of John Grant and Thomas West, as well as my other colleagues in the University of Dallas Politics Department. Christopher Burkett provided much appreciated editorial assistance in the final stages of production.

I very much appreciate the time and energy spent by the editors of the American Intellectual Culture series at Rowman & Littlefield, and I am especially grateful to Wilfred McClay, who helped motivate me to write this book and remained a constant source of assistance and encouragement.

Finally, anyone who writes on Wilson these days would be remiss if he or she failed to acknowledge a debt to the late Arthur S. Link, Wilson's biographer who headed the effort to produce the sixty-nine-volume *Papers of Woodrow Wilson*, completed in 1993. While I never met Link and while my perspective on Wilson no doubt differs substantially from his, it is nonetheless the case that writing my book would have been impossible without the Wilson papers.

Introduction

Wilson, the Founding, and Historical Thinking

Woodrow Wilson is an important figure in American politics and history for many reasons. Most obvious, he served two terms as the twenty-eighth president of the United States—a presidency most known for its stewardship of American involvement in the First World War and for Wilson's failed attempt to sign America on to the League of Nations. Wilson also served a partial term as governor of New Jersey before he became president in 1912.[1] But in addition to his political life, Wilson was a prolific scholar and successful academic for more than two decades; he was, in fact, the only professional political scientist ever to become president of the United States. He taught at his alma mater, Princeton University, and became president of that institution in 1902. Before this, Wilson held academic posts at Bryn Mawr College and then Wesleyan University.

From the perspective of American domestic politics, Wilson may be most interesting as a key figure in the election of 1912. That election represented, arguably, the high-water mark of national progressive politics, the culmination of a decades-long intellectual movement that had been born in the latter part of the nineteenth century. Traditionally, the 1912 election is understood as a contest between the champion of nationalist progressivism, Theodore Roosevelt, and the relatively conservative Wilson. Wilson is viewed as wary of the vast discretionary power that Roosevelt proposed to give to national administrative agencies, and of the threat Roosevelt's program posed to the rightful role of the states in the American system of government. Progressive historians have even applied the "Hamiltonian versus Jeffersonian" distinction to portray the differences between Roosevelt and Wilson,[2] further cementing the image of Roosevelt as an ardent nationalist bent on empowering the administrative apparatus of the national government, and the image of Wilson as Roosevelt's states'-rights-oriented critic. One scholar even sees in

Wilson's 1912 victory the very end of the progressive movement,[3] a movement whose ideals would have to wait until the New Deal to see the light of day again, and even then in an altered form.

I take a different view of the 1912 election, one that sees the principles shared by Wilson and Roosevelt as far more significant than the particular policy stands that divided them in the rhetoric of the campaign.[4] As I will explain when the book returns to 1912 in the conclusion, the rhetorical policy differences between Wilson and Roosevelt collapse almost immediately after Wilson's victory, with Wilson adopting and implementing major portions of Roosevelt's New Nationalism. This is because both Wilson and Roosevelt subscribed to the ideas of progressivism; indeed, while both men were important parts of the progressive movement that led up to the 1912 campaign, the reason for this book's interest in Wilson is that he was far more relevant to the intellectual development of progressivism in America. In order to understand this, we must examine Wilson's substantial body of work prior to his entry into politics. Such an examination is the focus of this book.

While much scholarly work has been written on Wilson's presidency, especially in its international aspects, this book is interested in Wilson because he was a progressive thinker, and because of the important place of progressivism in the development of American political thought. This place can best be understood by seeing through the traditional "Hamiltonian" and "Jeffersonian" labels for figures in the progressive era, and understanding instead that in spite of their obvious differences, Hamilton and Jefferson had much more in common with each other than either of them had with the principles of progressivism. The ideas shared by Wilson and Roosevelt were very different from those shared by Hamilton and Jefferson. This is because progressivism—certainly as Wilson expounded it—understood itself as presenting a rationale for moving beyond the political thinking of the American founding. The aim here is to understand Wilson as he understood himself. And while it is no doubt the case that Wilson often understood his vision as one that was not inconsistent with the democratic *spirit* of the founding, his intellectual work also makes very clear that Wilson was engaged in a self-conscious rejection of the *theory* that had animated the founding era.

A prerequisite for national progress, Wilson believed, was that the founding be understood in its proper historical context. The principles of the founding, in spite of their claims of universality, were intended to deal with the unique circumstances of that day. And so Wilson looked instead to what he believed to be the democratic spirit of the founding—one that launched national government as a work-in-progress, a government that would require continual adjustment to historical circumstances as it tried to fulfill the broad democratic vision of the founders. But this interpretation of the founding ran up against the founders' own self-understanding, as Wilson well knew. This is why much of his scholarship is devoted to a reinterpretation and critique of both the political theory of the founding, and of the implementation of that theory in the institutional design of the national government. In other words, both the Declaration of Independence and the Constitution had to be understood anew through a progressive lens. In order to understand Wilson's reinterpretation of these documents, it is first necessary to discuss, with admitted brevity, how the founders themselves understood them.

THE FOUNDING

Even among those scholars who seek to understand the founders as they understood themselves, there is much debate over the meaning of the founding. Some scholars focus on the more abstract and universal language of the Declaration of Independence as the leading characteristic of the founding era,[5] while others look to the political science of the Constitution as more important.[6] But Wilson believes that these two elements of the founding go together, and he therefore finds it necessary to address himself to both. For this reason, we will do likewise.

With respect to the Declaration, Wilson addressed himself to the transhistorical nature of the document's opening. The Declaration defines the purpose and the role of government not as contingent upon historical circumstance but instead as universal and applicable to all men by virtue of their common nature. In particular, the Declaration says that the purpose for which "Governments are instituted among Men" is to secure "certain unalienable Rights." These rights do not come from a particular regime or tradition—they do not vary from one point in time to another. Instead, the rights are granted to men by their "Creator," and therefore "entitle them" to a government that will protect their individual rights, which come from "the Laws of Nature and of Nature's God." In addition to being integral to the founders' own self-understanding, the transhistorical nature of the Declaration's principles was also a consistent and prominent feature in the speeches of Abraham Lincoln, who often argued that the nation's history had led it away from the natural-rights principles of its founding. Lincoln saw it as his duty to restore those principles to their rightful place in the public mind. Of the Declaration and its primary author, he said, in 1859: "All honor to Jefferson—to the man who, in the concrete pressure of a struggle for national independence by a single people, had the coolness, forecast, and capacity to introduce into a merely revolutionary document, an abstract truth, applicable to all men and all times."[7] It was this dedication to the "abstract truth" of securing natural rights that Wilson found troubling and that was a primary object of his historical reinterpretation of the founding's meaning.

Wilson focused on what he considered to be the abstract character of the Declaration's natural-rights teaching, warning against it by equating it with the philosophic radicalism of the French Revolution. But this interpretation did not reflect the founders' own understanding of the Declaration, since the founders were practical men and understood the role of prudence in politics. The revulsion in the bulk of the American founding generation to the events in France demonstrates that the Americans did not see in the French Revolution their own understanding of natural rights. Even Wilson's hero, Edmund Burke, whose condemnation of French revolutionary principles is famous, did not equate France and America. For the Declaration of Independence lays out the rights principle in its first two paragraphs, and then proceeds to take into account the specific circumstances of the case of America's relationship to England in the remainder of the document. In other words, the Declaration can arguably be understood as an example of prudent statesmanship—of looking to principle, and then prudently combining this principle with a sound appreciation of convention in order to arrive at the best course of action given the circumstances. The Declaration of Independence, in its second paragraph, is explicit in this regard: "Prudence, indeed, will dictate that Governments long established should not be changed for light and transient causes; and accordingly all experience hath shown, that mankind are more disposed to suffer, while evils are sufferable, than to right themselves by abolishing the forms to which they are accustomed."

Furthermore, the universal principles of the Declaration are put into practice through a Constitution animated by a sober appreciation for the dangers inherent in the same human nature that entitles all men to certain unalienable rights. The Americans are careful to be guided not only by ideas but by the experience of political development, as can be seen in *Federalist* 9 with the dependence upon the historical "improvements" in the science of politics, as well as in *Federalist* 85 with the reference to David Hume's exhortation to rely on experience. And Publius also understands that experience will allow continued improvement to the institutional means by which the fixed ends of American government can be achieved, writing in *Federalist* 82 that " 'Tis time only that can mature and perfect so compound a system."[8] This argument of *The Federalist* is why Harvey Mansfield has written that the universal ideas of the Declaration are made particularly American through the prudence of the Constitution, which turns Americans into a "constitutional people."[9] It is in this way that the Americans distinguish themselves from the "revolutionary people" of France.

Indeed, Wilson, too, understood the important relationship between the Declaration and the Constitution, seeing that the institutional arrangement contained in the Constitution was made necessary by the natural-rights teaching of the Declaration. That teaching, as the founders understood it (and as the French revolutionaries failed to understand it), requires limited, constitutional government.[10] The proposition of the Declaration—that the purpose of government is to secure the natural rights of citizens—makes it imperative that the government be carefully restrained and checked, since it is a constant danger that the power of the state may be employed to the detriment of the rights of individual citizens. Hence, for the founders, the greatest threat to democratic government was the threat of faction—that a majority might use the power of the state to violate the rights of the minority. Majorities, therefore, had to be limited in the ways that they could employ the powers of government, and government itself had to be checked and limited by a variety of institutional restraints. The founders were also clear, as explained in *Federalist* 6 and 10, that the threat of faction is *permanent*—it does not recede with time or with the march of history, because faction is grounded in human nature. *Federalist* 10 explains that "the latent causes of faction are thus sown in the nature of man."[11] And *The Federalist* maintains that human nature does not improve, that there is no progress to a point where we can stop worrying about the factious nature of men and the pernicious ends toward which it might direct the power of the state. Hence, the need to limit government and circumscribe carefully its authority is permanent. In *Federalist* 6, Publius criticizes those who fail to see the permanent dangers of human nature by saying that they are "far gone in utopian speculations." He cites as evidence all of human history, making clear that there has not been, nor will there be, any progress on the question of faction, and therefore there is no justification for relaxing our guard. Human nature does not change, governments must be structured accordingly, and to think differently is to be subject to the delusions of a "benevolent and philosophic spirit."[12] It is this "antiprogressive," or ahistorical, account of human nature that Wilson found most necessary to reinterpret, as it served as the foundation of the very limits within the Constitution that progressive reforms sought to transcend.

The founders' constitutionalism, ultimately, is designed to limit the power of government over the rights of individuals, even when that power is energized by a majority. Several institutional features were implemented to achieve this purpose. Each of these features, to Wilson's mind, made American government inflexible and incapable of adjustment to necessary historical change. First, *The Federalist* praises the diversity of interests that will comprise an extended republic such as the United States. Publius relies on this diversity of political interest, which will be a permanent feature of an extended republic, to keep faction in check, since it will be practically difficult for a coordinated, factious majority to arise over such a large territory out of so many diverse elements. Second, the power of the government must be restrained in order to prevent a factious majority from using that power to "execute their plans of oppression."[13] One way of doing this is to divide the power of government between different levels of authority—as is the case in the American system of federalism, which divides power between the states and the national government. Another way is to divide power further within the national government itself, so that no one set of hands can exercise the whole power of governing. This is the genesis of the separation-of-powers system, the very backbone of the founders' constitutionalism, which was made efficacious by giving to each branch of government a series of checks over the other branches.[14] It was the separation of powers that, among all of the objects of Wilson's criticism in the founders' Constitution, caused him the greatest distress and occupied much of his attention. For Wilson, the separation of powers, and all of the other institutional remedies that the founders employed against the danger of faction, stood in the way of government's exercising its power in accord with the dictates of progress.

Wilson, therefore, sought a reinterpretation of the founding—a reinterpretation grounded in historical contingency. To the founding's ahistorical notion of human nature, Wilson opposed the historical argument that the ends, scope, and role of just government must be defined by the different principles of different epochs, and that therefore it is impossible to speak of a single form of just government for all ages. This was a self-conscious reinterpretation, as Wilson even suggested in one speech that the Declaration ought to be understood by excluding from it the theoretical arguments of the first two paragraphs. In a 1911 address Wilson remarked that "the rhetorical introduction of the Declaration of Independence is the least part of it. . . . If you want to understand the real Declaration of Independence, do not repeat the preface."[15] It was this assertion of historical contingency over the permanent principles of American constitutionalism that animated the main tenets of Wilson's thought.[16] Each of these tenets will be developed in the chapters to follow.

Briefly put, those tenets rest on a coupling of historical contingency with a faith in progress. Wilson believed that the human condition improves as history marches forward, so protections built into government against the danger of such things as faction become less necessary and increasingly unjust. Ultimately, the problem of faction is solved not by permanently limited government but by history itself; history brings a unity of sentiment and fundamental will to the nation. Whereas *The Federalist* asserts that a diversity of interest will always underlie the extended republic, Wilson contended that history would overcome such particularism with an increasing unity of mind. So for him, the latent causes of faction are *not* sown in the nature of man, or if they are, historical progress will overcome this human nature. With the unity of national sentiment, political questions become less contentious and less important. We cease to concentrate on the question of what should be done, and more on the question of how we should do it. This is the principle behind Wilson's suggestion that the modern age is one of administration, where we seek to find the specific means to achieving the ends that we all agree we want. Government in such an age of unity is not a threat to the individual that has to be checked; rather, the state is an organ of the individuals in society — "beneficent and indispensable,"[17] as Wilson described it. The distinction and tension between the individual and government, a primary feature of early liberalism to which the American founders at least partly subscribed, are made largely extinct by the progress of history. Instead, the state becomes one with the unified will of the people; it becomes the organic manifestation of their spirit. The state must therefore be unfettered so that it can effect the will of the people. It makes no sense to limit the government in an effort to protect the people from the very manifestation of their own organic will. This need to unfetter the state, so that its scope can become whatever the current historical spirit demands, means undoing the various institutional limits that early American constitutionalism had placed on state power. The state must move beyond the narrow and outdated role assigned to it by the founding generation, taking instead an institutional form more appropriate for its new mission. This project was the focus of Wilson's writings, and this book is about understanding Wilson's project and how he wanted to go about effecting it institutionally.

The argument of this book is different than most in that it asserts that Wilson's progressive mission was, in its essential parts, consistent from his earliest writings and throughout his academic and political career. Many accounts of Wilson suggest that he ultimately converted to progressivism and to advocating centralized state power (although they differ on when such a conversion actually took place), but I will endeavor to show that there is a continuity in the main tenets of Wilson's thought, and that these principles are visible in the different stages of his intellectual and political work. Such an argument, which rests on Wilson's historical thinking, necessitates an examination of his substantial corpus of academic work. Therefore, the academic work occupies the bulk of my attention. But to understand Wilson's historical thinking requires at least a brief account of the intellectual roots of historical thought that influenced him.

THE ROOTS OF WILSON'S HISTORICAL VIEW

Wilson's discomfort with the founders' liberalism of natural rights reflects the influence of historical thinking that was becoming prominent during the time when he undertook his education. The historical view, in general, rejected the possibility of transcending the historical environment in order to grasp universal political principles; instead, politics had to be guided by the spirit of the current historical age, and political change was to be grounded in evolution from one historical spirit to the next. The historical view was, therefore, antithetical to the notion that one could permanently fix the scope and purpose of government. There were two important strains of historical thinking prominent in Wilson's time, and both influenced his thought: the *Historical School*, with roots in both England and Germany, and *historicism*, which came more squarely out of German idealism. Similar in many respects, particularly on the question of historical contingency, the two strains nonetheless contain critical differences, as the explication below will illustrate. My argument is that Wilson's constitutional thought imported much from the English Historical School, but that Wilson took his historical thinking in a more explicitly idealistic and historicist direction. So while Wilson's thought is perhaps most obviously influenced by Burke and Walter Bagehot, both members of the English Historical School, Wilson goes beyond their evolutionary conservatism to adopt a historicism most directly attributable to Hegel.

Wilson was exposed to historical thinking, especially of the German variety, during his graduate education at Johns Hopkins University, where he matriculated in 1883. While Wilson had read heavily from the English historical writers prior to his graduate study, it was at Hopkins that he became seriously educated in the historical tradition. In his history of Hopkins, Hugh Hawkins remarks on the prevalence of historical and evolutionary thinking: "No department, no vocabulary, no body of thought escaped the mark of evolutionary theory."[18] Wilson's teachers at Hopkins were all educated in Germany and in the tradition of German state theory and philosophy of history. The professors who seem to have influenced Wilson most were Richard T. Ely and Herbert Baxter Adams. Ely and Adams had both been hired in 1881, four years after the university's opening, as the university's first full-time professors of social science. Both Ely and Adams had studied at the University of Heidelberg and received their doctorates there in the 1870s, and both had studied under Johann K. Bluntschli. Bluntschli was a prominent Hegelian state theorist, and his papers were housed at Hopkins in 1883—the same year that Wilson entered and in the same seminar room where Wilson studied and participated in the Johns Hopkins Seminary of History and Politics.[19] Henry Wilkinson Bragdon characterizes Ely as "one of the first American economists to break away from orthodox Manchester liberalism."[20] Ely not only studied in Germany but remained there for a period of three years in order to write what was to be his most important book, *Property and Contract*. He was particularly interested in civil-service reform, municipal reform, and city planning. As Joseph Dorfman suggests, Ely believed that the German historical view "gave a more concrete interpretation of economic history, by attempting to understand past doctrines in the light of their environment." And William Diamond identifies Ely as not only a progressive but also as a radical, contending that he was one of the few on the Hopkins faculty who was openly hostile to the notion of private property.[21] Wilson's teacher Adams was one of the most influential American historians of his time. He clearly imparted to Wilson, who frequently wrote with great admiration about foreign systems of government, the "comparative method" of studying history and politics. As Adams elaborates: "Perhaps the grandest result of the comparative method, while broadening the areas of human knowledge[,] was the breaking down of that middle wall of partition between nations once thought to be widely different in language, religion, law and government."[22]

Wilson's own work certainly reflected the foreign influence exerted on him at Hopkins. His book *The State*, by far his most comprehensive and theoretical treatment of political principles, draws heavily from his study of foreign systems and German writers. In discussing his work on *The State*, Wilson even complained that he "wore out a German dictionary while writing it."[23] In general, Wilson's works are well known for their comparison of American government to foreign systems and for urging the adoption of features of foreign governments. Some of this foreign influence was apparent even before Wilson entered Hopkins: he wrote essays calling for the adoption of a parliamentary model as early as 1879,[24] was an avid reader of British authors as an undergraduate,[25] and believed that American scholarship compared very unfavorably to European scholarship—especially English and German.[26] In 1891, Wilson provided a list of books he thought essential for students of politics, naming the works of Bagehot, Burke, John Fiske, James Bryce, and his own *Congressional Government* and *The State*. He did not mention any early American standards such as *The Federalist*, instead focusing on contemporary works that emphasized the historical and evolutionary foundations of politics.[27] In a bibliography compiled around the same time, Wilson listed the titles that seem to have been most relevant to his work on administration and state theory. Most are German and French, including the works of Bluntschli, Heinrich Marquardsen, Hegel, Herbert Spencer, and Francis Lieber.[28] Wilson consciously adopted the historical method of writing about politics. In explaining his plans for writing on the modern state, he mentioned Sir Henry Maine's *Popular Government* as an important influence, but made clear that his own work would be more truly historical.[29] He explained that the historical view

> furnishes me with *method*. I want to come at the true conception of the nature of the modern democratic state by way of an accurate exposition of the history of democratic development. I want to keep safely within sober induction from concrete examples of political organization and of realized political thought. I

would read the heart of political *practice*, letting political theory wait on that practice and carry weight only in proportion to its nearness to what has been actually accomplished.

As he explained in more concise terms, "The true philosophy of government can be extracted only from the true history of government."[30]

The historical, evolutionary, progressive mode of thinking was sweeping through American higher education at the time Wilson began his studies. Robert Nisbet attributes the influence of these new ideas to two central figures—Hegel and Spencer—and notes their connection with the founding of the various social sciences during this same period.[31] Laurence Veysey's history of higher education cites the immediate post–Civil War period as revolutionary in terms of the dominance of historical and evolutionary thinking. He remarks that "the American university of 1900 was all but unrecognizable in comparison with the college of 1860," and he traces the roots of this transformation back to the early part of the century, when academics began going to Germany for study as early as 1816.[32] Bernard Crick's history of political science in America traces the origins of the discipline to the development of the faith in progress that became prominent in the latter part of the nineteenth century.[33]

As mentioned above, the rise to prominence of faith in progress and of historical thinking in America owes itself to two strains of thought: the English Historical School and the doctrine of historicism. The Historical School was influenced largely by evolution, and it developed into an application of evolutionary theory to history and politics, an application made perhaps most famously by Spencer. The British authors admired by Wilson, especially Bagehot, fall mostly into this category. Historicism became prominent through the influence of Hegel's writings. Both the English Historical School and the doctrine of historicism rest on historical contingency, denying the possibility of transcending history, tradition, or custom. But unlike the Historical School, the doctrine of historicism is idealistic. For Hegel and his fellow historicists, history is rational, and it culminates in a rational end-state. Given their influence on Wilson, each of these strains of historical thinking must be briefly examined in order to understand the development of his thought.

The English Historical School

Wilson's absorption of the Historical School was a consequence of his affinity for British writers. Most relevant to a discussion of Wilson and the Historical School are Burke, Spencer, and Bagehot. Burke was probably the earliest and most obvious influence on Wilson, who most admired Burke's criticism of abstract principles in politics. Burke's *Reflections on the Revolution in France* focuses its criticism of the French Revolution on the abstract notion of liberty inherent in the French understanding of the Rights of Man. To conceive of liberty in an abstract mode was ahistorical, Burke observes, and therefore dangerous and revolutionary.[34] Instead of speaking of the Rights of Man in general terms, Burke suggests that it was more proper to speak, for example, of one's rights as an Englishman. In other words, political principles ought to be grounded in the concrete historical reality of one's own time and place.[35] Burke therefore is skeptical of grounding government on natural rights, perceiving that natural rights are a foundation of social compact theory. Social compact theory was responsible for the doctrine of the right to revolution, which was antithetical to Burke's evolutionary conservatism.[36] Wilson's historical argument in *The State* draws on all of these points from Burke's critique of the French Revolution.

Spencer is an important figure not so much because of what Wilson learned directly from his writings (although he certainly did read and learn from Spencer), but because of the influence that Spencer had on the Historical School of writers who were most important to Wilson, particularly Bagehot. Bagehot's presentation of the English constitutional tradition, and his conception of politics in general, fell squarely in the mode of applying evolutionary thinking to social phenomena. This is a mode of thinking made popular by Spencer's application of Darwin's ideas. It was through Spencer, and especially through Spencerians in America, that the evolutionary theory of Darwin was brought into the service of the doctrine of progress. Spencer's influence in the latter part of the nineteenth century would be difficult to overstate, especially in the founding of the social sciences and in the faculties of American universities. Two of Spencer's works epitomize his impact. *Social Statics*, originally published in 1850, was first made available in an American edition in 1866. Spencer's other influential book, *The Man Versus the State*, was published in 1884. In these works, and in a variety of essays, Spencer takes evolutionary theory and applies it to general social development. He contends that political bodies, like their biological counterparts, are organic; they grow and evolve in response to environmental stimuli.[37] Spencer's thinking was essentially a variant of English utilitarianism, with a more developed argument on progress through evolution.[38] In America, Darwin and Spencer were taken in both laissez-faire and statist directions. William Graham Sumner (*What Social Classes Owe to Each Other*, 1883), for example, argues that government ought to get out of the way, since social evolution leads to progress. Lester Frank Ward (*Dynamic Sociology*, 1883), by contrast, contends that progress needs the superintendence of an educated class trained for leadership.

But Wilson was more taken with English scholarship than American, and so the arguments of Darwin and Spencer and the evolutionary school came to Wilson primarily through Bagehot, whose work much of Wilson's early scholarship imitates.[39] In *The English Constitution* (1867), from which Wilson drew his understanding of the parliamentary system, Bagehot places the English constitution within a broad pattern of historical development. This is a continually unfolding constitutional tradition, one that follows a rough pattern.[40] In his introduction to the 1872 edition of the book, Bagehot even uses the phrase "living constitution" to refer to British tradition, noting that his account is a study of "a Constitution that is in actual work and power."[41] The phrase "living constitution" is, of course, an important one in the lexicon of liberal and progressive interpreters of the American Constitution, and it is also central to understanding Wilson, who contends that we must take our cue from the reality of the Constitution's development, not from theories of what the Constitution was meant to be in the abstract. Bagehot also writes of the need for constant "adjustment" in the laws. The purpose of law is shaped by the current historical environment, and as that environment changes the laws must follow accordingly. Bagehot suggests that, due to the power of human passion in earlier periods, there may once have been a place for fixed laws that sought to keep dangerous changes in check. But since civilization has evolved, and presumably the danger from the passions has decreased, a permanent legislature is required in order to constantly "adjust" the laws to new circumstances.[42] As we shall see, *adjustment* was an important term to Wilson, who shared Bagehot's rejection of the American founders' belief that human nature does not change, and therefore that the passions are an ever-present threat to democratic government.

Bagehot's emphasis on adjustment shows his affinity to John Stuart Mill, another prominent member of the English Historical School. But as R. H. S. Crossman notes in his introduction to *The English Constitution*, an important difference between Bagehot and Mill was the former's emphasis on the cabinet. For Bagehot, unlike Mill, the cabinet was vital to ensuring the efficiency of the parliamentary system; it coordinated between the legislature and the executive ministries. This coordination is important to understanding Wilson, because like Bagehot he was concerned primarily with the *efficiency* of the parliamentary system, not merely its representativeness.[43] Bagehot contrasts himself with Mill throughout his book, even beginning the work with a quote from Mill and laying out how his own work will be different. Bagehot distinguishes between the "living reality" of the British constitution and the "paper description" of it. His account, unlike Mill's, will focus not on an abstract discussion of the British constitution but on the historical reality of how that constitution has actually developed.[44] Here we see the roots of what will come to be called Wilson's "liberal realism" or "historical realism."

While Bagehot's *The English Constitution* gives an historical account of the development of the British system, his subsequent *Physics and Politics* (1873) more broadly paints the history of political development using the terms of evolutionary biology. This work is a perfect illustration of how the Historical School naturally came under the influence of social Darwinism; Bagehot himself cites several prominent evolutionary writers in the opening chapter: Thomas H. Huxley, Francis Galton, Maine, Spencer, and others.[45] Bagehot addresses several evolutionary developments in politics, especially the growth of "national character." Because of necessities that nations have faced and the environments in which they have developed, a distinct national character emerges as a nation becomes less primitive.[46] It is in this regard that Bagehot frames evolution as occurring through conflict. Nations and peoples grow by virtue of a kind of natural selection—superior peoples are victorious in the conflicts of history, and inferior peoples are assimilated.[47] As Bagehot explains, in the process of history, "The best nations conquered the worst; by the possession of one advantage or another the best competitor overcame the inferior competitor." Those regions remaining backward are generally so because they have not come into contact (and conflict) with the more advanced nations of civilization.[48] Bagehot, and like him Wilson, relies heavily on Maine's account of the development of primitive political societies in *Ancient Law: Its Connection with the Early History of Society, and Its Relation to Modern Ideas* (1861). Bagehot cites Maine's phrase suggesting that the early law rested "not on contract but on status,"[49] which is exactly the phrase Wilson employed in *The State*.

It is important to note that Bagehot's evolutionary language, while certainly connected to the idea of progress, stops short of the idealistic account of history that one finds in the doctrine of historicism. In *The English Constitution*, for example, there is much talk of how evolution *has* taken place in the development of English government, but there really is no talk about the future—about where evolution might be going. There is not a discussion of a particular end that is necessitated by the process of historical development. And as Bagehot explains in *Physics and Politics*, "There was a considerable, *though not certain*, tendency toward progress" in history.[50] Unlike an historicist, Bagehot is both less emphatic on what "progress" really means or how it will end up, and less sure that there has been great progress or that there will be progress in the future. As he concedes: "In fact any progress is extremely rare. As a rule . . . a stationary state is by far the most frequent condition of man, as far as history describes that condition; the progressive state is only a rare and an occasional exception."[51] This is where Wilson would part company and take up instead the historicist's faith in the progress of history and its end-state.

Historicism

Commenting on Bagehot's *Physics and Politics*, Wilson remarked that "for my part, I acknowledge, I religiously believe most that the book contains." But Wilson's criticism of the book is critical to understanding his departure into historicism. He did not believe that Bagehot's evolutionary theory provided a sufficient model for political change. In particular, Wilson made the historicist's critique of Bagehot by contending that "he does not construct for the future."[52] And that is, in essence, the distinction between historicism and the Historical School. Wilson, and the historicism to which he subscribed, understood history not only as organic and evolutionary but as rational and powerful. Consequently, history was leading to a specific end. To gain a more complete understanding, then, of Wilson's intellectual roots, it is necessary to examine the main points of the historical argument of Hegel, who had given rise to historicism in the nineteenth century.

To attribute Wilson's historical thinking to Hegel is not to suggest that Wilson absorbed all of his argument directly from the German thinker. There is no doubt that Wilson learned many Hegelian precepts as they were adopted by other English and German historical writers whom he read. But as Nisbet points out, the evolutionary understanding of politics that became a trademark of the Darwinists and the Historical School did not originate with Darwin. Rather, it had its roots in philosophers—notably, Hegel—who preceded Darwin. So, while Darwin was responsible for the idea of natural selection, the broader notion of social evolution had already been launched by this older Hegelian tradition.[53] In addition to drawing Hegelian concepts from members of the Historical School whom he read, Wilson certainly learned much from Hegel directly, as will be demonstrated in the chapters that follow. Wilson even mentioned Hegel in a love letter to Ellen Louise Axson, commenting that Hegel "used to search for—and in most cases *find*, it seems to me—the fundamental psychological facts of society."[54]

Hegel agrees with the basic precept of the Historical School that one cannot transcend one's own historical environment. Historical contingency makes it impossible to ground politics on an abstract principle. Wilson cited Hegel directly in making this same point in his essay, "The Study of Administration." The political principles of any age, Wilson contends, are nothing more than reflections of its corresponding historical spirit. Wilson claimed that "the philosophy of any time is, as Hegel says, 'nothing but the spirit of that time expressed in abstract thought.' "[55] This reference is taken from the preface to Hegel's *The Philosophy of Right*, where Hegel argues that philosophy cannot be abstract in the traditional sense; rather, philosophy properly understood does not suggest what "ought" to be but reflects instead historical reality. So in explaining the philosophy of the state, Hegel contends, one does not attempt to derive some transhistorical principle and use it as a guide or standard (i.e., to distinguish between nature and convention); rather, the philosophy of the state is simply a clear understanding of the actual state that history has bequeathed. As Hegel explains, his work is

> poles apart from an attempt to construct a state as it ought to be. The instruction which it may contain cannot consist in teaching the state what it ought to be; it can only show how the state, the ethical universe, is to be understood. . . . To comprehend what is, this is the task of philosophy, because what is, is reason. Whatever happens, every individual is a child of his time; so philosophy too is its own time apprehended in thoughts. It is just as absurd to fancy that a philosophy can transcend its contemporary world as it is to fancy that an individual can overleap his own age.[56]

We are trapped with the reality that history gives to us or, as Hegel summarizes, "*What is rational is actual and what is actual is rational.*"[57] As he explains in *The Philosophy of History*, each age has its own morality or spirit, which is made manifest by the particulars of that age. History is a progression of such epochs; the spirit of each age is different and more advanced than the one preceding it.[58] More advanced historical spirits replace inferior ones through a dialectical process, where progress is the result of great clashes, conflicts, and struggles. The consequence of this dialectical process of historical advance is that progress is based upon peoples or races. Advanced races come into conflict with inferior ones, defeating them and either leaving them behind or assimilating them. This is why, for example, Hegel contends that the slave trade was truly liberating for Africans. Slavery may have meant defeat and subjugation on one level, but to Hegel it marked historical progress because it brought the African race into contact with more advanced civilization. Hegel asserts that the Africans were, through their enslavement by the races of the West, literally freed from their historical backwardness.[59] For Hegel, depending upon the spirit of one's people, one either is or is not on the forefront of world history. Therefore, the best thing that can happen for an historically inferior people is for it to be defeated by one that is more advanced, thus facilitating liberation by an historically superior spirit. History advances by the progress of certain peoples or races, for whom the time is ripe. For Hegel, there are real differences between peoples, and these differences have world historical significance.

The primary difference between Hegel and the English Historical School is that for Hegel, history is going somewhere. There is a particular end-point toward which world history is directed, and the particulars of history's advance happen in order to bring about that ultimate end. The fundamental premise of history for Hegel is that "Reason is the Sovereign of the World," and history presents us with a rational process.[60] So unlike the ideas of Bagehot, whom Wilson complained did not present an adequate model for the future, historicism has a particular future in mind, and progress is all about reaching it. Providence guides historical progress, and history represents the gradual unfolding of the Divine Idea on earth and ends in the modern state, which is the culmination of God's plan. As Hegel explains, "The State is the Divine Idea as it exists on Earth. We have in it, therefore, the object of History in a more definite shape than before; that in which Freedom obtains objectivity, and lives in the enjoyment of this objectivity."[61]

Hegel's end-state is arrived at through the actions and leadership of so-called "world-historical individuals." Such leaders are on the forefront of history. People follow the world-historical individual because they see their own spirit in him. This leader has in him the vision of the people's future. "Their fellows, therefore, follow these soul-leaders; for they feel the irresistible power of their own inner Spirit thus embodied."[62] Wilson laid out a similar concept of democratic leadership in his essay "Leaders of Men," which will be discussed in chapter 6. As Hegel explains, leadership is necessary in order to uncover and bring to the surface the people's true will, which becomes increasingly manifest as history progresses. Underneath the apparent clash of subjective interests and passions, there is a true, unified, and objective will. Leadership finds this true will and points it out to the people. The modern state represents the unity of the people's objective will, "For Truth," Hegel explains, "is the Unity of the universal and subjective Will; and the Universal is to be found in the State, in its laws, its universal and rational arrangements."[63] Politically, this means that one cannot develop individually outside of a devotion to the state and without the state's guidance. As Hegel makes clear, "All the worth which the human being possesses—all spiritual reality, he possesses only through the State."[64] He elaborates in *The Philosophy of Right*: "Since the state is mind objectified, it is only as one of its members that the individual himself has objectivity, genuine individuality, and an ethical life. Unification pure and simple is the true content and aim of the individual."[65] Real "self-development," as Wilson will call it, can take place in the state only at the end of history.

Because the ideal constitution can only be the product of gradual historical development, Hegel explains that government cannot simply be "created," as social compact theory suggests. Contrary to the method of Thomas Hobbes and John Locke, and to that of the American founders, one cannot simply transcend the historical environment, look to the abstract nature of man, and create a new government based upon principles derived thereby. The most rational government is the one that history has currently provided, since "Reason is the Sovereign of the World,"[66] and *"What is rational is actual, and what is actual is rational.*"[67] Fundamentally, it makes no sense to speak of the "best" constitution; one cannot choose one's constitution but must instead accept as just the choice that history has made.[68] As Hegel explains in *The Philosophy of Right*, "It is absolutely essential that the constitution should not be regarded as something made, even though it has come into being in time. It must be treated rather as something simply existent in and by itself, as divine therefore, and constant, and so as exalted above the sphere of things that are made."[69] We will see the same mode of constitutional thinking in Wilson, who eschews a fixed view of the U.S. Constitution's meaning and instead suggests that the Constitution must mean what the times require of it.

Since government cannot be understood to come from anything other than the concrete reality of what history has provided, there can be no principled or universal notion of liberty or rights. Liberty, and any doctrine of rights based upon liberty, must always be contingent upon the historical environment. Rights cannot be, therefore, "natural" or "unalienable," as the American founders believed, but must come from the conventional situation itself—from the current state. "The State," Hegel explains, "its laws, its arrangements, constitute the rights of its members. . . . All is their possession, just as they are possessed by it; for it constitutes their existence, their being."[70] The entire method of the Declaration of Independence, for instance, would be impossible. The Declaration contrasts the contemporary practice of government in British North America to the rights to which all men by nature are entitled. For Hegel, such a contrast is impossible. It leads to mere subjectivity, where one's own individual claims take precedence over the common good. He criticizes American constitutionalism for this very problem, suggesting that in North America,

> Universal protection for property, and a something approaching entire immunity from public burdens, are facts which are constantly held up to commendation. We have in these facts the fundamental character of the community—the endeavor of the individual after acquisition, commercial profit, and gain; the preponderance of *private* interest, devoting itself to that of the community only for its own advantage.[71]

This false subjectivity is the result of social compact theory and, as Hegel argues, there really can be no clear distinction between public and private such as the social compact understanding implies. Since one cannot have abstract rights against the historical state, there is no effective boundary that the state cannot cross. Hegel plainly says that the state can have no limits placed upon it—at least not limits that are concretely defined in principle. Since the state is simply the embodiment of the objective will of the people, it is nonsensical to suggest that the people need to be protected against the manifestation of their own unified, objective will. Even though Hegel's rational state is composed of different institutions, he makes clear that there can be no separation of powers in the American sense—no separation of powers in an effort to check or restrain the power of government. A separation of powers makes people suspicious of the state and sets them apart from it; it gets in the way of the state's efficiently putting the objective will of the people into practice.[72] All of these criticisms of social compact theory, abstract liberty, and the checking of government through the separation of powers are employed, in precisely the same terms, by Wilson in *The State,* as well as other works.

Since the state, according to Hegel, is the manifestation of the people's objective will, it must be managed by those who best understand that will and best know how to put it into practice. This is the role played by the bureaucracy, which has the keenest insight into the spirit of the age and the most efficacious means of effecting it in public policy. Hegel explains that the bureaucracy can best understand the objective will because it is not attached to any particular subjective interest in society. This objectivity is accomplished by giving to the bureaucracy insulation from the pressure of these interests— in the form of income and life tenure. Since they have been materially taken care of, the bureaucrats can then see more objectively what must be done and how to do it.[73] The bureaucracy, for instance, is to have a superintendence over corporations by exercising the right to approve or reject the appointment of corporate officers, thereby making sure that they operate in accord with the objective will.[74] Wilson's view of the civil service, like Hegel's, is premised on the irony that the bureaucracy can best understand and reflect the true public will by being insulated from public accountability—in Wilson's case, this insulation is achieved by nonpartisan, competitive examinations and life tenure.

Wilson seems to have adopted Hegel's notion of the state not only directly but also through the state theory of Bluntschli. Bluntschli, in *The Theory of the State*, emphasizes that the state embodies a unified national will that is more fundamental than any clash of subjective interests that might appear on the surface. "The one national will," he explains, "which is different from the average will of the multitude, is the will of the State."[75] Bluntschli employs the Hegelian understanding of how the state comes to be, writing, "States have a development and growth of their own. The periods of national and political history are to be measured by great eras which far surpass the age of individual men. . . . Every period again has its special character."[76] History is powerful and progressive, bringing about increasing unity of will not only in an individual nation, but also eventually between nations. In an argument that certainly bears on Wilson's internationalism, Bluntschli contends that "unconquerable time itself works on unceasingly, bringing the nations nearer to one another, and awakening the universal consciousness of the community of mankind."[77]

Wilson unquestionably adopted the primary tenets of historical thinking that had become prominent in Europe and America in the latter half of the nineteenth century. To the extent that one wants to distinguish between the influence of German historicism and the less idealistic English Historical School, it is important to keep in mind that Wilson, unlike so many members of the English Historical School whose works he read, was no conservative and no opponent of state power. Burke, Spencer, and Bagehot, in contrast, generally employ evolutionary arguments in a conservative way, in defense of a laissez-faire, Manchesterian economic thinking. Even if their evolutionary brand of conservatism itself offers no principled defense of individual liberty, so that any understanding of liberty does not stand on its own but is instead historically contingent, the members of the English Historical School were by no means statists. As this book endeavors to show, the same cannot be said of Wilson. The influence on Wilson not just of historical thinking but also of full-blown historicism is highly relevant to Wilson's constitutional thought. For Wilson, like the historicism to which he subscribed, was much more idealistic than the Historical School, holding great faith in progress and in the powerful, rational end-state toward which history was moving civilization.

SCHOLARLY INTERPRETATIONS

In suggesting that Wilson surpasses evolutionary or historical thinking and reaches a more idealistic historicism, this book differs from most scholarly interpretations of Wilson's thought. In general, such interpretations either find difficulty in identifying a consistent theme, or they attribute Wilson's thinking to the general, evolutionary arguments of Darwinism and the Historical School. And while several writers make connections of one kind or another between Wilson and historicism, the only work of which I am aware that makes an explicit and sustained connection between Wilson and Hegel is that of Scot J. Zentner. Zentner examines Wilson's Hegelianism in a series of articles on Wilson's understanding of executive leadership.[78]

Of the interpretations attributing Wilson's thought to the influence of the Historical School, the most important are probably those of Bragdon, Dorfman, Diamond, Niels Aage Thorsen, and Richard J. Stillman. Thorsen emphasizes Wilson's roots in the economic historians.[79] For Bragdon, Wilson's experience at Johns Hopkins is crucial in turning him away from Manchesterian liberalism and toward Darwinism. He cites especially Ely's influence on Wilson, and also mentions Wilson's careful reading of Bagehot, Spencer, and Maine.[80] Diamond makes a similar argument, contending that "the Wilson who left Hopkins was not the Wilson who entered the Baltimore university in 1883." While the young Wilson had entered Hopkins as a devotee of classical economics, the influence of Ely and others led him subsequently to embrace the role of "positive governmental action in the interests of society."[81] Stillman credits the English Historical School, especially Bagehot, with inculcating in Wilson a "conservative, evolutionary view of society."[82] For Dorfman, in contrast, it is the German Historical School, especially as it came to prominence in the 1870s and 1880s, that was highly influential on American progressives. It was under German historical thinking that "progressive-minded economists began to question the adequacy of traditional, classical economic theory which dominated America."[83]

John M. Mulder is one of those interpreters who finds it difficult to point to a single set of sources for Wilson's thought. His work instead describes the great variety of writers whom he believes played a role in shaping Wilson. "The sources of Wilson's political thought," Mulder argues, "are so complex and intertwined that it is an impossible, indeed fruitless, task to sort them out." In particular, Mulder sees in both Wilson's political and educational thought a "profound tension between individualism and organicism."[84] Mulder is joined by Wilson biographer Arthur S. Link, who interprets Wilson's progressivism late in his career as a major philosophical change. "Wilson's political thought," Link contends, "simply cannot be studied as a whole. There are too many incongruities, too many contradictions."[85]

Just as the question of Wilson's intellectual roots gives rise to multiple interpretations, there are several schools of thought on the broader question of Wilson's political principles. Although now largely abandoned, some scholars have attempted to understand Wilson through a psychological mode of analysis. The so-called "psychobiographical" approach is employed by Alexander and Juliette George, by William Bullitt and Sigmund Freud, and by James David Barber.[86] Much of the work on Wilson has come out of the discipline of history, most prominently by such historians as Charles Beard,[87] Richard Hofstadter, Louis Hartz, John Milton Cooper, August Heckscher, Kendrick A. Clements, and Link.[88] The interpretation of Wilson presented by these historians is generally one of Wilson as a progressive who was important in moving the nation away from its older political principles, particularly with regard to the presidency and its place in the constitutional order. While the works in this school disagree on the question of when in his career Wilson embarked upon his progressivism—some see the early Wilson as a "Jeffersonian," states'-rights conservative who subsequently saw the light—all generally concur that his turning away from the traditional constitutional order and moving the country toward a more modern understanding of government was both good and necessary. Wilson is seen as transforming and enlarging the role of presidential leadership, in particular, in order to make the government take on the role required of it by twentieth-century circumstances.

There is a more recent school—consisting largely of political theorists—who agree with the interpretation of Wilson as a progressive who helped turn the nation away from its traditional political order. But unlike the progressive historians, these political theorists look at Wilson from the perspective of the founding, and consequently see in him a dangerous departure from sound political principle. Writers in this school include James W. Ceaser, Jeffrey K. Tulis, Paul Eidelberg, Robert Eden, and Charles R. Kesler.[89] As Kesler explains the distinction between the principles of the founding and those espoused by Wilson, "Nothing could be further removed from the reverence for the Constitution recommended by the Framers and encouraged by the separation of powers than the tone adopted by the chief architect of the administrative state, Woodrow Wilson."[90] A challenge to this interpretation—which I address in detail in chapter 5—has been made by Stephen Skowronek and Terri Bimes, who suggest that Wilson had much more respect for traditional constitutionalism than these political theorists contend.[91]

However, not all scholars agree that Wilson was even a progressive. Contrary to those who see Wilson as a convert to progressivism after an early adherence to conservative principles, Eldon J. Eisenach sees no such conversion. Instead, he holds Wilson responsible for derailing the advance of progressivism, claiming that "many of the key values, interests, and hopes of the most profound and creative of the Progressive intellectuals were *lost* with the election of Woodrow Wilson."[92] In particular, Eisenach argues that the coherence of progressivism was undermined by Wilson, and that modern liberalism still suffers from this incoherence. Eisenach does not even include Wilson in his list of the nineteen "authors of progressive public doctrine" (yet Wilson's teacher Ely is on the list).[93] In Eisenach's view, Wilson was a thoroughgoing conservative, especially in the way he opposed the expansion of national power and fought to preserve the party system. Eisenach rests part of his case on what he calls Wilson's "reactionary" view of the Constitution's interstate commerce clause, a view set out in *Constitutional Government* that countered "more than two decades of economic teaching in America exposing the moral bankruptcy and intellectual absurdity of laissez faire as a national economic policy."[94]

In his early works, Link seems to agree with the interpretation of Wilson as a conservative. His biography paints Wilson as a states'-rights conservative and a defender of laissez-faire economics. Link contrasts Wilson to the more aggressive elements of the progressive movement, characterizing the early years of the Wilson presidency as an attempt to defend the New Freedom against these more liberal elements.[95] However, the more Link wrote on Wilson the more he saw him as a progressive, and the first-time publication of many of Wilson's political writings in Link's sixty-nine-volume collection of Wilson's papers seems to indicate this shift. In part, this is the problem with Eisenach's characterization of Wilson as a consistent and staunch conservative: it cites only one of Wilson's works—*Constitutional Government*.

The two most substantial and recent works that scrutinize Wilson's political thought are Thorsen's *The Political Thought of Woodrow Wilson, 1875–1910*, and Daniel D. Stid's *The President As Statesman*. Thorsen sees three basic tenets of Wilson's thought: first, a call for the growth of national power in response to the "social and economic diversification" of the modern era; second, a focus on political leadership as a key remedy to the problems of American democracy; and third, Wilson's call to understand politics scientifically. Directing his argument against those historians who believe that Wilson underwent a radical conversion to progressivism, Thorsen asserts instead that there is a continuity in the development of Wilson's thought.[96] Thorsen identifies "the most important Wilsonian legacy" as his fight against the traditional opposition to state power inherent in American political culture.[97] I find this interpretation largely persuasive as far as it goes, and the arguments developed in my book will generally support it. My work will depart from Thorsen's by approaching Wilson's thinking from the perspective of the principles of the American founding; my interest in Wilson lies in understanding how the traditional view of the constitutional order was transformed under his influence. I also disagree with Thorsen's representation of Wilson's intellectual roots, particularly by suggesting Hegel as a vital source for Wilson's approach to politics. And while he notes the importance of political leadership to Wilson, Thorsen does not see Wilson's leadership doctrine in terms nearly as radical as mine. The focus of my analysis, while grounded in Wilson's broad base of ideas, is on Wilson's new constitutionalism. Accordingly, as one would expect from a work by a political scientist, I am much more interested in his arguments on American national institutions, their arrangement, and their relationship to the ends of republican government. In this regard, I devote some brief attention to Wilson's presidency, examining the relationship of his political ideas to the policies he pursued in office.

It is on the question of Wilson's presidency that I would take issue with one of Stid's major theses. Stid suggests that there was a sharp discontinuity between Wilson's early views on separation of powers and how Wilson came to understand the matter during his own presidency. While Wilson as a scholar embraced a parliamentary system as a means of undermining the founders' scheme of separation of powers, Stid contends that as president Wilson moderated his position. This "change in tack" came from President Wilson's appreciation of an independent and energetic executive, and his conclusion that separation of powers could prove advantageous.[98] To the extent that Wilson did endorse the independence of the president once he assumed the office himself, I would question whether such an endorsement really constituted any significant shift in his fundamental constitutional thought. Did Wilson not instead simply see presidential independence as an expedient means of putting into practice the political ideas he continued to espouse? I argue that Wilson's presidency does not represent a newfound respect for the traditional constitutional order but is instead a fulfillment of his long-held philosophy of politics.

A SNAPSHOT OF WILSON'S WORK

Because a primary argument of this book is that Wilson's thought is, at its core, essentially consistent throughout his career as a scholar and public figure—and also because this book is not a history of Wilson but is instead an analysis of his political thinking—the work does not proceed in a strictly chronological fashion. The chapters are based on key themes in Wilson's political thought, and, in expounding its particular theme, each chapter draws from a variety of his writings. It will thus be evident that from Wilson's earliest through his most mature works, there is often a strong continuity in his thinking on these key themes. Since this book is not a strictly chronological account of Wilson's work, some brief overview of the main periods and works seems appropriate here.

Wilson's early essays and letters, written during his time in college, law school, and graduate school, largely fall into one of two categories. One of these addresses religious questions, like the brief but interesting series including "Christ's Army" and "Christian Progress" that he penned during the fall and winter of 1876. The other concerns Wilson's ideas for reforming American government—ideas that emerge in his account of British history and important British historical figures. Wilson's reflections on John Bright and William Gladstone (1880) fall into this category, as do such essays as "Cabinet Government in the United States" (1879). These essays are built into what eventually becomes Wilson's most well-known book, *Congressional Government*, which served as his doctoral dissertation and was published in 1885.

As a young professor—especially at Bryn Mawr and Wesleyan—Wilson devoted much of his energy to developing a theory of the state. This energy manifested itself in essays like "The Modern Democratic State" (1885) and, ultimately, in the book *The State* (1889). As an academic, Wilson also developed a line of thinking on the science of administration. This thinking was launched by his well-known "Study of Administration" in 1886 and continued through Wilson's time at Princeton. From 1888 to 1897, Wilson took off from his home institution to teach an annual five-week lectureship on administration at Johns Hopkins, and his notes from these lectures are a rich source for scholars of Wilson's thoughts on administration. While teaching at Princeton, Wilson also wrote three American histories: *Division and Reunion* (1893), *George Washington* (1896), and the five-volume *History of the American People* (1902). Once Wilson became president of Princeton in 1902, he stopped producing scholarly writings but gave several important lectures and addresses. Of these, the series of lectures he delivered at Columbia University in 1907 was among the most interesting, and it became widely known when it was published in 1908 as a book, *Constitutional Government in the United States*. Wilson, of course, delivered many speeches as a candidate or officeholder, and his 1912 presidential campaign speeches were edited and put into book form under the title *The New Freedom* (1913).

THE ARGUMENT AND STRUCTURE OF THIS BOOK

I have structured this book to examine Wilson's understanding of the foundations of government, and then to see how that understanding becomes manifest in his arguments on the Constitution and its institutional arrangements. In chapters 1 and 2, Wilson's understanding of the state is addressed. I contend there that he has an organic concept of the state, grounded in historicism— especially in historicism's rejection of natural-rights theory. Wilson's organic view of the state leads him to advocate increased national power, conceiving of a more powerful, more centralized state as the natural consequence of America's historical development. This vision of the American national state is taken up in chapter 3, which also lays out the criticism of the Constitution essential to moving beyond the notion of limited government to one more compatible with expanded and efficient state power. Wilson calls for the flexibility to interpret the Constitution in accord with new conditions, and criticizes the narrow and mechanical separation-of-powers constitutionalism. In its place, he wants to institute a separation of political and administrative questions in government. Chapter 3 outlines this broad vision of separating politics and administration in the American national state, and subsequent chapters address the specific institutional forms that the new vision was to take.

Wilson's earliest institutional plan for effecting his political ideas, as described in chapter 4, is for the adoption of something approaching a parliamentary system of government. A great admirer of the British political tradition, especially its parliamentary orators, Wilson called for breaking down the separation between legislative and executive branches so that Congress could take the lead in politics. A parliamentary system would also be ideal because it would extricate the political branches from the day-to-day details of governing and turn such matters over to the permanent civil service. Wilson later found this particular institutional mechanism unlikely to succeed, so he turned instead to proposing a new institutional arrangement that would feature strong presidential leadership. This change in institutional thinking, addressed in chapter 5, was a change in means only; it did not reflect new views on the principles of politics but was instead a different institutional way of putting into practice the organic state theory to which Wilson continued to subscribe. Political and administrative questions were still to be separated under this new arrangement, which would feature presidential supremacy over a reconstituted party system, and an activist judiciary as a partner in keeping the system responsive to the spirit of the times. Chapter 6 examines Wilson's leadership doctrine in more detail, suggesting that his visionary concept of leadership is grounded in historicism and is central to transforming the institutional expectations for the American presidency. I also argue in this chapter that Wilson's leadership doctrine—indeed, his new constitutionalism as a whole—is not as democratic as it seems, but instead amounts to elite governance under a veneer of democratic rhetoric. An essential part of this elite governance is the role of the bureaucracy, which is taken up in chapter 7. Wilson wants to free administration from the pressures—and accountability—of politics, and to grant to a nonpartisan civil service greater discretion to manage the complex machinery of the modern American state. Here Wilson's contributions to the origins of public administration are addressed, as is the question of the relationship of Wilson's thought to Hamilton's.

Having relied substantially on Wilson's work prior to his entry into public life, the book concludes with a brief look to 1912 and beyond. While any thorough treatment of Wilson in political life lies well beyond the scope of the book, the conclusion will address some particular issues from 1912 and beyond as they might relate to the book's substantive themes. The relationship of Wilson's thought to Roosevelt's, for example, which is often the foundation for characterizations of Wilson as an antiprogressive, will be addressed, as will be the potential relationship of Wilson's political thought to his subsequent internationalism. It is with these questions that the book will conclude its argument that Wilson, as a consistent progressive, engaged in an important, powerful, and fundamental rethinking of the presuppositions of American republicanism.

NOTES

1. Technically, the first public office held by Wilson was not the New Jersey governorship but membership on the New Jersey Commission on Uniform State Laws, to which he was appointed in 1906.

2. See, generally, the work of Charles Beard, esp. Charles A. Beard and Mary R. Beard, *The Rise of American Civilization*, vol. 2 (New York: The Macmillan Company, 1930). Wilson's contemporary, Herbert Croly, also used this language to distinguish the New Nationalism from the New Freedom, although Croly also seems to have an appreciation for the fact that Wilson may have been philosophically closer to him and Roosevelt than the New Freedom let on. See Croly, *Progressive Democracy* (1914; repr., New Brunswick, NJ: Transaction Publishers, 1998), 15–18.

3. Eldon J. Eisenach, *The Lost Promise of Progressivism* (Lawrence: University Press of Kansas, 1994), 3.

4. There are some scholars who are dubious of significant differences between Roosevelt and Wilson. See Sidney M. Milkis, *The President and the Parties* (New York: Oxford University Press, 1993), 22; Kendrick A. Clements, *The Presidency of Woodrow Wilson* (Lawrence: University Press of Kansas, 1992), 27–28; John Milton Cooper Jr., *The Warrior and the Priest: Woodrow Wilson and Theodore Roosevelt* (Cambridge, MA: Belknap Press, 1983), 219.

5. See, for example, Harry V. Jaffa, "Equality as a Conservative Principle," in *How to Think about the American Revolution* (Durham, NC: Carolina Academic Press, 1978), 13–48.

6. See, for example, Harvey C. Mansfield, *Taming the Prince* (1989; repr., Baltimore: The Johns Hopkins University Press, 1993), 250–57, 289–92; "Returning to the Founders: The Debate on the Constitution," *The New Criterion* 12:1 (September 1993): 48–53; "The Unfinished Revolution," in *The Legacy of the French Revolution*, ed. Ralph C. Hancock and L. Gary Lambert (Lanham, MD: Rowman & Littlefield, 1996), 19–41.

7. Abraham Lincoln to Henry L. Pierce and Others, April 6, 1859, in *Abraham Lincoln: Speeches and Writings, 1859–1865*, ed. Don E. Fehrenbacher (Library of America, 1989), 19.

8. Publius, *The Federalist Papers*, ed. Charles R. Kesler and Clinton Rossiter (New York: Mentor, 1999), 9:40, 85:494–95; 82:459. I am indebted to James R. Stoner for his suggestion of these passages to me.

9. Mansfield, "Unfinished Revolution," 33. In general, see Mansfield, *America's Constitutional Soul* (Baltimore: The Johns Hopkins University Press, 1991), 1–17.

10. It is on the question of the compatibility of the Declaration and the Constitution where my argument differs from Mansfield's. While Mansfield agrees that the prudent political science of the Constitution is a vital aspect of the founding, he suggests that this is because the Constitution is more about changing the tenor of the founding than it is about completing the mission of the Declaration. In particular, Mansfield contends that the potentially dangerous implications of the Declaration's equality doctrine are moderated by the Constitution, and in this sense America has a "constitutional soul" as opposed to a soul based on the political theory of the Declaration. The Constitution, then, does not so much complete as it does correct the Declaration, inculcating a "constitutional culture" to counteract the Declaration's Lockean, revolutionary culture. See, for example, Mansfield, "Returning to the Founders," 50–53; *Taming the Prince*, 289; "Unfinished Revolution," 22,

35. My own view, as I endeavor to demonstrate here, is that the institutional political science of the Constitution follows quite naturally from the political theory of the Declaration, since the natural-rights doctrine of the Declaration necessitates the institutional restraints that one finds in the Constitution. This is why Wilson—along with most progressives—found that he could not critique the limited character of the Constitution without also critiquing the natural-rights teaching on which it is based. Wilson saw that one could not be fully understood without the other. Even in defending the Constitution itself during the ratification debate, James Madison made clear in *Federalist* 43 that the forms of the Constitution exist only to serve the ends of the Declaration: "The transcendent law of nature and of nature's God," wrote Madison, "declares that the safety and happiness of society are the objects at which all political institutions aim, and to which all such institutions must be sacrificed." *Federalist* 43:247.

11. *Federalist* 10:47.

12. *Federalist* 6:22, 24.

13. *Federalist* 10:51.

14. See *Federalist* 48 and 51.

15. Wilson, "An Address to the Jefferson Club in Los Angeles," May 12, 1911, in *The Papers of Woodrow Wilson* (hereafter cited as *PWW*), 69 vols., ed. Arthur S. Link (Princeton: Princeton University Press, 1966–1993), 23:33–34. Quotations from Wilson's writings will be modernized as necessary for grammar and especially spelling, as Wilson liked to Anglicize his words. Emphasis will be in the original unless otherwise specified.

16. There will be those who will object to the contrast between Wilson's historicism and the political theory of the American founding, and will argue instead that the differences between the two are not fundamental but are, instead, a matter of degree. Such a view is often based upon one of the common interpretations of Leo Strauss's *Natural Right and History* and *What Is Political Philosophy?* This interpretation leads to the proposition that by accepting the ideas of the Enlightenment, the American founders unwittingly signed the country on to the logical—if not necessary—progress in modern political thought from Machiavelli and Locke to Rousseau and Hegel, and ultimately even to Nietzsche and Heidegger. That an American progressive should move away from Locke's concept of the social contract to Hegel's idea of the state will not, according to this argument, seem so arbitrary. This is, of course, a huge question in political philosophy and American political thought—one that has been ably taken up on all sides and which lies well beyond the scope of this book. About it I will say only that the rejection of nature and the reliance on the will in idealism and nihilism seems to represent something more than a minor distinction between the likes of Hegel on the one hand and Locke on the other.

17. Wilson, *The State* (Boston: D. C. Heath, 1889), 658–59.

18. Hugh Hawkins, *Pioneer: A History of the Johns Hopkins University, 1874–1889* (Ithaca, NY: Cornell University Press, 1960), 300.

19. Richard J. Stillman II, "Woodrow Wilson and the Study of Administration: A New Look at an Old Essay," *American Political Science Review* 67 (June 1973): 583. For further information on Wilson's background at Hopkins, see John M. Mulder, *Woodrow Wilson: The Years of Preparation* (Princeton: Princeton University Press, 1978), 75; Henry Wilkinson Bragdon, *Woodrow Wilson: The Academic Years* (Cambridge, MA: Belknap Press, 1967), 103.

20. Bragdon, *The Academic Years*, 104.

21. Joseph Dorfman, "The Role of the German Historical School in American Economic Thought," *American Economic Review* 45 (May 1955): 25; William Diamond, *The Economic Thought of Woodrow Wilson* (Baltimore: The Johns Hopkins Press, 1943), 27–28.

22. Herbert Baxter Adams, "New Methods of Study in History," *Journal of Social Science* 18 (1884): 218. Some have suggested that Wilson was disappointed with his experience at Hopkins, given complaints he makes during correspondence at this time (see, for example, "To Richard Heath Dabney," February 17, 1884, in *PWW* 3:25). But Wilson did not complain about what it was he was learning; rather, he seems most distressed about the separation from Ellen Louise Axson, to whom he had become engaged shortly before entering Hopkins.

23. Bragdon, *The Academic Years*, 173. Wilson's comments were made to Charles H. McIlwain, whom Bragdon interviewed.

24. See, for example, "Cabinet Government in the United States," August 1879, in *PWW* 1:493–510.

25. See Wilson's undergraduate Commonplace Book, in *PWW* 1:87–88, 94–98, 106–7, 110–12.

26. "True Scholarship," May 24, 1877, in *PWW* 1:268.

27. "The Study of Politics," September 1891, in *PWW* 7:280–83.

28. "A Working Bibliography," March 27, 1890, in *PWW* 6:562–606. In the general category of "administration," there are fourteen entries—six are in German, five are in French, and the remainder are English translations of books written by the German Rudolph Gneist. The entries for Bluntschli are *Lehre com mordernen Stat*, *Staats und Rechtsgeschichte von Zurich*, *Geschichte der Republik Zurich*, and *Geschichte des Sweizerischen Bundesrechts*. Under the category of "Constitutional History—America," Lieber's *The Rise of Our Constitution* is listed, along with Karl Friedrich Neumann's *Geschichte der Vereinigten Staaten von Amerika*. The single entry on "Modern Constitutions" refers to the series by Heinrich Marquardsen entitled *Handbuch des Oeffentlichen Rechts der Gegenwart*. Of the three entries for "Democracy," two are French and the third is Herbert Spencer's essay "The Great Political Superstition." The entries for Hegel include the English edition of *The Philosophy of History* and the German edition of *The Philosophy of Right*.

29. Wilson to Horace Elisha Scudder, May 12, 1886, in *PWW* 5:218.

30. Wilson to Horace Elisha Scudder, July 10, 1886, in *PWW* 5:303–4.

31. Robert Nisbet, *History of the Idea of Progress* (New York: Basic Books, 1980), 171.

32. Laurence R. Veysey, *The Emergence of the American University* (Chicago: University of Chicago Press, 1965), 1, 10–11.

33. Bernard Crick, *The American Science of Politics: Its Origins and Conditions* (Berkeley: University of California Press, 1964), 37. An important article on the role of the American university in the nineteenth-century development of progressivism has been written by John Marini. Titled "Theology, Metaphysics, and Positivism: The Origins of the Social Sciences and the Transformation of the American University," the essay will be available in Ronald J. Pestritto and Thomas G. West, eds., *Challenges to the American Founding: Slavery, Historicism, and Progressivism in the Nineteenth Century* (Lanham, MD: Lexington Books, 2005).

34. Edmund Burke, *Reflections on the Revolution in France* (New Rochelle, NY: Arlington House), 19.

35. Burke, *Reflections*, 44.

36. Burke, *Reflections*, 72–75, 109–10.

37. In addition to *Social Statics* and *The Man Versus the State*, see Spencer's essays "The Social Organism" and "Progress: Its Laws and Cause" for an elaboration of these basic themes.

38. Crick, *American Science of Politics*, 41–46. Crick points out that Darwin's theory itself was not explicitly progressive, but that the line between evolution and more full-blown theories of progress was very much blurred in America, particularly among devotees of Spencer. This helps to explain Wilson's apparent oscillation between the evolutionary thinking of the Historical School and the more idealistic and historicist concept of progress.

39. The earliest reference to Bagehot in Wilson's work that I have found is from 1879: "Cabinet Government," in *PWW* 1:501.

40. Walter Bagehot, *The English Constitution* (1867; repr., Ithaca, NY: Cornell University Press, 1981), 252.

41. Bagehot, *The English Constitution*, 267.

42. Bagehot, *The English Constitution*, 243.

43. Bagehot, *The English Constitution*, 8–9.

44. Bagehot, *The English Constitution*, 59. Wilson himself was critical of Mill. In a reflection on Macauley's account of Mill, Wilson commented: "How absurd Mill's theory of government was[,] to be sure." *PWW* 1:155. Entry on July 19, 1876.

45. See the first chapter of Walter Bagehot, *Physics and Politics* (1872; repr., Chicago: Ivan R. Dee, 1999), 3–38.

46. Bagehot, *Physics and Politics*, 34.

47. Bagehot, *Physics and Politics*, 46.

48. Bagehot, *Physics and Politics*, 75–76.

49. Bagehot, *Physics and Politics*, 140.

50. Bagehot, *Physics and Politics*, 75. Emphasis added.

51. Bagehot, *Physics and Politics*, 187.

52. "Wilson's Critique of Bagehot's *Physics and Politics*," July 20, 1889, in *PWW* 6:335.

53. Nisbet, *History of the Idea of Progress*, 174–75.

54. Wilson to Ellen Louise Axson, March 1, 1885, in *PWW* 4:317. In the scholarly literature, Scot J. Zentner makes the most explicit case for Wilson's Hegelianism. Zentner catalogues the following instances of Wilson's directly citing Hegel in his writings: *PWW* 1:89, 3:428, 4:317–18, 5:361, 6:586, 8:129. See Zentner, "President and Party in the Thought of Woodrow Wilson," *Presidential Studies Quarterly* 26:3 (Summer 1996): 676 (note 12).

55. "The Study of Administration," November 1886, in *PWW* 5:361.

56. G. W. F. Hegel, *The Philosophy of Right*, trans. T. M. Knox (Oxford: Oxford University Press, 1967), 11.

57. Hegel, *Philosophy of Right*, 10.

58. G. W. F. Hegel, *The Philosophy of History*, trans. J. Sibree (New York: Dover Publications, 1956), 17–18.

59. Hegel, *Philosophy of History*, 91–96.

60. Hegel, *Philosophy of History*, 9.

61. Hegel, *Philosophy of History*, 39.

62. Hegel, *Philosophy of History*, 31.

63. Hegel, *Philosophy of History*, 39.

64. Hegel, *Philosophy of History*, 39.

65. Hegel, *Philosophy of Right*, sec. 258.

66. Hegel, *Philosophy of History*, 9.

67. Hegel, *Philosophy of Right*, 10.

68. Hegel, *Philosophy of History*, 44–46, 52.

69. Hegel, *Philosophy of Right*, sec. 273.

70. Hegel, *Philosophy of History*, 52.

71. Hegel, *Philosophy of History*, 85.

72. Hegel, *Philosophy of Right*, sec. 272.

73. Hegel, *Philosophy of Right*, sec. 294.

74. Hegel, *Philosophy of Right*, sec. 288.

75. Johann K. Bluntschli, *The Theory of the State*, 3rd ed. (1852; repr., Oxford: Clarendon Press, 1921), 19–20.

76. Bluntschli, *Theory of the State*, 21.

77. Bluntschli, *Theory of the State*, 31.

78. Scot J. Zentner, "Liberalism and Executive Power: Woodrow Wilson and the American Founders," *Polity* 26:4 (Summer 1994): 579–99; Zentner, "President and Party."

79. Niels Aage Thorsen, *The Political Thought of Woodrow Wilson 1875–1910* (Princeton: Princeton University Press, 1988), 229.

80. Bragdon, *The Academic Years*, 51, 115, 175.

81. Diamond, *The Economic Thought of Woodrow Wilson*, 37. Diamond also points to the heavy influence on Wilson by British authors, most importantly Burke and Bagehot, but also William Gladstone, Charles Fox, Richard Cobden, and John Bright. See note 18.

82. Stillman, "Wilson and the Study of Administration," 583.

83. Dorfman, "The German Historical School," 17.

84. Mulder, *Years of Preparation*, 104, 165.

85. Arthur S. Link, *Wilson: The Road to the White House* (Princeton: Princeton University Press, 1947), 31.

86. I am indebted to Daniel D. Stid's account of this school in *The President as Statesman: Woodrow Wilson and the Constitution* (Lawrence: University Press of Kansas, 1998), 3 (note 6). See Alexander George and Juliette George, *Woodrow Wilson and Colonel House: A Personality Study* (New York: Dover Publications, 1964); William Bullitt and Sigmund Freud, *Thomas Woodrow Wilson, Twenty-Eighth President of the United States: A Psychological Study* (Boston: Houghton Mifflin, 1967); and James David Barber, *Presidential Character* (Englewood Cliffs, NJ: Prentice Hall, 1972).

87. As Thorsen explains, Beard himself never wrote much on Wilson, but he was responsible for the familiar "Jeffersonian versus Hamiltonian" dichotomy used to describe Wilson's transformation from a states'-rights Jeffersonian conservative to a progressive, nationalist Hamiltonian. Beard is important, too, because of his influence on his student William Diamond, who writes an early economic interpretation of Wilson. See Diamond, *The Economic Thought of Woodrow Wilson*. See also Thorsen, *The Political Thought of Woodrow Wilson*, 235.

88. Richard Hofstadter, *The American Political Tradition* (New York: Vintage Books, 1974), 308–67; Louis Hartz, *The Liberal Tradition in America* (New York: Harcourt, Brace & World, Inc., 1955); Cooper, *The Warrior and the Priest*; August Heckscher, *Woodrow Wilson* (New York: Scribner's Sons, 1991); Clements, *Presidency of Woodrow Wilson*.

89. James W. Ceaser, Glen E. Thurow, Jeffrey Tulis, Joseph M. Bessette, "The Rise of the Rhetorical Presidency," *Presidential Studies Quarterly* 11 (Spring 1981): 158–71; Ceaser, *Presidential Selection: Theory and Development* (Princeton: Princeton University Press, 1979); Tulis, *The Rhetorical Presidency* (Princeton: Princeton University Press, 1987); Paul Eidelberg, *A Discourse on Statesmanship: The Design and Transformation of the American Polity* (Urbana: University of Illinois Press, 1974); Robert Eden, *Political Leadership and Nihilism: A Study of Weber and Nietzsche* (Tampa: University of South Florida Press, 1983); Eden, "Opinion Leadership and the Problem of Executive Power: Woodrow Wilson's Original Position," *Review of Politics* 57 (Summer 1995): 483–503; Eden, "The Rhetorical Presidency and the Eclipse of Executive Power: Woodrow Wilson's *Constitutional Government in the United States*," *Polity* 18:3 (Spring 1996): 357–78; Charles R. Kesler, "Separation of Powers and the Administrative State," in *The Imperial Congress*, ed. Gordon S. Jones and John A. Marini (New York: Pharos Books, 1988), 20–40; Kesler, "The Public Philosophy of the New Freedom and the New Deal," in *The New Deal and Its Legacy*, ed. Robert Eden (New York: Greenwood Press, 1989), 155–66.

90. Kesler, "Separation of Powers," 31.

91. Terri Bimes and Stephen Skowronek, "Woodrow Wilson's Critique of Popular Leadership: Reassessing the Modern-Traditional Divide in Presidential History," *Polity* 29:1 (Fall 1996): 27–63.

92. Eisenach, *Lost Promise of Progressivism*, 3.

93. Eisenach, *Lost Promise of Progressivism*, 31–36.

94. Eisenach, *Lost Promise of Progressivism*, 124–25. For a different view of Wilson on the commerce clause, see Eric R. Claeys, "The Living Commerce Clause: Federalism in Progressive Political Theory and the Commerce Clause after *Lopez and Morrison*," *William and Mary Bill of Rights Journal* 11 (January 2003): 403–63.

95. Arthur S. Link, *Wilson: The New Freedom* (Princeton: Princeton University Press, 1956), 241.

96. Thorsen, *Political Thought of Woodrow Wilson*, x–xii.

97. Thorsen, *Political Thought of Woodrow Wilson*, 233.

98. Stid, *President as Statesman*, 2–4.

Chapter One

Historicism and Wilson's Critique of the Social Compact

Wilson's understanding of the modern state and the principles that underlie it is laid out most thoroughly in his 1889 work, *The State*.[1] It is this book that Wilson biographer Arthur Link says is "probably Wilson's greatest scholarly achievement."[2] This is no doubt true, especially since the work that Wilson had long planned as a comprehensive statement of his political principles—"The Philosophy of Politics"—was never published and, for the most part, never written. But Wilson's theory of the state, and especially the historical thinking that serves as its backbone, is also evident in a number of shorter, although important, writings. *The State* itself also represents the development of several earlier pieces of writing, most notably Wilson's 1885 essay, "The Modern Democratic State," and reflects research that Wilson had undertaken for his annual five-week lectureship on administration at Johns Hopkins University.[3] As explained in the introduction, my contention is that Wilson's fundamental view of the state and its principles does not change substantially from one work to another. Certainly Wilson's other major, published works also reflect the same basic political thinking that one finds in *The State*. This is the case, for example, with Wilson's famous essay, "The Study of Administration" (1886). While most scholars who write on this essay focus their attention on its second part, with its famous separation of politics and administration and the consequence of that dichotomy for public administration, the first part of the essay is highly significant for the historicism that Wilson boldly employs as the philosophical grounding for his vision of the modern democratic state.

It is no accident that Wilson's theory of the state is influenced heavily by historical thinking, since such thinking was dominant among those from whom he learned about politics. The overwhelming majority of these sources were foreign. While some suggest that Wilson's extensive reliance upon foreign sources bordered on plagiarism, Wilson himself frequently and frankly acknowledged that much of his writing on the state was derivative. Perhaps most striking is the extent to which Wilson drew upon the series on modern governments by Heinrich Marquardsen, titled *Handbuch des Oeffentlichen Rechts der Gegenwart*, in writing *The State*. Wilson remarked in the preface that it would have taken him twice as long to write the book had it not been for the Marquardsen series.[4] Perhaps the best evidence of Wilson's dependence upon the series is the omission of Italy and Russia in his discussion of foreign governments in *The State*—the books on these governments had not yet been published in the Marquardsen series, so Wilson could not write about them in his own work. Ironically, for all of Wilson's reliance on German sources, he was apparently not terribly well skilled in reading the German language. He complained in several letters about the length of time it took him to read German sources due to his limited ability,[5] and he thought seriously about going to live in Germany, at least in part to acquire a stronger competency in the German language.[6] As will be discussed in chapter 7, Wilson's limited ability in German seems to have been the source of his misinterpretation of an important argument of Johann K. Bluntschli on the relationship between politics and administration.

WILSON'S HISTORICISM

The principles that underlie Wilson's theory of the state heavily reflect Hegel and the tradition of historicism. Throughout his writings, Wilson constantly referred to government as something that is living and must adapt and grow in accord with the progress of history. This organic concept of government is most thoroughly explained in *The State*, where Wilson sought to refute the static view of the polity and replace it with one that understands government as constantly developing. He explained that progress comes through the gradual and organic change of history. Such a view encompasses a key tenet of historicism: that human choice has but a small role to play in politics. As Wilson said in an explication that is worth quoting at length, men in politics are confined to adaptation, working within the confines of their particular historical environment, unable to transcend it:

> From the dim morning hours of history when the father was king and priest down to this modern time of history's high noon when nations stand forth full-grown and self-governed, the law of coherence and continuity in political development has suffered no serious breach. Human choice has in all stages of the great world processes of politics had its part in the shaping of institutions; but it has never been within its power to proceed by leaps and bounds: it has been confined to adaptation, altogether shut out from raw invention. Institutions, like

morals, like all other forms of life and conduct, have had to wait upon the slow, the almost imperceptible formation of habit. . . . Revolution has always been followed by reaction, by a return to even less than the normal speed of political movement. Political growth refuses to be forced; and institutions have grown with the slow growth of social relationships; have changed in response, not to new theories, but to new circumstances.[7]

Such a vision of political development precludes grounding politics upon theory or abstract notions of right; instead, politics must take as its guide the historical spirit of its own particular epoch. This is a recurring theme in Wilson's theory of the state, and it is why he insisted that it is impossible to talk about societies as just or unjust in any absolute sense. To do so would require some abstract principle that could serve as a standard for such a judgment. Instead, Wilson asserted, some societies are simply more historically advanced than others. Wilson reasoned that the more advanced societies had simply been able to shed their attachment to historically obsolete principles—escaping from the "tutelage of inexorable custom"—and had adapted their politics to fit modern ideas. Wilson observed that even in advanced nations, political principles tend to lag behind historical reality and need to catch up—our political "oughts" need to take their bearing from what actually "is."[8]

Wilson also adopted the framework of historicism in describing how history brings about progress. Advance in history comes out of conflict, a dialectical process where opposing conventions or customs meet, with the historically superior convention winning out over and assimilating the inferior. Wilson traced this dialectic back to what he considered the early history of the state—the primitive family or tribe. Families would develop different customs, he explains, and through the clash of opposing families and customs, progress would result. This clash of customs was more severe in primitive history because custom was normally a matter of religious belief, and consequently worth a fight to the death. The result of such clashes, whether between primitive families or between modern civilizations, is that "the better prevail."[9] The just cause and the historically victorious cause are one and the same. "In this war," as Wilson elaborated in his lecture notes on state theory, "groups with the best customary law, with the best family organization, the best religion, prevailed. . . . The 'competitive examination of constant war' promoted general progress by making the best drilled and the best bred groups of men predominant."[10] As chapter 3 will discuss in detail, Wilson applied this framework to the American Civil War. For him, the result of the war represented a major step forward for America; it marked the country's moving from an historically inferior, decentralized system of government to a true national system. As he explained in a review of James Bryce's account of the Civil War, it is not sufficient to suggest that the Union cause prevailed. The result was not simply a victory for one of the combatants' positions—in this case, the idea of union over the idea of states' rights. Instead, what emerged from the Civil War was something more advanced than anything that had existed prior to it. According to Wilson, the problem with Bryce's *The American Commonwealth* is that a reader might "get the impression that our civil war, which was a final contest between nationalism and sectionalism, simply confirmed the Union in its old strength, whereas it in reality, of course, confirmed it in a new character and strength which it had not at first possessed, but which the steady advance of the national development, and of the national idea thereby begotten, had in effect at length bestowed upon it."[11] To put this idea in terms of the Hegelian dialectic, out of the clash between thesis and antithesis comes synthesis, the rising up of a newer, more advanced stage of history. In this respect, the particular events of the Civil War, as well as the events leading up to it, were necessary and good: they served the cause of historical utility by forcing America's growth as a nation.

For Wilson, the key persons and events of history are part of the providential plan for progress. Providence, through the particulars of history, gradually brings about the development of man from infancy to adulthood, so men must be constantly aware of this need to adapt and grow. A good example of this view is Wilson's corpus of work on George Washington. For Wilson, it was not mere fortune that led to a man of Washington's unique abilities to occupy a position of leadership at a crucial juncture in the history of American political development. Rather, Washington was God's way of using history to push America to its next step in the path of progress. "Washington was neither an accident nor a miracle," Wilson wrote. "Neither chance nor a special Providence need be assumed to account for him. It was God, indeed, who gave him to us; but God had been preparing him ever since English constitutional history began."[12] Wilson made the same argument about Napoleon as he did about Washington. In discussing the growth and development of administration in "The Study of Administration," Wilson saw Napoleon's despotism as historically necessary for the advance of administration in France.[13] Hegel himself uses Napoleon in much the same manner, asserting that in spite of the despotism of his rule, Napoleon served the cause of historical utility by helping to usher in a new historical age.[14] So history—its persons and events—is a means by which God's plan for human progress is put into practice. History is therefore not accidental or random; it is rational, powerful, and has a specific end in mind.

Wilson made clear that the development of nations does follow a general pattern, and even though some may follow it more speedily than others, all will eventually undertake it and reach its predetermined end. He explained that there are "periods of growth through which government has passed in all the most highly developed of existing systems, *and through which it promises to pass in all the rest.*"[15] This argument about the necessity of historical development is found not only in Wilson's early academic writings like "The Study of Administration" and *The State*, but also in his later work *Constitutional Government in the United States*. In that book, he said that there are four stages through which *all* governments pass: (1) government is the master and people are its subjects; (2) government remains the master, not through force but by its fitness to lead; (3) a stage of agitation, when leaders of the people rise up to challenge the government for power; and (4) the final stage, where the people become fully self-conscious and have leaders of their own choosing.[16] Regarding Wilson's seeing every event in history as a necessary part of God's plan for progress, Link makes the following telling observation:

> [Wilson] raised every issue and conflict to a high stage upon which the human drama was being played out. Were the citizens of Trenton about to vote upon the adoption of commission government? Then they were confronted with an opportunity to show the world whether Americans were capable of enlightened self-government! Were the American people about to enter a war? Then they were privileged to give their blood and treasure to make the world safe for democracy and to extend the dominion of righteousness throughout the earth!

Link attributes Wilson's approach to his being a "romantic moralist."[17] But this is, of course, a quality that makes perfect sense for someone with Wilson's idealistic brand of historicism. This outlook views the facts of history in light of their world-historical significance—that is, their role in helping to bring about the ultimate rational end toward which all of history is directed.

Wilson describes in Hegelian terms the progress of human history toward a rational end: the history of human progress is the history of the progress of freedom. Wilson explained that, as history has moved forward, people have become increasingly "conscious" of their freedom, and this evolution has led them to translate this consciousness into written constitutions. Significantly, Wilson does not say that modern, written constitutions show that people have become especially cognizant of their individual rights; instead, they have become more conscious of their freedom to direct the government. So mature freedom is not understood in terms of the freedom of the individual from state action but the freedom of a people to direct the power of the state.[18] Mature freedom is also not understood in terms of the rights with which one is endowed by nature (as the Declaration of Independence understands it), but as becoming more capable of overcoming or making use of nature. "Progress," Wilson wrote, "lies in the growth of man's ability to make more of himself and to make more out of nature."[19] Thanks to this increase in freedom, we become more fully human; history, by bringing about this increasing consciousness of freedom, makes us more human. "Who can doubt," Wilson asked, "that man has grown more and more human with each step of that slow process which has brought him knowledge, self-restraint, the arts of intercourse, and the revelations of real joy?" Furthermore, with each new age, humans must make sure to grow and adapt accordingly. As Wilson noted,

> In a new age we must acquire a new capacity, must be men upon a new scale and with added qualities. We shall need a new Renaissance, ushered in by a new "humanistic" movement, in which we shall add to our present minute, introspective study of ourselves, our jails, our slums, our nerve-centers, our shifts to live, almost as morbid as mediaeval religion, a rediscovery of the round world and of man's place in it, now that its face has changed.

If history is the process of men becoming fully human, then the end of this process is what Wilson called "self-liberation." History brings us into full realization of our freedom.[20]

When men realize their freedom at the end of history, they do so not as isolated individuals but as unified parts of a nation-state. History moves the state along through the state's own process of growth—from its roots in the primitive tribe to its mature status as a highly centralized and unified living organism. In his account of the state's development, Wilson made clear that history does have a definite end. He remarked that "no one who comprehends the essential soundness of our people's life can mistrust the future of the nation. He may confidently expect a safe nationalization of interest and policy in the end, whatever folly of experiment and fitful change he may fear in the meanwhile."[21] Wilson's proof that history is a powerful force—that it will certainly lead to the just and rational end—is the history of the United States. How else, Wilson asked, could the United States have survived and grown as a nation under a decentralized form of government with no real place for dynamic leadership, if not for the providential force of history? Wilson reasoned: "Unquestionably we believe in a guardian destiny! No other race could have accomplished so much with such a system."[22]

The historicism that underlies Wilson's theory of the state is perhaps most evident in the historical contingency through which he views all principles of government. As history moves forward, Wilson contended, one cannot speak of a single just or best form of government, because there is no accessible universal standard for such a government. Instead, the best government is the one that best reflects the spirit of a nation at a particular time and place.

> Nation differs from nation, in habits, aptitudes, ambitions, needs, desires, and a system of politics which will suit one nation may be eminently unsuitable for

another, its neighbor. *There is*, accordingly, *no one best system of government*, but for each nation there is some sort of government which is best adapted to its wants and capacities, most appropriate and helpful in its present stage of development. When once this idea is fully accepted, as it must be by every student qualified to judge, it is impossible to be doctrinaire, to travel any longer the "high priori" road of political speculation.[23]

One cannot do, therefore, what the American founders presumed to do in finding in nature the universal principles of just government. This is because, according to Wilson, government must represent not some ideal ethical form, but the current thought or will of the people. And while the founders certainly understood that the practical application of universal principles would depend and even vary on the basis of a prudent grasp of the circumstances, Wilson contended that the ethical forms themselves were simply a product of the historical mind. The implication of this argument is that for less advanced peoples—who are likely to have a spirit that is despotic—the best form of government may very well be a despotism; despotism would be the form of government most reflective of that people's contemporary thought or will. As Wilson explained, "The reason why one polity suits one nation and another, another, is that institutions match the thought of the people to which they belong."[24]

Wilson confirmed this notion of historical relativism in *The State*, where he asserts that there is no such thing as a universal law that transcends time and place. The only law is conventional, contingent upon particular customs, traditions, and environments. "Law thus normally speaks the character, the historical habit and development of each nation," Wilson wrote. "*There is no universal law*, but for each nation a law of its own which bears evident marks of having been developed along with the national character, which mirrors the special life of the particular people whose political and social judgments it embodies."[25] Wilson added a small qualification to his rejection of universal law, noting that there are certain common concepts or beliefs that can come to gain universal status. However, these concepts become universal not because they are grounded in some transcendent principle, but only because they have come to be accepted conventionally in most places in any given time.[26] This qualified notion of universal "conceptions" is applied to the realm of international law, which is where Wilson used the term *Law of Nature*. Here again, the Law of Nature is simply a precept that has gained its status because most have assented to it.[27]

In applying this framework to America, Wilson concluded that American law is simply a reflection of the spirit of the American people, and this spirit is contingent upon history. "If the American spirit is different from the spirit of any other nation," Wilson reasoned, "it is so because of the history of

America."[28] Problems in American government, consequently, result from a reticence to adjust our political principles to the new spirit that history is bringing forth. Wilson worried about the tendency in America, as in all nations, to have an unthinking reverence for the past, and complained that "we have ourselves in a measure canonized our own forefathers of the revolutionary era, worshipping them around fourth of July altars."[29]

HISTORICISM AND WILSON'S RELIGION

In several of Wilson's earliest writings, historical progress is characterized in explicitly religious language, and progress itself becomes something of a divine mission to be pursued with religious fervor. In keeping with a primary tenet of historicism, Wilson saw God's divine plan coming to fruition on earth. The final victory of good over evil is not something that transcends the earthly regime; instead, God uses human history to bring about the triumph of good here on earth, in the form of the ideal state at the end of history. There was an important utopian element to progress for Wilson and many others, and this feature distinguishes their brand of historical thinking from the less idealistic Historical School: paradise was not to be achieved in the next life but in this one. Earthly politics, therefore, takes on very high stakes, with each obstacle to progress seen as an obstacle to God's plan for the final victory of good over evil.[30]

The theme of progress as a religious battle, where God gradually triumphs on earth through the works of men fighting for progress, is emphasized in an early Wilson essay, "Christ's Army." Wilson depicted the fight for progress as a battle between the forces of righteousness and the devil's army of darkness, which is "marshaled by fiends under the dark banners of iniquity." In the early stages of the battle, the dark army scores many successes over the forces of good, but over time the righteous army becomes increasingly triumphant. "Thus," Wilson wrote, "the battle of life progresses and the army of Saints ever gains ground under divine generalship."[31] The culmination of Wilson's battle in the final earthly victory of good over evil coincides with Hegel's argument that the process of historical progress represents the gradual actualization of God's divine plan on earth. In a persuasive article on the historicist nature of Wilson's civic theology, Gregory S. Butler emphasizes the importance of unity. History gradually brings about a unity of will and thought. The role of God, Butler explains, is to move history in such a way that this unity is ultimately achieved. The history of America is particularly important—America was a key battleground in the victory of good over evil: "The organic conception of politics means that America had been assigned a special civilizational destiny by divine providence, and that American history was the story of a slow but inevitable unfolding of that destiny." This historicist civic theology was also part of Wilson's idealism for the entire world. Once America had become united from within, it could then turn to the outside world and lead it down the path to righteousness. "This was America's holy mission,"[32] an important connection between Wilson's domestic progressivism and his visions for a new world order. Butler also raises a good question: How does one reconcile Wilson's historicism, which seems to forbid looking beyond the concrete particulars of one's own time, with the abstract character of Wilson's idealistic theology? The answer lies in Wilson's adherence to German idealism, where history is seen as the unfolding of the divine idea on earth. Utopia is the *result* of concrete human history; it is not brought about by transcending human history. As Butler contends, Wilson's "organic view of American politics was grounded in a philosophy of history in which a pre-existing, divinely-inspired revolutionary plan was seeking its fulfillment, and was destined to triumph in the fullness of time."[33]

Since progress for Wilson is divinely ordained, one's participation in progress takes on the form of an obligation to God. This also means that those opposed to progressive ideas are also opposing God's plan for the earth. Wilson made clear that there can be no compromise on these matters: one is either for God or against Him, either for progress or against it. Certainly this attitude is familiar to those who study Wilson as a public figure, where Wilson was often inexplicably intransigent on issues where compromise would seem to have been the only means to at least partial success. But from Wilson's perspective, there can be no compromising with the divinely ordained plan for progress, and no questioning of someone who is an agent of this divine mission. As he wrote in "Christ's Army," in the battle for the ultimate victory of good over evil, "There is no middle course. No neutrality."[34] Wilson contended in another early essay, "Christian Progress," that men have a divine obligation to engage in "soul-progress." This soul-progress is idealistic in that it can move in only one direction, because God is in control. The man engaged in this journey can never go backwards: "There is no armor for his back . . . to retreat is death."[35] The religious understanding of the drive for progress in politics often led Wilson to see himself as the embodiment of God's vision for effecting righteousness on earth—a view that John M. Mulder calls "the Wilsonian synthesis of personal religion and political power." As Mulder rightly contends, this view was often naïve and overbearing, since it made it impossible to question "a leader who claimed to be serving the people while aggrandizing his own power."[36] To question a leader who sees himself on a divinely inspired mission is to question the will of God.

Following Hegel's model in *The Philosophy of History*, religion and politics for Wilson become indistinguishable. Belief in the ultimate victory of good over evil means believing in this victory being accomplished by history through the concrete particulars of earthly politics—especially in the final ideal state toward which history is progressing. One cannot understand the fulfillment of God's plan outside of the earthly state, and so religious faith requires a belief that the state is the fulfillment of God's plan on earth. Richard J. Bishirjian makes this point in describing the progressive vision of America's civil religion—particularly that of Wilson and Herbert Croly. The progressive civil religion, Bishirjian explains, was utopian. It required a faith that a good end on earth is preordained and that the power of the state must be used to make it come about. Religion, in this sense, is essentially a faith in the state. Croly even speaks of secular saints and a leader-messiah who "will reveal the true path" and direct the state.[37] Wilson himself was sharply critical of anything that might detract from one's faith in and obedience to the state. In the political realm, this led him to attack individualistic conceptions of rights—or any concept like the social compact that emphasized a distinction between the sphere of the state and the sphere of the individual. In the young Wilson's religious writings, these ideas occasionally manifested themselves in his criticism of Catholicism. In a series of letters to newspaper editors, Wilson characterized the Catholic Church as "an organization which, whenever and wherever it dares, prefers and enforces obedience to its own laws rather than to those of the state."[38] For Wilson, the Catholic religion detracted too much from civic religion—from the faith one ought to have in the state.

For a man of his strict religious upbringing (Wilson's father was a minister) and for someone who had to operate under the eyes of religiously minded university trustees, Wilson was bold in embracing both Hegelian themes and those of evolutionary thinkers. This boldness is noted by Laurence R. Veysey, who remarks on Wilson's unrestrained embrace of Hegelianism—and especially the Hegelian philosopher Josiah Royce.[39] Wilson also had considerable sympathy for his uncle, Dr. James Woodrow, who was educated at German universities and came to adopt Darwinian principles. Woodrow's ideas caused a scandal at Columbia Presbyterian Seminary, where in 1884 he was tried and convicted for heresy on the basis of his evolutionary views. Woodrow was subsequently ousted from the Presbyterian Church and fired from his seminary position. Wilson, a great admirer of his uncle, was appalled at the church's treatment of him.[40]

Wilson's religious views—particularly his belief that religious faith required a commitment to fulfilling God's plan here on earth—naturally raise questions about his connections to the Social Gospel movement. While some explicitly reject any such connection,[41] there are certainly thematic similarities between Wilson and the Social Gospel movement's combination of Unitarianism and Hegelianism. Social Gospel embraced a version of Christianity that focused on social salvation in this world, one where the Christian religion becomes the motivation for a kind of social work. While espoused most famously by Walter Rauschenbusch, Social Gospel was embraced by some people closer to Wilson, including his teacher at Hopkins, Richard T. Ely. Moreover, Wilson's religious essays do argue that we must carry out the work of Christ in our everyday lives, particularly through service to others.[42]

HISTORICISM AND THE QUESTION OF RACE

While Wilson's troubling views on the race question are occasionally, albeit quietly, acknowledged in some of the better histories, it is much rarer to see Wilson's racism connected with his historicism. The standard assumption is that because Wilson was a southerner, his racism must have had its roots in his southern upbringing. Such assumptions are normally found in those accounts of Wilson that see him as a conservative, states'-rights Jeffersonian. Just as this general interpretation of Wilson as a proponent of states' rights is fundamentally flawed (I will explain why this is so in chapter 3), so too are those accounts that attribute Wilson's racial views wholly to his southern heritage.[43] Wilson did not, in fact, subscribe to the "southern" position on most political questions; his views on race, while certainly consistent with those held by most southerners of the time, are mostly attributable to the historicist nature of his political philosophy.

For Wilson, the modern state results from the progress that history brings about. Progress in history is based upon the advance of certain races. Individuals advance as part of particular races, peoples, or civilizations. In *The State*, Wilson explained that certain races had been "progressive," and that all governments must have had their historical foundations in the beginnings of these "progressive races."[44] He traced the roots of modern government to the development of three races in particular: Aryan, Semitic, and Turanian.[45] Elaborating in "The Study of Politics," Wilson wrote that in studying how politics has advanced over the course of history, the student will see the historical superiority of some races over others. Recall Wilson's argument that there is no single best form of government but instead a government is best when it conforms most precisely to the particular historical spirit of its people. Here Wilson explained that superior races have a modern spirit, and hence the best form of government for them is modern democracy. Inferior races are mired further back in the process of history, and so the spirit of an inferior race may be a perfect match for an autocracy. In other words, some races, by virtue of their historical superiority, deserve a more advanced form of government. Compared to his own race, Wilson contended, "Other races have developed so much more slowly, and accomplished so much less."[46]

Wilson adopted the Hegelian model of historical progression: advance arises from clashes between major peoples or races, with the superior people defeating the inferior, and world history moving forward as a result. As explained in the introduction, this is why Hegel saw slavery as a positive development for Africans; he claims that it liberated them in the sense that they were subjugated by a superior race, and the result of this conquest was historical progression. Since history represents the gradual advance of freedom, to engage in progress—even if forced to do so by subjugation—is to become more free. In *The State*, Wilson commented on certain "stagnated nationalities." These are races or peoples who have not come into conflict with their superiors and consequently have not progressed beyond a primitive stage of development.[47] He cited as an example the way progress came to Chinese civilization: "The nation which is most likely to linger until it stagnates is the caste nation, caught in a crust of custom which it is almost impossible to break or even to alter, unless some irresistible force from without break and destroy it, as the force of the western nations has so ruthlessly broken the ancient forms of Chinese life."[48] So Wilson's racism lies at a much more fundamental level than mere prejudice. For him, some races are advanced historically and others are backward; the best thing that can happen to the inferior races and peoples is to be defeated and assimilated by their historical superiors. This stance echoes a central premise of Hegel's *The Philosophy of History*.

In the context of his historicism, Wilson's observations on the race issue in America can be understood in their proper light. One finds very little direct commentary on slavery itself in Wilson's papers. He did denounce slavery in an early marginal note, commenting that "surely there is some statesmanlike way of ridding a state of such a curse as slavery is—a curse to industry and a curse to morals."[49] Yet he also defended the general way in which slaves were treated, even while admitting that conditions for slaves could certainly be bad in exceptional cases.

> Books like Mrs. Stowe's *Uncle Tom's Cabin*, which stirred the pity and deep indignation of northern readers, certainly depicted possible cases of inhuman conduct towards slaves. Such cases there may have been; they may even have been frequent; but they were in every sense exceptional, showing what the system could produce, rather than what it did produce as its characteristic spirit and method.[50]

While Wilson's commentaries on slavery were relatively few, the same cannot be said for his views of Reconstruction. And Wilson's view of blacks as an inferior race was central to his frequent criticism of Reconstruction. Wilson detested Reconstruction policy because it put southern governments under the control of blacks. In his five-volume American history, Wilson contended that "the white men of the South were aroused by the mere instinct of self-preservation to rid themselves, by fair means or foul, of the intolerable burden of governments sustained by the votes of ignorant negroes and conducted in the interest of adventurers."[51] In a marginal note, he explained that Reconstruction government was detestable "not because the Republican Party was dreaded but because the dominance of an ignorant and inferior race was justly dreaded."[52] Wilson's primary objection to the political power of blacks in the south seems to have been his estimation that they were far too uneducated to be given a role in governing. A massive education effort would be required so that the black race could be "reclaimed from ignorance and indolence."[53] Wilson also raised a practical objection to the new political power of blacks in the postwar South: it led directly to the prevalence of carpetbagging, which was having a deleterious effect upon the southern economy.[54]

When Wilson reflected on the end of Reconstruction in *Division and Reunion*, he saw it as a turning point in American history, where the country had finally turned away from the old conflict and could now progress as a true, united "nation." This moving forward as a nation also meant a return to the rule of whites in the South: the whites had finally overcome the various Reconstruction barriers and regained control. According to Wilson's assessment, "Negro rule under unscrupulous adventurers had been finally put an end to in the South, and the natural, inevitable ascendancy of the whites, the responsible class, established."[55] For Wilson, national development could move forward now that the historically superior race had regained the upper hand.

THE SOCIAL COMPACT

Wilson contended that in order to progress, America had to leave behind its attachment to the historically inferior principles of social compact theory. He offered his historical view of American principles as a "destructive dissolvent" to the social compact theory of such thinkers as Richard Hooker and John Locke, which was so influential on the early Americans.[56] While social compact theorists like Locke looked to an abstract account of human nature in order to frame the purpose and scope of civil government, Wilson countered that the foundation of government can be uncovered only by looking to the actual history of its development, not to conjecture or theory. He admitted that our historical knowledge of society's actual beginnings may be limited, but even limited historical knowledge is far superior to engaging in "a priori speculations" about the origin of government. Moreover, Wilson asserted that "modern research" had rendered historical knowledge more reliable, making the knowledge of the true foundations of government more accurate as well. This stance contrasts with the theory of social compact, which "simply has no historical foundation."[57] Social compact theory rests upon a universal account of human nature, one that can be inserted into any particular historical environment as a standard for just government. Yet Wilson reasoned that looking at our contemporary human nature tells us nothing about human nature in past ages; this is why he contends that any theory of government "founded upon our acquaintance with our modern selves" cannot be universal.[58] Social compact theory is best understood as a product of the particular age in which the social compact philosophers promulgated it. The mistake of the social compact theorists—much like the mistake of the American founders—was not in establishing certain principles of government for their own age, but in thinking that such historically contingent principles could in fact transcend history and define just government for all ages.

The contention that the true principles of government come from history led Wilson to launch into a long discussion of the origin and history of the major tribes and peoples of the world—a discussion that occupies the bulk of Wilson's energy in *The State*. In looking to the actual history of human development, Wilson found that social organization originated in the history of "kinship." Because he viewed the family as the first state, Wilson investigated the characteristics of the primitive family and concluded that the modern state grew gradually out of the patriarchal family. The state's actual historical origins in the family disprove the notion of a voluntary contract as the basis for government or for any relations among individuals in society. Historically speaking, individuals in the families and tribes that constituted early societies were not radically autonomous and were not free to contract agreements. They were born into relations with and obligations to others over which they had no control. Hence, the "law of status"—not contract—governed the early conceptions of social order.[59]

In turning away from conjecture about a state of nature and looking instead to history for his understanding of government, Wilson launched into a critique of individualism. For Wilson, the patriarchal family was the historically true original condition of man. In such a condition, there is no concept of individualism. "All that [the individual family members] possessed, their lives even and the lives of those dependent upon them, are at the disposal of [the] absolute father-sovereign." Wilson contrasted this factual beginning of society with the radical autonomy posited by social compact theory, and concluded that the state-of-nature concept has led to an unfounded emphasis on the individual. The modern state originated in the historical structure of the family, Wilson argued, and is, therefore, a cohesive and fundamental political unit in its own right. The historical reality of the state's origins undermines the claim of "Locke and Locke's co-theorists" and shows how the individual was really an indistinguishable part of a larger community. Even as society developed in history, Wilson claimed, "it grew without any change of this idea."[60] As Wilson explained in his later work *Constitutional Government*, the mistaken emphasis on individualism in America comes out of an abstract notion of individual rights that is grounded in social compact theory. The problem with an abstract doctrine of rights is that it is not real and therefore can never form the basis of genuine political principles. Taking aim directly at the language of the Declaration of Independence, Wilson wrote:

> No doubt a great deal of nonsense has been talked about the inalienable rights of the individual, and a great deal that was mere vague sentiment and pleasing speculation has been put forward as fundamental principle. The rights of man are easy to discourse of . . . but they are infinitely hard to translate into practice. Such theories are never "law." . . . Only that is "law" which can be executed, and the abstract rights of man are singularly difficult to execute.[61]

In contrast to a government founded on the vague and speculative doctrine of abstract rights, real governments are practical, adjusting their principles to fit the current circumstances.

The argument against social compact theory also requires Wilson to discuss the role of natural law and the theorists who promoted it, whom Wilson identified as Hooker, Locke, and Thomas Hobbes. Social compact theory, according to Wilson, follows from the state-of-nature argument that the original or natural condition of human life was individual autonomy, from which, "as a result of deliberate choice, in the presence of the possible alternative of continuing in this state of nature," commonwealths "came into being." Political society, under such an account, is a human construct that is circumscribed by the more fundamental and ahistorical law of nature. Such a view of government, Wilson asserted, gives far too much credit to human choice. The social compact theorists "bring the conception of conscious choice into the history of institutions. They look upon systems as *made*, rather than as developed." Here Wilson's criticism of social compact theory reflects Jean-Jacques Rousseau, who argued that the early contractarians had erred in their conception of government by ascribing many things to the state of nature that were, in fact, the product of man's historical development. Wilson seems to have been conscious of the Rousseauan nature of his argument, since the conclusion to the section of *The State* in which Wilson discusses social compact theory is made up entirely of a long citation from John Morley's book on Rousseau.[62] Other sharp criticisms of the early social compact thinkers appear in works of Wilson's besides *The State*. In an early comment on Locke, for example, Wilson attributed Locke's influence not to the latter's theoretical arguments about the social compact but to the fact that Locke's opinions happen to have fit well with the spirit of his times. Locke was popular, in other words, "notwithstanding the introduction of the unnecessary fiction of social compact."[63]

Wilson put this mistaken, ahistorical notion of the social compact at the center of the French Revolution, and he joined the conservative critics of the Revolution by focusing on the pernicious influence of abstract theory. Government, Wilson reasoned, cannot be properly founded on revolution, which attempts to overturn the historical order; it must instead develop out of the gradual, organic process of historical evolution. Europe had suffered from a failure to recognize this distinction. "Democracy in Europe, outside of Switzerland, has acted always in rebellion, as a destructive force: it can scarcely be said to have had, even yet, any period of organic development." Only through a gradual process of evolution can government be founded on a unified common will, which Wilson contrasted to the passions of "Parisian mobs."[64]

The basic problem with democratic revolutions, Wilson contended, lies in their characterization of democracy as a universal principle; in fact, no government can be founded on the notion of principle. The fathers of democracy put it forth as "the single principle and crown of government," while the truth is that government develops out of the reality of history, not the spontaneous proposing of principles or theories. "The construction of government," Wilson wrote, "is not a matter of inspiration; reform is not a matter of invention." Historical contingency must be recognized: "Never a doctrine arrogated to itself absolute truth and perfect nutritiousness for all men alike but was eventually convicted of being only relatively true, and nutritious only under certain conditions and for certain persons." Even democracy itself, Wilson reasoned, "has proved only a relative, not an absolute, good." This is why Americans still do not have an accurate conception of democracy. Their understanding, based upon the rhetoric of the founding, conceives of democracy from the perspective of "abstract principles." So Wilson sought to correct this misunderstanding by showing how democracy evolved through a long history of political development, from an evolutionary "order in which democracy may be seen to be but a single term."[65] Wilson employed the British model of democracy to correct the mistaken early American view precisely because British democracy evolved gradually from historical tradition.

Wilson contrasted the "slow and steady stages of deliberate and peaceful development" of democracy in England with the notion of democratic "revolution." A nation cannot simply adopt a government by choice, Wilson contended, so England's route to democracy distinguishes it from other nations. "The English alone have approached popular institutions *through habit*. All other races have rushed prematurely into them through mere impatience with habit: have adopted democracy instead of cultivating it." Wilson cited Burke as a champion of his organic understanding of the democratic state and used Burke to attack the "theoretical democrats" who rely on principle divorced from history. Democracy must be seen as "the result of history, not of theory."[66] Wilson elaborated:

> The historical view of government is in any case the only fully instructive view; in the case we are considering—the case of history's latest political fruit, democracy—it is the only view not utterly barren. Only history can explain modern democracy either to itself or to those who would imitate it.[67]

The historical view of democracy has an important meaning for American institutions. If we cease to understand our democracy as one founded on timeless principles and instead adopt the evolutionary conception of democracy, we free ourselves to make fundamental institutional alterations. If we "extend those lines of development" of which American democracy has been a part, Wilson argued, we will realize that we "can make further permanent advances. We have not broken with the past: we have, rather, understood and obeyed it." One does not break with the past, in other words, when one understands that the past represents constant change and development. The only way one breaks with the past, ironically, is by maintaining a misguided faith in the timelessness of its principles. Wilson noted that the written constitution, which distinguishes America from England, has exacerbated this problem of misguided faith. Written constitutions are misleading in that they appear to endorse the social compact concept of government. Wilson explained that given the founding generation's social compact understanding of constitutionalism, it was only natural for this generation to see its forms of government as "definite creations." Unfortunately, such a view has proved an impediment to growth in later generations of Americans. The difficulty of the amendment process aggravates the problem by reinforcing the idea that change and adaptation are generally to be avoided. "We have been too much dominated," Wilson concluded, "by the theory that our government was an artificial structure resting upon contract only," and have been insufficiently cognizant of the true historical foundation for the state.[68]

The disdain that Wilson showed in these academic works for the theory upon which the American system was founded, as well as his preference for the evolutionary character of the British tradition, can be traced to his earliest days of thinking about such questions. His early diary reflections on the anniversary of American independence, for instance, certainly prefigure his scholarly work. "How much happier [America] would be now," Wilson wrote, "if she had En-gland's form of government instead of the miserable delusion of a republic. A republic too founded upon the notion of abstract liberty! I

venture to say that this country will never celebrate another centennial as a republic. The English form of government is the only true one."[69] Wilson explained in "The Study of Administration" that the English were superior because they had bowed to the movement of history. England had abandoned her
undemocratic forms, but unlike other nations she had not done so radically,
abruptly, or through violence. Instead, England had "simply tempered the
severity of the transition . . . by slow measures of constitutional reform."[70] The
English ability to be flexible, to adapt along with the gradual march of history,
stems from the fact that the English constitution is not grounded in abstract theory. The English, consequently, have not had to encounter obstacles to progress
that constantly impede the theoretically inflexible doctrines of other governments that eschew historical reality for vague notions of universal right.[71]

In laying out the virtues of the organic British constitutional tradition, Wilson made frequent and sharp contrasts between it and democracy in France.
The French had not adopted their system of government as a result of gradual adjustment to the historical environment but had instead transcended
their own historical conditions to impose a radically new regime. For Wilson,
a nation cannot adopt a system of government for which history has not yet
prepared it. As he argued in an essay praising the English constitution,
"Nothing but long habit will avail to steady and energize free institutions.
You can teach a savage in a single day how to use a rifle; but not even a hun-
dred years of persistent practice has taught Frenchmen how to behave in a
House of Commons."[72] The French did not undertake the evolutionary approach to constitutional change, and the result has been that in spite of their
having nominally established a democracy in the late eighteenth century,
they are still working on making democracy a reality because history has not
yet caught up.[73]

Wilson clearly articulates his attack on the revolutionary nature of French
democracy in an important early essay entitled "Self-Government in France."
In it, one can see the foundations for his subsequent embrace of organicism
in *The State*. One can also see that the roots of Wilson's historical thinking
were present well before he began his graduate education at Hopkins. This
historical thinking seems to have come from his early exposure to the English
Historical School—especially through Walter Bagehot's account of the
British constitution and other works on important British figures—and seems
to have made Wilson ripe for the more full-blown historicism that he was subsequently to encounter and embrace. In "Self-Government in France," Wilson
asked readers to "contrast the orderly progress of reform in England with the
rush of revolutions in France."[74] The very notion of revolution is inherently
problematic, because it proceeds without the requisite historical conditions.
Revolution implies rashness, or what Wilson characterizes as an impatience

to reach the proper historical circumstances. The rashness of revolutions is fueled primarily by their foundation in abstract principles; liberty, Wilson believed, means nothing when it is derived abstractly.[75]

It should not be surprising that Wilson greatly admired Burke's attack on French revolutionary thinking. In an essay on Burke, Wilson portrayed him as the quintessential embodiment of English constitutional thought, and argued that a hatred of revolutionary change was the core of Burke's political philosophy. Burke's attack on revolutionary change, according to Wilson, fit perfectly with Wilson's own rejection of the social compact and of founding governments on principle as opposed to historical circumstance. Burke "hated the French revolutionary philosophy and deemed it unfit for free men," Wilson wrote.

> And that philosophy is in fact radically evil and corrupting. No state can ever be conducted on its principles. For it holds that government is a matter of contract and deliberate arrangement, whereas in fact it is an institute of habit. . . . It assumes that government can be made over at will, but assumes it without the slightest historical foundation.[76]

Wilson even warned that the European continent—particularly France—was so filled with the spirit of revolution that America ought to guard against too much immigration from Europe. Wilson contended that immigration policy should favor people of the English historical spirit, for whom constitutional growth comes in an organic, evolutionary manner.[77]

For Wilson, what really mattered in Burke was his attack on the role of abstract theory in politics. This does not mean, however, that Wilson embraced Burke's conservatism. What Wilson seems to have taken from the English Historical School was the premise that we cannot transcend our historical environment and adopt universal or ahistorical principles. But Wilson, like Hegel, was utopian about the direction of history in a way that is absent from Burke and the other historical writers. Burke's conservatism, therefore, was too resistant to the kind of change that Wilson wanted to see taking place in politics—change that would need to occur in order for history's predestined end to come about. Wilson complained that "Burke was doubtless too timid, and in practical judgment often mistaken. Measures which in reality would operate only as salutary and needed reformations he feared because of the element of change that was in them."[78]

What Wilson loved about Burke was what Wilson considered to be his attack on reason, and his assertion of the superiority of custom and tradition. Wilson confessed that "there are no parts of Burke upon which I more love to dwell than those in which he defends prejudice against the assaults of the rational and expediency against the haste of the radical."[79] Wilson contended that reason is too private; the individual is isolated with his own reason, without the context of the environment in the community around him. For Wilson, the private reason of the average man is highly suspect (he calls it "unlearned" and "undisciplined"), and therefore he wanted most men to rely upon the customary prejudices of their communities. And in case there were any doubts as to what Wilson thought of the natural-rights doctrine of the American founders, Wilson blames the use of reason for such dangerous and radical doctrines as "socialism" and "natural rights." He conflated the two concepts by seeing in them the same key characteristic: an abstract idea of equality that eschews any kind of historical reality. He also saw both socialism and natural rights as fundamentally selfish.

Significantly, Wilson did not object here to socialism because of its statism and the centralized control it gives to the government over the individual. Instead, he saw the populist labor movements that are often motivated by socialism as means of individual laborers attempting to get something that they do not deserve. As he explained,

> The program of the average labor organization, made up of distorted bits of economic truth, mixed with many of the cut and dried formulas of rationalistic socialism, represents an attempt to replace in the mind of the laborer the virtues of patient industry and reverence for law which had taken such deep root there, with calculated polices which ignore law and would substitute the natural rights of man. It is a perilous attempt to train the unlearned and the undisciplined to "live and trade each on his own private stock of reason." Its success is due to the fact that it uses these theories of natural right which chime in with selfish desire and so establishes passion at the same time that it overthrows habit.[80]

The problem with socialism is that it is fundamentally revolutionary. It is grounded in abstract theorizing and is not content to adjust policy gradually to fit the evolving historical environment. This criticism is important to understanding the policies Wilson later advocated as a public figure. Wilson, like the socialistic labor movement, was looking for a way to depart from the laissez-faire system of the founders' liberalism and adopt a system that would empower the state to manage the new economic conditions of modern times. But Wilson was too much of an elitist and too fearful of populism to embrace the labor movement fully. He wanted to avoid doctrines that were based on abstract ideas and that would attempt to transcend the customs and prejudices of the community. In no way, however, does his approach preclude a substantial expansion of state power over the economy and the individual, so long as the expansion is accomplished gradually in accord with the demands of the current historical spirit.

Burke's virtue, for Wilson, is that he took the current historical realities as the fundamental guide in his statesmanship. Burke did not theorize about what politics ought to be in form; instead, he constantly adjusted to fit changing circumstances. In his essay on Burke, Wilson identified a series of key issues that Burke confronted during his career.[81] Wilson contended that Burke approached each of these issues in a consistent manner: He "had no system of political philosophy" but was guided instead by the circumstances of each case. This is evident in the practical policy he advocated in Parliament with regard to the American colonies. Burke urged England to consider the particular circumstances in America instead of trying to govern each of her possessions in the same, uniform manner. The historical reality was that America was unique—too big and too successful to be suppressed in the manner of India. England ought to recognize this and make peace with the Americans on favorable terms.[82] In his five-volume American history, Wilson blamed the onset of hostilities between Britain and the American colonies at least partly on the Crown's failure to adopt Burke's position. Burke was wise to argue that England should abandon its focus on the legal and theoretical status of the colonial legislatures. Regardless of who was right on matters of form, Burke contended that the legislatures were legitimate because England had allowed them to exist for some time and the historical fact of their existence must now be recognized. Wilson contrasted what he calls the strict lawyer's view of the question to Burke's organic view.[83] This is a contrast that is highly relevant to Wilson's view of the American constitution, where he urged that the document be interpreted not according to some strict or theoretical account of its meaning, but in accord with the evolving demands of the time. For Wilson, and for Wilson's Burke, it is the actual practice of government, not its form, that matters most.[84]

THE DECLARATION OF INDEPENDENCE AND WILSON'S IDEA OF LIBERTY

If government must constantly adjust its principles and practices to the evolving spirit of the times, what of seemingly timeless principles like liberty? The idea of liberty is certainly central to the American system of government, as Wilson himself repeatedly recognized. He stated in *Constitutional Government* that liberty is the cornerstone to the meaning of a constitutional government. But as we learn in *Constitutional Government* and elsewhere, to say that the principle of liberty is the central feature of American government is not to say that the meaning of liberty is static. In a fundamental criticism of the ideas of the American founders, Wilson took great care to contend that liberty cannot be permanently defined. It must instead take its meaning from the historical spirit in which it operates, so as history moves forward, the definition of liberty must move accordingly.[85] Wilson explained that, at the founding, we did not discover the ultimate or permanent meaning of liberty. We discovered instead a definition of liberty that fit well with the historical circumstances of the founding—one that our subsequent progress as a nation has superseded. Wilson contended that "liberty is not something that can be laid away in a document, a completed work. It is an organic principle, a principle of life, renewing and being renewed. Democratic institutions are never done—they are, like the living tissue, always a-making."[86] He pointed to the French Revolution as an example of what can happen if a nation grasps at an understanding of liberty outside of the current historical environment.[87]

This historically contingent view of liberty certainly runs Wilson afoul of the first two paragraphs of the Declaration of Independence, which grounds liberty in the transhistorical "Laws of Nature and of Nature's God." But Wilson argued that these passages of the Declaration were meant to be understood practically, not theoretically. They express a particular idea of liberty that was appropriate for the circumstances of the time—in this case, for providing a vehicle of separation between Britain and the colonies. In *Constitutional Government*, Wilson explained that the liberty spoken of in the Declaration is nothing more than the liberty of successive generations of men to define liberty as they please, according to the spirit of their own times:

> We think of [the Declaration] as a highly theoretical document, but except for its assertion that all men are created equal, it is not. It is intensely practical, even upon the question of liberty. . . . It expressly leaves to each generation of men the determination of what they will do with their lives, what they will prefer as the form and object of their liberty.

Wilson utilized Burke's evolving concept of liberty as support, contending that "every generation, as Burke said, sets before itself some favorite object which it pursues as the very substance of its liberty and happiness. The ideals of liberty cannot be fixed from generation to generation." In explicit opposition to the Declaration's natural law foundation for liberty, Wilson responded that "liberty fixed in unalterable law would be no liberty at all."[88]

In stating that liberty means different things in different times, Wilson turned the practical effect of the Declaration's liberty doctrine on its head. For the framers of the Declaration, the natural-rights concept of liberty translated into a protection of the individual against the tyranny of government, even when such a tyranny might be powered by a majority—hence the clear emphasis in *The Federalist* on mitigating the effects of majority faction. For Wilson, the founders' view of liberty was, in fact, impeding the freedom of majorities to rule unfettered. So liberty in the new conditions of modern times, Wilson explained, must be understood as the liberty of majorities to use the power of government as they see fit. In *Constitutional Government*, Wilson wrote that "political liberty is the right of those who are governed to adjust government to their own needs and interests."[89] The problem during Wilson's time was that progressives wanted to use the power of government to manage a whole host of new social and economic problems; Wilson recognized that the old understanding of individual liberty against the power of the state was impeding the prospects for the progressive agenda. Because liberty is often at the center of Wilson's arguments on government, some scholars conclude mistakenly that he is concerned with defending the individual against the power of the state. But Wilson was concerned not with the liberty of the individual, but with the liberty of individuals as part of a majority to direct government in a manner that they believe the times demand. In an 1891 essay, he offered a particularly Hegelian understanding of what this modern concept of liberty actually means. Liberty, he explained, is not found in freedom from state action but instead in one's obedience to the laws of the state. Since the laws of the state are, in themselves, nothing but the manifestation of the free will of the people, obeying the state is the fulfillment of true freedom. Wilson contended that "law is the *external organism of human freedom*."[90]

Wilson's redefinition of liberty makes complex his various commentaries on the Declaration of Independence. On the one hand, the sharp critique of abstract notions of liberty certainly makes Wilson a critic of the Declaration's theoretical premise. Yet on the other hand, Wilson often praised the Declaration by glossing over the document's theoretical premise. So when Wilson was interpreting the Declaration as a practical continuation of an organic tradition—an evolutionary document—he praised it. When he interpreted the Declaration as abstract and revolutionary, he attacked it. Such is the case in Wilson's history *Division and Reunion*, where Wilson holds the Declaration responsible for the importation of pernicious French theories about the rights of man. Wilson wrote that "French doctrines of the 'rights of man' crept in through the phrases of the Declaration of Independence."[91] The implication is that abstract ideas about the rights of man were not originally part of the American founding tradition.

For the most part, Wilson offered a favorable view of the Declaration by reading the theoretical premise out of it. Around the same time that he wrote *Constitutional Government*, Wilson made the book's themes more developed and explicit in an address on the authors and signers of the Declaration. The basic argument is that the Declaration was a practical document, reflecting the particular needs of the era in which it was written. "It is common to think of the Declaration of Independence as a highly speculative document," Wilson claimed, "but no one can think it so who has read it. It is a strong, rhetorical statement of grievances against the English government."[92] He contended that the Declaration cannot be seen as espousing a transhistorical understanding of liberty, because each generation must determine for itself what it is that liberty actually means. In a subsequent address, as mentioned in the introduction, Wilson even went so far as to suggest that the first two paragraphs of the Declaration be omitted when reading it. Wilson is often characterized as a Jeffersonian, but his argument with regard to the Declaration shows that if this characterization were accurate, it was so only insofar as Jefferson is redefined to mean something different than what he meant in his own time. "The business of every true Jeffersonian," Wilson contended, "is to translate the terms of those abstract portions of the Declaration of Independence into the language and the problems of his own day. If you want to understand the real Declaration of Independence, do not repeat the preface."[93] The business of every true Jeffersonian, in other words, is to redefine Jefferson according to one's own terms.

Wilson was conscious that he understood the founders differently than they understood themselves. He explained that his departure from the founders lay in his critique of their static and universal understanding of liberty; to Wilson, real liberty means that the people must be left free to make government whatever they currently want it to be. He elaborated:

> We are not bound to adhere to the doctrines held by the signers of the Declaration of Independence: we are as free as they were to make and unmake governments. We are not here to worship men or a document. But neither are we here to indulge in a mere rhetorical and uncritical eulogy. Every Fourth of July should be a time for examining our standards, our purposes, for determining afresh what principles, what forms of power we think most likely to effect our safety and happiness. That and that alone is the obligation the Declaration lays upon us.[94]

Wilson argued here that the founding principles themselves require us not to revere them but to change them in accord with the dictates of history.

At the root of Wilson's reinterpretation of the founding principles is a rather questionable understanding of the American Revolution. His commentaries on Burke are revealing in this regard, particularly where he echoed and reinforced Burke's criticisms of the French Revolution. It is certainly the case, as explained in the introduction, that the American and French revolutions were distinct in several critical ways. Yet there were similarities as well, and Wilson often critiqued those very elements of the French Revolution that were most similar to America's own. Wilson, for example, saw as a fatal flaw that the French Revolution relied upon a doctrine of the rights of man derived from an account of nature.[95] And while it made all the difference in the world that the Americans had a sounder and more sober grasp of human nature and an appreciation for the role of prudence in politics that the French lacked entirely, both revolutions looked to abstract principle as a foundation—just the kind of foundation that Wilson excoriated through his praise of Burke.

Wilson's preference for the evolutionary tradition of the British constitution over the revolutionary principles of France also manifested itself in his histories of America, where he commented on the leading figures of the American Revolution. Wilson singled out for praise those leaders who were not abstract in their rhetoric and who were not overly hasty in calling for a clean break with Britain. This is an important theme of Wilson's biography of Washington, whom Wilson found to have been the model of deliberateness and caution. In discussing the colonial leadership of Virginia in 1773, Wilson contrasted Washington with the likes of Jefferson, Patrick Henry, Richard Henry Lee, and Dabney Carr, whom he called "radicals all."[96] He further praised President Washington for his rebuff of the French revolutionaries and for resisting those in America who were more sympathetic to the cause of France.[97]

Wilson certainly connected Jefferson to the ideas of the French Revolution. And while some scholars characterize Wilson as a Jeffersonian (doubtless fueled by Wilson's own use of that label when it was to his political advantage), Wilson in his histories went so far as to say that Jefferson's abstract political philosophy meant that he really was not a true American. He stated that "Jefferson was not a thorough American because of the strain of French philosophy that permeated and weakened all of his thought." For Wilson, abstract political thought is un-American, because it contradicts his own conception of America as an organic part of the British constitutional tradition. Therefore, Jefferson's abstract thought "was un-American in being abstract, sentimental, and rationalistic, rather than practical. That he held it sincerely need not be doubted; but the more sincerely he accepted it so much the more thoroughly was he un-American."[98] Wilson was so intent on reading the doctrine of natural rights out of the American founding that anyone who subscribed to the doctrine—even the author of the Declaration himself—was not genuinely or fully part of the founding.

This attempt to read natural-rights theory out of the American tradition extends to Wilson's analysis of Abraham Lincoln, whom he seems to have misread. While there is genuine scholarly debate as to how central natural-rights theory was to the founding of America, it is hardly debatable that Lincoln relied heavily on natural-rights theory in his own statesmanship. Both Lincoln's admirers and detractors recognize that his arguments on slavery and equality rested squarely on a natural-rights interpretation of the founding and that his speeches were full of natural-rights rhetoric. Yet Wilson praised Lincoln for precisely the opposite quality—for eschewing abstract theory and being guided instead by the circumstances of the time. Wilson simply denied that

Lincoln was guided by theoretical principles: "What commends Mr. Lincoln's studiousness to me is that the result of it was he did not have any theories at all. . . . Lincoln was one of those delightful students who do not seek to tie you up in the meshes of any theory."[99] Lincoln was repeatedly held up by Wilson as a model Burkean statesman—one who never tried to draw on abstract notions of equality and liberty but instead embraced the practical model of evolutionary change.

THE AMERICAN TRADITION AS BRITISH TRADITION

If Wilson were such a strong critic of revolutions and abstract notions of liberty, embracing instead the evolutionary or historical mode of political change, his analysis would seem to put the American Revolution in a rather unfavorable light. Indeed, this is frequently so, as he criticized the abstract theory of the American Revolution. Yet Wilson often praised the American Revolution as well, doing so by portraying it not as a radical change founded on abstract ideas but instead as a natural and gradual outgrowth of the British constitutional tradition. There is much good sense to such an interpretation, of course, as the American political tradition has inherited elements of the British tradition. But the Americans also self-consciously broke from key elements of the British tradition, and it is these departures that Wilson either criticized or ignored.

The characterization of America as an heir to British constitutionalism is made in several of Wilson's most well-known works. In *Constitutional Government*, Wilson placed the origins of America's constitutional government in the British tradition. He placed emphasis on the Magna Carta, which wisely avoided any abstract language in its granting of certain liberties and avoided giving any permanent meaning to the idea of liberty itself. It is this conception of political rights, and not one grounded in natural law, that is the key to understanding the genuine constitutional tradition of America.[100] In "The Study of Administration," Wilson contended that there was no fundamental difference between the political principles of America and England; he asserted that American government simply represented a gradual development out of the British mode of democracy. "We borrowed our whole political language from England," Wilson explained, "but we leave the words 'king' and 'lords' out of it. What did we ever originate, except the action of the federal government upon individuals and some of the functions of the federal supreme court?"[101] Although the founders instituted a separation-of-powers system as opposed to a parliamentary system in order to protect the natural rights of individuals from majority tyranny, Wilson contended that this choice represented a minor difference of institutional means. The basic principles of American government were essentially British, and had been imported into the Constitution by way of imitating the state governments, which had taken British institutions as their guide. But even if the states had been models of British constitutionalism (itself a debatable proposition), Wilson chose not to emphasize *The Federalist*'s clear discomfort with both the form and practice of state governments under the Articles of Confederation. Wilson emphasizes the Magna Carta as a foundation for the American understanding of rights, choosing not to rely on the argument of *Federalist* 84, where Alexander Hamilton lays out in detail the reasons why the Magna Carta has "no application to" American constitutionalism.[102] Yet Wilson persisted: "Fortunately, there was nothing novel in the details of the government proposed. Every practical provision in it, almost without exception, had been borrowed from the experience of the colonies themselves, or from English experience equally familiar."[103]

Not only did Wilson believe that the basic principles of American government are drawn from the British tradition, but he also suggested that the particular institutions of government are essentially the same. There are certainly some obvious differences in form, but such differences were alleged to have arisen out of special circumstances in America and did not amount to much. "The political institutions of the United States," Wilson asserted, "are in all their main features simply the political institutions of England . . . worked out through fresh development to new and characteristic forms." He contended that not only are the institutions similar but that the Americans also adopted large elements of the British common law. While Wilson conceded that the American version eliminated various hereditary and aristocratic privileges, he believed that these divergences were not nearly as important as the substantial continuity.[104] Such a claim ignores, of course, the radical difference in political principles implied by the American rejection of aristocratic privilege. While the Americans understood such a rejection as the key tenet of republicanism—of the idea that political power originates from the people who, by nature, are the source of government—it was for Wilson little more than a cosmetic change.

Wilson's early and sustained fascination with and admiration for British constitutional history helps to explain why he was so ready to understand American government in light of it.[105] In general, Wilson believed that by learning more about the history of foreign governments, we could learn much that would be of use to our own. This was particularly true of what Americans could learn from English history. Wilson thought that we could borrow a great deal from the British tradition because it was so similar to our own.[106] Governments, according to Wilson, are not as unique as is frequently believed.

This is an important premise of *The State*, as Wilson explained in the book's preface. He employed his "historical-comparative method," which demonstrates that all governments are best understood in their historical context and as continuing an evolving tradition. While governments may be at different stages in historical development, they are all on essentially the same path.[107] Hence, for example, America can learn much from England since England simply represents a more advanced version of American constitutionalism. America is simply following the course laid out by the advance of the British constitutional tradition. This is why scholars like Wilson, who want to have some idea of America's future, must study the history of England. Such historical knowledge can then shed light on the reforms that need to be undertaken in America. Wilson's analysis of Congress illustrates this argument: to remedy what ails it, Congress should follow the path of development already taken by its historical predecessor, Parliament. Referring to the English Revolution of 1688, Wilson wrote:

> That Cabinet government is the form which does combine strength, wieldiness, and efficiency more completely than any other form of government yet devised or known appears not only from the discussions of the foregoing chapters but from the history of the English race and from the modern assent of all enlightened nations. The lesson of English history is very plain to this effect. The British House of Commons, the great prototype of our own Congress, passed, almost two centuries ago, through just such a season of inadequate organization as that in which Congress now languishes.[108]

Wilson constantly referred to changes in English history as inevitable, or the result of fate, or part of the irreversible development of British government. He also emphasized how America is bound up with this fateful development of the British tradition.[109] The English constitution is simply more advanced historically and is therefore a beacon of guidance for less-developed systems.[110]

The overall organization of Wilson's five-volume American history is useful in understanding the extent to which he sees American political development as a continuation of the British tradition. Of the five volumes, fully two of them are dedicated to colonial history—that is, to the history of the American people as British subjects. So Americans' history as a people does not begin with the principles of 1776; that date, instead, is simply a part of the long development of the English tradition of government in North America. In fact, much of Wilson's attention in the first two volumes of the history focuses on an account of political events *in England* involving the Crown and Parliament. The first volume of this American history, for example, concludes with a chapter on "the revolution"—not the *American* Revolution, but the *English* Revolution of 1688. Wilson's histories also take great care to note the similarities between the cultural settings of the colonies and England. This is particularly true of the southern colonies, as Wilson explained in his biography of Washington. He noted there that the colony of Virginia strongly resembled England, and that this similarity was an important influence on Washington. Moreover, the Virginia colony is contrasted to northeastern colonies, which were in most cases founded by people who left England because of differences with the Crown. Not coincidentally, according to Wilson, the northeastern colonies were also the most radical.[111]

Fundamentally, Wilson understood American government as an outgrowth of British government because all political systems are the product of historical development. No government, properly understood, can transcend its own historical heritage and environment. Consequently, one can comprehend American government only by grasping the history that led up to it and recognizing that the system itself is bequeathed by history. As Wilson explained in explicitly historicist language, it is the particulars of history, not abstract ideas, that inform the political system:

> [American institutions] are, in other words, English institutions as modified by the conditions surrounding settlements effected under corporate charters, in separate but neighbor colonies; above all as dominated by the material, economic, and social conditions attending the advance of the race in America. *These conditions it is, not political principles, that have controlled our intellectual as well as our political development.*[112]

This historicism is the lynchpin for Wilson's thinking on American government. As he argued in *The State*, the principles of the American system are historically contingent, as are the liberties that most Americans consider fundamental.[113] This is because liberties do not come from nature or anything else that transcends the current historical environment. Under this view, the role of the state is not permanently limited, but can instead become whatever the times are said to demand.

NOTES

1. Portions of my presentation of Wilson's state theory are drawn from my chapter "Woodrow Wilson, the Organic State, and American Republicanism," in *History of American Political Thought*, ed. Bryan-Paul Frost and Jeffrey Sikkenga (Lanham, MD: Lexington Books, 2003), 549–68.

2. Arthur S. Link, *Wilson: The Road to the White House* (Princeton: Princeton University Press, 1947), 21.

3. See, for example, Wilson's lecture notes on "Functions of Government," which were taken largely intact and put into *The State*'s chapter "Functions of Government." Arthur S.

Link, ed., *The Papers of Woodrow Wilson* (hereafter cited as *PWW*), 69 vols. (Princeton: Princeton University Press, 1966–1993), 5:669–90. Quotations from Wilson's writings will be modernized as necessary for grammar and especially spelling. Emphasis will be in the original unless otherwise specified.

4. Wilson, *The State* (Boston: D. C. Heath, 1889), xxxvi. Link explains Wilson's use of the Marquardsen series in an editorial note to the Wilson papers; see *PWW* 6:245.

5. Wilson to Edwin Robert Anderson Seligman, April 19, 1886, in *PWW* 5:163; Wilson to Richard Heath Dabney, November 7, 1886, in *PWW* 5:385.

6. Wilson to Dabney, November 7, 1886, in *PWW* 5:385.

7. *The State*, 575.

8. *The State*, 21.

9. *The State*, 24.

10. "Notes for Four Lectures on the Study of History," September 24, 1885, in *PWW* 5:19–20.

11. "Bryce's *American Commonwealth*," January 31, 1889, in *PWW* 6:74.

12. "A Commemorative Address" (lecture, Middletown, CT, April 30, 1889), in *PWW* 6:178.

13. "The Study of Administration," November 1886, in *PWW* 5:366.

14. G. W. F. Hegel, *The Philosophy of History*, trans. J. Sibree (New York: Dover, 1956), 31.

15. "Study of Administration," in *PWW* 5:365. Emphasis added.

16. Wilson, *Constitutional Government in the United States* (New York: Columbia University Press, 1908), 28.

17. Arthur S. Link, *Wilson: The New Freedom* (Princeton: Princeton University Press, 1956), 149.

18. "Political Sovereignty," November 9, 1891, in *PWW* 7:335.

19. "Notes for Four Lectures," in *PWW* 5:18.

20. "On Being Human," October 2, 1897, in *PWW* 10:249–51.

21. "The Making of the Nation," April 15, 1897, in *PWW* 10:231.

22. "Making of the Nation," in *PWW* 10:235.

23. "The Study of Politics," September 1891, in *PWW* 7:279. Emphasis added.

24. "Study of Politics," in *PWW* 7:279.

25. *The State*, 622. Emphasis added.

26. *The State*, 625.

27. *The State*, 628.

28. "The True American Spirit," October 27, 1892, in *PWW* 8:37.

29. *The State*, 19.

30. This point is echoed nicely by Richard J. Bishirjian, whose article on Wilson and Herbert Croly describes their civil religion as believing in God as the director of history, moving it toward an ideal outcome. Richard J. Bishirjian, "Croly, Wilson, and the American Civil Religion," *Modern Age* (Winter 1979): 36.

31. "Christ's Army," August 17, 1876, in *PWW* 1:180.

32. Gregory S. Butler, "Visions of a Nation Transformed: Modernity and Ideology in Wilson's Political Thought," *Journal of Church and State* 39 (Winter 1997): 40–42.

33. Butler, "Visions," 45.

34. "Christ's Army," in *PWW* 1:181.

35. "Christian Progress," December 20, 1876, in *PWW* 1:235.

36. John M. Mulder, *Woodrow Wilson: The Years of Preparation* (Princeton: Princeton University Press, 1978), 150.

37. Bishirjian, "American Civil Religion," 35.

38. Wilson to the Editor, North Carolina *Presbyterian*, January 25, 1882, in *PWW* 2:97–98.

39. Laurence R. Veysey, "The Academic Mind of Woodrow Wilson," *The Mississippi Valley Historical Review* 49 (March 1963): 626.

40. Wilson to Ellen Louise Axson, June 26, 1884, in *PWW* 3:216–18. For an account of this episode, see George C. Osborn, *Woodrow Wilson: The Early Years* (Baton Rouge: Louisiana State University Press, 1968), 115–16.

41. Mulder, *Years of Preparation*, 85, 151.

42. See, for example, "Work-Day Religion," August 11, 1876, in *PWW* 1:176; and "A Christian Statesman," September 1, 1876, in *PWW* 1:188.

43. Mulder claims that Wilson "adopted his father's allegiance to the South" and contends that Wilson retained certain southern prejudices. He does recognize, however, that Wilson was not a supporter of the Confederacy. Mulder, *Years of Preparation*, 33. Henry Blumenthal's essay on Wilson and race frames the issue more in terms of the practical politics of Wilson's day, and avoids getting into the principles that might underlie Wilson's racial views. Blumenthal does well to note, however, that Wilson thought the white and black races were progressing at different rates, and he is also properly critical of the simplistic assumption that Wilson's southern roots were determinative of his politics and philosophy. Henry Blumenthal, "Woodrow Wilson and the Race Question," *The Journal of Negro History* (January 1963): 1–10. The earlier writings of Link tend to rely heavily on the assumption that Wilson's racial views were grounded in his southern heritage, contending, for example, that Wilson "remained largely a southerner on the race question." See Link, *Road to the White House*, 502; Link, *The New Freedom*, 246. Yet Link's later scholarship on this issue—no doubt having benefited from his working on the multivolume collection of Wilson's papers—shows a much greater appreciation for how much Wilson departed from the traditional southern worldview. See especially Link, "Woodrow Wilson: The American as Southerner," *The Journal of Southern History* 36:1 (February 1970): 6, where Link writes: "During his youth and early manhood, when his political opinions and ideology were being formed, Woodrow Wilson not only failed to think and act like a southerner but, in his strident affirmation of American nationalism and condemnation of sectionalism, indeed went far toward repudiating identification with the South." Link does in this essay, however, give Wilson more credit for a favorable view of the black race than I believe is warranted by the evidence.

44. *The State*, 17.

45. *The State*, 2–3.

46. "Study of Politics," in *PWW* 7:280–81.

47. *The State*, 24.

48. *Constitutional Government*, 29. Nisbet rightly points to the racism that is inherent in the idea of progress—especially what he calls the "progress-as-power" doctrines of statists like Hegel. Robert Nisbet, *History of the Idea of Progress* (New York: Basic Books, 1980), 286–95.

49. "Marginal Notes on John B. Minor," November 10, 1879, in *PWW* 1:583.

50. Wilson, *Division and Reunion: 1829–1889* (1893; repr., New York: Longmans, Green, and Co., 1901), 126–27.

51. Wilson, *A History of the American People*, 5 vols. (New York: Harper & Brothers, 1902), 5:58.

52. "Marginal Note on A. H. H. Stuart," February 5, 1881, in *PWW* 2:19.

53. "Stray Thoughts from the South," February 22, 1881, in *PWW* 2:29.

54. "Stray Thoughts from the South," in *PWW* 2:27.

55. *Division and Reunion*, 273. In addition to the racism inherent in Wilson's historicism, Wilson was not known for favorable treatment of blacks in his public policy. Blumenthal writes that Wilson's 1912 campaign had given blacks some cause for hope, but they were then disappointed by his presidency, especially with its dominance by southern men and policies of segregation. Blumenthal, "Wilson and the Race Question," 5. For confirmation, see Kendrick A. Clements, *The Presidency of Woodrow Wilson* (Lawrence: University Press of Kansas, 1992), 45; Anthony Gaughan, "Woodrow Wilson and the Legacy of the Civil War," *Civil War History* 43:3 (1977): 236–37.

56. *The State*, 11. For another discussion of Wilson and social compact theory, see David Steigerwald, "The Synthetic Politics of Woodrow Wilson," *Journal of the History of Ideas* 50 (July/September 1989): 471–72.

57. *The State*, 13–14.

58. *The State*, 2.

59. *The State*, 3–4, 9–10.

60. *The State*, 7, 17–18.

61. *Constitutional Government*, 16.

62. *The State*, 12–15.

63. "Marginal Notes on Theodore D. Woolsey," May 8, 1883, in *PWW* 2:345. See Wilson to Horace Elisha Scudder, July 10, 1886, in *PWW* 5:303–4, for another of Wilson's critiques of the social compact thinkers.

64. "The Modern Democratic State," December 1885, in *PWW* 5:67, 75.

65. "Modern Democratic State," in *PWW* 5:61–63.

66. "Modern Democratic State," in *PWW* 5:63–65.

67. "Modern Democratic State," in *PWW* 5:65.

68. "Modern Democratic State," in *PWW* 5:65, 67–68.

69. "From Wilson's Shorthand Diary," July 4, 1876, in *PWW* 1:148–49. For similar sentiments, see the diary entry on July 10, 1876, in *PWW* 1:151.

70. "Study of Administration," in *PWW* 5:364.

71. "The English Constitution," October 1890, in *PWW* 7:44.

72. "English Constitution," in *PWW* 7:14–15.

73. "Self-Government in France," September 4, 1879, in *PWW* 1:515.

74. "Self-Government in France," in *PWW* 1:518.

75. "Self-Government in France," in *PWW* 1:522–38. Wilson succinctly lays out his argument from "Self-Government in France" in a letter to Robert Bridges (August 8, 1879, in *PWW* 1:512–13). See also Wilson's marginal notes on John Richard Green (September 4, 1879, in *PWW* 1:542). Niels Aage Thorsen also finds "Self-Government in France" an important essay; see his discussion of it in *The Political Thought of Woodrow Wilson 1875–1910* (Princeton: Princeton University Press, 1988), 36.

76. "Edmund Burke: The Man and His Times," August 31, 1893, in *PWW* 8:341.

77. "Commemorative Address," in *PWW* 6:181.

78. "Edmund Burke: The Man and His Times," in *PWW* 8:340. Thorsen has a sound account of what Wilson took from Burke and what he did not. See Thorsen, *Political Thought of Woodrow Wilson*, 158–59.

79. "An Address to the Princeton Alumni of New York," March 23, 1886, in *PWW* 5:138.

80. "Address to Princeton Alumni," in *PWW* 5:138.

81. (1) England's policy toward the American colonies, (2) administrative reform in the English government, (3) reform in the government of India, and (4) the threat posed by the spirit of the French Revolution.

82. "Edmund Burke: The Man and His Times," in *PWW* 8:334–36.

83. *History of the American People*, 2:217.

84. "Edmund Burke: The Man and His Times," in *PWW* 8:342.

85. *Constitutional Government*, 3.

86. "Commemorative Address," in *PWW* 6:180.

87. "From Wilson's Confidential Journal," December 29, 1889, in *PWW* 6:464.

88. *Constitutional Government*, 4.

89. *Constitutional Government*, 4.

90. "Democracy," December 5, 1891, in *PWW* 7:364.

91. *Division and Reunion*, 111.

92. "The Authors and Signers of the Declaration of Independence," July 4, 1907, in *PWW* 17:248.

93. "An Address to the Jefferson Club of Los Angeles" (lecture, Los Angeles, CA, May 12, 1911), in *PWW* 23:34.

94. "Authors and Signers of the Declaration," in *PWW* 17:251.

95. "Edmund Burke: A Lecture" (lecture, Baltimore, MD, February 23, 1898), in *PWW* 10:414–15.

96. Wilson, *George Washington* (1896; repr., New York: Schocken Books, 1969), 133, 146. See also *History of the American People*, 2:183.

97. *George Washington*, 296.

98. "A Calendar of Great Americans," September 15, 1893, in *PWW* 8:373–74.

99. "Abraham Lincoln: A Man of the People," February 12, 1909, in *PWW* 19:39.

100. *Constitutional Government*, 2, 8.

101. "Study of Administration," in *PWW* 5:378.

102. Publius, *The Federalist Papers*, ed. Charles R. Kesler and Clinton Rossiter (New York: Mentor, 1999), 84:480–81.

103. *History of the American People*, 3:76. See also "Democracy," in *PWW* 7:350; "True American Spirit," in *PWW* 8:37.

104. *The State*, 449, 468.

105. See, for example, these 1876 entries from Wilson's "Shorthand Diary": June 3–13, June 29, July 4, in *PWW* 1:132–40, 147, 149.

106. "Government by Debate," December 1882, in *PWW* 2:205–6.

107. *The State*, xxxv.

108. "Government by Debate," in *PWW* 2:254.

109. *History of the American People*, 1:34.

110. "English Constitution," in *PWW* 7:12.

111. *George Washington*, 9.

112. "Bryce's *American Commonwealth*," in *PWW* 6:71.

113. *The State*, 464.

Chapter Two

The Modern Democratic State and the New Political Science

The previous chapter detailed Wilson's criticism of the social compact and the abstract theory of rights upon which it is based.[1] In making his critique, Wilson seems to sound certain themes of classical democratic theory. He attacked, for instance, the speculative "state of nature" that serves as a foundation for the social compact, contending that such a state is purely imagined and has no basis in historical fact. Wilson also argued that the real origins of government lie not in the autonomous individual, as social compact theory maintains, but in the historical family or tribe. Yet it is clearly the case that, in rejecting social compact theory as a foundation for modern democracy, Wilson was not advocating a return to a more classical or Aristotelian concept of politics. Instead, he offered a vision of the modern state that rejects both classical and early modern theories of democracy.

CLASSICAL VERSUS MODERN DEMOCRACY

Even though Wilson's grounding of society in the family or tribe sounds certain Aristotelian themes, Wilson is just as critical of ancient thought as he is early modern thought. Of the latter, he remarked that the "theory simply has no historical foundation"; the former, according to Wilson, "exaggerates the part played by human choice."[2] Here Wilson refers to the ancient account of the origin of regimes, which emphasizes the statesmanship of the lawgiver as fundamental. He explained that the ancient idea of social organization relies too heavily on the exercise of prudence by certain great individuals or on the ability of human choice to affect historical events. Human thought and action are conditioned by their historical environment, and the ancient notion of statesmanship makes the mistake of assuming that great individuals can transcend

67

that environment. Contrary to the classical account of prudence, a statesman does not take some universal idea of the good and apply it as best he can in a particular historical situation; rather, the historical situation itself gives rise to its own principles.[3]

Wilson was also critical of the Aristotelian cycle of regimes, and he wished "to contrast the later facts of political development with this ancient exposition." While the Aristotelian cycle had suggested a continuous model of regime change based both upon chance events and the prudent (or imprudent) choices made by individuals, Wilson argued that history, in fact, leads to the *permanent* victory of modern democratic government. "Democracy seems about to universally prevail," Wilson contended, because the democratic form of government is the most consistent with the spirit of modern times. The idea of democracy has triumphed, and this is why, unlike earlier forms of democracy, modern democracy is permanent. Wilson wrote that "the cardinal difference between all the ancient forms of government and all the modern" is that "the *democratic idea* has penetrated more or less deeply all the advanced systems of government."[4] This is where the earlier, American founding-era liberalism had an important role to play. While founding-era liberalism was imperfect because it emphasized the permanent status of the individual, its victory was an essential step in the eventual triumph of modern democracy. Modern democracy came to fruition through a dialectical process: earlier, more primitive forms of self-government had to rise up and subsequently fail in order for history to bear its final fruit. Such reasoning also leads Wilson to praise feudalism—not because there was anything inherently good about it but because of its historical utility: "Such a system was fatal to peace and good government, but it cleared the way for the rise of the modern State by utterly destroying the old conceptions." The founding-era notion of the primacy of individual rights—where the state exists for the individual—was, in turn, an "inevitable" reaction against feudalism and earlier forms of statism. That modern democracy has triumphed over its earlier forms "is thus no accident, but the outcome of great permanent causes."[5]

As Wilson explained in "The Modern Democratic State," the state's development culminates in modern democracy—there is no more advanced form of government. "Democracy is the fullest form of state life: it is the completest possible realization of corporate, cooperate state life for a whole people."[6] This is where Wilson's Hegelianism seems to win out over his Darwinism. Instead of an endless adaptation to essentially random changes in environment, Wilson consistently referred to democracy as the intended result of history, the final stage of historical progress. "Democracy is poison to the infant," Wilson wrote, "but tonic to the man." It "is a form of state life which is possible for a nation only in the adult stage of its political development." The idea that democracy is the permanent end of history is an important component of Wilson's rejection of the Aristotelian cycle. When history brings about conditions under which people act as a whole, with a unified will, true democracy has arrived for good. "The cycle of Aristotle," Wilson concluded, "is impossible. For this democracy—this modern democracy—is not the rule of the many, but the rule of the *whole*." The unity of will in modern democracy shows that society has put behind it the Aristotelian problem of the many ruling only for their own interest at the expense of the few. In modern democracy, Wilson explained, "Childish fears have been outgrown." The Aristotelian cycle—like all theories of government—reflected and was therefore contingent upon the historical realities of its own epoch. Aristotle had erected a "philosophy of politics upon generalizations rooted in the changeful fortunes of Hellenic states the old world over." But modern democracy is different; many political thinkers fail to grasp the distinction because they fail to take into account the different historical spirit of contemporary self-government. So while the history of the twentieth century subsequent to Wilson might be cause for reevaluation, Wilson contended that modern democracy would not degenerate into tyranny, even though "many theoretical politicians the world over confidently expect modern democracies to throw themselves at the feet of some Caesar."[7]

As Wilson asserted in a subsequent work on democracy, the course of democracy's development since the American founding had been tremendously positive. The trend of history had been to move away from the founding's conception of democracy, and this trend was a true sign of the nation's growth into a modern democratic state.[8] Wilson made a criticism of Andrew Jackson's presidency in order to support this point. Jackson, Wilson argued, was essentially an autocrat and posed a real threat to the Constitution. Yet even Jackson could not upset the forward movement of history and the concomitant development of immature democracy into modern democracy. In spite of Jackson's "childish arrogance and ignorant arbitrariness," Wilson claimed, the regime survived and progress was not sidetracked.[9] This example offers more proof to Wilson that the Aristotelian cycle of regimes was an outmoded means of analysis, since history assures us that there will be no degeneration of democracy back into tyranny.

Wilson's contention that modern democracy is the final result of history reveals the underlying Hegelianism of his democratic theory. For Wilson, the modern democratic state is the preordained end of history. The history of regimes had not signified mere random adaptation, as a Darwinian analysis might suggest, but had instead been leading up to the permanent victory of modern democratic ideas. In early essays such as "The Art of Governing," Wilson commented that history points to the development of a single kind of government.[10] And in later works such as *The New Freedom*, Wilson laid out his vision of modern democracy as the end-state of historical progress. He used "parables" to communicate his vision. In this case, he likened the development of modern democracy to the building of a house:

> What we have to undertake is to systematize the foundations of the house, then to thread all the old parts of the structure with the steel which will be laced together in modern fashion, accommodated to all the modern knowledge of structural strength and elasticity, and then slowly change the partitions, relay the walls, let in the light through new apertures, improve the ventilation; until finally, a generation or two from now, the scaffolding will be taken away, and there will be the family in a great building whose noble architecture will at last be disclosed, where men can live as a single community, co-operative as in a perfected, coordinated beehive, not afraid of any storm of nature.[11]

In this parable, Wilson not only depicts a highly centralized, perfected, final end-state, but also employs the Hegelian understanding of the end of history. Hegel argues in *The Philosophy of History* that men caught up in the process of history cannot transcend it and therefore cannot see clearly their own role in the great historical unfolding of God's plan for development. Yet when the rational end-state is reached, history has fully revealed the plan, which exists for those at the end of history to look back upon and behold. Wilson's vision of a perfected community whose "noble architecture will at last be disclosed" certainly strikes a similar theme. And Wilson reassured his audience that the triumph of democracy at the end of history is guaranteed and irreversible: "Nor need any lover of liberty be anxious concerning the outcome of the struggle upon which we are now embarked. The victory is certain."[12]

It is history that makes modern democracy superior to classical democracy. History has borne a set of conditions that guarantee the permanency of the modern democratic state. In *The New Freedom,* Wilson explained that modern democracy is possible because the people themselves are in a far more advanced condition than they were at earlier stages of history. The common people are more interested in serious and open discussion of public issues, and are more inclined and prepared to participate in what Wilson called "common counsel." He contrasted these conditions, which are ripe for modern democracy, with the historical setting of earlier democracies, where genuine discussion was absent.[13] In "The Modern Democratic State," Wilson had also argued that a society would know that it had reached "manhood" if the historical conditions were conducive to genuine common counsel. This meant open and serious debate, as opposed to a simple aggregation of variegated interests.[14] In reaching modern democracy, history had also left behind the small-scale democracy of earlier periods. Modern democracy takes place on a national scale, reflecting the unified sentiment of a vast people.[15] This is why Wilson saw administration as a key part of modern democracy, since a modern democratic nation requires a centralized regulatory apparatus.

UNITY AND DEMOCRACY

If the primary difference between modern and classical democracy is the permanence of the former, what is it that makes modern democracy permanent? In a word, its unity. Wilson argued that the dialectical process of the state's development, having progressed beyond the "disintegration of feudalism," has led to a unity of will that underlies modern democracy. Wilson characterized modern society as "the whole" that "has become self-conscious, and by becoming self-directive has set out upon a new course of development."[16] The "common will" underlying modern democratic government is what distinguishes it from ancient democracy, where the spirit of the times was not ripe for genuine democratic institutions. The real authority behind any government, Wilson explained, is the common will or spirit of the society. Even the despotic governments of past ages were based upon the common will of society, insofar as one understands the common will as an implicit expression of the spirit of the age. Wilson applied this notion of implicit will to the American founding. The founding generation was under the impression that it made a conscious choice of the form of government. Wilson conceded that there may have been some genuine choice exercised over minor issues— "modifications" on questions of detail—but in general, the founders' "choice" was a reflection of the epoch's spirit.[17]

The premise behind Wilson's concept of unity is that, in spite of obvious conflicts of special interests on the surface of society, there is a more fundamental unity of will and spirit that is implicit in the most advanced societies. Here Wilson adopted an important theme of German idealism—that history brings about a unity or objectivity of will, and it is this implicit will that must govern the direction of society. The implicit will of a modern society is not equivalent to majority opinion, which exists merely at a surface level and is often beset by contending passions. A true, modern democracy is governed not necessarily by popular majority but by a leadership that can best discern the implicit, historically conditioned will that lies beneath ordinary political competition. This is why, as will be explored more fully in subsequent chapters, Wilson's model of political leadership requires, above all, that the leader hold visionary qualities that enable him to read the historical spirit and discern what the true, objective will of the people really is. Wilson's essay "Democracy" explicates the distinction between rule by majority opinion and rule by the implicit, objective will of society. Wilson called it merely an "assumption, still more curious when subjected to analysis," that "the will of majorities,—or rather, the concurrence of a majority in a vote,—is the same as the *general* will." He further explained that

> the will of majorities is *not* the same as the general will: that a nation is an *organic* thing, and that its will dwells with those who do the *practical* thinking and organize *the best concert of action*: those who hit upon opinions *fit to be made prevalent*, and have *the capacity to make them so.*[18]

Wilson conceded that his conception of modern democracy—where leaders must discern the implicit will of society—did not comport with the traditional understanding of democratic government. To make his point, he provided a highly revealing example of his idea of democracy: the civil service. Wilson admitted that from the perspective of traditional democratic thinking, the civil service seems undemocratic, in that its members are not elected and it elevates the educated man over the common man. But he contended that this governance by educated experts is democratic in a much higher sense: the experts in the civil service will not be distracted by the contending of special interests in majoritarian politics, but will instead discern the true and implicit unified will of the nation. The civil service will thus be in the best position to adjust governmental policy to the evolving will of society. This vision of the role of the civil service is strikingly similar to that put forth by Hegel in *The Philosophy of Right*, where he suggests that the bureaucratic class, even though unelected, sees most clearly the implicit objective will of society. Wilson, for his part, argued that his democratic conception of the civil service "is *not* democratic in the sense in which we have taught our politicians wrongly to understand democracy. It *is*, nevertheless, *eminently democratic*, if we understand democracy as history has given it to us." He added that the civil service is also democratic in the sense that its members—even though unelected and unaccountable—are drawn from the general mass of society.[19] (The implications of this conception of modern democracy for leadership and administration are discussed, respectively, in chapters 6 and 7.)

Wilson applied his idea of unity and modern democracy to the United States. After a series of significant steps in its political development, the United States either had arrived or at least was in the process of arriving at the point where it attained the primary condition for a modern democratic state: unity of implicit will. Wilson claimed that "the United States is singular and not plural. This makes it a united country."[20] A society can be said to have unity when it begins to think on a *national*, as opposed to local, scale. The gradual historical progression of America from a loose collection of localities into a single nation is a constant theme in Wilson's writings. It is also a necessary precondition for the progressive policies that Wilson was to advocate carrying out on a national scale. He explained that "the complete nationality of our law . . . had to await the slowly developed nationality of our thought and habit." This is why democracy, according to Wilson, is not simply a form of government that can be proclaimed or established at any time one wishes. Real democracy must be brought about by history, which gradually brings into being the necessary conditions of national unity. "Democracy," he explained, "is of course wrongly conceived when it is treated as merely a body of doctrine, or simply as a form of government. It is a stage of development. It is not created by aspirations or by new faith: it is built up by slow habit."[21]

Wilson contended that the absence of the proper condition for democracy—a unified democratic will—helps to explain the failure of the French Revolution. The French did not enjoy national unity, so the historical conditions were not ripe for true democracy. Wilson commented: "Paris rioted away the liberties of France at the Revolution because it was only in Paris that there was any life. The rest of the country, never having had imperative thoughts of its own as to the way in which it should be governed, could not have them now."[22] The *revolutionary* character of the French attempt at democracy, its failure to wait for it to evolve out of the proper historical conditions, doomed the effort from the start. A necessary condition for lasting democracy, Wilson argued, is "homogeneity of race and community of thought and purpose among the people." Wilson's historicism leads him to a form of corporatism—a democracy grounded in races or groups as the fundamental political entities. Wilson explained that "there is no amalgam in democracy which can harmoniously unite races of diverse habits and instincts or unequal acquirements in thought and action." Racial purity is important because democracy requires a "habit of concerted purpose and cooperate action," or a group that is "accustomed to act as an organic body."[23] History moves forward not on the basis of individual action but instead by the organic development of groups or races in their corporate capacity. The contrast with Publius's argument in *Federalist* 10 is important to note. For Publius, modern democracy can succeed only in a territory with many diverse interests, so that individual rights can be protected from majority faction. For Wilson, the focus is not on individual rights but on the unity of national will.

Sovereignty

The underlying historical spirit of a people—whether it be suited for democracy or despotism—is paramount in determining the government most appropriate for it. The best government, after all, is simply the one that reflects the historically conditioned will of a particular society. This notion is central to Wilson's argument on sovereignty. The real sovereign in any society, Wilson contended, is not the particular form of government and legal officers that it has but is instead the underlying will of society. Regardless of legal forms, government is always what the historically conditioned spirit of society calls for it to be. We see this point illustrated in *The State*, where Wilson distinguishes between legal sovereignty and real sovereignty. Legal sovereignty concerns the person or persons who can formally make law—a king or a legislature, for example. In reality, this kind of sovereignty has limits, even if in form it has none. Parliament may, for instance, be formally supreme, but Wilson pointed out that there are certain laws that the people, given their historical spirit, will simply not allow. Real sovereignty, then, regardless of legal sovereignty, lies in the will of the organic community. What is important is that law reflect the organic will of the community as opposed to some theoretical or formal structure.[24] Wilson's argument on sovereignty amounts to an argument that whoever exercises sovereign authority must do so by embodying the historical spirit of the people.

Wilson's account of sovereignty is grounded in his study of foreign writers. He cited discussions of sovereignty by the English author John Austin and the German jurist A. F. J. Thibaut. He also listed the key attributes of sovereignty, citing Johann Bluntschli as the primary source. Perhaps the most important of these attributes, at least for understanding Wilson's view of political institutions, is that there must be unity in the sovereign authority "because the state is organic."[25] In other words, as Wilson would say in a later critique of the separation of powers, a living thing cannot have its own organs offset one another. He agreed with Austin, Thibaut, and Bluntschli that legal or formal sovereignty lies in some governmental person or organ, but he stressed that such entities are always limited by what the organic will of the people will tolerate. Institutions and officials, in other words, are sovereign only insofar as they remain connected with the implicit will of the nation.[26] Sovereignty is founded not in God or in nature, but in will. Unlike God or nature, the will of the people is organic and historically contingent. There is a particular will for particular peoples. This is why law, which the sovereign makes on the basis of the organic will of the society, is itself contingent on the historical environment.[27] The English constitution that Wilson so much admired is a good illustration of his conception of sovereignty. Some might consider it a problem that the English constitution is unwritten, so that even its most fundamental liberties seem vulnerable to revocation by ordinary statute. A written constitution might seem to offer more formal protection. Yet Wilson responded that all constitutions, regardless of form, rest on the organic will of the particular society in which they operate. This underlying will is the true sovereign, and government will always reflect what it will and will not tolerate.[28]

The argument on sovereignty helps to show why Wilson was disdainful of constitutional formalism. Particular forms that outline legal sovereignty are effective only to the extent that they embody the community's organic will. This organic will is always evolving, and so particular forms must ultimately give way to the changing spirit of the times, which is far more fundamental. Applied to Wilson's understanding of America, this idea means that it is not terribly important to understand the particular founding intention behind the forms of the Constitution. That intention merely reflected the particular spirit that permeated the founding era; the organic will of American society, however, has evolved well beyond that stage. Wilson urged that the country be far more concerned with the more fundamental organic will of contemporary society—it is this will, and not the static forms of the Constitution, that holds real sovereignty in contemporary America. "Justly revered as our great constitution is," Wilson argued, "it could be stripped off and thrown aside like a garment, and the nation would still stand forth clothed in the living vestment of flesh and sinew, warm with the heart-blood of one people, ready to recreate constitutions and laws." This is why we must concentrate on the "practical spirit of democracy" and not on the misleading understanding of it that comes from constitutional formalism.[29]

Since the state is fundamentally a reflection of the current historical spirit, it cannot be understood as the creation of some particular constitution. The forms of a constitution cannot create a state. The state simply exists, whether formalized by a constitution or not, as an embodiment of the current organic will of society. Just as Hegel suggests that the current state is always just because it is what has been brought about by history, so too Wilson argues that the state is grounded in historical development and not in human choice or contract. " 'Constitutionality,' " he contended, "does not alter the nature of the (historical) state."[30]

An excessive focus on constitutional forms was the primary reason that Wilson was critical of another pioneer in the modern discipline of political science, John W. Burgess. Burgess's tendency to conflate political science and constitutional law indicated to Wilson a narrowness in Burgess's definition of political science—one that failed to understand that political science is much broader, encompassing "the forces of which laws are only the partial and temporary manifestations, while constitutional law is a study of conditions wholly statical."[31]

Government Not a Threat to Society

Since the real force or sovereign in any society is its organic will, government—whatever its particular form—is the creature of that will. Wilson made this point by characterizing government as the mere instrument of society's common will. The will of society evolves in accord with history, and government serves as the means by which society implements its organic will in a given era. It is therefore improper to characterize government as a necessary evil that poses a potential threat to society. Wilson asserted that government "is no more an evil than is society itself. It is the organic body of society: without it society would be hardly more than a mere abstraction."[32] This argument certainly does not mean that all governments in history—because they have been grounded in the organic will of the community—have also been democratic in form. What it means is that a particular society receives the kind of government that is the best reflection of its particular historical spirit. In the early stages of historical development, this usually meant that most societies were governed by despotisms, since the spirit of those peoples was fundamentally despotic.[33] This scenario demonstrates why one cannot transcend one's historical environment to claim that some particular form of government is either just or unjust. There is no single best form of government in history, since the ideal form of government for a particular people depends entirely upon the people's own historical epoch.

The unified will of modern society calls for development; government makes that happen. "Government is merely the executive organ of society," Wilson explained, the organ "through which [society's] will becomes operative." The will of society evolves historically; "Society, like other organisms, can be changed only by evolution," not revolution, which "is the antipode of evolution." As society evolves organically through the stages of history, its will informs and empowers different forms of government. Wilson admitted that the form of government during any given historical epoch is not of great importance, so long as the government is grounded in the spirit of that epoch; the forms of government "exhibit the stages of political development." Wilson cited John Morley's account of Rousseau on this point, asserting that the force employed by the government is always designed to harmonize the subjective interest of the individual with the will of society. Every form of government has such an aim: "The forms of government do not affect the essence of government: the bayonets of the tyrant, the quick concert and superior force of an organized minority, the latent force of a self-governed majority—all these depend upon the organic character and development of the community."[34]

Law, too, is tied to the organic will of the community, and so laws are contingent upon the historical environment. Wilson defined law as "the will of the State concerning the civic conduct of those under its authority." What, exactly, is the "will of the State"? It is the historically conditioned will of the organic community. The will is whole and unified. Law, therefore, is not based upon the clash of passions or interests, but instead upon the single organic will that underlies those passions or interests. In order for law to exist, there must be "an organic community capable of having a will of its own." This organic community comes into being through gradual evolution, and "law thus follows in its development."[35] The institutions and persons who formally make the law, therefore, simply embody the spirit of the age and translate it into formal, legal decrees. This is why Wilson characterized lawgivers as engaging in "formulation rather than . . . origination."[36]

For the purposes of understanding Wilson's politics, the most important consequence of his conception of government as the mere extension of society's organic will is that it makes no sense to place formal limits on the power of the state. According to Wilson, because the state is simply the instrument of society's will, it is both "beneficent" and "indispensable." Its regulatory power is not a potential threat to individual freedom, because that power is the organ of the people's own will. "If society itself be not an evil, neither surely is government an evil, for government is the indispensable organ of society."[37] As an indispensable and beneficent organ of society, Wilson contended that the state ought to enjoy a wide scope of power. Contrary to the founders' constitutionalism, Wilson's state does not operate under any permanent limits to its authority. Rather, the state is both empowered and limited by the common will of society. The extent to which this common will endorses state power is contingent upon the particular stage of society's historical development.

Wilson took up the American founding as an illustration. The founding generation's strict limits on state power were proper expressions of the spirit of the founding era. But contemporary state power, according to Wilson, needs to reflect the fact that the common will of society has evolved and that the country is operating within a more advanced historical spirit. The founders' mistake was to assume that their principles of limited government, which were appropriate for their own age, ought to serve as permanent limits to state authority in all ages. This mistake arises from the founders' reliance on ahistorical social compact theory for establishing the aims of government: this theory fails to ground state power in the actual history of its development. Consequently, Wilson reasoned, "Government does not stop with the protection of life, liberty, and property, as some have supposed." There is no permanent principle that mandates the protection of private property; the state may regulate property to varying degrees, depending upon the particular historical stage of development in which society finds itself. In principle, government is given broad power over an array of issues—Wilson named trade, labor, corporations, public works, sanitation, education, and sumptuary laws as examples. The extent to which government actually does exercise power over such issues is determined by society's historically conditioned will.

Even political liberties and privileges, Wilson asserted, are not immune from the exercise of state power if the will of the people in a particular age endorses state action. The fundamental point is that the scope of state power is not limited by a principle that transcends history. In this way, Wilson explains, there is no essential difference between modern liberal societies and ancient despotisms: in each, government exercises the power that the spirit of the times allows. As had been the case at every point in history, "Government does now whatever experience permits or the times demand; and though it does not do exactly the same things it still does substantially the same kind of things that the ancient state did."[38]

In his broad view of the scope of the modern state, Wilson envisioned a variety of tasks for which the state should be responsible. In several places in his lecture notes, he provided outlines of these responsibilities: the state (1) "conditions both the existence and the competence of the individual"; (2) "gives society the means of its self-knowledge through Statistics"; (3) protects against disorder; (4) promotes health; (5) serves as "economic guardian"; (6) serves as "spiritual godparent"; (7) promotes economic activity; and (8) protects property.[39] This array of tasks brings into question the place of the individual vis-à-vis the state, and Wilson's lecture notes make clear what that place is. He compared the relationship between the individual and the state to the relationship between local governments and the central government. In the latter relationship, Wilson explained, local governments are to have autonomy in those matters that do not interfere with the interests of the central government. The same principle applies to the individual: he is to have liberty insofar as that liberty does not interfere with the interests of the state.[40]

Wilson did speak of natural limits to state action. But these limits take on no formal or permanent status. Instead, state action is limited by the "necessary cooperation on the part of Society as a whole."[41] The scope of state action, in other words, can be only what the current historical spirit of society calls for it to be. If the historical environment is jealous of state power—as was the case during the American founding era—then the scope of government will be limited accordingly. But once history moves forward into an era where the organic will of society calls for greater state power over the individual—as Wilson asserted was the case during his own time—then the limits on the scope of government are loosened accordingly. This understanding does not change even in Wilson's writings and lectures on constitutional government, which appear in certain parts to offer individual rights as a reason to limit state power. Where do these rights come from? Wilson made very clear that they cannot come from reason or any permanent principle. He even cited Burke to this effect.[42] Instead, rights can only come from the experience that history provides. As historical experience evolves, so too must our conception of rights and how these rights limit or do not limit state action.

Wilson maintained that our historical spirit had reached the point where the state has been called upon to exercise greater power. His lecture notes on administration exemplify this idea. These lecture notes discuss the historical development of administrative power, as Wilson essentially provides an account of how much discretionary power the state was afforded during key epochs in history. Wilson broke the historical development into three basic stages: the Weal State, the Law State, and the Constitutional State. The Weal State was the earliest formulation of discretionary state power, where the scope of state action was virtually unlimited. Under the Weal State, the powers of government "extended to any and every act which would quicken the development of the community as a whole." Wilson made clear that the unfettered administrative discretion of the Weal State was, in principle, ideal. It was "at bottom unimpeachable: the State is an instrumentality for quickening in every suitable way . . . both collective and individual development." The problem with the Weal State was not, therefore, the extent of its powers, but rather that what it did with those powers did not coincide with the underlying organic will of society. This situation is what led to the onset of the Law State, which reflected the jealousy of state power then prevalent in the historical spirit. As Wilson himself explained, "The ideas of the 'Weal State' (*in themselves true*, but unsuited to an unreformed government) give way, therefore, to the ideas of the 'Law State.'" The Law State reflected the classical liberalism that dominated the American founding. But the Law State was inherently flawed, because it sought to "hold 'the government' in restraint, as something foreign, and even hostile, to the people." This is why the increased discretionary power of the modern state—which Wilson characterizes as the Constitutional State—is historically superior. The Constitutional State is essentially a resurrection of the discretionary powers of the Weal State, which Wilson thought "true," but now with the assurance of history that the state itself embodied the unified, organic will of the people.[43]

SOCIALISM AND WILSON'S DEMOCRATIC THEORY

Wilson's call for an expansion of the powers of the state raises the question of the relationship between his democratic theory and the theory of socialism. The socialist movement was certainly gaining strength during Wilson's rise to prominence, and it was connected in some ways with the populist and labor movements. There are two important points to be made with regard to Wilson and socialism. The first is that Wilson saw his progressivism as the only viable alternative to socialism. This is not to suggest that there were tremendous differences between Wilson and the socialists, as Wilson himself admitted. Both socialism and Wilson's progressivism found the traditional American political order outdated and unable to handle the new social and economic problems of contemporary times. Both looked to a sharp increase in the power of the state over private economic interests as a necessary step in enabling government to manage the modern world. The difference between the two, as Wilson understood it, was that his progressivism was organic and evolutionary, while socialism was abstract and revolutionary. Wilson saw his progressivism as a natural development or outgrowth of the new historical spirit. It was a way of transforming the government away from its founding principles and toward a new, energized role that would enable it to meet the demands of the current epoch. From Wilson's perspective, his model for change was conservative, insofar as it proposed an evolution in government in accord with the evolution of history. From this same perspective, socialism was radical. It sought an inorganic revolution of the American state on the basis of abstract doctrines of human equality. That the populist movement was tinged with a certain element of socialist thinking was an important factor in Wilson's distaste for populism—in spite of his tactical alliance with its leader, William Jennings Bryan, in the 1912 campaign. Given what Wilson believed was a significant change in the underlying historical will of the American people, he was certain that a corresponding change in government was going to occur and that the traditional constitutional order was going to be superseded. The only question for him was whether the change would be based upon his own evolutionary and organic model or upon the more revolutionary and abstract model of socialism. Considering Wilson's antipathy for revolutionary and abstract ideas, this was a question of the highest importance.

The second important point about the relationship between socialism and Wilson's theory of democracy is that, by Wilson's own account, there was little or no principled difference between the two ideas. Wilson's brief but significant essay, "Socialism and Democracy," makes this point clear. He begins the essay by defining socialism, suggesting that the doctrine embraces unfettered state power, which trumps any notion of individual rights. It "proposes that all idea of a limitation of public authority by individual rights be put out of view," and "that no line can be drawn between private and public affairs which the State may not cross at will." After laying out this clear definition, Wilson makes it equally clear that he finds nothing wrong with socialism in principle. He contended that socialism is much closer to his idea of true democracy than is any notion of government that attempts to limit the power of the state by protecting the sphere of individual rights. Socialism, Wilson explained, is simply the logical extension of genuine democratic theory—it gives all power to the people in their collective capacity to carry out their will through the exercise of governmental power, unlimited by any undemocratic idea like individual rights. He elaborated:

> In fundamental theory socialism and democracy are almost if not quite one and the same. They both rest at bottom upon the absolute right of the community to determine its own destiny and that of its members. Limits of wisdom and convenience to the public control there may be: limits of principle there are, upon strict analysis, none.[44]

Rights-based theories of self-government, such as the republicanism to which the American founders subscribed and of which Wilson was sharply critical, are far less democratic than socialism. Rights-based theories of government limit the state's sphere of action, thereby limiting the ability of the majority to implement its will.

The reason why Wilson did not embrace the socialist movement, even though he had no objection to socialism in principle, was that in practice men had not *yet* learned how to organize government so that it could efficiently handle all of the responsibilities that socialists wanted to give to it. The critical point is that Wilson did not suggest that it would be unjust to give the state unfettered control over both "public" and "private" spheres. Rather, he could not conceive of how government, at least at the present historical stage, could, as a practical matter, carry out such control. He emphasizes that this point is the only real objection:

> The difference between democracy and socialism is not an essential difference, but only a practical difference—is a difference of *organization* and *policy*, not a difference of primary motive. Democracy has not undertaken the tasks which socialists clamor to have undertaken; but it refrains from them, not for lack of adequate principles or suitable motives, but for lack of organization and suitable hardihood: because it cannot see its way clear to accomplishing them with credit.[45]

It is important to note that Wilson's only objection to the limitless role of the state envisioned by socialism was that the current organization of democratic government did not seem capable of handling it, especially in light of Wilson's focus on improving the science of administration. Yet while the *current* administrative apparatus of democratic government might not have been able to handle the broad aims for the state that socialists had in mind, one could certainly infer that Wilson's emphasis on improving administration in the modern state had the potential eventually to overcome this practical limitation; Wilson did repeatedly assert that the great questions of government in the twentieth century would be administrative. The inference is strengthened in the essay by the character the "democrat," who says to the "socialist":

> You know it is my principle, no less than yours, that every man shall have an
> equal chance with every other man: if I saw my way to it as a practical politi-
> cian, I should be willing to go farther and superintend every man's use of his
> chance. But the means? The question with me is not whether the community has
> power to act as it may please in these matters, but how it can act with practical
> advantage—a question of *policy*.

Wilson then goes on to suggest how such a practical impediment to the adoption of socialist policies might be overcome. The impediment is "a question
of policy primarily, but also a question of organization, that is to say of *administration*."[46] Improving administration is, of course, a primary focus of
Wilson's writing and teaching on government.

DEVELOPMENT AND THE MODERN STATE

As suggested in the introduction, Wilson's broad concept of state power in relation to the individual is embodied in his understanding of *development*—an
understanding that mirrors Hegel's political philosophy regarding the relationship between the individual and the state. The state, according to Hegel,
must allow for individual self-development, but this development can only be
fulfilled in the state, outside of which the individual has no real worth. For
Wilson, since the state is simply the extension of the organic will of society,
the state must superintend individual self-development in order to make sure
that it proceeds in conformity with social development. In his lecture notes on
administration, Wilson explained that the state—as the embodiment of society's organic will—is the natural completion of the individual. The individual's will becomes objectified by his participation in the state. Wilson contended that the state is "the eternal, natural embodiment and expression of a
higher form of life than the individual, namely, that common life which gives
leave to individual life, and opportunity for completeness,—makes individual
life possible and *makes it full and complete*."[47] Compare this language to
Hegel's in *The Philosophy of History*: "It is the moral Whole, the State, which
is that form of reality in which the individual has and enjoys his freedom. . . .
All the worth which the human being possesses—all spiritual reality, he possesses only through the State."[48] The role of the state, for both Hegel and Wilson, is to ensure that the development of the individual's subjective will conforms to the broader, objective will of the state; the state is to connect
individual development and social development.

In *The State*, Wilson explained the concept of development by contending
that government ties the individual to society by using its power to align individual self-development with societal self-development. Government is the

"means" by which "individual self-development may be made at once to serve and to supplement social development." Wilson even conceded his admiration for certain aspects of socialist government, which aims "to bring the individual with his special interests, personal to himself, into complete harmony with society with its general interests." Wilson wrote that such a harmony between the subjective and the general represents a "revolt from selfish, misguided individualism." The socialists are right, Wilson asserted, to criticize the modern industrial organization that has "magnified that self-interest which is grasping selfishness." The distinction that Wilson made between the socialists and himself was that the socialists attack all competition as leading to a magnification of selfishness, whereas he attacks only "unfair competition." Wilson's goal is to maintain individual self-development, but also to remedy the situation whereby individual self-development is encouraged at the expense of social development. History culminates in the unified will of modern society. Government, therefore, must protect society "against the competition that kills," and must reduce "the antagonism between self-development and social development to a minimum."[49]

The government provides for social development through "adaptation of regulation." The government, through regulation, enables the society to stay current with the historical development of its own will. Therefore, Wilson explained, "There must be constant adjustment of governmental assistance to the needs of a changing social and industrial organization." As Wilson made clear in his proposals for American institutions, the time had arrived for administration; the will of society was essentially unified in its understanding of the aims of government, so the most important task of government was to employ the necessary regulatory means to achieve the basic ends on which society was implicitly agreed. Wilson also reminded his audience that adaptive regulation implements the will of the *whole* society; we do not each individually choose our own way to evolve. We all face the same circumstances, and our common will must govern: "The circumstances of the case," Wilson contended, "are not, so far as government is concerned, the circumstances of any individual case, but the circumstances of society's case, the general conditions of social organization."[50] No individual can self-develop through excessive economic self-interest. We all must develop together, which means that society sets the parameters for development:

One of the most indispensable conditions of opportunity for self-development government alone, society's controlling organ, can supply. All combination which necessarily creates monopoly, which necessarily puts and keeps indispensable means of industrial or social development in the hands of a few, and those few, not the few selected by society itself but the few selected by arbitrary fortune, must be under either the direct or the indirect control of society. To society alone can the power of dominating by combination belong: and society cannot suffer any of its members to enjoy such a power for their own private gain independently of its own strict regulation and oversight.[51]

Private development, then, must be under the control of the state.[52]

WILSON'S REALISM AND THE HISTORICAL-COMPARATIVE METHOD

In order to be understood properly, Wilson contended, government must be seen as a product of historical development. This means that we can genuinely comprehend government not through a study of its theories and forms—which abstractly portray government as it ought to be—but instead by studying the actual history of what government has been and what it is. Since the best government, Wilson argued, is the one that best reflects the evolving spirit of history, then those who would gain expertise on government must study the particulars of history. These assumptions form the basis of Wilson's approach to studying politics, which, among other labels, is most commonly known as "realism," or the "historical-comparative" method. In essence, the method asserts that those who mistakenly believe that abstract ideas guide politics will study the theories and forms of constitutions; those who believe, instead, that politics takes its guidance from the particulars of the current historical epoch will study history and seek a deep knowledge of the spirit of the present age. The aim of a believer in the second method is not to change politics radically into something it "ought" to be, according to some principle or idea, but instead to know well the current historical conditions so that politics can be made to continuously keep up. Niels Thorsen describes this political realism in the following manner: "The political thinker was no longer to aim to transform political reality but instead simply to register its existing tendencies. His function was not to furnish new ways of grasping reality but to promote factualism in politics and to associate himself with the forces of progress and promote the general acceptance of expedient or inevitable changes."[53] Wilson certainly saw himself as just this kind of political thinker.

Instead of advocating that students of politics abstract about what institutions are supposed to be in form, Wilson urged them to see that institutions have a life—to see that institutions grow and evolve as history moves forward. Institutions have an "epochal" life, and students of politics must understand these epochs.[54] The realist method was to be the primary theme of Wilson's planned treatise "The Study of Politics." In essays that Wilson initially wrote with the intention of expanding into longer works, he emphasizes that traditional theories of politics and economics had proved far off the mark precisely because they ignored the empirical reality of government. Realism, Wilson explained, "sobers all constructors of systems. They cannot build in the air and then escape chagrin because men only gaze at their structures, and will not live in them. Closet students of politics are constantly having new drill in the same lesson: the world is an inexorable schoolmaster in these courses; it will have none of any thought which does not recognize *it*."[55] This was the problem with traditional economic theories, which abstractly posited that all behavior was caused by narrow self-interest. Such an approach proved an unreliable tool for analyzing the life of a real state, Wilson contended, because it was simply a theory and not a reflection of reality.

Genuine understanding of government comes from an intimate acquaintance with its history, which has made the state what it is. Wilson argued that

> it should be the chief object of the student of politics to study the life of states, and, to that end, to comprehend their histories. And not to comprehend them merely, but also to get their spirit, if possible, into his brain, so that he may think of them as they think of themselves, perceiving the power of their ideals, feeling the compulsion of their fortunes, realizing the coherence and necessity of their characteristic developments.[56]

The expertise of the modern student of politics, therefore, is what Wilson characterized as "interpretation." It is a reading of the historical spirit for the purpose of adapting politics to it. Wilson saw himself, through his scholarly work on the history and spirit of the modern state, as the interpreter of the present age, asking, "Why may not the present age write, through me, its political *autobiography*?"[57] This is the method that Wilson employed in *The State*. In a letter to his publisher, Wilson explained that the approach he planned on taking in the book would be to "*tell the story of government* first and let the lessons in duty follow."[58] Wilson planned a textbook that would provide political lessons by way of an empirical study of the historical development of politics. Such lessons are not to be found, he argued, in a study of constitutional forms. Constitutions are, when properly understood, "broad inductions"—that is, they cannot be deduced from a priori principles but are instead conclusions drawn from empirical observations.[59] Since "our written constitutions are more or less successful generalizations of political experience," the fundamentals of government are best grasped by a study of that real experience.[60]

The historical-comparative method is important in understanding a common feature of Wilson's political writings: his assertion that we can learn and borrow from foreign systems of government, even though their constitutional principles may differ significantly from our own. It is this assertion, for instance, that underlies Wilson's numerous writings on administration, where he argues that we can borrow administrative models from nations like Prussia in spite of the obvious constitutional differences. The historical-comparative method allows such borrowing because its premise is that constitutional forms and ideas really do not matter in politics. Students of politics must study history and its current spirit, which are far more determinative of institutional life than are any theories of constitutionalism. Applied to the American situation, this means that those interested in guiding American politics should not take their cue from the intention and forms of the Constitution but from what the current historical spirit requires. If the current historical spirit requires a broader sphere of administrative power—as Wilson believed it did—then we can borrow from foreign systems of government with strong administrative models. Such is the reasoning behind the many chapters in Wilson's *The State* that provide an account of various governmental systems in modern Europe. This approach is also why some consider Wilson to be the founder of the field of comparative politics. In the preface to *The State,* Wilson declares that his approach will be a comparative one, and he recognizes that he will be entering upon new territory: "In preparing [the book] I labored under the disadvantage of having had no predecessors. So far as I have been able to ascertain, no textbook of like scope and purpose has hitherto been attempted."[61] Wilson explains elsewhere that the need to adapt to historical changes requires Americans to let go of their fixation on the 1787 Constitution and to learn from other systems. "To study one government alone," he contends, "is to understand none at all."[62]

Wilson's rejection of constitutional formalism, and his focus instead on studying politics according to a much more empirical method, leads to his often being associated with both the "realism" and the "scientism" that was predominant during his time. Yet there is a key difference between these two movements in political science, and the distinction is useful in comprehending Wilson's place in the discipline. While scientism tended to be abstract, Wilson and the realists were far more interested in the particular historical facts of particular nations and peoples. Realism was more closely grounded in historicism, where the historical events of various epochs must be understood in order to grasp the proper direction for politics. The departure of realism from scientism helps to illustrate how Wilson diverged from Darwinism in certain highly relevant respects. James Farr describes how the realism of Wilson and others—such as Burgess—differed from the trends of scientism. He explains that Wilson and the realists "were indeed more historical; thereby, they were more factual and statistical in their analyses of the state since, for them, history was a great repository of facts and events. And they were genuinely comparative in their focus, providing more or less systematic studies of American, British, French, and German institutions, practices, and laws. Thus their allegiance to the 'historical-comparative' method."[63] David Easton also has a sound account of the realism to which Wilson subscribed, emphasizing its focus on the actual history of institutions as opposed to the legal provisions that govern them. Easton connects American realism to historicists in Europe—especially to those like Marx, who asserted that political systems could not be understood without an examination of the underlying conditions.[64]

Wilson made his realism a prominent theme of his address to the American Political Science Association in 1910, when he was serving as president of that organization. Titled "The Law and the Facts," Wilson's address called for adjusting government and policy to the facts of the current historical period. In order to understand the current historical "facts," Wilson said that one had to read the true spirit of the people and their development. This is why so-called fact-finding cannot consist merely of science but must instead involve history, literature, and other means of determining the genuine spirit of a people. This rejection of scientism is what drove Wilson to remark: "I do not like the term political science." He preferred the term *politics*, which expanded upon the scope of analysis required to fully comprehend the spirit of a people.[65] One does have to be careful, however, of overstating the distinction between scientism and realism. In spite of the differences I have just described, both approaches are fundamentally empirical, not ethical. It is this ethical approach to politics—one where politics is guided, at least partly, on the basis of what ought to be as opposed to an observation of what currently is—that governed the political thought of the American founding generation and that both realism and scientism strongly rejected.

The realist rejection of abstract theory in politics certainly owes much to Walter Bagehot, as Easton has suggested. Bagehot, reflecting the English Historical School of which he was an important part, saw his realism as corrective of the more doctrinaire and theoretical forms of early liberalism.[66] Wilson himself credited not only Bagehot but Alexis de Tocqueville as the influences on his realist method. "Bagehot and de Tocqueville were not merely students," Wilson remarked, "but also *men of the world*, for whom the only acceptable philosophy of politics was a generalization from the actual daily observation of men and things. . . . They were men who, had they written history, would have written the history of peoples, and not of courts or parliaments merely."[67] Yet Wilson also departed from the realism of Bagehot in a significant way, for Wilson's study of history did not exist merely for the purpose of continuous adaptation. His history had a specific end toward which it was moving—the final state of modern democracy. Wilson, therefore, was utopian in a way that the realists of the Historical School were not. Easton's account of liberal realism makes clear that Bagehot rejected this kind of thinking. He writes that Bagehot "was exhorting liberals to transform themselves into realists, to convert their wishful thinking and utopianism to liberal realism."[68] Wilson's historical thinking, therefore, while certainly embracing a realist methodology in political science, also owes much to German thinkers like Hegel and their study of the state.[69]

Applied to students of American government, Wilson's methodology means that one must study not the American Constitution's forms or ideas, which are ahistorical and do not reflect living reality, but instead the history of the development of the American state. Wilson's chapter "The Government of the United States" in *The State* does not, accordingly, offer a detailed account of the provisions of the Constitution and the ideas and debates that informed it. Rather, it provides an historical account of how American institutions have grown and adapted to changes in circumstance.[70] As a young student of American politics, Wilson explained his interest in the Constitution this way:

> [I would] devote myself mainly to a study of the constitutional history of the United States and of their present actual constitutional system—as contradistinguished from the ideal Constitution of the books and of the lawyers' theories, which latter is only the Constitution of 1789, ornamented with many "wise saws and modern instances." Of course such a study would have to be comparative, lighted by illustrations and parallels, as well as by contrasts, furnished by the present constitutions of Europe and of England.[71]

The key to American democracy, Wilson argued, is that it has been *lived*, not theorized.[72] He praised those authors whose constitutional histories of America focus on the historical development of the nation's institutions and not on the mechanics of the text. Hermann von Holst's constitutional history of America was excellent, Wilson concluded, because the author had actually come to America to live. This experience enabled von Holst to experience the real spirit of the American Constitution.[73] Similarly, Wilson praised James Bryce's *The American Commonwealth* for employing the historical-comparative method of studying the Constitution in action. He commented that "Mr. Bryce does not treat the institutions of the United States as experiments in the application of theory, but as quite normal historical phenomena to be looked at . . . in the practical, everyday light of comparative politics." Wilson particularly liked Bryce's focus on the American states. The states, Wilson explained, had a long history in constitutional experimentation—in adapting forms and laws to changing historical circumstances. Instead of theorizing about ideal constitutional forms, Bryce points to the actual historical practice of state governments, from which we can learn much more of relevance to modern America.[74] A study of the actual experience of constitutions and laws in action is superior, because it takes into account how well the forms have changed to accommodate the progress of history. There can be no set or theoretical view of the law because, as Wilson asserted, "For this race the law under which they live is at any particular time *what it is then understood to be*."[75]

THE NEW POLITICAL SCIENCE

Wilson's employment of the realist, or historical-comparative, method was an important development in the study of politics in America. Approaching political questions empirically as opposed to ethically was the central feature of the new disciplines of social science that were being introduced to America by Wilson and the likes of Lester Frank Ward and Francis Lieber. Wilson's historicist approach to political phenomena meant that politics should be contingent upon the current will or spirit of the people, not on static theories of what government ought to be. The study of politics, consequently, must be twofold, as Raymond Seidelmann and Edward J. Harpham explain in their work on the roots of political science in the tradition of realism. First, the study of politics must find a way to best discern the true will or spirit of the people; second, the discipline must devise the best institutional arrangement for the implementation of that will.[76] Under this mode of looking at politics, the discipline moves away from the ethical question of what government ought to be and toward the empirical question of what the current historical spirit requires. Wilson's writings were among the first by an American scholar of politics to fit this new disciplinary model. As Albert Somit and Joseph Tanenhaus note, Wilson's work fit well with the new political science's "classic" early works, which had as their premise that empirical observation of phenomena could reveal lessons about political development.[77]

Because empirical methodology came to dominate in the social sciences, the study of social phenomena began to require expertise in particular fields. This requirement led to specialization, with the various subfields of social science becoming distinct from one another. The founding of the discipline of political science can be traced to its splitting off from the other social sciences in the last two decades of the nineteenth century and first decade of the twentieth century. It was at this time that discipline-specific associations began to form: the American Historical Association in 1884, the American Economic Association in 1885, the American Statistical Association in 1888, the American Sociological Society in 1903, and the American Political Science Association in 1903.[78] At Johns Hopkins, Wilson was, through his teachers, involved in the beginnings of the Economic and Historical organizations. He became president of the American Political Science Association in 1910.

The development of specialized disciplines within the social sciences took place during a time when German influence on American institutions of higher learning was at its height. Bernard Crick points out that after the conclusion of the Civil War, there was a considerable influx of German-trained thinkers into American academic circles at the same time that resources for higher education were being expanded. The German-trained educational leaders included both Charles W. Eliot and Daniel Coit Gilman; Eliot became president of Harvard in 1869 and Gilman became president of the newly founded Hopkins in 1876.[79] In the discipline of political science, both of the men who are considered the pioneers of the discipline—Lieber and Burgess—were heavily influenced by German thinking. Lieber came to America from Prussia in 1827, became chair of political science and history at Columbia in 1858, and ultimately played a leading role in the creation of political science as a separate discipline at Columbia. He is generally credited with liberating politics from ethics.[80] Burgess, who succeeded Lieber at Columbia, studied in Germany and, upon his return, established the School of Political Science at Columbia in 1880; Columbia was thus the first American institution to house a graduate program in political science. The American situation often proved frustrating for these German-trained political scientists, since the state model did not seem to fit easily into the American circumstance. The problem, as Crick observes, was that "the American *sittlichkeit* needed no State to express it."[81]

Wilson was an important part of the early development of American political science. He was both taught and influenced by German-trained pioneers of the new social sciences, and his work on state theory, administration, and American government formed some of the earliest American contributions to the new discipline. Yet just as Wilson, in his realism, departed from much of the scientific thinking prevalent in his day, his contribution to political science departed from the more "value-free" positivism of his contemporaries. The main distinction between Wilson and the more strictly scientific element of the new discipline was that he was an historicist. As such, he differed from his contemporaries in two ways. First, he was deeply interested in phenomena that went beyond mere statistical data. Wilson believed that in order to truly discern the historical spirit of a people, one had to look beyond "hard" data and study literature and other humanistic indicators. Second, for Wilson, the study of politics and history was also not value-free in the manner suggested by positivism. History had a definite end, and so phenomena in history were understood as leading up to that end. Wilson was not neutral as to the outcome of history; for him, it led to the final victory of modern democracy, which was the most advanced regime. Each of these two differences between Wilson's political science and the more positivistic version of the discipline needs to be considered in further detail.

Wilson's literary essays are perhaps the best place to see how he rejected the purely scientific approach to politics. In "Mere Literature," one can observe that Wilson's critique of positivism is grounded in historicism. Positivistic social science, Wilson explained, is mere form and has no content of spirit. He attacked the "scientific and positivistic spirit of the age" because it does not grasp the underlying spirit of an historical people. The whole point of the historical-comparative method, by contrast, is to uncover the true spirit of an age so that politics can adjust itself accordingly. To uncover such a spirit requires an examination of writings that the positivists reject as "mere literature"—"the literature which is not an expression of form, but an expression of spirit."[82] The shortcomings of scientism are especially present in the reading of history. The reading of history is vital to an historicist like Wilson, who saw in history the gradual unfolding of the Providential idea for man. Scientism cannot perceive the unfolding of this idea, and cannot see the underlying spirit revealed by history. As he elaborated:

> In narrating history, you are speaking of what was done by men; in discoursing laws, you are seeking to show what course of action and what manner of dealing with one another men have adopted. You can neither tell the story nor conceive the law till you know how the men you speak of regarded themselves and one another; and I know of no way of learning this but by reading the stories they have told of themselves, the songs they have sung, the heroic adventures they have conceived. . . . Their jural relationships are not independent of their way of living, and their way of thinking is the mirror of their way of living.[83]

A literary, as opposed to scientific, mode of reading history is one that comprehends the true spirit of the people who constitute it.

Wilson's second difference with the more scientific of his contemporaries is that his mode of analysis is value laden. His empirical observations of various events and institutions are designed to justify his vision of where history is taking the political order. Like Hegel, who read back into human history the justification for his own vision of the rational end-state, Wilson looked at political phenomena in history as leading up to his vision for modern democracy. This is why Wilson's historical accounts and empirical observations—again like Hegel's—are often far from scientific. Wilson's writings on American history, for instance, are notorious for their errors. But this is because Wilson is more interested in seeing in history a pattern that culminates in his vision for the future than he is in laying out the actual "facts" accurately. The same observation can also be made of *Congressional Government*, about which Easton remarks that Wilson "sets the cart before the horse. He wants to discover how to achieve a given goal without first having discovered the way in which the institutions he wishes to manipulate do in fact operate."[84] Crick notes that

Wilson's more value-laden, even religiously oriented, empiricism is bypassed by the more strictly scientific and amoral pragmatism of William James, John Dewey, and others.[85] As we will see in chapter 7, Wilson's science of administration also comes under heavy criticism by subsequent theorists, who consider it insufficiently value free.

WILSON'S EDUCATIONAL VISION

Wilson's model for education is grounded in the historical approach he takes to politics. Since politics must be constantly on the move, adjusting itself to the evolving historical circumstances, education must be put in the service of politics. For those who are entrusted with guiding the state, the most important thing to know is not what is just according to nature, but what the current historical spirit is and what it requires of the current government. Education, therefore, must center on gaining a knowledge of the historical spirit. The educated class must be able to interpret where history is and where it is going, and be able to direct government accordingly. Knowledge of theories and forms is essentially useless; instead, a close discernment of the various facets of historical life must be the primary focus of education. Wilson incorporated this vision of education in his campaign for a teaching job at Princeton. In several essays during this period, he argued that the most important task for colleges was to ensure that students properly interpret the contemporary historical environment. He wrote that the teaching of politics, consequently, could not occupy itself merely with theory; it must instead provide historical context. Wilson argued that a college—Princeton in particular—could accomplish this educational mission by hiring a professor of politics who would teach students about the historical spirit of contemporary government.[86] History, according to Wilson, is "a record of the human spirit." Understanding the historical particulars of an era is the best way to uncover "the life of the day, the impulses that underlie government and all achievement, all art and all literature, as well as statesmanship."[87]

What kind of education is best suited to helping students uncover the current historical spirit? Wilson argued that a liberal education is the best means of exposing students to the variety of factors that constitute the historical spirit in the life of a people. He was sharply critical of the narrow, vocational university curricula that had been becoming more popular during his day. Much as he did in his realist critique of scientism, Wilson argued that specialized training at the undergraduate level leaves students without a full or genuine appreciation of the life and spirit of a people. This was the theme of Wilson's inaugural address as president of Princeton.[88] It was also the theme of an earlier address where Wilson argued that a broad liberal education needed to precede any specialized training—in this case, legal training. He asked:

> What can [the student of law] know but the forms and the tricks of the law if he know nothing of the law's rootage in society, the principles of its origin and development; how it springs out of material and social conditions which it is the special task of economy and political science to elucidate, out of elements which run centuries deep into the history of nations? No mere technical training can ever make a first-rate lawyer.[89]

Wilson certainly advocated specialized training for those who were to lead the nation, but he believed that this training should come in graduate school, after a broad, liberal education had ensured that the student was sufficiently steeped in the general historical spirit of the day. In this way, future leaders could be fully prepared for their twofold task: (1) to have a broad knowledge of the historical spirit and what it requires of government, and (2) to have the specialized knowledge of the specific means required to adjust government accordingly.[90]

Although Wilson opposed the rising trend of vocational training for undergraduates, he did not do so because he believed that education should be an end in itself. Quite to the contrary, Wilson's entire vision of education was grounded in his desire to put education in the service of the nation's progress. Wilson wanted a broad, liberal education for undergraduates precisely because he believed that it was this kind of education that would best enable students to serve their nation in the future. Only with a comprehensive knowledge of the historical spirit can future leaders know the direction in which politics must be adjusted. Wilson explained that "scholarship is something more than an instrument of abstract investigation merely. . . . It is the object of learning . . . to advance civilization." The need to educate students in the history of their state and in the current historical spirit gives rise to the need for a common core curriculum. Since the underlying spirit of society is unified and organic, students must approach understanding it from a common perspective. Wilson suggested the compulsory study of English literature as a means of accomplishing this aim, since English literature captures the full historical spirit and development of the English race.[91]

Wilson's writings on education are put into context by Laurence R. Veysey's work on Wilson's life as an academic. Veysey outlines the four most prominent educational visions during Wilson's time. He characterizes the first view as that of "academic conservatives," who defend the traditional mission of education to discipline the mind and inculcate religious piety. Beginning in the late 1860s, the traditional view was challenged by reformers who wanted a more practical or vocational orientation. The reformers promoted elective curricula, where students could take those courses that would train them for the specific career they had in mind. Such curricula were promoted by Eliot at Harvard and by Andrew D. White at Cornell. While neither of these first two educational visions was based upon the German model for universities, the third and fourth were. Veysey attributes the third view to Americans who received Ph.D.s in Germany and who became influential in the 1870s and 1880s. These academics advocated an "abstractly scientific" mission for the university, one that promoted "original investigation, conducted for its own sake." The final vision grew up at the conclusion of the nineteenth century, and Veysey attributes it to both the English historical model and to "the Germany of Hegel and Goethe." The key for those subscribing to this vision was unity of the mind and of the academic experience. They opposed elective curricula, and were very much concerned with connecting the university with service to the political world. This group tended to include "philosophers of Kantian or Hegelian leanings."[92] Wilson clearly belonged to this final group, as Veysey rightly suggests. Students under this final educational model would be trained to uncover the underlying, unified spirit of the age, and to guide the state accordingly.

NOTES

1. Portions of my presentation of Wilson's state theory are drawn from my chapter "Woodrow Wilson, the Organic State, and American Republicanism," in *History of American Political Thought*, ed. Bryan-Paul Frost and Jeffrey Sikkenga (Lanham, MD: Lexington Books, 2003), 549–68.

2. Wilson, *The State* (Boston: D. C. Heath, 1889), 13–14. Quotations from Wilson's writings will be modernized as necessary for grammar and spelling. Emphasis will be in the original unless otherwise specified.

3. Wilson also points to other obvious differences between classical and modern democracy, such as the lack of special class requirements for citizenship in modern democracy. See "The Real Idea of Democracy," August 31, 1901, in Arthur S. Link, ed., *The Papers of Woodrow Wilson* (hereafter cited as *PWW*), 69 vols. (Princeton: Princeton University Press, 1966-1993), 12:177–78.

4. *The State*, 600, 603–5.

5. *The State*, 607–9.

6. "The Modern Democratic State," December 1885, in *PWW* 5:92.

7. "Modern Democratic State," in *PWW* 5:71–74, 76, 80–81.

8. "Democracy," December 5, 1891, in *PWW* 7:351. In an editorial note, Link comments that this lecture—"Democracy"—seems to have been Wilson's favorite to deliver in the 1890s. It was the one that he gave most frequently (*PWW* 7:344).

9. "Modern Democratic State," in *PWW* 5:81.

10. "The Art of Governing," November 15, 1885, in *PWW* 5:53.

11. Wilson, *The New Freedom* (New York: Doubleday, Page, 1913), 51–52.

12. *The New Freedom*, 245. While Scot Zentner's work rightly points to historicism as the distinguishing feature between Wilson's thought and that of the American founders, he also suggests that Wilson's "thought prefigures the 'pragmatic liberalism' associated with certain Progressive thinkers." I would contend that such a view does not give sufficient recognition to the certainty with which Wilson envisioned the culmination of history in the modern democratic state, and I would thus disagree with Zentner's statement that "Wilson's theory of government lacks any determinate end." Scot J. Zentner, "Liberalism and Executive Power: Woodrow Wilson and the American Founders," *Polity* 26:4 (Summer 1994): 589.

13. *The New Freedom*, 95.

14. "Modern Democratic State," in *PWW* 5:90.

15. "Democracy," in *PWW* 7:347.

16. *The State*, 609.

17. *The State*, 594–95, 597.

18. "Democracy," in *PWW* 7:355.

19. "Democracy," in *PWW* 7:356. This novel defense of bureaucracy as fundamentally democratic is adopted in the scholarly literature by John A. Rohr and, to a certain extent, by Herbert J. Storing. Their arguments are discussed in chapter 7.

20. "Lecture at the New York Law School," March 11, 1892, in *PWW* 7:475.

21. "Bryce's *American Commonwealth*," January 31, 1889, in *PWW* 6:74.

22. "Modern Democratic State," in *PWW* 5:82.

23. "Modern Democratic State," in *PWW* 5:74–75.

24. *The State*, 624–25. See also "Democracy," in *PWW* 7:352–54, 359.

25. "Notes for Lectures at the Johns Hopkins," February 1, 1892, in *PWW* 7:432.

26. "Political Sovereignty," November 9, 1891, in *PWW* 7:326–33.

27. "Political Sovereignty," in *PWW* 7:337.

28. "The English Constitution," October 1890, in *PWW* 7:44.

29. "Modern Democratic State," in *PWW* 5:69–70. In his outline to "The Philosophy of Politics," Wilson emphasizes the difficulty arising from "formalism," which creates an impediment to "reading the growth of national sentiment in the U.S." January 12, 1891, in *PWW* 7:98.

30. "Notes for Lectures at the Johns Hopkins," January 26, 1891, in *PWW* 7:128–29.

31. Review of *Political Science and Comparative Constitutional Law*, by John W. Burgess, May 1891, in *PWW* 7:196–97.

32. *The State*, 658.

33. *The State*, 594–96.

34. *The State*, 598.

35. *The State*, 610.

36. *The State*, 619.

37. *The State*, 658–59. See also "Notes for Lectures," in *PWW* 7:157. Richard Hofstadter contends that one reason Wilson and other progressives were not fearful of state power was that they feared private power even more. Hofstadter, *The Age of Reform* (New York: Alfred A. Knopf, 1961), 229.

38. *The State*, 647–54.

39. "Notes for Lectures," in *PWW* 7:122–24.

40. "Notes for Lectures at the Johns Hopkins," February 1, 1892, in *PWW* 7:385.

41. *The State*, 664.

42. "Notes for Lectures in a Course on Constitutional Government," September 19, 1898, in *PWW* 11:28.

43. "Notes for Lectures," in *PWW* 7:125–26. See also "Notes for Lectures," in *PWW* 7:382-3; and "Notes for Lectures on Public Law," September 22, 1894, in *PWW* 9:11–12. Emphasis added.

44. "Socialism and Democracy," August 22, 1887, in *PWW* 5:561.

45. "Socialism and Democracy," in *PWW* 5:561–62.

46. "Socialism and Democracy," in *PWW* 5:562. Wilson employs a similar argument in *The State*, when expressing his preference for regulation of privately owned interests as opposed to direct government ownership. He raises no principled objection to direct government ownership, contending instead that it is simply not the best practical way to manage affairs. *The State*, 662–63.

47. "Notes for Lectures," in *PWW* 7:124. This argument is repeated, nearly verbatim, in the lecture notes at 7:382.

48. G. W. F. Hegel, *The Philosophy of History*, trans. J. Sibree (New York: Dover, 1956), 38–39.

49. *The State*, 658–60.

50. *The State*, 660–61.

51. *The State*, 661.

52. See the work of Zentner for an argument that Wilson's doctrine of development makes him an "individualist"—in other words, that the power of the state must be focused on ensuring the proper development of the individual. Zentner reasons that such a role for government requires a powerful executive. Consequently, he connects Wilson and Hobbes. Zentner also explains that Wilson's individualism is different from the traditional liberalism of the American founding. Traditional liberalism held that individual rights limited the power of the state, whereas Wilson's liberalism liberates the power of the state on behalf of the individual. Zentner, "Liberalism and Executive Power," 581–83, 599.

53. Niels Aage Thorsen, *The Political Thought of Woodrow Wilson 1875–1910* (Princeton: Princeton University Press, 1988), 216. See also Raymond Seidelmann and Edward J. Harpham, *Disenchanted Realists: Political Science and the American Crisis, 1884–1984* (Albany: State University of New York Press, 1985), 44–45.

54. "Of the Study of Politics," November 25, 1886, in *PWW* 5:397.

55. "Of the Study of Politics," in *PWW* 5:395–96.

56. "The Study of Politics," September 1891, in *PWW* 7:283.

57. "From Wilson's Confidential Journal," December 28, 1889, in *PWW* 6:463.

58. Wilson to Daniel Collamore Heath, March 30, 1886, in *PWW* 5:150.

59. Wilson drafted a selection that was to be part of his teacher Ely's book on the history of political economy in the United States (the book was never finished). In it, Wilson embraces the *inductive* method of the new economics—a method that assumes that economic theories, to the extent that they are useful, must come from particular historical facts and conditions, as opposed to a priori speculation. In the editorial note to this selection, Link agrees that this stance is evidence of Wilson's preference for the new economics. This view contradicts that of William Diamond, who also argues that the manuscript in question actually represents little or none of Wilson's own thought. "Wilson's Selection for a 'History of Political Economy in the United States,'" May 25, 1885, in *PWW* 4:630–63.

60. "Responsible Government Under the Constitution," February 10, 1886, in *PWW* 5:107. Wilson's essay on self-government in France is a good illustration of his employing the historical-comparative method. See "Self-Government in France," September 4, 1879, in *PWW* 1:517. See also Wilson to Robert Bridges, August 8, 1879, in *PWW* 1:513.

61. *The State*, xxxiv.

62. "Study of Politics," in *PWW* 7:280.

63. James Farr, "Political Science and the State," in *Discipline and History: Political Science in the United States*, ed. Farr and Raymond Seidelmann (Ann Arbor: University of Michigan Press, 1993), 75.

64. David Easton, *The Political System: An Inquiry Into the State of Political Science* (New York: Alfred A. Knopf, 1967), 161–62.

65. "The Law and the Facts," December 27, 1910, in *PWW* 22:264–71. Wilson seems to have taken his realism to heart, suggesting at several points that, in order to fully understand the foreign governments about which he was to write, he would need to travel abroad so that he could come to know the full historical spirit of the peoples in question. See Wilson to Robert Bridges, November 28, 1886, in *PWW* 5:410. He was never able to make any such trip, due to finances and his wife's health. See also John M. Mulder's account of the early part of Wilson's teaching career: Mulder, *Woodrow Wilson: The Years of Preparation* (Princeton: Princeton University Press, 1978), 93.

66. David Easton, "Walter Bagehot and Liberal Realism," *American Political Science Review* 43 (1949): 17–18, 36. Easton, "The Political System," 163.

67. "Of the Study of Politics," in *PWW* 5:397.

68. Easton, "Bagehot and Liberal Realism," 36.

69. See Charles R. Kesler, "The Public Philosophy of the New Freedom and the New Deal," in *The New Deal and Its Legacy*, ed. Robert Eden (New York: Greenwood Press, 1989), 158.

70. *The State*, 449–570.

71. Wilson to Richard Heath Dabney, February 17, 1884, in *PWW* 3:26.

72. "The True American Spirit," October 27, 1892, in *PWW* 8:37.

73. "Review of *The Constitutional Law of the United States of America*, by H. von Holst," April 17, 1887, in *PWW* 5:491.

74. "Bryce's *American Commonwealth*," in *PWW* 6:62, 66.

75. *The State*, 475–76.

76. Seidelmann and Harpham, *Disenchanted Realists*, 41.

77. Albert Somit and Joseph Tanenhaus, *The Development of American Political Science: From Burgess to Behavioralism* (Boston: Allyn & Bacon, 1967), 23. Seidelmann and James Farr, in their history of the political science discipline in America, name three specific ways in which this new empiricism manifested itself: (1) some connected political science to the natural sciences, (2) some grounded their political studies in collections of statistics and other data, and (3) some grounded their political studies in an observation of history. See Farr and Seidelmann, "Introduction" to part I, Farr and Seidelmann, eds., *Discipline and History*, 16.

78. Somit and Tanenhaus, *Development of American Political Science*, 22.

79. Bernard Crick, *The American Science of Politics: Its Origins and Conditions* (Berkeley: University of California Press, 1964), 19.

80. Crick, *American Science of Politics*, 15–17.

81. Crick, *American Science of Politics*, 26–30.

82. "Mere Literature," June 17, 1893, in *PWW* 8:240–42.

83. "Mere Literature," in *PWW* 88:245.

84. Easton, *The Political System*, 82–83.

85. Crick, *American Science of Politics*, 73–75.

86. "An Address to the Princeton Alumni of New York" (lecture, March 23, 1886), in *PWW* 5:139–41.

87. "The Variety and Unity of History," September 20, 1904, in *PWW* 15:474, 77. See also William Diamond, *The Economic Thought of Woodrow Wilson* (Baltimore: The Johns Hopkins University Press, 1943), 39–41; Thorsen, *Political Thought of Woodrow Wilson*, 187; Samuel J. Rogal, "From Pedagogue to President: Thomas Woodrow Wilson as Teacher-Scholar," *Presidential Studies Quarterly* 24 (Winter 1994): 52–53.

88. "Princeton for the Nation's Service," October 25, 1902, in *PWW* 14:170–85. See also "The Relation of University Education to Commerce," November 29, 1902, in *PWW* 14:228–45.

89. "Should an Antecedent Liberal Education Be Required of Students in Law, Medicine, and Theology?" (lecture, July 26, 1893), in *PWW* 8:289. See also "Education and Democracy," May 4, 1907, in *PWW* 17:133–36.

90. Johns Hopkins University, where Wilson received his specialized training to become a political scientist, was founded explicitly to achieve the second of these educational tasks. For an account of the university's founding and purpose, see Hugh Hawkins, *Pioneer: A History of the Johns Hopkins University 1874–1889* (Ithaca, NY: Cornell University Press, 1960), especially 7, 22–33, 108.

91. "University Education and Citizenship," June 20, 1894, in *PWW* 8:588–90.

92. Laurence R. Veysey, "The Academic Mind of Woodrow Wilson," *The Mississippi Valley Historical Review* 49 (March 1963): 615–17.

Chapter Three

Beyond the Separation of Powers: The New Constitutionalism and the Growth of the American National State

The first two chapters have addressed Wilson's belief that America during his time had come to an essential unity of will or spirit. America now had, or was about to have, the necessary unity to become a full-fledged, organic state—a true nation. How had this come about? How did America change from a fragmented country dominated by individualism to a nation where the public mind was essentially unified on the direction it wanted its government to take? Wilson found the answer to these questions in history. History was not simply a story of past events, but was instead a powerful force that had made the country increasingly unified over the progression of its great epochs. Evidence of this view can be found throughout a wide cross-section of Wilson's writings, but it is especially clear in the books on American history that he wrote in the last decade of the nineteenth century. These histories—*Division and Reunion* (1893), *George Washington* (1896), and *A History of the American People* (1902)—have not been explored to any significant extent by scholars of Wilson's political thought.[1] Many believe that Wilson diverted into writing histories in the 1890s at least partly because he needed to earn more money; this is a belief that is supported by the fact that the histories themselves are more popular than scholarly.[2] Yet Wilson's political philosophy manifests itself clearly and consistently in the histories, and one can see in them his vision of how the progressive force of history brought America out of mere subjectivity and into a moral state of national unity and objectivity. In addition, under Wilson's vision, the method by which history effects progress is decidedly Hegelian. Progress, in Wilson's tale of American history, occurs through a series of conflicts that mark the decay of one epoch and rise of the next. The Civil War, as we will see, was a key component in the progress of American history because it did away with the old order of fragmented localism and ushered in the age of national unity. So not in spite of,

but because of, the great conflicts of American history, America had been unified into a true national state. This new condition also laid the groundwork for
significant transformation of American political institutions.

PROGRESS AND THE DIALECTIC OF AMERICAN HISTORY

The very title of Wilson's first major historical work—*Division and
Reunion*—evidences the progress that he read into the key historical events of
the nineteenth century. Underlying the story that Wilson tells in this book is
the Hegelian understanding of history—that it proceeds by way of a progression of great epochs, that movement from one epoch to another takes place
by way of a major conflict, that each epoch has its own spirit that cannot be
transcended, and that each spirit is more advanced than the one preceding it.
Division and Reunion tells the story of America from 1829 to 1889. The year
1829 marks the beginning of new epoch of increased unity; that unity is challenged by sectional conflict and the Civil War, and out of that conflict
emerges a confirmation of and progression in national unity. Wilson explained that 1829 marked a progression into a new epoch partly because of
the settlement of the American West that was taking place. This settlement
represented progress because, as a nation grows, it must overcome nature.
Wilson argued that "for the creation of the nation[,] the conquest of her proper
territory from Nature was first necessary." This conquest helped to signify the
necessary move from rough and uncultured conditions to new conditions in
American life. That year also marked the passing of the last remnants of the
founding generation and the founding spirit. Wilson characterized this event
as a "change in *personnel* and in spirit. . . . Colonial America, seeking to construct a union, had become national America, seeking to realize and develop
her united strength, and to express her new life in a new course of politics."[3]
The nineteenth century introduced improved material conditions. These conditions, in turn, led to more advanced thought. Progress in underlying conditions, explained Wilson, leads to progress of thought and ideas.[4] So as American history moved forward, America's political ideas had to become
correspondingly more modern.

 The premise that political ideas must advance as history moves forward is
confirmed in many of Wilson's subsequent writings, including *Constitutional
Government*. There Wilson devoted an entire chapter to "the place of the
United States in Constitutional Development"—in other words, he believed
that one could understand the principles of American government only by understanding the historical pressures on their evolution. In that chapter, Wilson
stated that the most important fact to know about the American Constitution

is that its meaning is contingent upon history, and that its meaning and our understanding of it had changed and grown significantly since the time of its establishment. According to Wilson, the single most relevant historical development that can lead to a proper understanding of the Constitution is the fact that America had escaped the narrow individualism of the founding and had grown into a genuine nation. He elaborated:

> Our life has undergone radical changes since 1787, and almost every change has operated to draw the nation together, to give it the common consciousness, the common interests, the common standards of conduct, the habit of concerted action, which will eventually impart to it in many more respects the character of a single community.[5]

Such an account of America's historical development led Wilson to conclude that the Constitution, if read in light of these developments, must allow for a greater sphere of central government power. A new understanding of American constitutionalism is a mark of progress. Wilson explained that "we are a strengthened, elevated, matured nation. We have triumphed over difficulties, not by steadfastness merely but by progress also. We have had the best evidence of health, namely growth."[6] Wilson viewed the nation as having overcome its difficulties not by sticking to its original principles, but by submitting to progress and growth, by adopting new methods and new political ideas to meet new historical circumstances. History would continue to bring improvement to America precisely to the extent that the nation was willing to eschew its original principles. Ultimately, Wilson possessed the confidence of an historicist that America would make the necessary adjustments and that history would culminate in the ideal end-state. "No one who comprehends the essential soundness of our people's life can mistrust the future of the nation," Wilson reasoned. "He may confidently expect a safe nationalization of interest and policy in the end, whatever folly of experiment and fitful change he may fear in the meanwhile." We could have the confidence that history would create a true and complete nation, Wilson explained, because one could see how far the country had come toward this end in spite of an ill-designed, fractured government with little or no energetic leadership. He proclaimed: "Unquestionably we believe in a guardian destiny! No other race could have accomplished so much with such a system."[7]

The Historical Utility of the Civil War

In terms of key historical events that had helped move America toward its ideal end as a true nation, the Civil War seems to have been the most significant to Wilson. In his historical writings he certainly devoted a great deal of attention to the conflict, consistently portraying it as having been absolutely essential to America's progress. Similar to Hegel's characterizations of the great conflicts of human history in *The Philosophy of History*, Wilson saw the destruction and decay wrought by the Civil War as regrettably necessary in a world-historical sense; without the war, the old order would not have been defeated, and America could not have taken the steps necessary to mature. As Wilson summarized in *The State*, the "Civil War completes the Union,"[8] by which he meant that the conflict had swept away the last vestiges of the old order, which had stood in the way of progress.

That the Civil War was a decisive step forward in America's progress as a nation is an important theme of Wilson's five-volume work, *A History of the American People*. The significance of the change that Wilson attributed to the war cannot be overstated. The following passage captures the sense of the war's importance to Wilson:

> The nation, shaken by those four never to be forgotten years of awful war, could not return to the thoughts or to the life that had gone before them. An old age had passed away, a new age had come in, with the sweep of that stupendous storm. Everything was touched with the change it had wrought. Nothing could be again as it had been. The national consciousness, disguised, uncertain, latent until that day of sudden rally and call to arms, had been cried wide awake by the voices of battle, and acted like a passion now in the conduct of affairs. All things took their hue and subtle transformation from it: the motives of politics, the whole theory of political action, the character of the government, the sentiment of duty, the very ethics of private conduct were altered as no half century of slow peace could have altered them.[9]

This characterization of the war's significance contains several noteworthy points. First, once the war was concluded, there was no returning to the old order or old political ideas; the conflict had eradicated the old historical spirit. This is why major conflicts are essential for an historicist such as Wilson—it is only by something as cataclysmic as a war that history can thoroughly free itself from the old ideas and move forward. As Wilson himself explained in the passage, everything about the country was transformed in a way that could not have been accomplished by fifty years of peacetime development. One ought also to note that once the old historical spirit—"the national consciousness"—has been replaced by a new one, everything changes. Politics, political theory, government, duty, and ethics—all are contingent upon the historical spirit and become transformed when that spirit advances.

Wilson's five-volume history goes on to portray the postwar American spirit as truly national. This new national spirit manifests itself especially in the new mode of understanding the Constitution. Modern America had moved beyond the narrow, legalistic constitutionalism characteristic of the founding generation. Wilson explained that in the new era, the forms of the Constitution cease to be the main focus of national life. Instead, what really matters is the unity of will in the nation, and the government's reflection of that new will. In this regard, the war had "disclosed the real foundations of the Union; had shown them to be laid, not in the Constitution, its mere formal structure, but upon deep beds of conviction and sentiment." What became most important in national politics was not the Constitution's protection of individuals, but its ability to put into action "the passionate beliefs of an efficient majority of the nation." The war helped to overcome an excessive fixation on the forms of the Constitution because the prosecution of the war itself often required that those forms be disregarded. Once the fighting stopped, the nation was conditioned out of its slavish reliance on the legalisms of the Constitution, and there was no looking back. In this way, the legal formula of federalism gave way to a national spirit that invigorated central government.[10]

In his political writings, Wilson often pointed to the Civil War as evidence that the particular historical purposes for which the original Constitution had been instituted had been superseded. The Civil War represented to Wilson the final battle over the old constitutional ideas. In the conflict, two fundamentally different views of America's basic principles had collided, with one emerging as the victor and the other having been permanently vanquished. The conclusion of the war meant, therefore, that the fundamental constitutional questions of the country had been decided. As a result of the conflict, the country had reached a basic unity of opinion on what the ends of government were. Now that this question had been settled, the pressing issue of the day was not what the government ought to do, but rather what specific means ought to be employed to achieve the ends on which all were now agreed. As Wilson proclaimed in "Government by Debate," "The construction of the Constitution is settled now, settled once and for all by the supreme arbitrament of war."[11] In other words, in the debate over the country's fundamental political principles, history had made the decision. Since history is inherently progressive, the outcome of the war necessarily led to the adoption of superior principles.

The Epochs of American History

Wilson applied the framework of historicism to each of the main epochs in American history that he addressed. In his *New Freedom* campaign, Wilson asked rhetorically what the attitude of progressives ought to be toward the symbols of the founding political order—especially toward the Constitution and the individualistic understanding of it that dominated the founding era. His answer was that the forms and principles of the founding era were appropriate and necessary for their time. Without them, later developments in modern liberalism could not have taken place. Wilson explained that modern democracy could not simply be installed in a country that had had no experience at all with self-government; to do so would be inorganic and revolutionary. The founders' primitive, individualistic liberalism—while outdated for the present circumstances—had been historically necessary. It was part of history's overall plan for the progressive development of America into a modern state.[12] This argument formed an important part of many of Wilson's campaign speeches and allowed him to urge the abandonment of the founding political order by way of giving it apparent praise.

Wilson's argument that the ideas of the founding were outmoded for modern times is why he and other progressives who wrote about the founding era tended to focus on biographical and historical accounts and avoid a discussion of principles. Such an approach permitted Wilson to praise the great figures of the founding as appropriate and significant for their own age while he maintained that their political principles did not carry over into modern times. So Wilson, in his histories, spent significant time discussing the heroes of the founding, while in his political writings he made clear his objection to the founding's central ideas. Here again the contrast between Wilson's and Lincoln's reflections on the founding is instructive. Lincoln's speeches refer frequently to the founders precisely for the purpose of explicating their ideas and returning those ideas to their proper place in the public mind. For instance, as discussed in the introduction, Lincoln's references to Jefferson point out the transhistorical nature of Jefferson's political principles; Lincoln makes these references in order to support his argument that the principles of the founding are just as applicable in the antebellum period as they were during the founding era. On the other hand, Wilson mentioned Jefferson and others of the founding generation for the purpose of understanding that time's historical spirit by showing how it was manifest in the period's leading statesmen. He wrote that "Mr. Jefferson spoke the spirit of the day, its only acceptable principle in affairs."[13]

Wilson also saw in both Hamilton and Madison a manifestation of the historical spirit of the founding. That spirit, according to Wilson, was essentially British. He saw the early American political tradition, as explained in chapter 1, as essentially a continuation of British constitutional development. Hence, he characterized Hamilton and Madison as English in spirit, by which he meant that their constitutional ideas were conditioned by the English tradition that was dominant at the time. This is why Wilson, in his "Calendar of Great Americans," claimed that neither Hamilton nor Madison was truly "American."[14] He also claimed that America, while having adopted the British tradition in the founding of its institutions, failed to understand those institutions as part of a continuing pattern of development. The British government that the Americans copied in 1787, Wilson argued, was itself in the process of growth and change. While the British adjusted their government in accord with the forward march of history, the Americans of the founding generation believed that their forms were appropriate not only for their own generation but for future generations as well.[15]

Development began in America during the era of Jeffersonian democracy. The year 1800 marked an important turning point, Wilson reasoned, because democratization had overcome aristocratic Hamiltonianism.[16] This development simply reflected the forward march of history, which was moving America down the road of becoming a modern democratic state. Wilson's account of the rise of Jeffersonian democracy is dialectical. The radical spirit of the Jeffersonians, Wilson explained, dominated the revolutionary period. That radical spirit subsided during the rise of the federalists in the 1780s. In 1800 it rose again, but this time it was more moderate and responsible, and reflected the true underlying spirit of the people.[17] Jeffersonian democracy, then, represented a change for which the time was ripe. Yet it required the antithetical historical event of the federalist period in order to take hold and represent genuine progress.

Wilson saw American development in the first half of the nineteenth century as a struggle between the forces of what he called *originalism*, which wanted to keep the country fragmented, and the forces of *union*, which advocated progress. In writing about the conflict between these opposing forces, which ultimately led to and was resolved by the Civil War, Wilson called John Marshall and Daniel Webster the first true "American" statesmen. They were true Americans because they fought for national unity, which conformed to the future for which America was destined. In his "Calendar of Great Americans," Wilson reserved some of his strongest praise for Marshall and Webster, particularly because they did not feel constrained by an overly legalistic interpretation of the Constitution. Instead, Wilson contended, they were gifted at taking the written Constitution and reading into it whatever the times required. Wilson characterizes this mode of interpretation as an ability to find "life" in the Constitution. Marshall and Webster "viewed the fundamental law as a great organic product, a vehicle of life as well as a charter of authority; in disclosing its life they did not damage its tissue; and in thus expanding the law without impairing its structure or authority they made great contributions alike to statesmanship and to jurisprudence."[18] Marshall and Webster were uniquely American, Wilson explained, because they had to practice a form of statesmanship that formulated broad national policies within the tight framework of a written constitution. His praise for Marshall and Webster stands in contrast to his sharp criticism of figures like John C. Calhoun. Calhoun did not represent the American spirit of national unity, instead fighting against union by refusing to abandon the originalism of fragmented power and weak national government. So while Marshall and Webster were genuine Americans who supported historical progress, Calhoun was reactionary and "provincial."[19]

To understand the significance of the union issue to Wilson's conception of American politics, and to understand why Wilson was no southern partisan, it is vital to know that, for Wilson, it was the southerners who were the constitutional originalists. In other words, the forces of states' rights and secession, as Wilson understood them, represented the founders' constitution as it was originally intended to be—one that placed strict limits on the sphere of federal authority. Those who favored national unity and the cause of the North, then, were the progressives. The progressive, pro-union forces really advocated a departure from the original constitutional understanding and an embrace of national unity and expanded national government. The pro-union forces were progressive because they wanted to adjust political principles to the advances and new circumstances brought about by history. They understood that America was growing and evolving, and they wanted to read the Constitution accordingly. The southerners, technically speaking, held the correct view of the original Constitution, and they wanted the country to stick to it. Secession, therefore, was not an attack on the Constitution, but rather a movement of reactionary forces who wanted to restore the original constitutionalism in a fight against progress.

In *Division and Reunion*, Wilson expressed his approval of Webster's pro-union argument—"that the Constitution had created, not a dissoluble, illusory partnership between the States, but a single federal state, complete in itself." But he contended that this interpretation, however much he embraced it, was probably *not* the view of those who framed the Constitution: "It may, nevertheless, be doubted whether this was the doctrine upon which the Union had been founded." While the states'-rights view of the southerners may have been the one that most accurately reflected original intent, it was inferior historically and opposed the march of progress, since "Webster's position was one toward which the greater part of the nation was steadily advancing."[20] Wilson explained in a subsequent essay that, in spite of its inferiority, Calhoun's "doctrine of the ultimate sovereignty of the States was not new. It had once been commonplace to say that the Union was experimental, to speak of circumstances in which the contracting States might deem it best to withdraw." The historically inferior understanding of federal power that animated the founding generation simply reflected the particular historical environment in which this understanding grew up—one where it was simply more common for the focus to be on the states and their primacy.[21] In the face of this undue attachment to original forms, those who favored a national union adopted what might be called today a "living constitution" understanding of government. Wilson explained: "The legal theory upon which [secession] was taken was one which would hardly have been questioned in the early years of the government. . . . But constitutions are not mere legal documents: they are the skeleton frame of a living organism; and in this case the course of events had nationalized the government once deemed confederate."[22] In the dialectical contest between the forces of the old order and those of the new, history inevitably and necessarily resolved differences in favor of the side representing progress. Wilson commented in a letter on the war that "*I think the North was wholly right then*, and that the South paid the inevitable penalty for lagging behind the national development, stopping the normal growth of the national constitution."[23]

Wilson's conception of the antebellum period, which portrays as outmoded originalists those who wanted to maintain strict limits to federal authority, explains his hostility toward Andrew Jackson. Especially in his histories, Wilson went out of his way to attack Jackson because he saw Jackson's strict constructionism as a reactionary doctrine aimed at turning the clock back on progress and returning to the founders' constitutionalism of limited government. This view of Jackson comes out most clearly in Wilson's discussion of the national bank. While Wilson conceded that the bank was of dubious constitutionality if one were to take the narrow view of it that animated the founding, it was a mark of national progress that the Supreme Court in the *McCulloch v. Maryland* decision had interpreted the Constitution liberally to allow for this increased role of the federal government. *McCulloch v. Maryland*, in other words, represented an important historical advance beyond the principles of the founding. Jackson's reopening of the question of the bank's constitutionality represented to Wilson an attempt to erase a significant step forward in expanding national power. Wilson targeted Jackson's disregard for Supreme Court precedent, because in this case the precedent marked a major departure from the narrow, formulaic constitutionalism of the founding and embraced a significant expansion of national powers.[24] Wilson's criticism of the Jacksonians in the election of 1824 was also fueled by his support for those who wanted to "grow" the Constitution beyond the narrow conception of 1787. Wilson characterized Jackson's opponents in 1824—Henry Clay and John Quincy Adams—as proponents of the more liberal mode of interpreting the Constitution. He commented that "Mr. Clay stood in all his thought for the same principles of liberal construction in applying the constitution and for the same purposes of legislative action in furthering national interests that Mr. Adams frankly avowed and earnestly advocated."[25] Anyone who wanted to use the Constitution as a means of reining in national power—which is how Wilson interpreted Jackson—was an enemy to the progressive, pro-union forces.

Some misunderstand Wilson's attack on Jackson, pointing to it as evidence that Wilson wanted to defend the traditional constitutional order against Jackson's populism.[26] Wilson, for example, criticized Jackson's crusade against the legitimacy of the 1824 election, which Wilson noted was conducted precisely according to the electoral college provisions of the Constitution. Yet Wilson did not make this observation because he himself was a defender of the Constitution's forms against Jackson's irresponsible populism. Rather, Wilson clearly was interested in portraying Jackson as a hypocrite. He mocked Jackson's alleged strict constructionism by pointing out that Jackson did not hesitate to attack the provisions of the Constitution when they did not coincide with his own interests.[27] This is a sound criticism of Jackson's position on the 1824 election, but it does not mean that Wilson himself supported strict constructionism. His attacks on Jackson's national bank policy show that the contrary is true.

Wilson also criticized Jackson because he associates him with the origination of the spoils system. The system, by law, had been in place since the Tenure of Office Act of 1920, which limited many civil servants to four-year terms. But Wilson pointed out that it was not until Jackson that the law's provisions were widely used for the distribution of spoils. He complained that, under Jackson, the merit of the incumbent civil servants received no consideration; instead, the political loyalty of the replacements was the only factor involved in removing the incumbents from office:

> Not only those who sought appointment to the better sort of offices came, but the politically covetous of every degree. Jackson saw to it that they got all that there was to give. For the old office-holders there set in a veritable reign of terror. Official faithfulness and skilled capacity did not shield them. . . . Friends were to be rewarded, enemies punished; and inasmuch as the number of needy friends greatly exceeded the number of avowed enemies to be found in office, even those who could not be shown to deserve punishment were removed, to provide places for those who were deemed to deserve reward.[28]

It was for this reason that Wilson detested Martin Van Buren perhaps even more than he did Jackson, for he blamed Van Buren (first as Jackson's secretary of state, then as vice president in the second term) as being primarily responsible for putting Jackson's spoils policy into wide and vigorous effect. It was Van Buren, according to Wilson, who created a party system based upon spoils and patronage.[29]

Ultimately, in spite of his sharp criticisms, Wilson viewed Jackson through the lens of historicism: Jackson may have been destructive and dangerous, but such degradation was necessary and useful at the time for the purposes of spurring further historical development. Wilson contended that the national spirit grew during the antebellum period, seemingly both because of and in spite of Jackson's often reckless and crude presidential policies and postures. "Whatever harm it may have done to put this man into the presidency," Wilson concluded, "it did the incalculable good of giving to the national spirit its first self-reliant expression of resolution and of consentaneous power."[30] Jackson's raw populism may simply have been the expression of the new democratic spirit that was gaining strength at the time. While certainly this raw spirit needed to be, and was, subsequently refined by Wilson's own modern democratic vision, Jackson played the role assigned to him by history.

The Jacksonian period and the years leading up to the war, according to Wilson, were signs of progress because the institution of slavery was coming under increased skepticism. Wilson concluded that this skepticism signaled the new democratic spirit of the times.[31] Yet Wilson's assumption here seems vulnerable to Lincoln's criticism of Chief Justice Roger B. Taney. In the *Dred Scott* decision, Taney made the progressive assumption that the public's attitude toward slavery was much enlightened compared to the attitude prevalent during the days of the founding. In commentary on that decision, Lincoln points out that Taney's assumption of progress is mistaken, and that the status of the black race in America was much worse because the natural-rights principles of the Declaration had lost their place in the public mind.[32] Lincoln, as opposed to both Taney and Wilson, maintained that "progress," properly understood, constituted nothing more than a continuing public dedication to the transhistorical political principles instituted at the founding. Wilson's entire corpus of work, in contrast, asserts that progress is defined precisely by how willing the nation is to reconsider the principles of its founding and adopt instead a more modern outlook. This is why Wilson's frequent praise of Lincoln as a model statesman and champion of national progress seems rather misplaced.[33] Lincoln devoted many of his speeches to defending the timelessness of the founders' principles and argued that a return to those principles was the only way out of America's crisis in the mid-nineteenth century; Wilson's solution to the crisis involved transcending those very same principles.

Even Wilson's criticism of slavery and his native South is grounded in this understanding of progress. Wilson believed that the principles of slavery and states' rights were the outdated principles of early America. By maintaining its attachment to slavery, the South impeded its own progress. While other parts of the country were advancing, slavery cemented the old class order in the South and caused resistance to change and development. This was the great crime of the South—not because slavery violated the natural rights of the slaves, but because the South itself resisted progress: "Southern society had from the first resolutely, almost passionately, resisted change. It steadily retained the same organization, the same opinions, and the same political principles throughout all the period of seventy-two years that stretched from the establishment of the federal government to the opening of the war for its preservation."[34] The Civil War, therefore, was a fight between two principles—between the principles of reaction and old traditions on the one hand, and the principles of progress, growth, and development on the other.[35] Wilson's criticism of the South, placed in this perspective, is easy to understand. Even in his earliest writings, Wilson conceived of the South's defeat as essential for America's progress as a nation. In an essay on John Bright, Wilson contended that the defeat of the South, contributing as it did to national progress, benefited the South itself. "*Because* I love the South," Wilson wrote, "I rejoice in the failure of the Confederacy."[36]

The period of Reconstruction after the war was almost as important, in Wilson's mind, as the conflict itself. Many of the passages in Wilson's writings where he attacks the North and appears to be defending the South come from his sharp criticism of Reconstruction policy. Much of this criticism, however, is not a defense of the southern cause but is instead a protest against the extent to which Reconstruction had allowed blacks to rule over whites in the South. He justified southern antipathy for the Republican Party by explaining that the southerners were "bound for the preservation of their own liberties and in the interests of self-government to maintain an united resistance to the domination of an ignorant race."[37] For Wilson, the war had marked the defeat of the old order, and the postwar period should have been a time for progress as a unified nation now that the forces of states' rights had been vanquished.

In spite of his criticism of Republicans for Reconstruction, Wilson also reasoned that the antagonisms fostered by Reconstruction were perhaps necessary from the perspective of historical utility. He explained that Reconstruction brought about the "permanent" effect of nationalization in American government:

> The national government which came out of Reconstruction was not the national government which went into it. The civil war had given leave to one set of revolutionary forces; Reconstruction gave leave to another still more formidable. The effects of the first were temporary, the inevitable accompaniments of civil war and armed violence; the effects of the second were permanent, and struck to the very centre of our forms of government.[38]

It was during the Reconstruction period, Wilson argued, that America really progressed beyond a narrow, legalistic constitutionalism. The war and Reconstruction had forced the country to abandon some traditional constitutional protections, and the benefit of this action was the discovery that the principles of the country were not grounded in the static Constitution but in historically evolving public sentiment. The war and Reconstruction had the effect of liberating the country from its constitutional shackles and placing public sentiment squarely in charge. Wilson explained that "civil war discovered the foundations of our government to be in fact unwritten, set deep in a sentiment which constitutions can neither originate nor limit. The law of the Constitution reigned until war came. Then the stage was cleared, and the forces of a mighty sentiment, hitherto unorganized, deployed upon it." Adopting the framework of historicism, Wilson contended that through the major antagonisms of the war and Reconstruction, history had brought into realization a public mindset that had hitherto been only potential. "The sentiment of union and nationality," Wilson argued, "never before aroused to full consciousness or knowledge of its own thought and aspirations, was henceforth a new thing, aggressive and aware of a sort of conquest." The North's victory "naturally deemed nationality henceforth a thing above law."[39] Constitutional forms would no longer be allowed to hinder national progress. As Wilson claimed in *Division and Reunion*, 1876 marked the beginning of a new era in American history. The date signified not only the end of the war itself, but also the end of the battles over Reconstruction. Now the newly unified nation was free to move forward.[40]

The Current Historical Spirit and Wilson's Idea of Patriotism

In the concluding volume of *A History of the American People*, Wilson summarized his view that the antagonisms of the nineteenth century had resulted in the manifestation of a truly national spirit in the country:

> A full century had gone by since the government of the nation was set up. Within that century, it now began to appear, fundamental questions of governmental structure and political authority had been settled and the country drawn together to a common life. Henceforth matters were to be in debate which concerned the interests of society everywhere, in one section as in another, questions which were without geographical boundary, questions of the modern world, touching nations no less than communities which fancied themselves to lie apart.[41]

And as Wilson explained elsewhere, the evolution of public sentiment made possible the adoption by the country of a genuinely national outlook on policy and law. This national outlook could not simply have been proclaimed at the country's inception; it had to wait for history to bring about the proper conditions in the underlying public will.[42] Wilson's argument that the country had progressed into a nation as a consequence of the Civil War and Reconstruction laid the groundwork for his political writings. In those writings, when calling for a variety of institutional changes, Wilson's method is to argue for adaptation of government to historical changes that he has observed in the country at large. This approach occasionally lends books like *Congressional Government*, for example, a tone of simply observing changes that have already taken place, as opposed to urging the transformation of the current order.

Wilson's historical argument about the new public sentiment that had emerged from the Civil War also lays the groundwork for his discussion of patriotism. Wilson's speeches and writings on this theme employ patriotism as a means of encouraging devotion to the idea of a unified nation along with devotion to a truly national government with expanded powers to meet modern exigencies. Wilson wrote that patriotism is grounded in "unselfishness." One who is patriotic will focus less on himself, deemphasizing the notion of individualism, and will instead consider himself a part of a unified national society.[43] This notion of patriotism informs Wilson's treatment of "Americanism," which he defined by eliminating any sentiment that detracts from national unity and cohesiveness. Any person who would stand in the way of America's progress as a united nation, Wilson claimed, is not truly an American. Americanism, he wrote, is "above all things, a hopeful and confident spirit. It is progressive, optimistically progressive, and ambitious of objects of national scope and advantage. It is unpedantic, unprovincial, unspeculative, unfastidious; regardful of law, but as using it, not as being used by it or dominated by any formalism whatever."[44] True Americans, Wilson implied, are those who will not let individualism and legal formalism supersede a true national spirit and the vigorous action that it requires from government.[45]

FEDERALISM

Wilson's portrayal of American history does provide a clearer picture of his views on the cause of states' rights. It also helps to lay the groundwork for an understanding of his view of states in the newly nationalized, postwar political order. It is often asserted that Wilson was a staunch defender of federalism in the face of the rising tide of national power.[46] Such assertions are frequently based on Wilson's *Constitutional Government*, where statements such as "it would be fatal to our political vitality really to strip the States of their powers and transfer them to the federal government" appear to form a defense of states' prerogatives.[47] While some of this debate will be taken up in the concluding chapter, it is important to note here that Wilson's genuine teaching on federalism is rooted in his portrayal of American history as triggering progress by overcoming decentralization and inculcating a true spirit of national unity. He did acknowledge and concede that the legal framework of federalism is still in place.[48] But much of his writing is based upon the premise that the nationality of public sentiment that had been brought about by the conclusion of the war was more fundamental than, and had moved the country beyond, the narrow legalisms that had hitherto impeded energetic action by the national government.

In *The State*, Wilson contended that modern Americans understand the nature of their government differently than did the founding generation. Given the change in public sentiment that history had caused, Wilson asserted that modern men see the government as more representative of a national whole, whereas the earlier generation of men conceived of government much more in terms of a federation. Progress had caused this new outlook. Wilson explained that "at first neither love nor respect shielded the federal authorities from the jealousies and menaces of the states. The new government was to *grow* national with the growth of a national history and a national sentiment." He emphasized that what matters in government is not the forms on which it is legally constructed but the understanding of it in the public mind. The public mind had come to a new understanding that liberated the national government from the earlier constraints of the federal model.[49] Even as a young southern writer, Wilson frequently defended the increased scope of the national government vis-à-vis the states. He remarked that the nationalizing effects of the war's conclusion were beneficial for the states themselves. And he chastised fellow southern writers for fearing the power of the national government.[50]

Wilson urged readers simply to acknowledge the reality that history had brought forth, regardless of the legal mechanisms of federalism. The reality of circumstances required the national government to expand its sphere of authority. Since the best government, according to Wilson, is the one that best adjusts itself to the current historical epoch, increased national power ought to be accepted and embraced. In *Congressional Government*, he conceded that the original intention behind the law of the Constitution had been to reserve significant power for the states. But he reasoned that abandoning that original intention was a matter of acquiescing to the changing conditions and necessities of contemporary society.[51] Wilson was candid that one of the adjustments that government would have to make was to allow a much greater sphere of administrative authority for the national government than the Constitution seems to allow on its face. He explained that the increased role of the national government could by accomplished "only by wresting the Constitution to strange and as yet unimagined uses." Wilson provided very little commentary on this

necessary change in government—it was simply a change required by historical reality, and there was nothing to do but to submit and accept it.[52]

The reason why Wilson was not hesitant about fundamental changes in the
American system of government was that he believed that the system itself is
not grounded in any universal principle but instead only in the historically
conditioned sentiment of the public. This is certainly the case with the system
of federalism. Even in *Constitutional Government*, which is often seen as a
defense of federalism, Wilson made clear that there is no principled foundation to the federal system, and that the idea of limiting national government
through federalism was not good or just absolutely. Rather, the federal system
was merely the product of the particular historical forces at play during the
time that the Constitution was framed. And while Wilson did praise various
facets of state government, the clear implication is that, as the old historical
circumstances pass away, so too must a strict understanding of the federal
system.[53] As Wilson proclaimed in a lecture, "The only historical reason for
the existence of a federal arrangement is that there are peculiar historical circumstances back of them making the several pieces jealous of one another."
He explained that he did not necessarily advocate a completely nationalized
system, but also admitted that such a system seemed to be the end that history
had in mind: "I am free to say that I do not wish to see our government completely nationalized if it is too complex, but I do say that we must face the fact
that every federal government has had that history so far. It seems irresistible." Given Wilson's constant argument that government must acquiesce
to the changes brought about by history, such a statement can hardly be understood as a defense of federalism. The statement is immediately followed
by an observation that each generation seems to abandon older understandings of politics for new ones, and reference is made to the fundamental
changes caused by the Civil War.[54] Wilson's writings also teem with criticisms for those figures who do not want to acknowledge the reality of historical change and who resist acquiescing to it. We know that this was a primary
factor in Wilson's hostility toward Andrew Jackson, for example, whom
Wilson attacked for wanting to limit the power of the federal government vis-
à-vis the states.[55] Jackson, Wilson believed, was simply a reactionary who did
not want to acknowledge the progress that history had spawned.

On the practical side of the question, Wilson saw federalism as a system
that was too outmoded to handle the problems that had emerged from the development of history. He was particularly critical of the lack of uniformity in
state laws under the federal system, and he considered these inconsistencies
a hindrance to solving modern problems in a unified and national manner.
Federalism was simply not as administratively efficient as modern times
seemed to require. The system, Wilson wrote, "seems sadly at war with any

uniform administration of the laws such as good government seems to demand." He suggested that the solution might be to centralize more authority at the national level. As he explained:

> The evil that results to the nation at large from the exercise of this extensive legislative independence on the part of these forty-eight legislatures is a very serious one, and grows to more threatening proportions as the country increases in population and advances in wealth. It begins to become manifest that there are some public affairs, now left to the determination of local legislatures, which are of such vital and universal interest as to demand a *uniform and somewhat inflexible* policy in their administration.

Wilson conceded that under the forms of the Constitution, there existed a system of decentralized control over the matters about which he was concerned. He suggested that these constitutional forms must either be formally changed or read in light of a new historical perspective. Wilson cited, as examples of issues that require uniform national treatment, such matters as railroads, criminal law, and marriage law. He believed the regulation of railroads to be an obvious case for national regulation. He was distressed that some states might take it upon themselves to abolish capital punishment, and that others were making divorce too easy; to him, these practices called out for federal intervention.[56] Part of Wilson's concern with the practice of state government had to do with his belief that the quality of state legislatures was low. He considered the legislators in those bodies to be narrow-minded and overly focused on particular interests, while the times demanded a more national outlook.[57]

Since to Wilson the times appeared to require a more expansive national government, the question became how such a role was to be put in force in light of the Constitution's forms. Here Wilson emphasized the need for an historically conditioned reading of the Constitution. The document ought to be read, Wilson argued, as outlining certain general principles while allowing for the adaptation of those principles to vary with the circumstances. In *Constitutional Government*, he applied this reasoning to the division of authority between the states and the national government, employing what might today be characterized as a "living constitution" mode of interpretation:

> The general lines of definition which were to run between the powers granted to Congress and the powers reserved to States the makers of the Constitution were able to draw with their characteristic foresight and lucidity; but the subject-matter of that definition is constantly changing, for it is the life of the nation itself. Our activities change alike their scope and their character with every generation. The old measures of the Constitution are every day to be filled with new grain as the varying crop of circumstances comes to maturity.

Here Wilson repeated the argumentation employed in his definition of liberty, where he contended that the ideas and principles are clear, but that they must be understood differently at different times. The idea of federalism, Wilson contended, is clear from the Constitution, but it is up to the people of each generation to determine the necessary scope of national power. Such is the "defense" of the federal system put forth in *Constitutional Government*.[58]

Wilson reasoned that historical changes directly affect the amount of power Congress must exercise vis-à-vis the states. While he devoted much energy in *Constitutional Government* to citing specific examples of the kinds of matters into which the federal government should not intrude, these exceptions are undermined by his own general argument that the particular lines of demarcation are to be determined by each generation and are not matters of principle. Wilson questioned, for example, whether such matters as child labor should fall under the scope of congressional authority. He contended that they should not, but his contention was based not upon the strict limits that must be imposed on federal power but upon the prevailing historical conditions. As Wilson elaborated in explaining the division of authority between states and the national government, it is clear

> that what are the general commercial interests, what the general financial interests, what the general economic interests of the country, is a question of fact, to be determined by circumstances which change under our very eyes, and that, case by case, we are inevitably drawn on to include under the established definitions of the law matters new and unforeseen, which seem in their magnitude to give to the powers of Congress a sweep and vigor certainly never conceived possible by earlier generations of statesmen.[59]

So Wilson's claim that he did not want the federal government to expand at the expense of the states is coupled with an historicist reading of the Constitution that makes just such an expansion perfectly legitimate. He commented on the Constitution's provisions for federalism: "As the life of the nation changes so must the interpretation of the document which contains it change, by a nice adjustment, determined, not by the original intention of those who drew the paper, but by the exigencies and the new aspects of life itself."[60]

Since determining the role of the federal government would be a matter of interpreting the Constitution in light of "the new aspects of life," Wilson was fully cognizant of the importance this determination places on the federal judiciary. He acknowledged that the courts are the key in the federalism question, since they will ultimately decide whether certain national measures are permissible under the Constitution. The judiciary's reading of the Constitution, consequently, must be based upon the evolving historical spirit; it is essential for judges to reflect what it is that each generation wants out of government, and not to be stuck on an outdated understanding of the purpose and role of government. In an argument remarkably similar to Justice William Brennan's call for judges to read the Constitution as twentieth-century Americans, Wilson explained that "the members of the courts are necessarily men of their own generation: we would not wish to have them men from another." He recognized that all debate about the extent of federal power would come down to an interpretation of the interstate commerce clause, and those interpreting the clause must do so through the lens of the current historical spirit, not the one that informed the framing of the Constitution.[61]

THE RECEDING THREAT OF FACTION

In advocating a wider scope of power for the national government, Wilson consciously challenged the principle of limited government inherent in the constitutionalism of the framers. The framers had limited the scope of government through various institutional mechanisms, primarily because of the threat of faction—especially the possibility that a majority faction, gaining control of the government, could use its power in a democracy to tyrannize other groups or individuals. Wilson no longer saw the need for limited government because he believed that faction was no longer a threat in modern democracy. His view of American history, whereby the country progressively becomes united as a single nation in its fundamental will, was an essential foundation for his belief that faction was no longer a threat. The unity of will that is brought about by history meant that the threat of one faction using its power to tyrannize others had receded. In the days of the nation's founding, when historical circumstances were such that individuals and groups were focused on their own special interests and not on the nation as an organic whole, faction was a real threat, and so the institutional remedies the founders employed were appropriate for those times. Yet with the subsequent growth and development, the previously individualistic and fragmented public mind had matured into a cohesive, unified, objective will. Wilson made this very point in *Congressional Government*, which is more explicitly historicist than the several earlier essays upon which it is based. Whereas the model of government expounded in *The Federalist* relies upon a competition of diverse interests in order to check the dangerous exercise of centralized power, Wilson explained in *Congressional Government* that "there has been from the first a steady and unmistakable growth of nationality of sentiment."[62] This growing nationality of sentiment, he contended, must serve as the foundation for an increasingly unfettered national power. In particular, this evolution spawns a national government that can enact policy more efficiently by eliminating such mechanisms as the separation of powers that serve as obstacles to efficiency.

Because Wilson believed that progress had reduced or eliminated the threat of faction, he estimated that majorities were no longer the problem that they once had been in democratic government. Whereas the various institutional mechanisms of the founders' Constitution were designed to "refine and enlarge" the public view in order to ensure that it was not factious, Wilson's vision of modern government eliminated these restraints on majority rule. Wilson noted that, in the past, Americans had been taught to fear "partisan majorities." Yet in modern democracy, restraining such majorities is tantamount to denying the very principle of self-government. As Wilson argued, "It is the present custom of unthinking newspaper writers, insincere demagogues, and utopian philosophers to denounce, in tones of righteous wrath, what they call 'the tyranny of partisan majorities,' and at the same time, almost in the same breath, to speak the praises of 'true representative government.' They do not dream that they are laughably inconsistent the while."[63]

Since history had guaranteed that the public sentiment was inherently just, there was no longer any reason to be concerned with the possibility of any excesses. Wilson noted that the primary difference between American and English government—a difference that decidedly favors the English—is that the English do not fear majority tyranny. In fact, the term *majority tyranny* does not even make sense to the English, since they understand that the very definition of self-government is rule by majorities.[64] As Scot Zentner persuasively argues, Wilson did not see majority faction as a threat because, unlike the founders, he did not see a conflict between reason and will.[65] And Niels Thorsen explains that Wilson's theory of constitutional government represented a "decisive break with past liberal understandings" because constitutionalism no longer served as protection for the individual against tyrannical majorities, but instead served "as a political authorization of the growth and development of national power."[66]

A problem with limited government, from Wilson's perspective, was that wealthy special interests had been using it to protect their own privileged status and to prevent the majority from governing for the common good. The founders' preoccupation with faction, viewed in this light, merely masked the maintenance of the wealth and status of a few. This is why Wilson called Hamilton a "great man" but "not a great American." According to Wilson, Hamilton believed that only the wealthy had a stake in government and that government, therefore, should be designed with a view toward protecting their interests. There is a loose connection here to Wilson's 1912 campaign rhetoric, where he claimed that such an understanding still plagued the country, in the form of the "guardianship" of wealthy trusts. Wilson wanted to oppose his theory of genuine constitutional government to the "guardianship theory" of government by special interests. Under the "guardianship theory"—which Wilson identified with the Republican Party—the wealthy special interests prevent government action that is desired by the majority of average people.[67] Wilson essentially identified the "guardianship theory" as the limited-government theory of the founding and called for it to be replaced by true representative government.

WILSON'S EVOLUTIONARY CONSTITUTIONALISM

In urging Americans to advance beyond the limited-government constitutionalism of the founding, Wilson suggested a more flexible interpretation of the Constitution—to see it not as a set of firm rules and restrictions, but as a vehicle for adapting governmental institutions to the new conditions of modern life. In the New Freedom campaign, Wilson exhorted Americans to replace the rigid, mechanical "Newtonian" constitutionalism of the founding generation with a "Darwinian" mode of interpretation that could serve the needs of modern life. Mechanical Newtonianism was a logical constitutional perspective for the founding generation because of the dominance of Newtonian thinking during that age. "The Constitution of the United States had been made under the dominion of the Newtonian Theory," Wilson explained. "You have only to read the papers of *The Federalist* to see that fact written on every page." Yet while Newtonian thinking suited the founding generation, members of that generation were mistaken in their belief that such constitutional thinking was universal—that it ought to apply not only during their own time but to governments of all ages. Wilson blamed the French philosophers for influencing the founders to think in terms of universal theories. He explained: "The makers of our Federal Constitution read Montesquieu with true scientific enthusiasm. They were scientists in their way,—the best way of their age,—those fathers of the nation. Jefferson wrote of 'the laws of Nature,'—and then by way of afterthought,—'and of Nature's God.' And they constructed a government as they would have constructed an orrery,—to display the laws of nature." This thinking in terms of universal theories—instead of historically contingent principles—created significant problems for modern government, which Wilson believed was impeded from growing and adapting as new circumstances required. Placing rigid limitations on the power and role of government was not a means of protecting liberty, Wilson reasoned, but a prescription for choking the life out of our governing institutions.

> The trouble with the theory is that government is not a machine, but a living thing. It falls, not under the theory of the universe, but under the theory of organic life. It is accountable to Darwin, not to Newton. It is modified by its environment, necessitated by its tasks, shaped to its functions by the sheer pressure of life.[68]

The language Wilson employed in arguing for a more flexible reading of the Constitution resembles Johann Bluntschli's language on the state as an organic entity. Bluntschli wrote that "the State is in no way a lifeless instrument, a dead machine: it is a living and therefore organized being. This organic nature of the State has not always been understood." As an organism, Bluntschli continued, all of the parts of the state must work together, in unity. "In the State spirit and body, will and active organs are necessarily bound together in one life."[69]

New conditions necessitate a new understanding of government. Wilson explained that "our life has broken away from the past. The life of America is not the life that it was twenty years ago; it is not the life that it was ten years ago. We have changed our economic conditions, absolutely, from top to bottom; and, with our economic society, the organization of our life." Consequently, the old principles of government can no longer be employed to manage the new conditions. Political principles need to be redefined, since "the old political formulas do not fit the present problems."[70] Constitutions, Wilson reasoned, cannot be understood as laying down a rigid set of rules. Instead, the demands of the age must drive them.[71] This is why American greatness comes not from remaining true to the original forms and ideas of the Constitution, but from realizing the necessity of departing from these forms and ideas and being willing to do so. To the extent that we had succeeded as a nation, Wilson argued, our success had been rooted not in our ideas and institutions themselves, but in our willingness to adapt those ideas to the evolution of history.[72] A potential threat to this evolutionary model of constitutional interpretation is the legal profession, Wilson contended, because lawyers tend to become obsessed with the technical details of the law at the price of missing its overall organic character. Hence, Wilson frequently argued that legal education ought to incorporate more historical study so that lawyers would come to have an appreciation for the law as a part of a broad pattern of historical development.[73]

The practical meaning of Wilson's historically contingent constitutionalism is that government must constantly reflect the true public mind of any given age. This is why Wilson's definition of *constitutional government* does not stress the notion of a government whose role is defined or restricted by a predetermined set of rules. Rather, a constitutional government is one that is in tune with, and constantly adjusting itself to, the will of the people. Since the public mind continually changes and evolves, so too must our understanding of what government should do.[74] Hence, Wilson explained, "A constitutional government is one whose powers have been adapted to the interests of its people."[75] Institutionally, the organs of government must keep up with the times or be discarded if they no longer fit. "Whatever institutions,"

Wilson reasoned, "whatever practices serve these ends, are necessary to such a system: those which do not, or which serve it imperfectly, should be dispensed with or bettered."[76]

Wilson granted that constitutional government must always be focused on liberty, but liberty is an evolving concept and must be understood in the context of the current public mind. Public opinion about what liberty means in practice is constantly changing, and government must keep up with these changes. Wilson contended that a true constitution requires a community of opinion as its foundation. It is impossible to have a constitution based merely upon form. Rather, the constitution must represent or embody some organic community and must evolve as an organic community evolves. This is why "nothing but a community can have a constitutional form of government, and if a nation has not become a community, it cannot have that sort of polity." A true constitution represents a "common political consciousness."[77] Wilson made clear that an emphasis on constitutional forms offers no protection for liberty. Liberty, he explained, depends much more upon public opinion than it does upon constitutional mechanics. Wilson contended that in America, there had been a tradition of public self-restraint, which had been primarily responsible for the limited role of government. The foundation of this self-restraint had been public opinion. If the people change their view of what is required from government—as they are apt to do gradually—then their understanding of the Constitution itself must change accordingly.[78] This evolution of constitutional understanding will best be facilitated by putting public opinion more directly in control of governing institutions. Such reasoning fuels Wilson's support for the direct election of U.S. senators and his willingness to at least consider other progressive proposals for direct democracy.[79]

Wilson frequently criticized what he considered to be an unthinking fixation on the forms of the original Constitution. Such a fixation amounts to a "blind worship" of the Constitution and the principles that informed it, and impedes the adaptation of American government to the changes in historical conditions and the public sentiment. Wilson argued that opponents to the Constitution during the founding era, who wanted to ensure that the Constitution would not be interpreted as giving much power to the central government, initiated this worship. These detractors pounced on the Constitution's procedural provisions and elevated them in order to constrict the new government. Wilson claimed that this very narrow and erroneous view of the Constitution had persisted unchallenged for decades. He complained that "the divine right of kings never ran a more prosperous course than did this unquestioned prerogative of the Constitution to receive universal homage."[80] And he criticized America's "self-confidence"—the conviction that she had discovered a permanent answer to the problem of politics: "There was a time when America was blithe with self-confidence. She boasted that she, and she alone, knew the processes of popular government; but now she sees her sky overcast; she sees that there are at work forces which she did not dream of in her hopeful youth."[81]

The problem arises not only from America's "blind worship" of the Constitution, but also of the principles that informed the framing of the Constitution. Hence, Wilson attacked those who were devoted to the principles of the Declaration of Independence. He complained that "some citizens of this country have never got beyond the Declaration of Independence. . . . Their bosoms swell against George III, but they have no consciousness of the war for freedom that is going on today."[82] Wilson contended that the Declaration addressed only the specific historical circumstances of the founding era, and that its principles could not be translated literally into modern times. He saw hope in the fact this his own generation was really the first to question substantially the principles of the founding, and he encouraged others to join in:

> When grave, thoughtful, perspicacious, and trusted men all around us agree in deriding those "Fourth of July sentiments" which were once thought to hallow the lips of our greatest orators and to approve the patriotism of our greatest statesmen, it will not do for us, personifying the American eagle, to flap wing and scream out incoherent disapproval.[83]

That the principles of the founding can be called into question is a sign of America's maturity. As a mature nation, Wilson contended, we can look to the principles and practices of foreign governments to see how we might improve ourselves.[84] In fact, we must improve ourselves or risk perishing. As Wilson remarked in 1876, "The American Republic will in my opinion never celebrate another Centennial. At least under the present Constitution and laws."[85]

As Wilson himself matured, he began to package his calls for abandoning the principles of the founding in rhetoric that purported to be aimed at restoring the regime's true principles. This was certainly more the case in his political addresses than it was in his academic writings. Many of his political addresses argued that special interests had used the forms of the Constitution to inflate and protect their own status, but that his own proposals and those of other progressives were designed to recover the true spirit of republican government. As he contended in a representative passage from *The New Freedom*, "How absurd is the charge that we who are demanding that our government be made representative of the people and responsive to their demands,—how fictitious and hypocritical is the charge that we are attacking the fundamental principles of republican institutions!"[86] Wilson maintained that the principles of the country could best be preserved by adopting an historically contingent perspective on their meaning. Under this model, such ideals as liberty or Jeffersonianism, for example, can be upheld by having their meanings altered to accommodate the demands of the current age. Government, accordingly, becomes defined by whatever the people currently want (or are told that they want), instead of taking its direction from any permanent understanding of liberty or justice. As Charles R. Kesler explains, "The New Freedom means government . . . through the people rather than of, for, and by the people—government expressing the spirit of the age, rather than embodying the people's attempt to govern themselves in the light of certain self-evident truths." This is the crucial difference, Kesler points out, between Wilson's "New Freedom" and Lincoln's "New Birth of Freedom." Whereas Lincoln aimed to reawaken the original understanding of freedom that animated the founding, Wilson wanted to redefine the meaning of freedom to fit the change in historical circumstance.[87]

What is different about modern times that requires a more up-to-date application of the Constitution's principles? Wilson explained, in "The Art of Governing," that the fundamental difference between the modern period and the founding era is the present need for governmental efficiency, not the hindrance of state action. The constitutionalism of the founders aimed at limiting state action in order to uphold the individualistic notion of liberty prevalent at that time. Modern constitutionalism, in contrast, ought to reflect the people's desire to see their will efficiently implemented by their government. Hence, Wilson claimed that "the period of constitution-making is passed now. We have reached new territory in which we need new guides, the vast territory of *administration*."[88] The efficiency required by administration stands directly at odds with the operative principle of the primary institutional feature of the founders' Constitution—the separation of powers.

SEPARATION OF POWERS AS AN OBSTACLE TO PROGRESS

If Wilson's primary complaint about American constitutionalism was that it mistakenly aimed at protecting individual liberty by restricting the power of government, and that it consequently was both undemocratic and inefficient, then the primary institutional manifestation of this problem was the separation of powers. For Wilson, the separation of powers was the source of much of what was wrong with American government. As opposed to a democratic system that would quickly translate the current public mind into efficient government action, the separation-of-powers system, as Wilson understood it, was designed to protect the people from themselves; it would accomplish this by throwing up as many obstacles as possible to the implementation of the people's will. Such a system served only to impede genuine democracy, which Wilson wanted to restore by breaking down the walls between the branches, allowing them to work in close coordination in order to constantly adjust public policy to the current public mind. Wilson's antipathy toward the separation of powers was at the heart of his various proposals for a cabinet or parliamentary form of government in the United States, and for energetic popular leadership and broad administrative discretion. These institutional proposals are examined at length in the upcoming chapters. In general, Wilson saw the separation of powers as fundamentally contrary to his understanding of government as a living, organic extension of the people's own will. As he proclaimed in *The New Freedom*, "No living thing can have its organs offset against each other, as checks, and live."[89]

Wilson argued that the separation-of-powers system was both inefficient and irresponsible. It was inefficient because it prevented government from solving the problems of modern life in a coordinated way; instead, the various organs of government were busy attacking one another. Separation of powers was irresponsible because it made it difficult for the government to implement new public policy, even when the new policy reflected a clear new direction in public opinion. Unlike parliamentary government, where changes in public opinion could quickly effect a change in government and a change in policy, the separation-of-powers system prevented just that kind of responsiveness. Wilson elaborated on the problem of irresponsibility in *Congressional Government*:

> It is . . . manifestly a radical defect in our federal system that it parcels out power and confuses responsibility as it does. The main purpose of the Convention of 1787 seems to have been to accomplish this grievous mistake. The "literary theory" of checks and balances is simply a consistent account of what our constitution-makers tried to do; and those checks and balances have proved mischievous just to the extent which they have succeeded in establishing themselves as realities. It is quite safe to say that were it possible to call together again the members of that wonderful Convention to view the work of their hands in the light of the century that has tested it, they would be the first to admit that the only fruit of dividing power had been to make it irresponsible.[90]

Wilson's criticism of separation of powers from the perspective of responsibility reaches back to his earliest political writings of the 1870s.[91] Those writings consistently call for some form of cabinet government to be instituted in the United States—a form of government where a national legislature depends upon majority public opinion and the executive branch depends upon sustained support in the legislature. The key feature of such a system is that there is no separation between the legislative and executive branches—in fact, the leaders of the legislative branch also serve in the cabinet as leaders of the executive branch. Wilson's writings make clear that the only remedies to the problems of American government are "certainly none other than those which were rejected by the Constitutional Convention." The most obvious error of the convention was Article I, Section 6 of the Constitution, which prohibits members of Congress from serving simultaneously in the executive branch. In his essay "Cabinet Government in the United States," Wilson explicitly called for the repeal of this section of the Constitution.[92] In a comment elsewhere, he decried "the folly of America in taking away from the national assembly the reverent custom of appointing the great officers of state!"[93] In his marginal notes to several papers of *The Federalist*, Wilson frequently wrote that cabinet government was the best solution to the various problems Publius mentioned. In particular, in response to those papers where Publius addresses the personal motivations of public officials and the self-interest that is fundamental to their human nature, Wilson commented that making public officials accountable to public opinion through a cabinet system of government could supply the proper motivations.[94] For Wilson, openness and accountability through a cabinet system are the solution for the potential self-interestedness of officeholders, whereas Publius suggests that channeling self-interest through a separation-of-powers system will lead to a situation where "the private interest of every individual may be a sentinel over the public rights."[95] For Wilson, such a system of ambition counteracting ambition will only prevent unity in government, and without unity there can be no real coordination and no real leadership.[96]

While Wilson's critique of the founding usually displays a solid grasp of what the founders were up to, he at times seems to misunderstand certain elements of the founding. His commentary on the separation of powers, for example, is partially founded on a flawed understanding of the intentions behind the system. He asserted that the framers thought they could rely upon mere "parchment barriers" for the system to work—that they could prevent corruption with a simple, formal separation of the branches. As Wilson claimed, "They thought, in their own fervor of patriotism and intensity of respect for written law, that paper barriers would prove sufficient to prevent the encroachments of any one department upon the prerogatives of any other." Wilson concluded that this belief blinded the framers to the dangers posed by the legislative branch. "In spite of constitutional barriers," he wrote, "the legislature has become the imperial power of the State, as it must of necessity become under every representative system."[97] Of course, the framers' view was exactly the opposite of the one that Wilson attributed to them. Publius himself, in *Federalist* 48, explains that mere "parchment barriers" will be insufficient to prevent one branch from encroaching upon the jurisdiction of the others. The whole point of *Federalist* 48 is, in fact, to demonstrate the need for checks and balances if the separation of powers is to be maintained. Furthermore, while Wilson comments that the framers were blind to the dangers of the legislature, Publius, to the contrary, identifies the legislature as the greatest threat among all the branches, calling it the "impetuous vortex" bent on drawing all power into its own sphere.[98] And in *Federalist* 51, Publius plainly recognizes that "in republican government, the legislative authority necessarily predominates."[99]

Wilson attributed part of the problem with the separation of powers to the fact that the framers took Montesquieu's teaching on the matter too literally. Wilson argued that Montesquieu's teaching on a strict separation of powers was written to apply to an "undemocratic state." The framers committed the great sin of taking Montesquieu's political ideas out of historical context. They should have considered how his broad ideas ought to be adapted to accommodate their own circumstances. The problem, Wilson explained, was that "we had no thought of reexamining his principles to see if they really held good for all cases. We simply accepted them, and, like practical men, thought that if they were good to use at all they were good to use in their plain literal meaning."[100] Wilson believed that the framers might have been more inclined to accept Montesquieu's separation-of-powers system because they had a distaste for anything British.[101] And ultimately, the examples of England and France prove Montesquieu's doctrine wrong. Wilson contended that the "partial union of branches has been effected directly in the face of the honored opinion of the great Montesquieu, if the later interpretations of that opinion are to be accepted."[102]

For Wilson, a fundamental quandary in continuing the separation-of-powers system in modern times is that the system is based on the principles of "older liberalism." This "older liberalism" holds that a division of power is necessary to keep the government from tyrannizing over the people. He identified the "theoretical basis" of the division as "Individualism versus State Power"—a basis that no longer applies to the modern epoch.[103] As Wilson had explained in *The State,* the state is not a threat to the individual but is, instead, essential to proper individual self-development. The real marvel for Wilson was that the American system of government had survived at all under the separation of powers. He cited Walter Bagehot's observation that Americans must have an excellent capacity for self-government because it seems they can make *any* system work—even one as inefficient as the separation of powers. Wilson concurred, but warned that even America would fail unless changes were made. He pointed to the British constitution as a model, particularly because of its cabinet system of interbranch cooperation. During the American founding era, Wilson pointed out, the English constitution was imperfect. But unlike its American counterpart, the English constitution was not subject to any formal restrictions on its growth and development, and so contemporary English government served as a model for modern democracy. As Wilson explained, if the English government "is now superior, it is so because its growth has not been hindered or destroyed by the too tight ligaments of a written fundamental law."[104]

SEPARATING POLITICS AND ADMINISTRATION

Based upon his general objection to the founders' understanding of government, and his particular objection to the separation of powers, Wilson put forth a series of institutional proposals designed in one way or another to overcome the fixed notion of politics that lies at the heart of limited government. Wilson's institutional substitute for the founders' separation of powers is best understood as the separation of politics and administration. The idea of separating politics and administration broadly defines the different institutional arrangements that Wilson suggested in his scholarship, although the specific institutional means for achieving the separation of politics and administration changed as Wilson progressed from his earlier to his more mature intellectual works.

For Wilson, the force of history had been forming a national unity of public will; the American nation had arrived at a point of fundamental agreement about politics or political justice, or at least it was in the final stages of doing so. Consequently, the vital task of government would become administration—which is simply the determination of the specific governmental means needed to achieve the political ends that we all agree we want. From the perspective of the American founders, Wilson might well have been characterized as "far gone in utopian speculations"[105] since the founders believed that political discord would always remain at the heart of republican government, or that the "latent causes of faction are thus sown in the nature of man."[106] Whereas the founders' constitutionalism had limited government in order to guard against majority groups of citizens implementing their own passionate view of political justice at the expense of the rights of other citizens, Wilson's constitutionalism did not need to limit or check government in such a way because national political unity had been achieved.

Wilson's vision of government seems to be one where the unified will of the public has a much more direct role to play in politics than the founders had envisioned. Yet politics, while increasingly democratized in Wilson's thought, also becomes much less authoritative. The emphasis in government shifts to administration. The key to Wilson's separation of politics and administration is to keep the former out of the latter's way. Administration, after all, is properly the province of scientific experts in the bureaucracy; the experts' competence in the specific technological means required to achieve those ends on which we are all agreed gives them the authority to administer or regulate progress, unhindered by the realm of politics. Politics can claim no such expertise.

Wilson's understanding of politics, and its separation from administration, requires a transformation in the traditional American thinking on legislative and executive power. Wilson proposed such a transformation. The story of how this transformation would unfold is essentially the story of how Wilson conceived of arranging the "politics" half of the politics-administration dichotomy. His proposed transformation manifests itself in two distinct forms: one of these forms is the product of Wilson's early political thought, where he emphasized the importance of Congress and a cabinet form of government responsible to a legislative majority; later, however, Wilson became disillusioned with Congress and looked instead to popular leadership under a strong presidency as the key to transforming American institutions. The following four chapters will examine each of these alternatives. After addressing Wilson's institutional proposals for Congress, the presidency, the judiciary, and the party system in chapters 4 and 5, the book will turn in chapters 6 and 7 to the question of how democratic Wilson's new institutionalism really is. It will examine the extent to which, under the separation of politics and administration, Wilson brings public opinion into more direct contact with politics while shifting much governing authority away from politics and into the bureaucracy. It will also address the extent to which Wilson's popular-leadership model, while democratic on the surface, is really a means for elites to govern the people.

NOTES

1. One recent exception is Terri Bimes and Stephen Skowronek, "Woodrow Wilson's Critique of Popular Leadership: Reassessing the Modern-Traditional Divide in Presidential History," *Polity* 29:1 (Fall 1996): 27–63. My reading of Wilson's histories leads me to very different conclusions than the ones reached by Bimes and Skowronek. I take up this argument in chapter 5.

2. See David Steigerwald, "The Synthetic Politics of Woodrow Wilson," *Journal of the History of Ideas* 50 (July/September 1989): 474–75.

3. Wilson, *Division and Reunion: 1829–1889* (New York: Longmans, Green, 1901), 4–9. Quotations from Wilson's writings will be modernized as necessary for grammar and spelling. Emphasis will be in the original unless otherwise specified.

4. *Division and Reunion*, 110.

5. Wilson, *Constitutional Government in the United States* (New York: Columbia University Press, 1908), 46–47.

6. "A Commemorative Address," April 30, 1889, in Arthur S. Link, ed., *The Papers of Woodrow Wilson* (hereafter cited as *PWW*) 69 vols. (Princeton: Princeton University Press, 1966–1993), 6:177.

7. "The Making of the Nation," April 15, 1897, in *PWW* 10:231, 235.

8. Wilson, *The State* (Boston: D. C. Heath, 1889), 480.

9. Wilson, *A History of the American People*, 5 vols. (New York: Harper & Brothers, 1902), 4:265.

10. *History of the American People*, 5:128–29. For a discussion of Wilson's vision of the Civil War as necessary for progress, see the following: Niels Aage Thorsen, *The Political Thought of Woodrow Wilson 1875–1910* (Princeton: Princeton University Press, 1988), 15; Anthony Gaughan, "Woodrow Wilson and the Legacy of the Civil War," *Civil War History* 43:3 (1977): 227–38; Steigerwald, "Synthetic Politics of Wilson," 476.

11. "Government by Debate," December 4, 1882, in *PWW* 2:232.

12. Wilson, *The New Freedom* (New York: Doubleday, Page, 1913), 43–44. This is precisely the argument on the founders' liberalism that John Dewey makes in "Liberalism and Social Action."

13. *History of the American People*, 3:173–74.

14. "A Calendar of Great Americans," September 15, 1893, in *PWW* 8:370.

15. *Constitutional Government*, 40–43.

16. *History of the American People*, 3:173.

17. *History of the American People*, 3:166.

18. "Calendar of Great Americans," in *PWW* 8:371.

19. "Calendar of Great Americans," in *PWW* 8:372.

20. *Division and Reunion*, 44–47.

21. "State Rights," December 20, 1899, in *PWW* 11:311–12.

22. *Division and Reunion*, 211.

23. Wilson to Hermann Eduard von Holst, June 29, 1893, in *PWW* 8:271–72.

24. *Division and Reunion*, 73–83. Wilson gives the same account of Jackson as a reactionary in *History of the American People*, 4:9, 18.

25. *History of the American People*, 3:276.

26. This is the argument made by Skowronek and Bimes, which I will take up in detail in chapter 5.

27. *Division and Reunion*, 18–21. Wilson makes the same argument in *History of the American People*, 3:274.

28. *Division and Reunion*, 27, 31.

29. *Division and Reunion*, 33. Insofar as Wilson credits Van Buren as the primary architect of the nineteenth-century party system, his analysis coincides with the judgment of James W. Ceaser in *Presidential Selection* (Princeton: Princeton University Press, 1979), 123–69.

30. *Division and Reunion*, 115. For a similar argument, see "Calendar of Great Americans," in *PWW* 8:377.

31. *Division and Reunion*, 119.

32. Lincoln, "Speech on the *Dred Scott* Decision," in *Lincoln: Selected Speeches and Writings* (Library of America, 1992), 117–22.

33. For an illustration of Wilson's praise of Lincoln as a champion of progress, see "Calendar of Great Americans," in *PWW* 8:378–79.

34. *Division and Reunion*, 105–6.

35. "State Rights," in *PWW* 11:345.

36. "John Bright," March 6, 1880, in *PWW* 1:618–19. In the scholarly literature, several writers have argued against the common assumption that Wilson was a southern sympathizer and a defender of states' rights. See Gaughan, "Wilson and the Legacy of the Civil

War," esp. 225–29; Arthur S. Link, "Woodrow Wilson: The American as Southerner," *The Journal of Southern History* 36:1 (February 1970): 3–17; John M. Mulder, *Woodrow Wilson: The Years of Preparation* (Princeton: Princeton University Press, 1978), 33; Harry Blumenthal, "Woodrow Wilson and the Race Question," *The Journal of Negro History* (January 1963): 1.

37. "Stray Thoughts from the South," February 22, 1881, in *PWW* 2:27–28.

38. "The Reconstruction of the Southern States," March 2, 1900, in *PWW* 11:460.

39. "Reconstruction of the Southern States," in *PWW* 11:474–75.

40. *Division and Reunion*, 273. Incidentally, as Wilson claims here, the return to normal at the conclusion of Reconstruction meant the return to the rule of whites in the South, who had finally overcome the various Reconstruction barriers to regain control. This, too, Wilson regards as a sign of progress. For a similar argument, see *History of the American People*, 5:300.

41. *History of the American People*, 5:198–99.

42. "Bryce's *American Commonwealth*," January 31, 1889, in *PWW* 6:74. Thorsen's commentaries on *The State* emphasize this point—that Wilson was attempting to reassert the legitimacy of national political authority in response to the war and Reconstruction. Hence, Wilson emphasizes national cohesion. Thorsen, *Political Thought of Woodrow Wilson*, 100.

43. "Spurious Versus Real Patriotism in Education," October 13, 1899, in *PWW* 11:245.

44. "Calendar of Great Americans," in *PWW* 8:374.

45. Thorsen connects Wilson's concept of patriotism to his concept of leadership—suggesting that the unity of patriotic sentiment seems to open up the opportunity for popular leadership. Thorsen, *Political Thought of Woodrow Wilson*, 166. Mulder is critical of what he calls the "facile" combination of patriotism and religion in much of Wilson's work. He argues that Wilson was "consistently using religious terms to describe allegiance to America." Mulder, *Years of Preparation*, 230–31.

46. Deil S. Wright suggests that Wilson is concerned with federalism and that his administrative arguments are not exclusively nationalistic. Yet he does concede that Wilson as president took positions that constituted "a frontal assault on the Madisonian doctrine of dispersed and fragmented power." Wright, "A Century of the Intergovernmental Administrative State: Wilson's Federalism, New Deal Intergovernmental Relations, and Contemporary Intergovernmental Management," in *A Centennial History of the American Administrative State*, ed. Ralph Clark Chandler (New York: The Free Press, 1987), 226, 231. Martha Derthick and John J. Dinan also suggest that progressives, including Wilson, wanted to preserve many qualities of the federal system. They cite Wilson's praise of the Senate in *Constitutional Government*. Derthick and Dinan, "Progressivism and Federalism," in *Progressivism and the New Democracy*, ed. Sidney M. Milkis and Jerome M. Mileur (Amherst: University of Massachusetts Press, 1999), esp. 91. Yet writers like Larry Walker and Jeremy F. Plant argue that Wilson was clearly a nationalist, and that his policies set precedents that eroded state authority for the sake of national administration. Walker and Plant, "Woodrow Wilson and the Federal System," in *Politics and Administration: Woodrow Wilson and American Public Administration*, ed. Jack Rabin and James S. Bowman (New York: Marcel Dekker, 1984), esp. 120–22. See also the argument of Kendrick A. Clements, who dismisses the notion that Wilson was interested in preserving the prerogatives of states. Clements, *The Presidency of Woodrow Wilson* (Lawrence: University Press of Kansas, 1992), 2–3.

47. *Constitutional Government*, 191.

48. See, for example, *The State*, 483.

49. *The State*, 476–81.

50. See, for example, "Marginal Notes on P. C. Centz," February 7, 1883, in *PWW* 2:301–3.

51. Wilson, *Congressional Government* (1885; repr., New York: Meridian Books, 1956), 34.

52. *Congressional Government*, 54–55.

53. *Constitutional Government*, 44.

54. "Lecture at the New York Law School," March 11, 1892, in *PWW* 7:476–77.

55. *Division and Reunion*, 38–53.

56. "Some Legal Needs," May 1, 1881, in *PWW* 2:60–63. Emphasis added. Wilson also criticizes the lack of uniformity in state laws in *The State*, citing marriage laws as a particular example. *The State*, 493–95.

57. "Some Legal Needs," in *PWW* 2:61. See also *Constitutional Government*, 191, 196–97.

58. *Constitutional Government*, 173.

59. *Constitutional Government*, 173–74, 177–79.

60. *Constitutional Government*, 192.

61. *Constitutional Government*, 185, 193.

62. *Congressional Government*, 42. Thorsen identifies national unity or integration as a key premise of Wilson's vision of national administration. See Thorsen, *Political Thought of Woodrow Wilson*, 117.

63. "Congressional Government," October 1, 1879, in *PWW* 1:550.

64. "Government by Debate," December 1882, in *PWW* 2:206.

65. Scot J. Zentner, "Liberalism and Executive Power: Woodrow Wilson and the American Founders," *Polity* 26:4 (Summer 1994): 595. Zentner also points out that Wilson's failure to see a conflict between reason and will also eliminates the concern with demagoguery, since unity of will means that one faction cannot be raised up against another by a demagogic leader. See Zentner, "President and Party in the Thought of Woodrow Wilson," *Presidential Studies Quarterly* 26:3 (Summer 1996): 669–73.

66. Thorsen, *Political Thought of Woodrow Wilson*, 203–4.

67. *The New Freedom*, 55–58. See also 242.

68. *The New Freedom*, 45–47. For a sound analysis of Wilson's interpretation of the Constitution, see Christopher Wolfe, "Woodrow Wilson: Interpreting the Constitution," *Review of Politics* 41 (January 1979): 131–33.

69. Johann K. Bluntschli, *The Theory of the State*, 3rd ed. (1852; repr., Oxford, UK: Clarendon Press, 1921), 18–19.

70. *The New Freedom*, 3–4. This argument is also made in *The State*; see 583.

71. "Leaderless Government," August 5, 1897, in *PWW* 10:299–300. As Robert Eden explains, Wilson "believes that a mature, self-governing people, are capable of *breaking* constitutions without losing respect for them. . . . The notion of a settled, essentially permanent constitution reflects the immaturity of a self-governing people. Wilson's synthetic, opinion-leading politics is intended to combine the primitive loyalty to fixed constitutional opinions with refined flexibility and openness to innovation." Eden, "Opinion Leadership and the Problem of Executive Power: Woodrow Wilson's Original Position," *Review of Politics* 57 (Summer 1995): 491.

72. "Commemorative Address," in *PWW* 6:179.

73. "Legal Education of Undergraduates," August 23, 1894, in *PWW* 8:648–53.

74. "Notes for Lectures in a Course on Constitutional Government," September 19, 1898, in *PWW* 11:4.

75. *Constitutional Government*, 2.

76. *Constitutional Government*, 14.

77. *Constitutional Government*, 25–26.

78. "Responsible Government under the Constitution," February 10, 1886, in *PWW* 5:109–10.

79. See, for example, *The New Freedom*, 231, 236–42.

80. *Congressional Government*, 27.

81. *The New Freedom*, 28.

82. *The New Freedom*, 48.

83. "Government by Debate," in *PWW* 2:207.

84. "Self-Government in France," September 4, 1879, in *PWW* 1:515.

85. "From Wilson's Shorthand Diary," June 19, 1876, in *PWW* 1:143.

86. *The New Freedom*, 243.

87. Charles R. Kesler, "The Public Philosophy of the New Freedom and the New Deal," in *The New Deal and Its Legacy*, ed. Robert Eden (New York: Greenwood Press, 1989), 155, 159. For the opposing view, see Howard Gillman, "The Constitution Besieged: TR, Taft, and Wilson on the Virtue and Efficacy of a Faction-Free Republic," *Presidential Studies Quarterly* 19 (Winter 1989): 191–92. Gillman argues that Wilson wanted to preserve the Constitution rather than usher a new political order.

88. "The Art of Governing," November 15, 1885, in *PWW* 5:52.

89. *The New Freedom*, 47.

90. *Congressional Government*, 187.

91. See, for example, "Some Thoughts on the Present State of Public Affairs," January 30, 1878, in *PWW* 1:348.

92. "Cabinet Government in the United States," August 1879, in *PWW* 1:497.

93. "Marginal Notes on John Richard Green," July 27, 1878, in *PWW* 1:387.

94. "Marginal Notes on *The Federalist on the New Constitution*," February/March 1880, in *PWW* 1:598–601.

95. Publius, *The Federalist Papers*, ed. Charles R. Kesler and Clinton Rossiter (New York: Mentor, 1999), 51, 290.

96. "Leaderless Government," in *PWW* 10:299. For an account of how Wilson believed separation of powers affected the potential for great leadership, see Daniel D. Stid, *The President as Statesman* (Lawrence: University Press of Kansas, 1958), 7–10.

97. "Cabinet Government in the United States," in *PWW* 1:497.

98. *Federalist* 48:276–77.

99. *Federalist* 51:290.

100. "Art of Governing," in *PWW* 5:51.

101. "Government by Debate," in *PWW* 2:167.

102. "Government by Debate," in *PWW* 2:165–66.

103. "Notes for Lectures at the Johns Hopkins," January 26, 1891, in *PWW* 7:134.

104. *Congressional Government*, 202–3.

105. *Federalist* 6:22.

106. *Federalist* 10:47.

Chapter Four

Congress as Parliament?

Woodrow Wilson saw the separation of powers as a key obstacle to America's progress as a nation. He believed that government should act as a coordinated extension of the organic will of the people, and that the separation of powers divided the government against itself and impeded the whole of government from implementing what the spirit of the times demanded. Throughout his career, Wilson proposed various institutional remedies for the separation of powers. While the specific institutional proposals changed as Wilson's career developed, the basic blueprint did not. He believed government ought to be designed to accomplish two tasks: (1) to embody public opinion and (2) to carry it out efficiently in day-to-day policy decisions. The best way to accomplish these aims, Wilson reasoned, was to divide the government itself into two basic categories: political and administrative. Unlike in the separation-of-powers model, the political element of Wilson's new scheme would be unified and coordinated, reflecting the nation's fundamental political unity. The task of the political element of government would be to connect with the historically conditioned spirit of the people—to embody it, and in certain ways educate and shape it. The political element of government would not really involve itself in day-to-day policymaking, leaving that instead to the administrators. Free from political pressures, the government's administrative half would focus on the efficient implementation of the public will by drawing on its expertise and using the advanced machinery of the modern state.

In devising a specific institutional scheme to put this general "politics-administration" dichotomy into effect, Wilson in his early writings focused on the legislature. Later in his career, he turned away from this plan and embraced instead strong presidential leadership. The following chapter will take up this focus on the presidency, while we turn our attention here to the early arguments on Congress.

Wilson's early writings envision Congress as the institutional leader of the "political" element of the national government. Congress would serve as the connection between the government and the organic will of the people. Breaking down any separation between the political branches of government would allow Congress—as the embodiment of the people's will—to superintend the whole of government. Wilson's model for such an arrangement was the British parliamentary system, which he enthusiastically admired. And so Wilson proposed in his early writings various schemes for cabinet government, arguing that the American separation-of-powers system ought to be replaced by one that brought the legislative and executive together in a manner that ensured the supremacy of the legislature.

While Wilson's proposals for Congress are best known though his book *Congressional Government* (until very recently, the only one of Wilson's books that remained in print), the primary arguments can actually be found in a few important essays that he wrote in the late 1870s and early 1880s— before the book and even before entering Johns Hopkins University as a graduate student. The book, with one or two important modifications, consists largely of sections from these earlier essays. Wilson's parliamentary scheme for the American legislature was first addressed in a major essay entitled "Cabinet Government in the United States," published in 1879 in the *International Review*.[1] Written during the summer between his graduation from Princeton and his entry into the University of Virginia Law School, this was Wilson's first major article for a national publication. Ironically, the editor of the journal who gave Wilson the opportunity to write the article was Wilson's future nemesis, Henry Cabot Lodge.[2] During his first year of law school, Wilson followed "Cabinet Government" with an unpublished essay entitled "Congressional Government," which mirrored the earlier essay.[3]

Wilson's most substantial and radical essay in this series came next, in the form of "Government by Debate" in 1882.[4] The essay was too radical to be published, as his friend Robert Bridges warned him. Bridges suggested that Wilson modify certain institutional proposals in the essay in order to make it more publishable, but Wilson initially refused to do this. Every detail in the proposal was necessary, Wilson claimed, writing to Bridges:

> I admit that you are right in calling the changes proposed *radical*—perhaps they are *too* radical; but if one goes one step with me, he cannot, as it seems to me, escape going all the way. To stop short of the length to which I carry the argument would be simply to be afraid of the legitimate and logical conclusions toward which it inclines with an inevitable tendency.

The exchange with Bridges is useful in showing that Wilson's call for major constitutional change was not merely a theoretical exercise. Wilson explained

that the essay's "conclusions do not stand a single inch beyond my convictions—my *deliberate* convictions."[5] He was ultimately able to get portions of
the essay published in another form, under the title "Committee or Cabinet
Government?"[6] and portions of both essays, in turn, became part of *Congressional Government*. Wilson's essay "Government by Debate" also gives us an
early indication that his observations on the workings of Congress were not
based upon his own visits to the institution. In describing a visit to the gallery
of the House of Representatives—a description that sounds much like a first-
hand account—Wilson cited news reports of congressional proceedings from
The Nation, among other publications.[7]

Congressional Government itself was written in the early part of 1884—
Wilson's first year in graduate school—and published in 1885. Like the earlier essays on which it was based, the book contained little original research.[8]
While aggressive in its attack on the separation of powers and on Congress in
particular, the book did not call for formal changes to the core of the Constitution in the way that Wilson's earlier essays had. Some scholars, among
them Louis Brownlow, speculate that Wilson moderated his dim view of the
presidency after being energized by Grover Cleveland's 1884 campaign.[9] Yet
others point out that the book was written in the early part of 1884, which
would have been too early for the Cleveland campaign to have affected Wilson's thought. Henry Wilkinson Bragdon suggests instead that Wilson simply
became more practical, taking a more cautious approach in the book in the
hopes that it would reach a wider audience and that his criticism of the American system would point the way to necessary changes.[10] Daniel D. Stid concurs, explaining that "Wilson faced the hard choice between theoretical rigor
and political relevance," and "he opted for the latter."[11] Ultimately, the book
served as Wilson's doctoral dissertation. Special arrangements were made for
Wilson to secure his Ph.D., since he had left Hopkins without it to begin
teaching at Bryn Mawr. Wilson realized that he needed the degree in order to
be promoted, so *Congressional Government* was accepted in partial satisfac-
tion for the degree requirements.[12] Although it is occasionally suggested that
Wilson subsequently turned away from the principles he espoused in *Congressional Government*, it is worth noting that Wilson himself suggested very
few modifications when he reflected on the book in the preface to the edition
printed in 1900.[13]

There can be no doubt that Wilson's reading of Walter Bagehot's *English
Constitution* heavily influenced *Congressional Government*. Wilson's call for
the implementation of parliamentary-style changes reflects almost exactly
Bagehot's description of the virtues of the British system.[14] In a letter to his
publisher that accompanied the submission of some sample chapters, Wilson
explained that "I have modeled my work chiefly on Mr. Bagehot's essays on

the English Constitution, though I have been guided in some points of treatment by the method followed in some of the better volumes of Macmillan's admirable 'English Citizen Series.' "[15] In addition to Bagehot, Gamaliel Bradford, a frequent contributor to *The Nation*, influenced Wilson's early work. Bradford was a retired banker who had devoted his postretirement life to civil service reform and to giving cabinet officers seats in Congress.[16] Wilson directly cited Bradford in *Congressional Government*, relying on the latter's work in laying out his criticism of congressional procedure.[17] The admiration, at least at this early stage of Wilson's career, was mutual. The review of *Congressional Government* published in *The Nation* reads: "We have no hesitation in saying that this is one of the most important books, dealing with political subjects, which have ever issued from the American press."[18]

Wilson thus develops his emphasis on congressional leadership in a parliamentary-style system in a series of essays that begins in 1879 and culminates with the publication of his book in 1885. The remainder of the chapter will address Wilson's argument on Congress as it is manifested in these essays and in *Congressional Government*.

CONGRESS TO CEDE RULEMAKING AUTHORITY

Wilson believed that the first step in reforming Congress—or any element of the government—was to make the institution understand its appropriate role in modern times. Under the politics-administration dichotomy, the legislature cedes rulemaking authority to the bureaucracy. Wilson urged Congress to take up this understanding and abandon its stubborn insistence on its constitutionally defined duty to legislate. Contemporary circumstances had led to a situation where the objects of legislation had grown enormously; modern law needed to encompass matters that were far too complex and broad for an institution like Congress to manage. "That [Congress] cannot regulate all the questions to which its attention is weekly invited is its misfortune, not its fault," Wilson reasoned. It was "due to the human limitation of its faculties" that Congress needed to step back from legislating.[19] As Wilson explained in "The Study of Administration":

> There is scarcely a single duty of government which was once simple which is not now complex; government once had but a few masters; it now has scores of masters. Majorities formerly only underwent government; they now conduct government. Where government once might follow the whims of a court, it must now follow the views of a nation. And those views are steadily widening to new conceptions of state duty; so that, at the same time that the functions of government are every day becoming more complex and difficult, they are also vastly

multiplying in number. . . . This is why there should be a science of administration which shall seek to straighten the paths of government, to make its business less unbusinesslike, to strengthen and purify its organization, and to crown its duties with dutifulness.[20]

Because the majority, according to Wilson, had come to a point in history where it was calling for a wider scope of governmental authority, only the scientific expertise of a businesslike bureaucracy was capable of handling the rulemaking function that had been Congress's responsibility in times when the scope of national power was much more circumscribed. This case for a transformation in the American understanding of the nature of government is confirmed in *The New Freedom*, where Wilson explained that he was "forced to be a progressive, if for no other reason, because we have not kept up with our changes of conditions, either in the economic field or the political field."[21] Wilson's problem with Congress was that it failed to recognize the change in conditions and acknowledge the need to cede its responsibilities to the administrative side of the politics-administration divide. Instead, Congress was continuing to take its mission from Article I of the Constitution—that is, to exercise the legislative power of the government. But, Wilson argued, "Whatever intention may have controlled the compromises of constitution-making in 1787, their result was to give us, not government by discussion . . . but only *legislation* by discussion, which is no more than a small part of government."[22] It is of course important to note that Wilson did not urge Congress formally to abandon lawmaking. But the clear import of his argument is that Congress needs to become so general or broad in its formal lawmaking that actual rules or policies of the national government will be set not so much by acts of the legislature as by acts of the bureaucracy. For this reason I use the terms *rulemaking* or *policymaking* to refer to the kinds of governing decisions that Wilson wanted the bureaucracy to make. Congress needs to focus its attention on other matters.

According to the political and administrative functions that Wilson assigned in his early arguments for reform, Congress was to serve as the lead political institution, embodying the public will; the executive, in contrast, was to operate as part of the apolitical administrative apparatus. Wilson ascribed to the president the attributes of a chief bureaucrat who guides the bureaucracy as it seeks the particular means necessary to achieve the broad political aims laid out by Congress. In the vision of the presidency explicated in *Congressional Government*, Wilson wanted to give to the president the qualities of a typical nonpartisan administrator, including long tenure. As he explained:

The business of the President, occasionally great, is usually not much above routine. Most of the time it is *mere* administration, mere obedience of directions from the masters of policy, the Standing Committees. Except in so far as his power of veto constitutes him a part of the legislature, the President might, not inconveniently, be a permanent officer; the first official of a carefully graded and impartially regulated civil service system, through whose sure series of merit-promotions the youngest clerk might rise even to the chief magistracy.

As for where the president fits in the politics-administration dichotomy, Wilson made clear that the president "is part of the official rather than of the political machinery of the government."[23] This is why Wilson praised Alexander Hamilton's role as secretary of the treasury. During Hamilton's tenure, Congress set the broad policy aims as the nation's political branch, while the executive focused on the tedious but important details of finance and administration.[24]

In *Congressional Government* and the earlier essays on which it was based, Wilson contended that the most important quality of a chief executive is administrative efficiency and competence. It is this administrative efficiency and competence that show why Congress should cede significant rulemaking authority to the executive and bureaucracy. The earliest mention of efficiency as the chief quality for the executive appears in "Cabinet Government," where Wilson recommended that executive ministers be given a greater share in policymaking because of their administrative expertise. He explained that "none can so well judge the perfections or imperfections of a law as those who have to administer it." Wilson was highly critical of Congress for its incompetence in policymaking, and reasoned that the nonpartisan executive is more suited for the task.[25] Since the key for the executive is not political accountability (Congress is the political branch) but efficiency, Wilson advocated longer terms for the president and other executive officers. Long terms are perfectly consistent with the principle of republicanism, Wilson explained, because the executive is not really part of the political arm of government. Accountability comes through politics, which is centered in Congress.[26]

The roots of Wilson's subsequent writings on administration are here in his early work on Congress. As Wilson would suggest in his administrative writings, we can borrow the administrative methods of monarchic systems without diminishing the republican nature of our political institutions, because politics and administration are two distinct categories of government. So all forms of government—republican and monarchic alike—should strive for the same qualities of efficiency and competence in their executive officers. "Efficiency," Wilson explained, "is the only just foundation for confidence in a public officer, under republican institutions no less than under monarchs; and short terms which cut off the efficient as surely and inexorably as the inefficient are quite as repugnant to republican as to monarchical rules of wisdom."[27]

In sharp contrast to later writings on the presidency, Wilson's portrayal of the office here constitutes a remarkable weakening of the office's stature, a clear step down even from its already anemic position in the latter part of the nineteenth century. In "Cabinet Government," Wilson painted a picture of an executive where each cabinet officer is more or less individually responsible for his own area of policy. What matters to the cabinet officer more than the support of the chief executive is the existence of majority support in Congress for his policy agenda. In addition, since Wilson proposed a cabinet composed of members of the majority party in Congress, the president might have to accept a cabinet consisting entirely of members of the opposite party. Wilson envisioned a system where there is no genuine separation of powers, but where the executive rests almost entirely upon the makeup of the legislature.[28]

In response to the charge that his plan would weaken the presidency, Wilson countered that under his scheme, the president would be better off because each of his cabinet ministers would also be a legislative leader. This would be an improvement upon the current system, where legislative leaders ran the congressional committees to which the president had no connection at all. As to the problem a president might face if he had to accept a cabinet composed entirely of members of the opposite party, Wilson reasoned that this was no worse than having a cabinet of friends who must nevertheless act according to the wishes of congressional leaders who are themselves members of the opposite party. Wilson argued that at least under his envisioned plan, when the president faces a Congress of the opposite party, he and his cabinet ministers would be present during legislative debates.[29]

THE PROBLEM WITH CONGRESS

If Wilson had a clear vision of what role Congress should play in modern government, he was equally clear that Congress as it stood in the 1880s was woefully unsuited for the task. Indeed, the picture of Congress that Wilson painted in the late 1870s and early 1880s represents a classic progressive critique on the institution. His discussion of Congress is driven by his search for an authority in the constitutional order that could serve as a superintending embodiment of public opinion; the purpose of such an authority would be to coordinate and direct the political component of the government. He praised the British Parliament because it fulfills such a purpose, and criticized the U.S. Congress because of its failure to perform in the same manner.

Congress is supreme in the American political order, yet, Wilson lamented, there is no real leadership in Congress; there is, therefore, no real leadership for the nation itself. Wilson was particularly critical of the internal organization of the House of Representatives, which, he believed, serves to confound control of the chamber by majority opinion. The House's structure prevents members from acting upon the policy preferences of their constituents. In "Cabinet Government," Wilson explained that the only way there can be accountability in the legislature is for there to be identifiable leaders whose positions on the key policy issues are made clear; in this manner, public opinion can serve as a force in the legislature by its approval or disapproval of these leaders and the parties they represent. The obvious leader in the House, Wilson contended, is the Speaker. Leadership can only come from such an identifiable person, as opposed to plural, secretive bodies such as committees. Yet, Wilson complained, the Speaker is not truly a public figure, and he is not held publicly accountable for his policies.[30] In "Government by Debate," Wilson used the example of tax legislation to show that the lack of leadership in Congress breeds a lack of accountability. He criticized the indirect method of taxation through tariffs, contending that such taxes benefit the manufacturing class at the cost of consumers. Direct taxation, which Wilson strongly promoted throughout his career, is preferable because the public knows how much it is being taxed and for what purpose. As Wilson saw it, indirect taxation was merely a symptom of the absence of leadership and accountability in Congress.[31]

Congress's disorganized structure also contributed to the lack of accountability. Complicated organization, Wilson argued, inhibits the tight connection that the House ought to have with public opinion; the public has little or no understanding of how the institution works. As Wilson explained, "It is too complex to be understood without an effort. . . . Consequently, very few people do understand it, and its doors are practically shut against the comprehension of the public at large."[32] Even a new member of the House would be confused by the arcane and secretive procedures. Wilson championed the plight of new members, whose efforts to seek open debate and consideration of their legislative proposals constantly ran afoul of the complicated rules, hierarchy, and standing-committee system:

> If [the new member] supposes, as he naturally will, that after his bill has been sent up to be read by the clerk he may say a few words in its behalf, and in that belief sets upon his long-considered remarks, he will be knocked down by the rules. . . . The rap of Mr. Speaker's gavel is sharp, immediate, and peremptory. He is curtly informed that no debate is in order; the bill can only be referred to the appropriate Committee. This is, indeed, disheartening; it is his first lesson in committee government, and the master's rod smarts.[33]

It is the system of legislation through standing committees that is the focal point of Wilson's attack on Congress. He contrasted the corruption of "committee government" with the openness and accountability of his proposed "cabinet government." The committee system, Wilson explained, hides legislation and keeps deliberation out of the public eye, detaching the members from those whom they represent. The part of the deliberative process that the public can see—the floor debates and votes—is little more than a rubber stamp for the real decision making that has already taken place behind closed doors in committee sessions. Wilson complained that Congress "legislates in committee-rooms; not by the determinations of majorities, but by the resolutions of specially commissioned minorities; so that it is not far from the truth to say that Congress in session is Congress on public exhibition, whilst Congress in its committee-rooms is Congress at work."[34] The effect of the committee system is that legislation becomes the product of just a few individuals. These individuals are powerful not because they enjoy public support for their views, but because they are successful at brokering power behind the scenes in the standing committees. As Wilson complained in "Government by Debate,"

> The theory of our government is, that the laws of the Union are made by the concurrent voice and the cooperative wisdom of the Senate and the House of Representatives. The practice of our government is, that the laws of the Union are made by the concurrent voice and the cooperating wisdom of fragments of the Senate and the House of Representatives. Committees make the laws and Congress votes them into currency and potency. Because, truth to tell, voting for laws is not making them. Those who frame measures, who fill them with their pith of policy, are the makers of the laws these measures embody when they have become Acts. The President does not make a law by signing it, nor Congress by voting for it. It is made by its originators. The committees are the lawmakers.[35]

For Wilson, the most offensive element of the standing-committee system is the secrecy of deliberation. This secrecy prevents Congress from having the necessary close connection to public opinion. He used railroad legislation as an example of the problem, arguing that deliberation in the committees over railroad rate regulation was almost entirely disconnected from the broad national will. He contended that when Congress was considering rate regulation, it invited committee testimony only from railroad executives.[36] He also pointed to the budget process as an example of deliberation plagued by secrecy: when the House does hear from the executive on budgetary matters, it is not in an open floor session as the cabinet model would have it, but behind the closed doors of committee rooms. Secret, committee-based budgeting, Wilson reasoned, leads to the prevalence of "logrolling," where members cast their votes on the basis of covert, special-interest deals with one another.[37]

Wilson's criticism of the secretive committee process did not fade later in his career. In his New Freedom campaign for the presidency, Wilson used his criticism of the committee process to push for the elimination of the tariff. When setting tariffs, Wilson explained, congressional committees meet in secret to dole out favorable rates to influential special industries, at the expense of the great mass of the people. He pointed out that the tariff schedules were set by the House Ways and Means Committee, which meets in secret and listens only to those interests who benefit from protection.[38]

In Wilson's early commentaries on Congress, the Senate comes in for nearly as much criticism as does the House. *Congressional Government*, for example, sees little difference between the two chambers. And for Wilson, it is not important that the two institutions be distinct from each other. This is a departure from the argument of Publius, who in *Federalist* 62 contended that the threat of both corruption and majority faction could be reduced by making the House and Senate as different from each other as possible. Publius had explained that "as the improbability of sinister combinations will be in proportion to the dissimilarity in the genius of the two bodies, it must be politic to distinguish them from each other by every circumstance which will consist with a due harmony in all proper measures and with the genuine principles of republican government."[39] Wilson, in contrast, championed the thinking of Bagehot, whose attack on bicameralism Wilson cited at length in *Congressional Government*.[40] Wilson did not disagree with Bagehot's critique of bicameralism; rather, he simply believed that since the House and Senate are not in reality terribly different, then bicameralism poses no significant threat to American institutions.

In *Congressional Government*, Wilson contended that the House and the Senate are equally flawed. He criticized the dominance of special interests over members of the House, and then reasoned that senators are no different in quality from members of the House. "There cannot be," he wrote, "a special breed of public men reared specially for the Senate [*sic*]. It must be recruited from the lower branches of the representative system, of which it is only the topmost part. No stream can be purer than its sources."[41] The Senate, while nominally a distinct institution, is subject to the same impediments as the House: namely, a system of standing committees and a lack of recognized party leadership. Wilson explained that even the Senate's longer terms do not serve to differentiate the two institutions significantly. Even though two-thirds of the Senate remains the same during each congressional election cycle, Wilson pointed out that the body must necessarily reorganize itself every two years to accommodate the new membership brought in as a result of the elections. The business of the Senate, therefore, is subject to the same interruptions as that of the House. At bottom, Wilson concluded, the Senate—like the House—simply reflected the current state of American public life, a state about which Wilson was considerably pessimistic. The conditions of public life, lamented Wilson, were simply not conducive to drawing the best men into politics. So while *The Federalist* had expected senators to be distinguished for their wisdom and prudence, Wilson observed that they had no greater sense of duty or national interest than did the average cross-section of citizens—an observation with which Publius himself might have agreed had he seen the Senate of that era.[42]

Wilson's view of the differences between the House and Senate did change by the time he wrote *Constitutional Government*, in which he claimed that the Senate "differs very radically from the House of Representatives."[43] He commented that the Senate's standing committees have much less control than the House's over the proceedings. Wilson explained that this is an advantage in that Senate committees play a more appropriate role; they help to organize and delegate work, without taking over the deliberative function of the entire body. Wilson also praised the Senate for having debates that are more open and lengthy than those of the House, even though he conceded that Senate debate is often "unprofitable."[44] He also approved of how the Senate, unlike the House, provides representation equally to all areas of the country, regardless of population. As Wilson elaborated, "It is of the utmost importance that its parts as well as its people should be represented; and there can be no doubt in the mind of any one . . . that [the Senate] represents the country, as distinct from the accumulated populations of the country, much more fully and much more truly than the House of Representatives." Wilson especially liked the Senate's regional representation because it gave the South and the West more representation than they would have under a system based solely upon population.[45]

Wilson's commentary in *Constitutional Government* also played down criticism of the appointment of senators by state legislatures. He did suggest that there were certain areas of the country where wealth had an undue influence in this process—not coincidentally, he believed that the problems arose in those areas where business interests were strong, and that the strength of business interests led to an abuse of democracy. He explained that "the purchasing power of money in politics is chiefly exerted where there is most money. The selfish influence of great corporations is most often exhibited where they have their seats of control, at the financial centers of the country. The processes by which men procure places in the Senate have been most often under suspicion where men buy most things."[46]

A MODEL FOR LEGISLATIVE REFORM

Given his criticisms of the institution, it seems obvious to ask whether Wilson saw any hope for redemption in Congress. While it is the case that the objections in *Constitutional Government* are more nuanced than those made in *Congressional Government*, one might well conclude that Wilson would have preferred to replace the institution with some other, more democratic body or process. Such a conclusion would be strengthened by the fact that many of Wilson's contemporaries in the progressive movement were calling for the implementation of mechanisms of direct democracy, at least at the state level, in order to circumvent incorrigible legislatures.[47] While Wilson's complex response to the direct-democracy movement will be taken up substantially in chapter 6, it is important to say here that he did not advocate circumventing the legislative process but rather wanted to work through the traditional institutions of government—if they could be appropriately reformed. Reform of the legislative process could take place, Wilson argued, if Congress would model itself after the British Parliament.

In this early stage of his scholarly career, where his criticisms of the U.S. Congress are particularly sharp, Wilson almost always compared the institution—unfavorably—with Parliament. In general, Wilson admired the parliamentary model because it fit perfectly with his scheme to separate politics and administration. On the one hand, Parliament is able to embody public opinion through its openness; on the other, it does not really involve itself in the details of governing, which are better left to the permanent bureaucracies. In *Congressional Government*, therefore, the model for reform is Parliament, where the public can actually have a genuine interest in and see what goes on. Not only the openness of debates, but also the strong principle of party government, ensures that the legislature is directly accountable to the public will.[48] Conforming to the character of much of his writings, Wilson attempted in his early works to convince his audience not to have an undue attachment to the forms of government simply because those forms are American. As he asked in "Government by Debate," where his parliamentary model for legislative reform is put in its most radical terms, "Shall the forms of federal administration be altered in accordance with a plan which has been tested and found best by our own ancestors and our own kinsmen, which is now the prevailing system amongst the most advanced nations of the world, and which both reason and our own experience recommend to our acceptance?"[49]

If, as Wilson suggested, the committee system is at the root of Congress's problems, then the solution to such "committee government" must be "cabinet government." The specific proposal for this change was first made in "Cabinet Government in the United States," where Wilson wrote:

> What, then, is Cabinet government? What is the change proposed? Simply to give to the heads of the Executive departments—the members of the Cabinet—seats in Congress, with the privilege of the initiative in legislation and some part of the unbounded privileges now commanded by the Standing Committees.

Wilson went on to clarify that, in selecting cabinet officers, the president would be required to choose from among the members of Congress; he could not, in other words, appoint new members of the legislature.[50] This proposal would accomplish at least two aims of great importance to Wilson. First, it would help to break down the separation-of-powers barrier between the legislative and executive branches, thereby facilitating a more efficient government response to the public will. Second, it would add a strong measure of accountability to the cabinet. Any cabinet officer under the proposed system would, Wilson suggested, resign from office if he could not maintain the support of a majority in Congress for the policies of his department. The cabinet officers, as leaders of departments that held jurisdiction over different areas of public policy, would essentially serve as responsible substitutes for the role then played by Congress's standing committees. Instead of secretive committees and their unaccountable chairmen directing policymaking, members of the cabinet would direct policy in a manner strictly accountable to majority sentiment. Wilson implied that under this plan, the president would have to choose his cabinet not only from among the membership of Congress, but from among the membership of the majority party in Congress. There could, of course, be no other way for the policies of each cabinet officer to maintain the support of a congressional majority. The suggestion, then, that a president might be forced to appoint a cabinet consisting entirely of members from the opposing party is an indication of the narrow view with which Wilson conceived of the presidency in these early essays.

In "Government by Debate," Wilson took the next logical step. While he never called for vesting the selection of the president in a congressional majority, Wilson did argue that both Congress and the president should rise and fall on their ability to maintain public support. He therefore attacked the idea of fixed terms of office, suggesting instead that the principle of accountability demands both longer terms for those who maintain public support and shorter terms for those who do not. He suggested, in particular, that it be possible to dissolve the House of Representatives if its majority party fell out of favor with the public.[51] In cabinet government, the House would lead; it would represent the unified nation, and through its dissolvability would rise and fall on the basis of national sentiment. The Senate could never take on such a role—at least not prior to the Seventeenth Amendment—since it represented the particular views of the state governments. While arguing that the Senate would maintain its dignity under such a system, Wilson nonetheless implied that the Senate would have to defer to the House because the House would speak for the nation as a whole. As represented in the Senate, the states qua states would have to give way to the national popular sentiment. As Wilson explained,

The object of dissolution would be to obtain an expression of opinion by the country; and it is hardly probable that Senators, with all their six-year security, would often care to brave the public sentiment by standing in the way of a policy sanctioned by the newly elected House. A new election would show them the temper of the country, and they would not be so blind as to ignore or antagonize it. The dissolution of the House would thus answer the purposes of a dissolution of both branches of Congress.[52]

To the charge that making the House dissolvable would lead to instability, Wilson responded that the system of fixed terms could also be unstable. It could lead, he reasoned, to forcing an election when there had been no change in national sentiment.[53]

"Government by Debate" takes Wilson's proposal for cabinet government even further by making the attack on the separation of powers explicit. Wilson called for the formal amendment of Article I, Section 6, Clause 2 of the Constitution, which prohibits a member of Congress from holding any civil office of the United States. Regarding the limitation on who can serve as a member of Congress, Wilson contended that the language of the clause should be amended to say: "And no other person holding any *other than a cabinet* office under the United States shall be a member of either House. . . ."[54] And in case there was any ambiguity as to Wilson's intentions, he made clear that the goal was to return to an idea, which was rejected at the constitutional convention, to make the executive subservient to the legislature: "The plain truth of the matter is that, if government is to operate smoothly, harmoniously, and efficiently, Congress must consent to the advice of Roger Sherman and choose its own executive servants. There can be no gain in winking facts."[55]

The reason for adopting such parliamentary-style changes to the American system was to effect in Congress the two principal virtues that Wilson saw in Parliament: (1) full and open debate, with a close connection to public sentiment; and (2) a reliance upon the expertise of the executive ministries to manage day-to-day policy decisions. Regarding the first of these advantages, Wilson explained, the English House of Commons is busy with debate and talk. It takes the time to examine carefully the merits of potential laws, and this examination is accessible to the public eye. The House of Representatives, in contrast, cannot take the time for careful debate because it is too busy writing the details of national policy, getting bogged down in the day-to-day rulemaking function of government.[56] For Wilson, a legislature can either busy itself conducting detailed legislative business, or it can engage in great open debates and discussions; it cannot do both. The English Parliament had chosen the latter of these options, leaving the details of rulemaking to the permanent ministries. The key is that the Parliament does not pretend to be the "government." The "government" sees to the details of policy, while Parliament debates its broad principles.[57]

The second principal virtue that Wilson saw in Parliament—its reliance upon the expertise of the executive ministries—is just as important as the openness of its debates. The executive ministers are responsible for considering the broad expression of the public mind and translating it into the specifics of policy. Wilson wrote of the role of the executive:

> Everywhere [outside of the United States] there is one form or another of ministerial leadership in the legislature. A body of ministers constitutes, as it were, a nerve center, or rather a sensitive presiding brain, in the body politic, taking from the nation such broad suggestions as public opinion can unmistakably convey touching the main ends to be sought by legislation and policy, but themselves suggesting in turn, in the light of their own special knowledge and intimate experience of affairs, the best means by which those ends may be attained.[58]

Such a system embodied all of the efficiency and accountability that Wilson found lacking in the traditional separation-of-powers arrangement. An accountable legislature gives broad guidance to those with expertise, and the experts respond to the legislature by seeing to the implementation of policy in accord with their intimate knowledge of public affairs. This system also highlights the superiority of the British prime minister to the American president. While the American president is merely a chief clerk, the British prime minister—because of his reliance upon the legislature's majority party—is an accountable public leader. Or, as Wilson explained, "A President's usefulness is measured, not by efficiency, but by calendar months. It is reckoned that if he be good at all he will be good for four years. A Prime Minister must keep himself in favor with the majority, a President need only keep alive."[59]

Wilson used the British system of setting budget policy as an example of both the system's openness and of its reliance upon executive expertise—in fact, large portions of *Congressional Government*'s second chapter on the House are essentially descriptions of the various facets of British financial policymaking. With regard to the first virtue, Wilson explained that when the ministers present their plan for revenue and expenditures to Parliament, they will resign if it is rejected. Instead of a secretive standing committee and its chairman holding the budget authority, as is the case in the American Congress, in the British system an accountable cabinet minister possesses this authority. That cabinet minister comes under the scrutiny of the entire Parliament, which can simultaneously rely on his expertise and hold him accountable to the broad national sentiment that has been uncovered in the course of parliamentary debate.[60] With regard to the attribute of expertise in financial policymaking, Wilson pointed out that the congressional system of budgeting is far too fragmented to create competent financial management. In the British system, in contrast, financial policy originates not in congressional committees but instead with the executive ministers who have expertise in such matters. The ministers know best the needs of their own departments, and they communicate those needs to Parliament. Wilson explained that "Parliament . . . simply controls, it does not originate, measures of financial administration. It acts through the agency and under the guidance of the ministers of the Crown."[61] In this account of the British system, Wilson called for an innovation in the American budget process. This suggestion would later be adopted under the Budget Act of 1921. It is a system where the American executive departments are made responsible for taking the initiative in budget policy, in accord with the virtues of the British system as Wilson described them in *Congressional Government*.[62]

Having made proposals for significant change in the constitutional order, Wilson found himself responding to criticisms that the ideas were too radical or simply not realistic. In responding to one such criticism, Wilson emphasized that there is a tremendous difference between the theory and form of American government, on the one hand, and the reality of how it works, on the other. As was previously explained, Wilson was critical of constitutional studies that focused on the static idea of how the system was supposed to work. Genuine constitutional study, he reasoned, was based upon an understanding of how American government had evolved in response to actual historical developments. Government was constantly evolving, and his ideas were merely part of that evolution.[63] Wilson contended that even without formal constitutional changes, the president could do much to set up responsible party government through an aggressive and creative use of his cabinet. Such a strategy would merely reflect the reality that the Constitution, "beside being a legal document, is also a vehicle of life."[64]

In enumerating the virtues of the parliamentary system as a model for legislative reform in America, Wilson was influenced at the earliest stages of his political thinking by a variety of British sources. There are several citations in his Commonplace Book, for instance, to Parliament and to the functions of representatives. Most frequently, Wilson cited Burke on these questions.[65] But there can be no mistaking the fact that Wilson understood Parliament through the writings of Bagehot—and through Bagehot's *The English Constitution* in particular. Even the mode of presentation found in *The English Constitution* served as a model for Wilson's comparison between Parliament and Congress. In his discussion of the cabinet, for example, Bagehot contrasts the parliamentary model with the American "presidential" model, providing a point-by-point explanation of the superiority of the British system in much the same manner that Wilson later adopted.[66] Bagehot's account emphasizes the British system's efficiency, which is made possible through the unity of the legislative and executive branches. As Wilson subsequently contended in his own works, cabinet government is, for Bagehot, a more mature form of democracy. This is so, Bagehot explains, because public opinion in cabinet government has a continuous voice—it may command changes any time there is a need for them. For both Wilson and Bagehot, then, the British model is the key to reforming the American legislature.

Accountable Parties as the Centerpiece of Legislative Reform

Wilson also used the parliamentary model to point out the weaknesses of the American party system and to suggest a restructured form of party government as an essential element in reforming the national legislature. If the general problem with Congress is its lack of real leadership, then much of the blame for this lies with the decentralized operation of the party system. In *Congressional Government*, Wilson complained that there was an absence of leadership in the national parties, and that dissent from party leadership was rampant. The party's officeholders were not held accountable for deviating from the platform on which the party campaigned, and therefore the party itself was not accountable to public opinion.[67] Even the Speaker—the only identifiable leader of the House—was not accountable to the nation for how he led his party or his institution. Instead, he was a mere power broker, limited by the power of the even less accountable standing committees and their chairmen.[68]

Wilson marveled that even given this decentralized leadership and lack of accountability, members of Congress nonetheless seemed to stick with their party cohort in casting votes. He noted that this trend was especially common in the House of Representatives, and reasoned that it could be attributed to committee government—that is, the real decisions are made in committee, with each committee having free rein in its own sphere, and so the floor votes in the House are merely formalities where party members generally vote the party line. Furthermore, the united front that parties display on the floor covers up not only the secretive committee process but also the legislative caucus. Rather than bare their differences in public floor debate, Wilson explained, the different factions within a party will fight things out behind closed doors in a legislative caucus. This privacy, he argued, undermines all accountability because it prevents the close superintendence of public opinion.[69]

A truly accountable party system in Congress—modeled after that of Parliament—is the remedy. Parties in the legislature, Wilson explained, should be clearly organized, under leaders whom the public easily recognizes. Voters could then, through their electoral support or rejection of these prominent party leaders, make known and felt their views on policy matters. Furthermore, prominent party leaders should fill the ranks of both the congressional leadership and the cabinet. Under such a system, Wilson believed that members of Congress would act with care—ever mindful that the public would be watching and would hold their party and its leaders accountable.[70] In this way, a national party, which would be accountable to the public will, could coordinate both the legislative and executive powers for an efficient implementation of the public views.

Wilson's subsequent, sharp criticism of President Grover Cleveland's cabinet was predicated on these basic ideas for reform. Wilson pointed out that Cleveland had appointed remarkably few prominent party leaders to his cabinet. Wilson framed the appointment of a cabinet as a choice between two alternatives: (1) a cabinet that is responsible to the party and, therefore, accountable to public opinion; or (2) a cabinet that is personally accountable to the president. He put the question in this way:

> What *is* the Cabinet? Is it the President's cabinet, or are the heads of the executive departments meant by the spirit of our national institutions to be real party colleagues of the President, in council, chosen by him, indeed, but from among men of accredited political capacity, not from among the general body of the citizenship of the country? It is a question fundamental to our whole political development, and it is by no means to be answered from out of the text of the Constitution simply.[71]

For Wilson—given what he claims is the vagueness of the Constitution on this question—the choice must be the one that will help to implement genuine party government in America: a cabinet consisting of the party leadership. He offered several reasons for this choice. First, party leaders are known and established, having built up reputations with the public over a long period of time. Personal appointments like those of Cleveland, in contrast, can be largely unknown and, consequently, unaccountable. Second, Wilson pointed out that cabinet officers must, by necessity, share a significant portion of the nation's executive power; this executive power must be exercised by officers who are accountable. Finally, Wilson explained that placing party leaders in the cabinet would enable a close cooperation between the executive and legislative branches, since the cabinet officers could work well with fellow party leaders in Congress. "No government can be administered with the highest efficiency," Wilson reasoned, "unless there be close cooperation and an intimate mutual understanding between its Administration and its legislature."[72]

The proposals for accountable party government that one finds in *Congressional Government* and in the subsequent criticisms of Cleveland's cabinet were developed out of an earlier series of essays on this subject. These earlier essays were usually more radical in their suggestions for institutional change. In one such essay, "Congressional Government," Wilson suggested that the key to reform is to restructure the party caucuses in Congress. The problem with party caucuses is that they are secretive and, therefore, unaccountable. Wilson proposed that the cabinet—which is to be made up of the national party leadership—also lead the majority party caucus in Congress. In this role, the cabinet would constitute a committee that would control and direct the various standing committees in Congress, appointing their chairmen. The powerful standing committees, then, which were at the heart of the secretive ways of Congress, would emerge into public view through their accountability to the party leadership.[73]

By the time Wilson wrote his book, he had softened several of these more radical proposals for party government. Nonetheless, the general effect of the ideas in both the book and the earlier essays on which it was based was, essentially, to elevate the cabinet to what would be called "the government" in the parliamentary model. To varying degrees, Wilson's early proposals for government reform seemed to turn the president into a mere appendage, perhaps along the lines of systems where the president serves as head of state while a prime minister runs the cabinet and oversees domestic policy. To the suggestion that such a vision for cabinet government might eviscerate the executive as an independent institution, Wilson responded that cabinet members would "surely be interested in preserving and fortifying the prerogatives of the Executive" because they themselves would lead the executive departments.[74] Wilson also did not see the apparent irony in his calls for using the party system as a tool for progressive national leadership, as he alternately criticized the spirit of party and the corruption of party officials, and discerned in political parties the means of reforming the government.

Ultimately, Wilson wanted a unified and cohesive legislature that would reflect the fundamental unity of will that he perceived in the public mind. If it were the case that history had brought the American mind to this condition of unity, then the legislature—the very embodiment of this public mind—must be made to overcome its disorganized and decentralized structure. The key is that the decentralized clash of interests in Congress did not indicate to Wilson that, perhaps, this diversity was also the true condition of the public mind. To concede that the condition of Congress was merely a reflection of the genuine diversity of views among the public would be, for Wilson, to abandon the primary tenet of his political thought: that history had overcome the factiousness of human nature. It was the American founders, after all, who had identified in human nature the permanent causes of faction and who had structured a limited system of government to control the effects of this ever-present problem. Wilson's critique of limited government was predicated on the assumption that history could and had overcome what the founders believed to be the permanent characteristics of human nature, and had led to a unity in the public mind that Wilson wanted to see reflected in the legislature.

The Informing Function of Congress

The accountable-party model is critical in making Congress an open institution whose deliberations can take place in close concert with public opinion. This view of the institution comports with Wilson's overall argument that the legislature should focus less on specific rulemaking—ceding such functions to "the government" or the executive ministries—and concentrate more on what he refers to as its "informing" function. Here Wilson envisioned Congress as a parliament—a grand debating body whose floor debates are its very purpose for existing. The open debates in such a legislature serve two important ends, as Wilson explained in "Government by Debate": First, they keep the legislature accountable to public opinion, since members know that the public is watching. Second, the debates themselves educate public opinion, focusing the public mind on the important issues and making public opinion worthy of its role in directing the state.[75]

Congress's informing function requires an openness that Wilson believed it sorely lacked. In *Congressional Government*, he cited the process of financial policymaking as a prominent example of the need for openness. The House and the Senate, for instance, resolved their differences over the budget in secret—through conference committees—not in open floor debate where members could both educate public opinion and be held accountable to that same public opinion. As Wilson further observed,

> After all the careful and thorough-going debate and amendment of Committee of the Whole in the House, and all the grave deliberation of the Senate to which the general appropriations are subjected, they finally pass in a very chaotic state, full of provisions which neither the House nor the Senate likes, and utterly vague and unintelligible to every one save the members of the Conference Committee; so that it would seem almost as if the generous portions of time conscientiously given to their consideration in their earlier stages had been simply time thrown away.[76]

It is through the budget that the nation sets its policy priorities. Yet the public is essentially shut out of this priority-setting function and learns little or nothing from the process of enacting a budget. Wilson was under little illusion as to the state of public opinion, understanding that it was for the most part woefully uninformed and unprepared for the role of superintending the direction of government. He conceded that "we lack in our political life the conditions most essential for the formation of an active and effective public opinion." It was through public debates in the legislature (and, later, through the visionary leadership of the president) that this deficiency was to be remedied. But if the public was shut out of the debates involved in setting the nation's financial policy, no such remedy could be forthcoming.[77]

Even as Wilson moved beyond *Congressional Government* and his other early writings on Congress, he continued to see Congress as an institution that should use its close connection to the public as a means of bringing public opinion to bear on the broad direction of the government. This remained the case even as Wilson outlined in works like *Constitutional Government* a new, grander role for presidential leadership. In that book, Wilson maintained that the purpose of a legislature should be to furnish "watchful criticism, talk that should bring to light the whole intention of the government and apprise those who conducted it of the real feeling and desire of the nation." He also emphasized again that "it was as far as possible from the original purpose of representative assemblies that they should *conduct* government."[78] As in his earlier study of Congress, Wilson argued in *Constitutional Government* that—in spite of his new vision for the president—Congress remained important in the connection between the people and their government. Congress needed, therefore, to remain open and responsive to the public mind, adapting itself to changes in the public mood.[79]

How did Wilson propose that Congress bring together, or "synthesize," public opinion and governing? He wrote in *Constitutional Government* that public opinion must always serve as a close "counsel" to the government. But this did not mean that the public was to have a direct role in policymaking (as was the case, for instance, with various direct-democracy proposals of other progressives). Wilson believed that institutions like Congress were still necessary, because of the distinction between what he called "aggregate counsel" and "common counsel." Aggregate counsel, Wilson explained, is the opinion of the people expressed through such directly democratic mechanisms as the ballot initiative, whereas common counsel is the voice of public opinion heard through the institutions of government. The second of these is to be preferred to simply aggregating the mass of public opinion.[80] This conception of representation sounds much like the vision of *Federalist* 10, where Publius explains that "the public voice, pronounced by the representatives of the people, will be more consonant to the public good than if pronounced by the people themselves, convened for the purpose."[81] Yet it is more accurate to say that Wilson's conception strikes a middle ground between the institutional deliberation envisioned by *The*

Federalist and the direct governance by the people envisioned by some of Wilson's contemporaries. Wilson explained that "common counsel" must be conducted by "men authorized to be the spokesmen of the voters and speaking with a constant sense of being held responsible for what they say." He continually emphasized the constant pressure of public opinion on the representatives and the need to constantly adapt to changes in the public mind.[82] This view is an important contrast to the view of representation espoused in *The Federalist*, especially with regard to the Senate, which is justified precisely as a "defense to the people against their own temporary errors and delusions" and "a safeguard against the tyranny of their own passions."[83] Wilson argued that far from being a body that can occasionally resist public opinion when necessary, Congress needs to be reformed so that it becomes more directly influenced by public opinion. The reason for this difference with *The Federalist*'s idea of representation is that, as explained in chapter 3, Wilson did not see the public's passions—or faction—as a perpetual danger to democratic government, and hence did not see it as a necessary or legitimate role of government to act as a filter for the public's passion. It is, therefore, from Wilson's perspective, a great weakness of Congress that its "counsel" is not open. "Open counsel" is the key to the success of Congress as a democratic institution; its ultimate failure to achieve the requisite openness is a main reason for Wilson's turn to the presidency as the primary institution responsible for informing and embodying public opinion.[84]

Even in *The New Freedom*, Wilson continued to emphasize the necessity of open debate and counsel in modern democracy. He explained that "the whole purpose of democracy is that we may hold counsel with one another, so as not to depend upon the understanding of one man, but to depend upon the counsel of all." Making the same distinction that he had previously made between "aggregate" and "common" counsel, Wilson declared that democracy is not to be based upon a mob but upon the people engaged in open discussion—what Wilson called a "parliament of the people."[85] This framing of public discussion as a "parliament" is important, because a parliament engages in debate on the broad issues of the day but is not really involved in "the government" of a nation. It is important to distinguish, in other words, Wilson's intensely democratic rhetoric from his understanding of who ought to be making the important decisions in government. In *The New Freedom*, in the context of criticizing the private interests that he claimed had taken hold of the institutions of government, Wilson made his call for openness and "common counsel." He called for "substituting the popular will for the rule of guardians, the processes of common counsel for those of private arrangement." Openness in government would be the chief means of eradicating corruption, and public opinion would serve as a "purifying" element in politics.[86] Wilson even cast the people's voice as a god that would recreate the world of politics:

Wherever any public business is transacted, wherever plans affecting the public are laid, or enterprises touching the public welfare, comfort, or convenience go forward, wherever political programs are formulated, or candidates agreed on,—over that place a voice must speak, with the divine prerogative of a people's will, the words: "Let there be Light."[87]

As was the case with much of what Wilson wrote about Congress in his early work, the terminology that Wilson employed in his vision of reforming Congress in accord with the parliamentary model contains obvious parallels to the writings of Bagehot. In *The English Constitution*, Bagehot contends that cabinet government is superior to presidential government because the former educates public opinion, elevating it through open parliamentary debates on the great issues of the day. Using language from which Wilson clearly drew, Bagehot argues that the legislature "expresses the mind" of the people, that it has a "teaching" and an "informing" function. Bagehot explains that in fulfilling its "teaching function," the legislature must feature great men engaged in open debate, thereby raising those who witness such debate to a higher level of understanding. Bagehot writes that in fulfilling its "informing function," the legislature must make the public aware of what is going on in the nation; it must bring to the nation's attention the various grievances and problems of different segments of society. He likens this "informing function" of the modern legislature to the responsibility of parliaments in times past to bring to the attention of the Crown the important grievances in society. The only feature that has changed in the modern circumstance is that the sovereign is the public mind itself, and this public mind is informed by the legislative debates. Bagehot's idea of the "informing function" seems to be different from his idea of the "teaching function" in that the informing function does not necessarily elevate the public with grand argument and rhetoric; instead, it simply calls attention to matters of which the public might otherwise be unaware. Bagehot also makes clear that these "teaching" and "informing" functions are far more important than any role the legislature might play in actual legislating. The legislative function, which Bagehot allows is still important, must be subordinated to "the political education given by Parliament to the whole nation."[88]

It is from Bagehot's subsequent book, *Physics and Politics*, that Wilson seems to have learned the phrase "government by discussion." Bagehot criticizes those societies that suffer from an undue attachment to the customs of the past; Bagehot is not opposed to custom per se, but to an attachment to it that inhibits the organic development of a people. He explains that the remedy for an undue attachment to custom is "government by discussion," which "at once breaks down the yoke of fixed custom."[89] "Government by discussion," which takes place through the debate in Parliament, advances the public by elevating it. And Bagehot explains that government by discussion will elevate the public to the extent that the institution focuses on great as opposed to trivial issues. A legislature, therefore, that mires itself in the details of policymaking cannot accomplish its more important task of teaching the public.

Great Oratory in a Reformed Legislature

If Congress is, through its floor debates, to carry out the function of "informing," "teaching," or "elevating" the public mind, it can do so only by elevating the quality of its own oratory. While Wilson subsequently turned to the popular rhetoric of the president as a means of teaching the public mind, in his early works he called for Congress to become the focal point of national, oratorical leadership. He explained in "Cabinet Government in the United States" that "the President can seldom make himself recognized as a leader; he is merely the executor of the sovereign legislative will." Congress was to be led, at least in Wilson's early essays, not by a popular president embodying the people's unified will but from within, by its own great oratorical leaders who could shine during the floor debates.[90]

Members of Congress, under Wilson's early vision, should reflect the great oratorical tradition of Parliament that he so admired from having read histories of British statesmen. Congress as an institution, therefore, needed to be reformed in order to provide an environment under which those most skilled in grand oratory could flourish. Indeed, providing the conditions conducive to statesmanship is, for Wilson, synonymous with providing the conditions conducive to grand rhetoric. Wilson called for the redesigning of the American government in order to develop "the conditions of statesmanship." The best system would be one where those most skilled in oratory would have the greatest share of ruling power.[91] This is so because, for Wilson, to both embody and teach the public mind is tantamount to staking a legitimate claim to rule. Whether it be through Congress or, later, the presidency, this connection to the people—and especially the ability to move them by utilizing rhetoric—becomes the most important quality of leadership. Cabinet government, by providing rhetorical leaders pride of place, will help to create what Wilson called a "ruling class" educated from youth in the tradition of great oratory.[92]

A Congress that features great oratorical leadership is also essential, Wilson argued, to managing the advent of universal suffrage. Wilson made clear that universal suffrage posed a grave problem to American democracy since the public was so poorly educated. A Congress that provided high oratorical debate was crucial to elevating the level of public education about the great issues of the day. He explained:

> In the severe, distinct, and sharp enunciation of underlying principles, the un-
> sparing examination and telling criticism of opposite positions, the careful,
> painstaking unraveling of all the issues involved, which are incident to the free
> discussion of questions of public policy, we see the best, the only effective,
> means of educating public opinion.

Wilson contended that high-quality, open debate in the legislature improves
both the public and the legislators themselves.[93] More to the point, he reasoned that an institution requiring great oratorical skill will weed out those
mere political managers who represent and pursue narrow, special interests—
the very people whom Wilson believed plagued the institution during his own
time.

How can America go about producing great orators? Wilson, from the very
first writings of his that are available, consistently called upon colleges and
universities to make rhetorical training an important piece of their curricula.
As an undergraduate at Princeton, he frequently pestered the institution to
provide greater support for those interested in debating and developing their
rhetorical skills. In one letter to the college newspaper, Wilson called for "a
complete system of vocal training" in the undergraduate curriculum.[94] He recognized that it was difficult to encourage intelligent young men to develop
their oratorical skills because the government itself did not offer such men the
reward that their skills merited. "What young man who is conscious of fine
abilities," Wilson asked, "will choose to enter public life when he knows that
no honorable exertion can secure for him any high station of authority in the
government of his country?"[95]

Wilson aimed to facilitate the development of American orators who could
meet with the success of the great British statesmen about whom he had read
a great deal during his formative intellectual years. Wilson particularly admired William Gladstone—precisely because it was Gladstone's oratorical
skill that propelled him to greatness. Wilson wrote that "it is as an orator that
Mr. Gladstone more forcibly appeals to our imaginations." He used Gladstone
to contrast England and America, lamenting the fact that American government prevents such orators from shining.[96] The greatest example, in Wilson's
mind, of an American orator who was stifled by the system of government is
Daniel Webster. Wilson's writings consistently praise Webster for his oratorical skill (it does not hurt, of course, that Webster was also an advocate of national power and a staunch opponent of states' rights). The American Constitution was flawed, Wilson reasoned, precisely because it failed to grant
significant power to great orators like Webster—power, Wilson emphasized,
"which would in any other country belong of right to one with like endow-
ments." Again, rhetorical skill is tantamount to a legitimate claim to rule. Wilson made this point by contrasting Webster and William Pitt, explaining that

the fundamental difference between the two was that Pitt operated in a system that recognized his rhetorical skill and thereby placed him in his rightful place of leadership.[97]

It was his admiration for Americans like Webster that led Wilson to comment more favorably upon the Senate than upon the House. While Wilson certainly opposed the undemocratic nature of the Senate and, as governor of New Jersey, urged the passage of the Seventeenth Amendment, the Senate, at least, had members who more closely fit Wilson's ideal for oratorical statesmanship. Wilson pointed out in *Congressional Government* that debate in the Senate is more open than in the House, where debate becomes subordinated to a maze of petty rules and secretive procedures. The Senate, in general, is more likely to feature genuine discussion, since its rules make it difficult for debate to be cut off or thoroughly controlled by committee chairmen. Wilson did not emphasize the powers of the Senate or its role in legislation; rather, the Senate is important because it is more open and rhetoric can have a place in its proceedings. Again, the point of Wilson's vision is not to bring the public mind into more direct participation in actual governing; what matters instead is that politics itself—separate from the actual administration of government—becomes more democratized. This democratization takes place—to a limited degree—in the Senate, which is known for its orators. The House, by contrast, does not require its members to have oratorical skill in order to have influence; there, one must merely be a skilled power broker.[98] Ultimately, Wilson wanted to change the grounds on which claims to rule are made. The formal assignment of powers by the Constitution becomes less important, while one's ability to read the spirit of the people—and to educate and shape it—begins to constitute the more legitimate mandate to lead. This is why, for Wilson, it is not terribly important which of the formal institutions of government (Congress or the presidency) actually takes the leadership role in politics. Whichever one can, through its rhetorical skill, come to embody the public mind is the one most entitled to lead. The following chapter addresses Wilson's determination that it is not Congress but the presidency that can stake the more legitimate claim to embody the public mind.

NOTES

1. "Cabinet Government in the United States," August 1879, in Arthur S. Link, ed., *The Papers of Woodrow Wilson* (hereafter cited as *PWW*), 69 vols. (Princeton: Princeton University Press, 1966–1993), 1:493–510. Quotations from Wilson's writings will be modernized as necessary for grammar and spelling. Emphasis will be in the original unless otherwise specified.

2. See Harry Wilkinson Bragdon, *Woodrow Wilson: The Academic Years* (Cambridge, MA: Belknap Press, 1967), 56.

3. "Congressional Government," October 1879, in *PWW* 1:548–74. John M. Mulder argues that there is an important difference between "Cabinet Government" and "Congressional Government," in that the latter essay maintained that the cabinet officers ought to be selected from Congress itself. But Wilson made this stipulation in the earlier essay as well. In "Cabinet Government," Wilson reasoned that the president should be required to choose his officers from among members of Congress, since it would never do in a republican government to have the president appointing new members of the legislature. See "Cabinet Government," in *PWW* 1:499. See also Mulder, *Woodrow Wilson: The Years of Preparation* (Princeton: Princeton University Press, 1978), 61.

4. "Government by Debate," December 1882, in *PWW* 2:159–275.

5. Wilson to Robert Bridges, February 5, 1883, in *PWW* 2:298.

6. "Committee or Cabinet Government?" January 1884, in *PWW* 2:614–40.

7. "Government by Debate," in *PWW* 2:160, 171, 196.

8. For example, see Wilson's response to a critic who had pointed out some factual errors in the work: "I thank you very much for calling my attention to the error in my book in the matter of the Supreme Court appointments of 1870. I am very much chagrined that I should have fallen into it. I did *not* examine original sources upon the point." Wilson to George Frisbie Hoar, February 16, 1885, in *PWW* 4:262. See also Richard J. Stillman II, "Woodrow Wilson and the Study of Administration: A New Look at an Old Essay," *American Political Science Review* 67 (June 1973): 585 (see note 21).

9. Louis Brownlow, "Woodrow Wilson and Public Administration," *Public Administration Review* 16 (1956): 78.

10. Bragdon, *The Academic Years*, 134.

11. Daniel D. Stid, *The President as Statesman: Woodrow Wilson and the Constitution* (Lawrence: University Press of Kansas, 1998), 21. For some criticisms of *Congressional Government* in the scholarly literature, see Roland Young, "Woodrow Wilson's *Congressional Government* Reconsidered," in *The Philosophy and Policies of Woodrow Wilson*, ed. Earl Latham (Chicago: University of Chicago Press, 1958), 203; Arthur S. Link, *Wilson: The Road to the White House* (Princeton: Princeton University Press, 1947), 15.

12. For details on Wilson's arrangement to secure his Ph.D., see the following correspondence in *PWW*: 5:150–51 (Wilson to Herbert Baxter Adams, April 2, 1886); 5:153 (From Daniel Coit Gilman to Wilson, April 5, 1886); 5:154–55 (From Herbert Baxter Adams to Wilson, April 7, 1886); 5:155 (Wilson to Herbert Baxter Adams, April 8, 1886).

13. "Preface to the Fifteenth Edition of *Congressional Government*," August 15, 1900, in *PWW* 11:569–70.

14. See, for example, Bragdon's side-by-side comparison of Bagehot's work and Wilson's *Congressional Government*. Bragdon, *The Academic Years*, 60.

15. Wilson to Houghton, Mifflin & Company, April 4, 1884, in *PWW* 3:111.

16. See Link's editorial note on Bradford in *PWW* 3:21.

17. Wilson, *Congressional Government* (1885; repr., New York: Meridian Books, 1956), 133.

18. "Gamaliel Bradford's Review of *Congressional Government*," February 12, 1885, in *PWW* 4:236. On the details of how Wilson's proposal for institutional change compares with Bradford's, see Stid, *President as Statesman*, 19.

19. *Congressional Government*, 193.

20. "The Study of Administration," November 1886, in *PWW* 5:362–63.

21. Wilson, *The New Freedom* (New York: Doubleday, Page, 1913), 34.

22. *Congressional Government*, 197–98. Wilson's reference to "government by discussion" is indicative of his admiration for the great oratory of the British parliamentary tradition. This tradition, which Wilson came to know principally through the work of Walter Bagehot and various English histories, occupied much of his attention as a young thinker. Wilson made British parliamentary leaders—and especially their acumen in debate—subjects of several of his early essays; see, for example: "John Bright," March 6, 1880, in *PWW* 1:608–21; and "Mr. Gladstone: A Character Sketch," April 1880, in *PWW* 1:624–42. This interest clearly led Wilson to admire those American statesmen whom he considered to excel in oratory, especially Daniel Webster. See "Daniel Webster and William Pitt," August 10, 1878, in *PWW* 1:396–97.

23. *Congressional Government*, 163, 170. See also Wilson to the Editor, *Bradstreet's*, February 24, 1885, in *PWW* 4:290–91. Wilson's depiction of the president as chief bureaucrat is also evident in his discussion of senatorial courtesy, where he advocated giving the president more complete control over the appointment of officers in the bureaucracy. See "The 'Courtesy of the Senate,'" November 15, 1885, in *PWW* 5:44–48.

24. *Congressional Government*, 128.

25. "Cabinet Government," in *PWW* 1:502–3.

26. *Congressional Government*, 170–71.

27. *Congressional Government*, 171.

28. "Cabinet Government," in *PWW* 1:498–99.

29. "Cabinet Government," in *PWW* 1:507–9. A similar argument is made in "Government by Debate," in *PWW* 2:244. For Niels Aage Thorsen's analysis of Wilson's weakening of the presidency, see Thorsen, *The Political Thought of Woodrow Wilson 1875–1910* (Princeton: Princeton University Press, 1988), 50–53.

30. "Cabinet Government," in *PWW* 1:495. This same point is made in "Government by Debate," in *PWW* 2:187, and in "Leaderless Government," August 1897, in *PWW* 10:298.

31. "Government by Debate," in *PWW* 2:187. Wilson frequently used financial policy as an example of Congress's defective organization. The third chapter of *Congressional Government* focuses on specific shortcomings in the manner in which Congress makes financial policy. Wilson seems to have gotten some of his information on Congress's financial policy from his former law partner, Edward I. Renick, who by that time had taken a civil-service position in Washington. Evidence of this derivation appears in the correspondence between Wilson and Renick that is contained throughout volume 3 of the Wilson papers.

32. *Congressional Government*, 57.

33. *Congressional Government*, 61–62. See also Wilson's account of the travails of the new member in "Government by Debate," in *PWW* 2:171–73.

34. *Congressional Government*, 69.

35. "Government by Debate," in *PWW* 2:200. See also "Cabinet Government," in *PWW* 1:495, where Wilson proclaimed that "our Government is practically carried on by irresponsible committees."

36. *Congressional Government*, 72.

37. *Congressional Government*, 116, 121.

38. *The New Freedom*, 126, 138.

39. Publius, *The Federalist Papers*, ed. Charles R. Kesler and Clinton Rossiter (New York: Mentor, 1999), 62:347.

40. *Congressional Government*, 150–52.

41. *Congressional Government*, 136.

42. *Congressional Government*, 135–36, 146, 152–56.

43. Wilson, *Constitutional Government in the United States* (New York: Columbia University Press, 1908), 112.

44. *Constitutional Government*, 134–35.

45. *Constitutional Government*, 116, 118.

46. *Constitutional Government*, 125.

47. See Herbert Croly, *Progressive Democracy*, ed. Sidney A. Pearson Jr. (1914; repr., New Brunswick, NJ: Transaction Publishers, 1998), 245–83; Theodore Roosevelt, "The Right of the People to Rule," in *Social Justice and Popular Rule* (New York: Charles Scribner's Sons, 1926), 151–71.

48. *Congressional Government*, 91–92.

49. "Government by Debate," in *PWW* 2:253.

50. "Cabinet Government," in *PWW* 1:498–99.

51. "Government by Debate," in *PWW* 2:202–3, 247.

52. "Government by Debate," in *PWW* 2:246–50.

53. "Government by Debate," in *PWW* 2:251.

54. "Government by Debate," in *PWW* 2:202.

55. "Government by Debate," in *PWW* 2:257.

56. "Government by Debate," in *PWW* 2:162.

57. "Government by Debate," in *PWW* 2:173.

58. "Bryce's *American Commonwealth*," January 31, 1889, in *PWW* 6:64.

59. *Congressional Government*, 167–68.

60. *Congressional Government*, 104, 121, 127.

61. *Congressional Government*, 103.

62. On the Wilsonian origins of twentieth-century budget policy, see John Marini, *The Politics of Budget Control* (Washington, DC: Crane Russak, 1992), 39–66.

63. "Responsible Government under the Constitution," February 10, 1886, in *PWW* 5:107.

64. "Mr. Cleveland's Cabinet," March 17, 1893, in *PWW* 8:173.

65. See, for example, "Wilson's Commonplace Book," February 1876, in *PWW* 1:109–13.

66. Walter Bagehot, *The English Constitution* (1867; repr., Ithaca, NY: Cornell University Press, 1981), 59–81.

67. *Congressional Government*, 210.

68. *Congressional Government*, 58.

69. *Congressional Government*, 210–12.

70. *Congressional Government*, 76-80.

71. "Mr. Cleveland's Cabinet," in *PWW* 8:175.

72. "Mr. Cleveland's Cabinet," in *PWW* 8:175–77.

73. "Congressional Government," in *PWW* 1:559–62. A difference between what Wilson proposed in "Congressional Government" and what he had proposed in his earlier essay "Cabinet Government in the United States" is that in "Congressional Government," the cabinet rises or falls as a single group, on the basis of congressional acceptance or rejection of its program as a whole. In "Cabinet Government," Wilson had proposed that each cabinet member rise or fall as an individual, depending upon congressional support for his particular program.

74. "Congressional Government," in *PWW* 1:562.

75. "Government by Debate," in *PWW* 2:199.

76. *Congressional Government*, 114–15.

77. *Congressional Government*, 129–31. This is a point Thorsen makes in his analysis of Wilson's early essays on Congress, casting them as "an attempt to reconcile the idea of the nation with the practice of universal suffrage." Expanding suffrage, Thorsen explains, is desirable as a means of legitimizing national power. But this legitimacy can arise only if public opinion is properly formed and educated. See Thorsen, *Political Thought of Woodrow Wilson*, 31–33.

78. *Constitutional Government*, 11.

79. *Constitutional Government*, 83.

80. *Constitutional Government*, 104.

81. *Federalist* 10:50.

82. *Constitutional Government*, 103.

83. *Federalist* 63:352.

84. *Constitutional Government*, 105, 110–11.

85. *The New Freedom*, 105, 109.

86. *The New Freedom*, 111, 115.

87. *The New Freedom*, 134–35.

88. Bagehot, *English Constitution*, 152–53.

89. Bagehot, *Physics and Politics* (1872; repr., Chicago: Ivan R. Dee, 1999), 143–46.

90. "Cabinet Government," in *PWW* 1:505.

91. "Cabinet Government," in *PWW* 1:496, 504–5.

92. "Government by Debate," in *PWW* 2:272.

93. "Cabinet Government," in *PWW* 1:500–501.

94. Wilson to the Editor, *The Princetonian*, January 25, 1877, in *PWW* 1:238–39.

95. "Government by Debate," in *PWW* 2:242. Wilson echoed this point in a letter to his future wife, explaining that he would prefer to remain outside of public service until the conditions of government "are altered radically and finally." Wilson to Ellen Louise Axson, March 3, 1885, in *PWW* 4:324.

96. "Mr. Gladstone, a Character Sketch," in *PWW* 1:637.

97. "Daniel Webster and William Pitt," in *PWW* 1:397. Wilson's admiration for Webster is also evident in his histories. See, for example, Wilson, *A History of the American People*, 5 vols. (New York: Harper & Brothers, 1902), 4:27.

98. *Congressional Government*, 144–45, 148, 150.

Chapter Five

The Presidency, the Parties, and the Judiciary

In continuing the analysis of Wilson's proposals for American national institutions, we must recall that such proposals constitute for Wilson specific attempts to implement his broad vision of separating politics and administration. As explained in chapter 3, such a vision entails substantially transforming the traditional conceptions of legislative, executive, and even judicial power. The evolution of Wilson's proposed reforms for American institutions—first with a focus on Congress and subsequently with a focus on the president—represents his search for some entity in the constitutional order to lead the "politics" half of his politics-administration dichotomy. His switch in emphasis from Congress to the president was a switch in means only. Wilson's broad vision for the transformation of American politics remained consistent: politics had to embody, and be guided by, the historically conditioned and unified will of the people. Only in this way could the government, and the principles upon which it rested, be constantly adjusted to fit the changing demands of historical progress.

Chapter 4 looked to Wilson's early thought, particularly as expressed in the book *Congressional Government* and the essays upon which it was based, and discussed how Wilson focused on Congress—as opposed to the presidency—as the leader of the political arm of government. This approach became manifest, in particular, in Wilson's call for instituting some form of parliamentary government in the United States. The present chapter addresses Wilson's focus on other institutions. As his thought matured, Wilson became more convinced that Congress would never be able to fulfill the new institutional role that he was contemplating for it. The impediments to national leadership that Wilson had seen in Congress in his early writings convinced the later Wilson that Congress would never sufficiently embody the unity of national will needed to lead the "politics" side of the politics-administration dichotomy.

This realization led to a second and somewhat different form of institutional political science, one that turned to the popular leadership of the president, with the assistance of a reconstituted party system and judiciary.

Wilson's shift to an institutional arrangement that featured the presidency is most commonly understood to come in *Constitutional Government in the United States*, although it is certainly evident in a broad cross-section of his writings from the first decade of the twentieth century. The book was based upon a series of lectures that Wilson delivered at Columbia University, where he was invited by university president Nicholas Murray Butler to inaugurate the Blumenthal Lecture Series. The contrast in Wilson's account of the presidency between *Congressional Government* and *Constitutional Government* is indeed striking. While the former had considered the president as little more than chief bureaucrat, the latter sees him as the primary means by which the historically conditioned public will is brought to bear on the direction of American government. But even more important than the stark differences between the two accounts of the presidency is what remains consistent in the two books: in both, regardless of which particular institution is looked upon to lead the political arm of the government, Wilson called for transferring policymaking authority from the political branches to the administrative departments.[1] In this respect, Wilson's view of Congress changed very little. He continued to call in *Constitutional Government* for Congress to become more open and accountable, while contending that it must abandon its stubborn insistence on being involved in the details of policymaking.

Even if Wilson's shift in emphasis from Congress to the president were a shift in means only, the question remains as to what, exactly, might have precipitated this clear modification in institutional tactics? Scholars have offered several possibilities, perhaps most common among them being the argument that specific presidencies during Wilson's own life changed his view of the institution. Daniel D. Stid, for instance, believes that the Cleveland presidency contributed to the evolution of Wilson's thought. Stid notes that the early (1893) Wilson was critical of Cleveland's efforts to "govern unilaterally from the executive branch." But by Cleveland's second term, Wilson was coming to see the possibilities for executive leadership, especially when considered in conjunction with the necessary reform of the party system. As Stid explains, "What was most impressive to Wilson was the way in which Cleveland had called into question the claim of *Congressional Government* that the president was simply a creature of—and could not begin to re-create—the pragmatic, parochial features of the American party system." Wilson admired the way in which Cleveland pursued certain policies even over the objections of his party's leadership—Stid mentions tariff reform, the repeal of the Silver Purchase Act, and the expansion of the civil service. He writes that "the 'singular independence and force of purpose' that Wilson detected in Cleveland's enduring refusal to play politics as usual on the tariff and his resolute stand on silver suggested to Wilson that a president could in fact set the legislative agenda, if not control it outright, in Washington."[2] Stid suggests that in addition to the Cleveland presidency, the Spanish-American War and the increasing focus on foreign affairs played a transformative role in Wilson's understanding of the presidency, particularly with regard to the American seizure of the Philippines, the administration of which would necessarily lead to the expansion of the American executive.[3] In considering what Wilson witnessed from specific presidencies during his own life and how that might have influenced the evolution of his thought on the presidency, Arthur Link points to the "revivification of the presidency" under Theodore Roosevelt as the main reason for the new direction in Wilson's views.[4] Kendrick Clements agrees that both the Roosevelt presidency and the Spanish-American War were important, and adds that Wilson's own presidency of Princeton helped to develop his argument on presidential leadership.[5]

These are valuable insights, as they certainly help to make sense of a rather remarkable shift in Wilson's proposed rearrangement of American national institutions. Yet it must be emphasized again that the shift was a change in tactics only—new and perhaps better ways of effecting through institutional reform Wilson's consistent view of how the theoretical foundations of American government had to be radically transformed. As Scot Zentner has contended, Wilson's shift to presidential leadership can be understood as a move to an institutional arrangement that fit more coherently with his broad conception of American government. "Wilson's turn to presidential government," Zentner explains, "was . . . a more adequate answer to his desire to have political leadership represent the nation's 'oneness of personality.' "[6] The president, in other words, was better suited than Congress to become the embodiment of the historically conditioned will of the people and, consequently, to lead the political arm of government.

What happened to Congress? How did it go from being the very institutional linchpin of Wilson's plan for reforming America to getting pushed aside by the president? Much of Wilson's discussion of Congress in *Constitutional Government* is nothing new and merely reiterates his contention from his early works that the main function of Congress is not to legislate but to keep in step with public opinion. Wilson called for Congress to extricate itself from day-to-day governing and concentrate instead on broad oversight. He emphasized that Congress must actually cease considering itself as part of "the government." The "government," understood in Wilsonian terms, is the bureaucracy that sees to the daily rulemaking and regulation of public life. The role of Congress must be to oversee this function, not to attempt to carry it out itself.[7]

Wilson conceded in *Constitutional Government* that the Senate does have some legitimate claim to being a part of "the government," as it must aid in the appointment of officials and other executive business.[8] The problem with the Senate was its tendency for independence. Much to Wilson's dismay, the Senate was in the habit of following the prescription of *Federalist* 51 that each branch of government exercise a "will of its own."[9] This would never do if the separation of powers were to be overcome by a system that was grounded in the cooperation of the branches in response to the unified public will. Wilson complained that "the Senate has a very stiff will of its own, a pride of independent judgment, very admirable in itself, but not calculated to dispose it to prompt accommodation when it differs in its views and objects from the House or the president. Its very excellences stand in its way as an organ of cooperation."[10] Wilson reasoned that the original intention behind the creation of the Senate had not been for it to function as a check against other branches of government, but instead to serve as a consultative body for the president. It is interesting, particularly in light of events at the end of Wilson's own presidency, that he wrote that the burden for resolving disputes between the legislative and executive branches lies with the president, who must make sure to coordinate his efforts with the Senate and to take into account its views in the conduct of executive affairs. He warned that presidents must not simply formulate conclusions or programs and then submit them to the Senate for its approval; the president should, instead, consult with the Senate in the construction of programs, so that senators will see themselves not as rivals but partners. As Wilson elaborated:

> There is another course which the President may follow, and which one or two Presidents of unusual political sagacity have followed, with the satisfactory results that were to have been expected. He may himself be less stiff and offish, may himself act in the true spirit of the Constitution and establish intimate relations of confidence with the Senate on his own initiative, not carrying his plans to completion and then laying them in final form before the Senate to be accepted or rejected, but keeping himself in confidential communication with the leaders of the Senate while his plans are in course . . . in order that there may be a veritable counsel and a real accommodation of views instead of a final challenge and contest. . . . If [the president] have character, modesty, devotion, and insight as well as force, he can bring the contending elements of the system together into a great and efficient body of common counsel.[11]

It is tempting to speculate that Wilson's own legacy may well have been different if he had adopted this same approach with regard to plans for the League of Nations. But Wilson offered a different interpretation of the Constitution during the League debate, one that insisted that the president take the lead and that the Senate play only a limited role—that of accepting or rejecting the treaty as devised by the president, without amendment. In *Constitutional Government*, Wilson does treat the Senate much more favorably than he had in earlier accounts. He even seems at points to adopt the traditional view of the Senate as a deliberative check against the House. Wilson's increasingly dim view of the House had much to do with this new tone.

Wilson's basic criticism of the House of Representatives in *Constitutional Government* remained fairly consistent with his earlier accounts. In particular, he reinforced the complaint that the House had an impatience for discussion, preferring instead to meddle in the details of policy that should be left to the administrative departments.[12] Wilson's account of the Speaker of the House was somewhat modified from what he had written in *Congressional Government*. In that earlier work, Wilson complained that the Speaker, in spite of serving as the only identifiable leader of the House, was not terribly powerful. The real power, instead, lay with the chairmen of the standing committees. But in *Constitutional Government*, more power is attributed to the Speaker directly. This observation is related to Wilson's comments on the new powers of the House Rules Committee, which Wilson explained had become a powerful tool for the majority party and, especially, the Speaker. In a reflection still applicable to today's House, Wilson reasoned that the Rules Committee provides the Speaker with a vehicle to curtail debate, shutting off the kind of discussion Wilson believed essential in Congress and allowing it instead to meddle in the details of legislation.[13] It also seems reasonable to infer that Wilson's expanded vision of the Speaker's role was influenced by the tenure of Thomas Reed and Joseph Cannon—two very strong Speakers who had come into office subsequent to the publication of *Congressional Government*.[14]

Unlike his earlier assessment of Congress, Wilson in *Constitutional Government* concluded that Congress simply could not be refurbished in the manner necessary for it to serve as the leader for the "politics" half of the politics-administration dichotomy. Given the various institutional obstacles, Wilson reasoned that it was impossible for Congress to establish a sufficient connection with the public will. In turning to the popular leadership of the president, Wilson explained that "the House seems to have missed . . . the right to be [the nation's] principal spokesman in affairs."[15]

THE POSTCONSTITUTIONAL PRESIDENCY

Just as his earlier proposal for reforming Congress had urged that the institution focus less on its constitutionally defined legislative powers and duties,

Wilson's new institutional vision for the presidency required the president to look beyond his role as it is defined in the Constitution. Wilson urged in *Constitutional Government* that the president concentrate on his role as the embodiment of the nation's popular will—the role Wilson had initially envisioned for Congress. In modern times, it was more important for the president to be leader of the whole nation than it was for him to be the chief officer of the executive branch. Wilson contrasted the president's duties as "legal executive" to his "political powers," advocating an emphasis on the latter as a means of using popular opinion to transcend the rigid separation-of-powers structure of the old "Newtonian" constitutional framework.[16] As opposed to remaining confined to the constitutionally defined powers and duties of his own branch, the president's role as popular leader means that he must, as the embodiment of the national will, coordinate and move Congress and the other parts of government.

The president's new role in Wilson's institutional plan is based upon the president's connection to public opinion. It is the duty of each president to adapt himself to the needs and interests of the day. This is why Wilson remarked that each presidency in American history had been unique: each presidency represents a different stage in the evolution of the American political order. Wilson said that "both men and circumstances" had created the unique characteristics of each presidency.[17] The president is uniquely situated to adapt himself to changes in the public mood (something Congress ultimately could not do because of its secrecy and disorganization) because he is the only official who has won a true national mandate through a nationwide election. Just as Wilson had praised the British Parliament for its connection to popular majorities, he said that the president "is at once the choice of the party and of the nation." The president "is the only party nominee for whom the whole nation votes. . . . No one else represents the people as a whole, exercising a national choice." The president is the "spokesman for the real sentiment and purpose of the country."[18]

Wilson emphasized the person of the president, not the office; it is the man himself and his personality that come to embody the national will. "Governments are what the politicians make them," Wilson wrote, "and it is easier to write of the President than of the presidency."[19] This is why a president's expertise in public affairs is not as important as his possession of a forceful personality and other qualities of popular leadership. It is, in other words, more important that the president be able to "feel the pain" of the people than it is for him to demonstrate competence in carrying out the duties of chief executive. What America needs, Wilson wrote, is "a man who will be and who will seem to the country in some sort an embodiment of the character and purpose it wishes its government to have—a man who understands his own day and the needs of the country."[20]

Wilson defined a constitutional government as one that can adapt itself to the changing interests of its people, and this adaptation can best be accomplished through the coordination provided by the president's leadership. As an embodiment of the public will, the president can transcend the government and coordinate its activities. Congress could not lead the whole of government because it had become too bogged down by competing narrow interests and by stubbornly confining itself to the details of policymaking. Wilson explained that "there can be no successful government without leadership or without the intimate, almost instinctive, coordination of the organs of life and action."[21] This is why it is wrong to limit the president with the traditional checks of the Constitution. The president is "the unifying force in our complex system" and must not be relegated to managing only one branch of it.[22] Even in *The State*, Wilson had criticized the distance in the practice of American government between the president and Congress. He implied there that this was a distance that was not necessarily mandated by the Constitution, arguing instead that it had arisen out of the circumstances of the Jefferson presidency. In fact, Wilson contended, the constitutional design left significant room for the president to extend his influence to other branches and work with them in a coordinated effort.[23] Just as a Parliament serves as the embodiment of the public will that guides the whole government, and just as Wilson had initially wanted the U.S. Congress to serve as the public's superintendent over the entire scope of political affairs, the president must lead America's politics in a direction that adapts itself to the changing sentiments and interests of the public mind.

While *Constitutional Government*—published in 1908—is frequently cited as an illustration of Wilson's postconstitutional understanding of the presidency, many of the key themes from this doctrine were actually laid out in primitive form in Wilson's 1897 essay on the Cleveland presidency. The essay represents a clear shift in Wilson's thinking from his earlier works that favored congressional government, and it gives credence to those who have pointed to the Cleveland presidency as transformative in Wilson's thinking on American institutions. In the essay, Wilson contended that the power of the presidency is really a reflection of the personality who occupies the office, and he cited Cleveland's personality traits as decisive in making the presidency prominent in American politics.[24] Wilson wrote admiringly of how Cleveland, through the force of his personality, made the presidency important once again in America: "It was singular how politics began at once to center in the President, waiting for his initiative, and how the air at Washington filled with murmurs against the domineering and usurping temper and practice of the Executive. Power had somehow gone the length of the avenue, and seemed lodged in one man."[25]

If Cleveland's presidency catalyzed Wilson's changed thinking on executive power, Wilson's own experience as a chief executive—in New Jersey and in Washington—offers clear evidence that he took this thinking to heart and implemented its key tenets in a variety of concrete ways. During his gubernatorial campaign in 1910, Wilson explained in a speech what kind of governor he would be. He criticized his opponent's pledge to be a "constitutional governor" who would refrain from infringing on the province of the legislature and from calling on it to enact specific pieces of legislation. Wilson countered that if refraining from pressuring the legislature was what it meant to be a constitutional governor, then he would be "an unconstitutional governor." Wilson promised to bring the pressure of public opinion to bear on the legislature if it failed to do its job.[26] This is a promise he fulfilled, as Wilson explained in a 1911 interview on the success of his program in the state legislature: "'A notion has gone abroad that I whipped the Legislature of New Jersey into performing certain acts,' said the Governor, 'but that view of the matter is not correct. I did appeal to public opinion, and public opinion did the rest.'"[27] Wilson described his position as New Jersey's chief executive as one where he embodied the will of the people, and then acted as the embodiment of the public will in guiding and superintending the disparate parts of state government. He noted in an address that someone had "referred to the Commission Government as the Governor's cause. I accept that characterization of it because I believe it to be the people's cause, and I am proud to have my name identified with anything that is their cause."[28]

One of the most interesting controversies in which Wilson became involved as New Jersey governor—the state's selection of one if its U.S. senators—is also quite instructive on Wilson's view of executive power. Wilson opposed the candidacy of one of New Jersey's major Democratic bosses, James Smith, and used his position as governor to work instead for the selection of James E. Martine, who had won the nonbinding Democratic primary for the office. Wilson explained that, as governor, he was responsible for ensuring that the people's will was implemented, and that they had expressed their will in the nonbinding primary. Reasoning that his role as governor extended well beyond its definition in the state constitution, he stated that "legally speaking, it is not my duty even to give advice with regard to the choice [of senator]. But there are other duties besides legal duties. The recent campaign has put me in an unusual position. I offered, if elected, to be the political spokesman and adviser of the people."[29] As the political spokesman of the people, Wilson planned and implemented an aggressive public-speaking campaign in the counties of key Democratic legislators, in order to pressure those lawmakers in their votes for U.S. senator.[30]

Wilson invoked a similar understanding of executive power in his 1911 campaign for the adoption of the Geran Bill, which was to establish the direct primary in New Jersey. Link reports that Wilson personally attended the critical meeting held by the Democratic legislative caucus for the purpose of deciding upon the legislators' strategy with regard to the bill. Some of the legislators objected on separation-of-powers grounds to Wilson's presence, but Wilson responded that his presence was proper under a broad construction of a provision of the state constitution that required the governor to recommend matters for legislation to the legislature. He also threatened to take the case directly to the people if the legislators failed to move on the bill.[31] As Wilson explained in a letter written around this time, "There is much balking [in the legislature] at the adoption of one of the chief bills pending, because it takes the control of things out of the hands of the politicians. I shall, apparently, have to use 'the big stick.' If necessary, very well!"[32]

When it came time for Wilson to test the waters for a presidential campaign, he forbade his advisers from gathering alliances and commitments from party bosses—this was the traditional way of "exploring" a potential run for the White House. As the editors of his papers explain, Wilson insisted (initially) that a campaign be conducted, instead, to both gauge and stimulate the support of public opinion for his candidacy.[33]

As president, Wilson maintained the same understanding of the executive as the embodiment of the public will that he had as New Jersey governor, and he used that understanding to superintend the whole operation of American government. Link explains that Wilson was heavily involved in negotiating the minute details of the major pieces of legislation enacted during his presidency, particularly the major reform measures of his first term. Before he was even inaugurated, Wilson crafted what was to become Congress's legislative agenda for 1913 and 1914, and this agenda was carefully implemented once he assumed office. On the tariff reform measure, Wilson even called a special session of Congress and broke long-standing precedent by addressing the special session in person.[34] Link's account of Wilson's involvement in legislative matters is instructive:

> In Trenton, before his inauguration, he took control by conferring in person and by correspondence with committee chairmen and Democratic leaders over the general structure of the legislative program. In Washington, he gave assiduous attention to the minutiae of legislation, conferred frequently at the Capitol and the White House, brought congressional and Cabinet leaders together, mediated when it seemed fundamental differences might disrupt the Democratic ranks, and, when necessary, cracked the patronage whip and used the House and Senate Democratic caucuses to force rebels into line.[35]

Wilson's practice of executive governance, in other words, largely corresponded to the doctrine he had developed in his writings, that the political arm of government needed strong leadership and that the president, as the embodiment of the historically conditioned will of the people, should use his position to direct a wide range of national political action.

The "Modern Presidency" Debate

Wilson's new institutional vision for the presidency, one that grounds the president's power in his connection to public opinion, raises several serious issues with regard to the increasingly rhetorical nature of the modern presidency. There is a school of interpreters who contend that Wilson's popularization of the presidency represents a substantial departure from the vision of the founders—indeed, the departure is so sharp that this school of interpretation identifies Wilson as the originator of a new conception of the presidency, the "modern presidency." According to the "modern presidency" argument, Wilson's new institutional vision has radically transformed presidential politics in contemporary America. The "modern presidency" argument points to the founders' fear of demagoguery, noting that the founders were careful to avoid the direct connection that popular rhetoric would create between the president and public opinion. Wilson rejected this fear of demagoguery, and he rejected the institutional design of the presidency that was based upon it.

Perhaps the first scholar to note the sharp distinction between Wilson's and the founders' understanding of presidential leadership was Paul Eidelberg. While the thrust of Eidelberg's analysis focuses on the question of statesmanship and leadership generally, he can nonetheless be considered a pioneer in the "modern presidency" school. Eidelberg gives an account of the decline of statesmanship in the American tradition, naming Wilson as a primary figure in transforming and popularizing the American presidency.[36] Eidelberg thinks this transformation pernicious, which is what distinguishes his commentary from that of Henry A. Turner, who was also among the first scholars to recognize Wilson's substantial departure from the founders' design of the presidency. Turner describes Wilson as one of the originators and first practitioners of the "modern presidency," which he sees as a perfectly natural and necessary development in American constitutionalism.[37]

The "modern presidency" thesis was pushed further in a landmark article by James W. Ceaser, Glen E. Thurow, Jeffrey K. Tulis, and Joseph M. Bessette, who point to the dangers inherent in Wilson's popularization of the presidency—particularly in the resulting emphasis on rhetoric as the primary feature of presidential government. The authors outline the three main factors in the rise of the modern presidency: the "modern doctrine of presidential leadership," the mass media, and modern campaigns. The most important of these is the first, for which the authors hold Wilson responsible. They contend that Wilson's legacy is still influential in contemporary presidential politics, again most particularly in the rhetorical nature of presidential campaigning and governance:

> Popular or mass rhetoric, which Presidents once employed only rarely, now serves as one of their principal tools in attempting to govern the nation. Whatever doubts Americans may now entertain about the limits of presidential leadership, they do not consider it unfitting or inappropriate for presidents to attempt to "move" the public by programmatic speeches that exhort and set forth grand and ennobling views. It was not always so. Prior to this century, popular leadership through rhetoric was suspect.[38]

In a subsequent book on the subject, Tulis explains how Wilson's rhetorical leadership model represents a departure from nineteenth-century presidents who understood their authority as coming from the Constitution and not the people directly. Nineteenth-century presidents, Tulis argues, did not use their rhetoric to connect directly with public opinion in an effort to move Congress. By contrast, as president, Wilson implemented several changes in presidential rhetoric designed precisely to fulfill the aims of enlarging the presidency that had been set out in *Constitutional Government*. As Tulis explains, Wilson focused on policy rhetoric, making it oral and delivered directly to the people (as opposed to written and delivered primarily to Congress). Wilson also introduced a new form of speech, where rhetoric was no longer constrained by constitutional tradition. The "visionary speech" and the "policy stand speech," each a standard element of today's presidential repertoire, originated with Wilson.[39] Charles Kesler takes the rhetorical presidency argument a step further, emphasizing Wilson's role in the origination of much that is novel in twentieth-century American politics; to the extent that he treats the presidency in particular, this stance places Kesler squarely in the "modern presidency" school of interpretation.[40]

In a pair of articles, Robert Eden shares the view of the "modern presidency" school that Wilson's turn to "opinion leadership" marked a substantial departure from the founders' vision, but Eden argues that it is wrong to see this change as responsible for enlarging the scope of executive power in the twentieth century. Eden reasons that by downplaying the formal powers of the executive, Wilson's rhetorical presidency actually weakened the institution. He notes that Alexander Hamilton desired an energetic presidency, and that Hamilton conceived of the president's considerable energy as deriving directly from the formal powers of Article II of the Constitution. By placing those formal powers "in commission," Wilson actually undermined executive authority.[41] Eden's analysis relies on the sharp distinction he makes between the political powers of the president (which come from "opinion leadership") and the executive powers (which come from the Constitution). He suggests that we must have one or the other, that we cannot have both, and that Wilson develops the former at the expense of the latter.[42] To the extent that the president's executive powers are defined in such narrow terms, it is no doubt the case that they are weakened by Wilson's emphasis on the president's political powers. But it is also the case that by emphasizing "opinion leadership," Wilson freed the president from formal constitutional restraints, and this liberation would seem to offer great—even frightening—potential for the enlargement of the president's power, generally speaking. Eden himself acknowledges this potential criticism by conceding that "Wilson's abandonment of the executive office may free presidents from the confines of the American constitutional tradition, and loosen the hold of many customary constraints that had deterred earlier presidents."[43]

While it is obvious that the argument of my book is largely sympathetic to the "modern presidency" thesis and its interpretation of Wilson, it is important to note some recent critiques of this school and its view of Wilson. Stid, for example, cautions that Wilson's use of popular rhetoric as a tool to move Congress can be overblown, and he suggests instead that Wilson thought it just as important—if not more so—that the president deal directly with Congress as a means of accomplishing his agenda. Stid does not see Wilson's leadership doctrine in terms nearly so radical as the modern presidency school; he contends that Wilson "saw real limits on the president's ability to rely on public opinion."[44] David K. Nichols goes so far as to challenge the very idea that there is a "modern presidency," contending instead that the elements of the contemporary presidency were present from the very formation of the Constitution itself. Wilson, in this regard, was mistaken if he thought that his vision of presidential leadership could be achieved only by transcending the Constitution.[45]

A recent article by presidential scholars Terri Bimes and Stephen Skowronek presents one of the more interesting challenges to the "modern presidency" argument—at least with respect to Wilson. Bimes and Skowronek assert that Wilson was more concerned with the constitutionally defined powers and duties of the presidency than were many nineteenth-century presidents. The approach of Wilson's critics, according to Bimes and Skowronek, leads to a "bifurcated frame" that erroneously portrays a "great divide" between Wilson and the constitutionalism that preceded him. Bimes and Skowronek find their version of Wilson in his histories.[46] They note that, in discussing past presidencies, Wilson was critical of the modes of popular leadership employed by the likes of Jefferson, Jackson, and Johnson. There is an "instinctive protection of institutions [that] is evident throughout Wilson's histories," Bimes and Skowronek contend, and this protection "lays a firm foundation for his defense of the Constitution." Wilson is portrayed as the defender of constitutional tradition against the democratic populism of many nineteenth-century presidents about whom he wrote. Jackson came in for particular criticism because of his extraconstitutional mode of leadership. Bimes and Skowronek assert that "Wilson's treatment of Jackson reads like a page out of current criticisms of his own leadership standards." Far from being the thinker and president who ushered in what is commonly referred to as the "modern presidency" and who played down the constitutionally defined role of the president, Bimes's and Skowronek's Wilson is someone who appreciated and defended the constitutional order.[47]

Yet when one considers Wilson's clear hostility toward federalism—toward any institutional arrangement that might detract from the unity of the nation—the attacks in Wilson's histories on Jefferson and Jackson become easier to understand. Bimes and Skowronek argue that Wilson defended the Constitution against the popular rhetoric of Jefferson and Jackson, and that therefore we ought not see Wilson as the key turning point from the constitutional rhetoric of the nineteenth century to the extraconstitutional popular rhetoric of the twentieth century. But what reason might Wilson have had for criticizing Jefferson and especially Jackson? As any examination of his commentaries on federalism (not to mention his lengthy writings promoting the science of centralized administration) will show, Wilson strongly advocated unifying power at the national level and staunchly opposed decentralizing power to the states. Jefferson and Jackson argued more forcefully than perhaps any other nineteenth-century presidents against the expansion of federal power. Wilson's use of *any* means of argumentation—including constitutional argumentation—to criticize these two presidents should not be terribly surprising. That Wilson criticized Jefferson's defense of states' prerogatives and praised his later "growth" in office—especially for the Louisiana Purchase in spite of its dubious (by Jefferson's own admission) constitutionality—seems only further evidence that Wilson's constitutionalism was subordinated to his desire to expand and transform the role of the federal government.

As I endeavored to show in chapter 3 in my analysis of Wilson's histories, Jackson came under heavy criticism there not so much for his popular style of leadership but because Wilson thought him a reactionary, the very antithesis of the unifying spirit of the nation that history was bringing about. In the same historical accounts of Jackson that are cited by Bimes and Skowronek, Wilson was most critical of Jackson's strict construction of national power, especially on the question of Congress's power to charter a national bank. Wilson conceded that a narrow view of federal power had been the dominant thinking behind the founding-era construction of the Constitution. But the nation had progressed since then, reflecting greater unity and coming to a more expansive view of federal power; this progress had already been confirmed in 1819 by the Supreme Court decision of *McCulloch v. Maryland*, which had read into the Constitution the power to charter a national bank. What Jackson wanted to do in unnecessarily digging up the bank issue was to turn back the clock on progress, to return to a constitutionalism that had already been overcome by our historical growth as a nation.[48] Such an antiprogressive sin was unpardonable to Wilson.

In addition to the "modern presidency" debate, Wilson's popularization of the presidency also raises the question of Wilson's doctrine of leadership. In particular, is the presidential leader, as the embodiment of the public will, a follower or a shaper of public opinion? Is Wilson's vision of leadership fundamentally democratic or elitist? Chapter 6 is dedicated to a consideration of these questions. The present chapter focuses on how Wilson's new understanding of the presidency manifests itself institutionally. It continues, accordingly, with a consideration of those institutional modifications necessary to effect the new, postconstitutional view of the president's role. If the president is to provide the kind of coordination and leadership that Wilson envisioned, if he is to overcome a rigid separation-of-powers structure that seeks to confine the president to his own branch, the president will need to employ some extraconstitutional tools in order to accomplish his mission. This is how the party system—radically transformed for its new role—comes to be employed as a key means of the president's national leadership.

THE PARTY AS NATIONAL LEADERSHIP TOOL

In the various iterations of Wilson's vision for American national institutions, political parties play a consistently strong and vital role. Since the Constitution separates the formal institutions of government from one another and places them at some distance from public opinion, Wilson looked for some extraconstitutional means of both securing greater coordination between the formal institutions and providing for the more efficient translation of public opinion into public policy. The party system plays just such a role. First, parties aid in making the connection between the people and their governing institutions more immediate and direct. Through their electoral endorsement (or rejection) of the specific policy platforms of the parties, the people make known their will to the government and send officials to their jobs with a specific mission. Second, once in office, parties provide a means by which public officials can coordinate their efforts across different branches. Parties become a tool for unifying their members even while those members serve in different institutions.

In order to carry out these functions, Wilson well understood that parties could not continue to act as they had during much of the nineteenth century. Unelected and, therefore, unaccountable party bosses could no longer be permitted to dominate public officials. Instead, parties had to be transformed; they needed to serve both the will of the people and the will of those whom the people had elected to lead them. Only by transforming itself in this manner could the party system play a central role in Wilson's vision for American institutions.

This central role for parties is one that evolves in two stages in Wilson's constitutional thought. The evolution of Wilson's views on parties mirrors the evolution of his views on Congress and the presidency. While Wilson always maintained the need for a strong party system, he first understood this system as being essential in the service of congressional government. The parliamentary framework that he employed in his early writings on American government clearly could not function without a strong party system. When Wilson moved away from his emphasis on parliamentary government and looked instead to presidential leadership, the parties remained vital. Accordingly, the second stage in Wilson's thinking on the party system was one where strong parties were to be put in the service of presidential government. Each of these stages is examined below.

The Party in the Service of Congressional Government

If Wilson, in his early works, calls for some form of parliamentary government, then he must also call for a strong party system, on which the parliamentary form of government naturally relies. As Wilson's early suggestions for modifying the president's cabinet demonstrate, he sought to break down the separation between the legislative and executive branches by making the executive accountable to the majority party in the legislature. In this way, parties—once they are free from the control of unelected party bosses—make the system as a whole much more accountable to public opinion. Chapter 4 discussed Wilson's call for each party to have clear and identifiable leaders in the legislature. Through its support of these party leaders, the public can give broad direction to the legislature, which in turn directs the executive.

Wilson well recognized that parties, as they functioned in the nineteenth century, impeded the accountability of public officials. He observed that public officials were more concerned with retaining the friendship of the corrupt party bosses who controlled their access to the ballot than they were with responding to the public will. In order for Wilson to implement his vision of the party system as a means of connecting public opinion with policymaking, the parties themselves had to be made accountable. Wilson complained bitterly, in essays like "Government by Debate," that the parties were designed more to perpetuate their own power than they were to carry out the people's will. He called for parties that would actually be aggressive in policymaking—in particular, he wanted the party in power to do something on behalf of the majority it represented. He commented that

> the present condition of parties in this country is such as to make the wish to be rid of them a very natural one, and such as very properly to quicken the anxiety of patriotic citizens. The spirit of faction seems to be running maddest riot. There is daily justification of the statement, now everywhere made and believed, that parties are organized merely to carry elections, not to carry measures of policy.[49]

Wilson's argument that parties ought to be more aggressive and prominent in governing—that they were the only way to achieve some unity among the national institutions—ran contrary to the reformers of his day who were calling for the elimination of parties altogether. Wilson certainly agreed with these reformers that parties as they operated in the nineteenth century had to go, but he considered it essential that the old, corrupt parties be replaced by stronger, more accountable ones. His early work on congressional government is based, in part, upon an attack on the antiparty reformers. In the essay "Congressional Government," Wilson contrasted his proposal for American institutions to that of Albert Stickney, who had contended that parties were irredeemably corrupt and had to be eliminated from the American system of government.[50] Wilson countered that "it is my present purpose to show that there is a method which, whilst it essentially involves party rule, is nevertheless a method which may not only deprive this rule of its depravity but even exalt it to a position of most salutary authority."[51] In his reflections on the electoral politics of his day, Wilson looked to his own Democratic Party as the potential vehicle for reforming the party system in general. This was particularly true of the Tilden-Hayes contest in 1876, about which Wilson remarked that "the salvation of the country depends upon the success of the Democratic cause."[52]

In "Government by Debate," Wilson argued that democracy itself—which rests fundamentally on the accountability of public officials to public opinion—relies on party government. The party system, in its proper role, could present the voters with a clear choice with regard to the direction of the nation. The party that won the support of the majority of voters could use that popular support to govern through something resembling a parliamentary system. The essential reform, then, was for political parties to be made accountable to public opinion; the party responsible for governing would need to move the government in the direction endorsed by the public will.[53] Wilson became more specific in 1886, when he complained that parties in America failed to stand up for clear ideas, and therefore the two parties did not offer the people two clear alternatives. This situation needed to change if elections were to become determinative of national policy. Wilson lamented that "a man must nowadays either belong to a party through mere force of habit, or else be puzzled to know what party he belongs to. Party platforms furnish no sort of chart by which he can shape his political course. Unless they are carefully labeled, he cannot tell which party speaks through them, for they all say much the same thing."[54] This is partly why Wilson admired Edmund Burke, whom Wilson praised for his loyalty to his party: in spite of the fact that Burke's party was primarily in the opposition and its leaders treated him poorly, he remained devoted to it. Wilson characterized Burke's devotion to his party as intellectual; Burke was devoted to its ideas, and this is the trait that Wilson believed essential if American parties were to be held accountable to public opinion.[55]

Public opinion could be brought most directly to bear on government if there were only two parties, each proposing to the public a clear and distinct direction for endorsement or rejection. An electoral victory for one of the parties could then be seen as a mandate from the public for the party members—regardless of the particular branch of government to which they belonged—to cooperate in implementing the party platform. Wilson's preference for such a two-party system was one of many reasons why England was to be contrasted favorably to France. While he admired certain elements of the French National Assembly—particularly that it adopted the form of cabinet government—Wilson complained that it had far too many parties, each representing a rather narrow perspective. French politics, therefore, offered no clear choice to the voters.[56] Even as late as 1907, Wilson was still complaining that the parties in America had not yet presented two distinct visions for the public's electoral endorsement. "It is manifest that we must adjust our legal and political principles to a new set of conditions which involve the whole moral and economic make-up of our national life," Wilson contended, "but party platforms are not yet clearly differentiated, party programs are not yet explicit for the voter's choice."[57]

In order for parties to become accountable to public opinion, they had to operate under recognizable and accountable leaders. This is how the early Wilson understood a reformed party system as integral to his vision of congressional government. Members of Congress and their parties needed to be held accountable for the policies they pursued. Such accountability required that the public be able to scrutinize congressional debates, see party leaders taking clear stands of principle in those debates, and endorse or reject those principles through elections. Such was the origin of Wilson's complaints about the Speaker of the House, whom Wilson believed should take on a much higher profile so that, though him, the public could hold the majority party in Congress accountable. The problem with American government was that it was "leaderless"; a reformed party system, therefore, must rely upon the emergence of identifiable leaders.[58]

Under such leaders, a new party system could arise. The new system would feature leaders with great oratorical skill—leaders whose participation in national debate would attract the public's attention and bring the public into closer connection with national policymaking. Debates in Congress could feature opposing party leaders who would eloquently articulate the principles of their respective parties. The public, attracted to these open and grand debates, would direct Congress by endorsing the principles outlined by these party leaders. The current state of affairs indicated to Wilson that such a reform had not even begun to take root: "Eight words contain the sum of the present degradation of our political parties: *No Leaders, No Principles; No Principles, No Parties.* Congressional leadership is divided infinitesimally; and with divided leadership there can be no great party units."[59] Yet the young Wilson had a plan for how government could be turned around, and his plan centered on the entrance into politics of a university-trained class of men, men whose oratorical skills would dwarf those of the petty legislative tacticians who had served as lawmakers for most of the nineteenth century. These young oratorical leaders would rise above the narrowness of partisan politics to lead their parties on the basis of broad principle or vision about the future direction of the nation. Wilson saw such men as the saviors of both the party system and American government itself:

> If the thirty thousand young men who are pursuing studies at the different colleges of this country would endeavor to throw off the party spirit which has been rooted in their natures by education and would undertake to study each political question for themselves, forming their opinions intelligently and independently, and would, moreover, strive to uphold and advance in every way within their power the principles which they have accepted only after mature consideration, there would be little to fear concerning America's future.[60]

As it stood, Wilson reasoned that the party system suppressed leadership. Party officials, desiring to preserve control over members of Congress, would resist any attempt by a gifted young leader to stick his head above the crowd, expound on principles with brilliant oratory, and attract public support to himself and to his party. According to Wilson, party officials resisted this because it would put elected leaders in charge of parties, as opposed to maintaining the dominance of party bosses. A "responsible" party system of the kind that Wilson envisioned would, by contrast, make parties accountable by ensuring that those who led them would have to stand or fall in the court of public opinion.[61] His plan for "congressional government" was one where the majority party governed the legislature and the executive in a coordinated fashion, and did so on the basis of public support that was to be garnered by the oratorical skills of the party's leaders in the legislature.

The Party in the Service of Presidential Government

As previously explained, Wilson moved away from his emphasis on parliamentary-style modifications to the institutional framework, focusing instead on the leadership of the president as a means of both connecting politics more directly to public opinion and enabling political leadership to overcome the separation of powers and mobilize the whole of government in a unified direction. Just as parties were essential to his parliamentary plan, they were also essential to Wilson's conception of presidential government; they were to be the tools or device by which the presidential leader superintended the whole of government and led it in the direction mandated by the public will—or at least his interpretation of the public will. It must be emphasized here that just as Wilson's shift in focus from congressional to presidential government constituted a change in means as opposed to ends, such is also the case with his understanding of parties. The party system remained, for Wilson, a chief means of national leadership.[62]

The connection that Wilson made between his vision for strong presidential leadership and his vision for a reformed party system appears primarily in *Constitutional Government*. As Wilson stated in that work's extensive discussion of presidential leadership and political parties, the leader needs to "make parties his instruments" in exercising disciplined control over the whole machinery of government.[63] No one part of the government— including its chief executive—could exercise enough control on its own without the aid of party discipline. As Wilson argued: "Not the authority of Congress, not the leadership of the President, but the discipline and zest of parties, has held us together [and] has made it possible for us to form and to carry out national programs."[64] The ideal for Wilson was the coordination in government exhibited in parliamentary systems, where the legislature and executive were engaged in a common effort to achieve a common party goal. The general view of Wilson on the role of parties, then, was that parties needed to be prominent, strong, and disciplined in the governing process—not as *masters* over the leader, however, but as his effective *instruments* or *tools* of leadership.

The legal system of the founders had served to isolate the various officials of government in their respective departments, and so Wilson reasoned that such a formal system could have been "solidified and drawn" into a coherent whole only "by the external authority of party." Precisely because parties stood outside the formal system of government, they were not affected by the forced fragmentation of the founders' constitutionalism. As Wilson wrote: "There must, therefore, be an exterior organization, voluntarily formed and independent of the law, whose object it shall be to bind [the branches] together in some sort of harmony and cooperation. That exterior organization is the political party."[65] The development of political parties is an important piece of the historical framework within which Wilson placed the progress of American politics. For Wilson, history had made parties necessary. History had brought about circumstances that could not be effectively addressed by the formal, fragmented system of the founders. And so the rise of parties in America as an extraconstitutional governing force was simply a natural consequence of history, which had placed parties in a role that led Wilson to characterize them as "instruments for progressive action" and the "means for handling the affairs of a new age."[66]

It is also important to keep in mind that Wilson's historical argument about America's progress led to his criticism of federalism, and a strong party system was an important means of overcoming the decentralization of authority that is at the heart of federalism. Wilson contended that the force of history had changed America from a disorganized collection of particular and local interests into a whole, organic nation. There was now, Wilson believed, a unified, national sentiment, or national will. This national will was embodied in the national government, which meant that it had been transformed by history into the organic whole of what Wilson called "the state." The decentralized forms of the Constitution's federalism, consequently, needed the external, extraconstitutional coordination and discipline of political parties if America were truly to overcome "localism" or "provincialism" in favor of "the nation." Wilson made this argument in *Constitutional Government*, where he remarked that without parties, "it would hardly have been possible for the voters of the country to be united in truly national judgments upon national questions." He commented that "it would be hard to exaggerate the importance of the nationalizing influence of our great political parties."[67] The division of political authority among the municipal, state, and federal levels, and the variety of elections required at each level, would make it impossible for the nation to come together as a whole without the unifying force of parties. Parties excel, Wilson reasoned, at a unified mastery of detail and personnel, or, as Wilson described it, "their control of the little tides that eventually flood the great channels of national action."[68]

Because of the ability of political parties to overcome both federalism and separation of powers, Wilson promoted strong and disciplined parties that would be involved in governing. It is for this reason that, unlike some other progressives (Herbert Croly and Theodore Roosevelt, in particular), Wilson was not a forceful advocate of removing local politics from the realm of partisanship or even national party affiliation. While Wilson admitted that it might be "desirable" to "separate matters of local administration from . . . choice of party" or to "obtain nonpartisan local political action," he concluded that such efforts were ultimately unworkable and would fail. Such nonpartisan local efforts would lead parties to lose "form and discipline altogether" and would undermine the unity and coordination that the system desperately needed from parties. Even local political machines, Wilson admitted, "whatever their faults and abuses," were "absolutely necessary . . . for keeping the several segments of parties together. No party manager could piece local majorities together and make up a national majority, if local majorities were mustered upon nonpartisan grounds."[69]

It is in connecting Wilson's view of political parties to his argument on the electoral system that we come to what seems to be a key paradox: Wilson wanted strong parties to play a prominent role in governing for the reasons that have been described, yet as his thinking evolved on this issue, he wanted to have parties and party leaders play a much subordinated role in candidate selection. The problem with parties, as Wilson saw it, was not in their strength or the prominence of their role in governing; instead, it was that parties were not nearly responsible enough to the public will. Precisely because the party system had grown up independent of and external to the formal institutions of government, party leaders were not subject to the same electoral accountability as public officials. And so with these two separate entities—the extraconstitutional party system on the one hand and the formal institutional system on the other—there was a situation that Wilson described as "the irresponsible dictating to the responsible." Under such a bifurcated arrangement, the people "have virtually no control at all over nominations for office, and . . . having no real control over the choice of candidates, they are cut off from exercising real representative self-government."[70]

This observation is what eventually led Wilson to lose confidence in party machines and nominating conventions, and to encourage more strongly the use of the primary for candidate selection.[71] Wilson's advocacy of a shift in the operation of parties is recounted in Ceaser's book *Presidential Selection*, where Ceaser connects the implementation of Wilson's vision for parties to a broader transformation in the nature of American politics. Ceaser contends that the nineteenth-century party system served to guard against the potential excesses of democracy. It maintained a distance between presidential candidates and the people, thus reducing the risk of demagoguery by discouraging candidates from resorting to the popular arts. By retaining significant control over the nomination process, party leaders ("regulars") constituted a powerful check on the presidency. It is precisely this control by party regulars—the "irresponsible," to use Wilson's term—as opposed to the people themselves that Wilson, in his vision for party reform, wanted to overturn.[72]

Wilson's call for taking the parties out of the hands of the bosses and placing them under the control of the candidates and those who support them becomes manifest in his reflections on the New Jersey governorship. Wilson was involved in fighting the Senate candidacy of James Smith, the Democratic boss of Newark, and promoting instead the winner of the nonbinding Democratic primary. The contest, Wilson explained, came down to a fundamental question:

> Does the Democratic party consist of a little group of gentlemen in Essex county? . . . Of whom does the Democratic party consist? The Democratic party does not consist in any portion of any organization; it consists of the men who vote the Democratic ticket. Organizations are instruments—instruments to serve the people or take the consequences.[73]

Wilson even referred at one point to the condition of the voters of New Jersey as "slavery" to the party bosses. The public, he reasoned, was not able to effect its will in state government because it could not hold the parties accountable at the ballot box.[74]

The campaign against party machines and for the institution of the primary was Wilson's way of merging the two key elements of governing—the informal party system and the formal institutional system—in a manner more responsible to the public. America was unique, Wilson observed, in that the party system was a "distinct authority outside the formal government." This situation led to a uniquely American distinction between the "politician" (by which Wilson meant the party manager) and the "statesman" (by which he meant the public official).[75] For Wilson, the next step for the party and selection system was to meld the politician and the statesman together into the single person of the *leader*. In this way, the corruption of unaccountable party managers could be eliminated and the strength and discipline of the party system put into the service of a responsible leader. The president, with his formal electoral connection to the national will, was the natural choice to both coordinate the government and manage the party. Through the president as both party manager and leader of the government, Wilson aimed to inject the strength, discipline, and coordination of the external party system much more directly into the formal governing process. This needed to be our aim, Wilson argued, if we were "ready to make our legislatures and our executives our real bodies politic, instead of our parties," and if we were willing to "think less of checks and balances and more of coordinated power, less of separation of functions and more of the synthesis of action."[76] And so by uniting the states-man and the politician in the person of the popular leader, Wilson hoped to accomplish two goals: first, to take advantage of party unity and discipline in order to help overcome separation of powers and federalism; and second, to make parties more responsible and less corrupt by bringing them into gov-ernment and making them accountable to public opinion through a modified candidate selection process.

As a matter of practice, how did Wilson pursue this vision of a reformed party system once he came into political power? As New Jersey governor, Wilson pushed for passage of the Geran Bill, which established direct pri-maries for governor, members of Congress, and state party committees. He fought with leaders in his own party over the bill, especially state party head James Richard Nugent. Wilson claimed that as the top state officeholder who had won the electoral support of the people, he had the right to set the party's legislative agenda, whereas Nugent claimed that Democratic officeholders had to answer to the organization itself.[77] As president, Wilson exercised firm control over the Democratic Party, using that control to move the government as a whole to adopt his policies. Link proclaims that "few presidents in Amer-ican history established so complete and far-reaching a control over political parties as did Woodrow Wilson during the first years of his tenure at the White House." Yet Wilson employed the traditional patronage practices to make the Democratic Party a tool for his leadership. Link explains that Wil-son initially talked about favoring progressive Democrats over the old con-servatives who had opposed his nomination. But he quickly realized that, if he wanted to win the cooperation of Democrats in Congress for his legisla-tive agenda, he would have to dole out patronage according to the wishes of the conservatives.[78]

One question that we might raise about Wilson's view of parties and selec-tion, and about his desire, on the one hand, for strong parties in governing and, on the other, for subordinated parties in candidate selection, is whether or not such a combination is feasible. Wilson himself realized that this is an important question, one that he answered confidently by asserting that "the time is at hand when we can with safety examine the network of party in its detail and change its structure without imperiling its strength."[79] Wilson did not worry that removing candidate selection from the hands of party leader-ship and placing it in the hands of the public through the primary process would undermine party discipline and cohesion. For Wilson, history had re-solved the unity issue. That is to say, history had brought the American nation to the point where there was a fundamentally unified public will. All that was necessary, therefore, was for that unified will to be left free to direct parties at the candidate-selection level, and then for the popular leader to use strong party discipline in governing as a means of moving in a coordinated way the otherwise fragmented system of the framers.

The issue all of this raises, both for Wilson and for analysts of contemporary politics, is how the leader can exert party discipline in governing while the party itself has a much diminished control over candidate selection. It seems fair to surmise that one of the reasons why the twentieth century has witnessed an erosion of the party strength that Wilson admired is precisely that parties have lost all real control over the candidate-selection process. This perhaps explains why Wilson emphasized the personal and charismatic traits of the president as popular leader. With the weakening of party discipline, the one way in which today's leaders can coordinate and move government is through popular rhetoric. The Wilsonian roots of this practice are examined in the following chapter.

Wilson's Vision of Parties: An Evaluation

A two-party system, properly reformed, was for Wilson a key means of national progress. Wilson's progressive account of the American nation, discussed in the early part of this book, requires that the role of government constantly adapt and change in order to keep pace with the evolving demands of history. A properly functioning party system is vital to this account of government because responsible parties under a popular leader are a tool for facilitating the changes demanded by the historically conditioned will of the people. The paradox here, as the next chapter will more fully explain, is that Wilson wanted to rely upon genuine party competition, yet he simultaneously maintained the position that history had brought about a fundamental unity in American national will. In an important essay on the nature of the American party system, Harry V. Jaffa explains how an understanding of parties that coincides with Wilson's view departs in an important way from the early American political tradition. While Jaffa does not specifically point to Wilson, his account of the traditional American view of parties is very much an indictment of Wilson's vision.

As Jaffa explains, the founding generation was generally wary of parties, but it is more accurate to say that it was wary of a particular kind of partisanship. Partisan competition among those who subscribed to the fundamental principles of the regime could be healthy, and so George Washington, for example, was not nearly as alarmed by the likes of James Madison and Thomas Jefferson as he was by some of the more radically partisan newspaper editors such as Benjamin Bache (*Aurora*) or John Fenno (*Gazette of the United States*). The kind of partisanship that was decidedly unhealthy from the perspective of the founding generation was precisely the kind of partisanship advocated by Wilson—that is, a partisanship that was a means of changing the fundamental principles of the regime and the basic understanding of the role of government. For Wilson, parties were of no use unless they served as tools for escaping the narrow constitutionalism of the founding generation. But Jaffa points out that a party system was healthy, from the founders' perspective, only to the extent that all sides were citizens of the same regime, which is to say that all sides were dedicated to government on the basis of majority rule circumscribed by the more fundamental duty of securing the natural rights of all individuals. For a party to serve as a potential means of departing from this original understanding of the purpose of government would have been viewed as highly pernicious.[80] On the basis of this distinction between healthy and unhealthy partisanship, Jaffa argues that the partisanship of Jefferson and Jackson was healthy, because it had as its end the restoration of original constitutional government.[81] The partisanship of Wilson, by contrast, had, as its aim, distancing the nation from the constitutionalism of 1787—an aim about which Wilson was abundantly clear and unapologetic.

In relying on a reformed two-party system as a key instrument for progress, Wilson was, of course, employing decidedly different means from other progressives who shared his understanding of the ends of government. In Wilson's public life, this was most famously true of his differences with Herbert Croly and Theodore Roosevelt, two prominent progressives who were also notorious critics of Wilson's partisanship. In the conclusion, I will explain why much more is made of these differences than is just (these progressives differed on the question of means only). Nonetheless, their differences on the question of whether parties were a tool of progress or an impediment to it were both real and instructive.[82]

Wilson, Croly, and Roosevelt all agreed that progress beyond the narrow constitutionalism of the founding generation was essential, and they also agreed that the strong, centralized leadership of a popular president was the proper means of effecting such progress. The only question was whether or not the two-party system could help the president's progressive leadership or hinder it. As explained above, Wilson saw the party system as a useful tool for the president—the means by which he could both connect to the public will and coordinate the whole of government in a unified direction. Croly and Roosevelt disagreed, contending that parties were simply obstacles to a direct connection between the leader and the people—they were an unnecessary and pernicious intermediate step between public opinion and the president. And while they agreed with Wilson that parties as they existed in the nineteenth century were corrupt and undemocratic, they did not share Wilson's belief that the system could be reformed and put to good use. The 1912 platform of Roosevelt's Progressive Party, for example, devotes an entire plank to "old parties," denouncing both of the traditional parties as irredeemably corrupt and as permanent barriers to democratic progress.[83] The platform endorses the various mechanisms of direct democracy that were designed to circumvent not only traditional governing institutions but also traditional partisanship itself.

Croly labeled Wilson's vision of parties "Jeffersonian." And while chapter 7 will explain why the Jeffersonian-Hamiltonian distinction did not amount to much, Croly was certainly using fighting words by employing the "Jeffersonian" label against Wilson. Croly meant by the allusion that Wilson's desire to maintain the party apparatus would inhibit centralized administrative power. In his book *Progressive Democracy*, Croly argued for the complete elimination of parties and partisanship from American politics, while maintaining the temporary usefulness of the Progressive Party as a means of achieving progressive aims under the current legal system of partisan competition. To Croly, Wilson failed to see that partisanship detracts from the loyalty that individual citizens must be encouraged to give to the state. Karl Marx had understood religion and property as private attachments that impeded individual devotion to the common will,[84] and Croly saw partisanship as just such a private attachment. Partisanship, Croly explained, "demands and obtains for a party an amount of loyal service and personal sacrifice which a public-spirited democrat should lavish only on the state." Croly also shared Roosevelt's objection that parties interpose themselves as mediators between the people and the national government.[85]

Wilson's doctrine of responsible party government, with its placement of parties at the very center of progressive political reforms, could not have been more at odds with the antiparty crusading of Croly and Roosevelt. Austin Ranney comments on how much faith Wilson placed in the perfectibility of the party system. Ranney finds fault with the doctrine, especially because Wilson did not, Ranney claims, take into account the role of the judiciary. He notes that the courts play a major role in American politics, yet judges have life tenure and no party accountability. Ranney reasons that this would seem to be a significant impediment to responsible party government.[86] Yet, while Wilson did not necessarily reconcile the role of the judiciary to his doctrine of party government, it is not correct to say that Wilson failed to account for the role of judiciary in American politics.

THE JUDICIARY AS AN AGENT OF PROGRESS

The national judiciary was indeed a part of Wilson's plan for American institutions, and it did fit within his broad vision for using the institutions as means of national progress. There can be no doubt that Wilson looked primarily to executive leadership as the instrument through which progress would be achieved; this is certainly reflected in the overall proportion of his writing dedicated to the executive. There can also be no doubt that the party system was to be a chief tool for the president in leading the nation and the government. While the judiciary—with its life tenure and lack of party accountability—does not fall under the umbrella of the president's partisan control, Wilson nonetheless saw it as an important partner in advancing the nation.

How did Wilson perceive the judiciary? What was it about the judiciary that made him believe it could be an institutional partner in stimulating progress? There are certain indications that have tempted some to portray Wilson's vision of the judiciary as rather conservative or traditional. He did comment negatively, for instance, on the popular election of judges, and seemed to support the federalist contention that life tenure for federal judges was important.[87] Such a position would seem to cut against the general progressive tenet of making governing institutions more directly accountable to the evolving public will. Perhaps this basic point is what the scholar Kent A. Kirwan was thinking of when he wrote that "*Constitutional Government* has [a chapter on the judiciary] that could have been written by the authors of *The Federalist*."[88] Yet the bulk of evidence from *Constitutional Government* suggests otherwise; it suggests, instead, a vision of the national judiciary as a key means of the nation overcoming and progressing beyond the constitutionalism of 1787.

Wilson begins his *Constitutional Government* chapter on the judiciary by proclaiming that the federal courts are central to the maintenance of individual liberty. He casts the judiciary as the keeper of the dividing line between the liberty of the individual and the power of the government. Both sides of the line are legitimate and worthy of defense—that is, the judiciary must not only focus on the liberty of the individual, but also ensure that government has the ability to carry out its proper function. He elaborated:

> The constitutional powers of the courts constitute the ultimate safeguard alike of individual privilege and of governmental prerogative. It is in this sense that our judiciary is the balance-wheel of our entire system; it is meant to maintain that nice adjustment between individual rights and governmental powers which constitutes political liberty.[89]

Put this way, the role of the judiciary is critical for Wilson's vision of progress. There is no question that the government will have to exercise increasing power if Wilson's vision is to be implemented. Therefore, the judiciary, as the arbiter of which governmental powers are legitimate and which cross the line into the sphere of individual liberty, must share in a broad sense the progressive understanding of the proper role of government. If the judiciary adopts too narrow or strict a view of the dividing line between the government and the individual, the nation will remain mired in the narrow constitutionalism of the founding and will be held back from the progress that is essential to national life. Wilson was fully aware of what was at stake:

> The federal government is, through its courts, in effect made the final judge of its own powers. . . . The whole balance of our federal system, therefore, lies in the federal courts. It is inevitable that it should be so. . . . Such a principle constitutes the courts of the United States the guardians of our whole legal development. With them must lie the final statesmanship of control.[90]

Wilson was adamant that if it is to determine which exercises of governmental power are legitimate under the Constitution, the judiciary must read the Constitution broadly. The Constitution must be read through the lens of historicism; its precepts cannot be interpreted to have a static meaning. So, the judiciary must interpret the clauses of the Constitution in accord with the historical spirit of the day—a mode of interpretation where powers that might have been considered illegitimate from the perspective of the founding spirit are considered legitimate in light of historical progress. Wilson made clear that that the judiciary must be willing to allow as constitutional many exercises of governmental power that would have astounded the founding generation:

> The Constitution is not a mere lawyers' document: it is, as I have more than once said, the vehicle of a nation's life. . . . We have read into the Constitution of the United States the whole expansion and transformation of our national life that has followed its adoption. We can say without the least disparagement or even criticism of the Supreme Court of the United States that at its hands the Constitution has received an adaptation and an elaboration which would fill its framers of the simple days of 1787 with nothing less than amazement. The explicitly granted powers of the Constitution are what they always were; but the powers drawn from it by implication have grown and multiplied beyond all expectation, and each generation of statesmen looks to the Supreme Court to supply the interpretation which will serve the needs of the day.[91]

The role of the federal judiciary is, as Wilson conceived of it, to grow and multiply the powers of the federal government to meet the demands of national development. The Constitution must be brought in line with these demands, and it is the job of the judiciary to make the necessary adjustments. Wilson was explicit that what is determinative is not what the Constitution says, but what the times demand. If the times demand something, the Constitution must be read to allow for it. It is the *Constitution* that must prove itself worthy of the times, and the courts "determine . . . the adequacy of the Constitution in respect of the needs and interests of the nation."[92] Wilson easily conceded that his account gave the judiciary an explicitly *political* character—it must be so in order to read from the current spirit the needs of the nation. To conceive of the judiciary differently would be to deny the judiciary's ability to make the Constitution an instrument of progress. "It is true," Wilson admitted of the courts, "that their power is political; that if they had interpreted the Constitution in its strict letter, as some proposed, and not in its spirit . . . it would have proved a strait-jacket, a means not of liberty and development, but of mere restriction and embarrassment."[93] So while Wilson had cast the judiciary as the protector of liberty, liberty itself is understood broadly, just as Wilson had suggested in his interpretation of the Declaration of Independence—that is, it is understood within the context of national development.

In *Constitutional Government*, Wilson praised the federal courts for adopting what might be called a "living" mode of constitutional interpretation. Without it, national progress would have been impossible. This led Wilson to single out for praise the Supreme Court justice whom he believed was responsible for the very broad construction of federal power—John Marshall—and led him to attack the figure whom he most associated with resisting Marshall's progressive interpretation of the Constitution—Andrew Jackson. The Marshall Court's expansive reading of federal power had been a key ingredient to national progress. The court under Marshall had fulfilled Wilson's vision of the judiciary—one where the courts grow and multiply the powers of the federal government. Marshall was able to do this, Wilson reasoned, because he interpreted the Constitution in light of his insight into the spirit of the times—a must for all judges. Wilson cited Marshall for having presided over the courts "during the formative period of our national life." Note that the "formative period" was not the framing of the Constitution itself, but was instead the application of that legal framework to the evolving demands of the nation. Fortunately, from Wilson's perspective, Marshall "saw in [constitutions] not mere negations of power, but grants of power."[94] Unfortunately, Marshall's accomplishments for progress had to withstand the challenge of the reactionary Jackson. Whereas Marshall had multiplied the powers of the federal government by reading into the Constitution the power to charter a national bank, Jackson wanted to turn back the clock on progress by refusing to defer to Marshall's interpretation in *McCulloch v. Maryland*.[95]

Conceived in this way, the judiciary joins the president as an institutional agent of national progress. Presidential leadership remains, of course, the central feature of Wilson's institutional plan. The next chapter takes up the question of the means by which the president connects to public opinion: popular leadership.

NOTES

1. Scot J. Zentner goes so far as to argue that even Wilson's views on executive power do not change significantly. See Zentner, "Liberalism and Executive Power: Woodrow Wilson and the American Founders," *Polity* 26:4 (Summer 1994): 593. Niels Aage Thorsen, in contrast, sees several key differences between *Congressional Government* and *Constitutional Government*, pointing out in particular that the focus of the latter was much more on the changing circumstances of the national economy, and the need to adjust government to these new economic realities. Oddly, Thorsen suggests that most scholars see *Constitutional Government* as a mere continuation of *Congressional Government*, while in fact such a view appears to be the exception rather than the rule. See Thorsen, *The Political Thought of Woodrow Wilson 1875–1910* (Princeton: Princeton University Press, 1988), 199–200.

2. Daniel D. Stid, *The President as Statesman: Woodrow Wilson and the Constitution* (Lawrence: University Press of Kansas, 1998), 36–39. In this last quote, Stid refers to Wilson's "Mr. Cleveland as President," January 15, 1897, in Arthur S. Link, ed., *The Papers of Woodrow Wilson* (hereafter cited as *PWW*), 69 vols. (Princeton: Princeton University Press, 1966–1993), 10:109–13. Quotations from Wilson's writings will be modernized as necessary for grammar and spelling. Emphasis will be in the original unless otherwise specified.

3. Stid, *President as Statesman*, 42–43.

4. Arthur S. Link, *Wilson: The New Freedom* (Princeton: Princeton University Press, 1956), 146.

5. Kendrick A. Clements, *The Presidency of Woodrow Wilson* (Lawrence: University Press of Kansas, 1992), 7. See also John M. Mulder, *Woodrow Wilson: The Years of Preparation* (Princeton: Princeton University Press, 1978), 242.

6. Scot J. Zentner, "President and Party in the Thought of Woodrow Wilson," *Presidential Studies Quarterly* 26:3 (Summer 1996): 674.

7. Wilson, *Constitutional Government in the United States* (New York: Columbia University Press, 1908), 82–85.

8. *Constitutional Government*, 86.

9. Publius, *The Federalist Papers*, ed. Charles R. Kesler and Clinton Rossiter (New York: Mentor, 1999), 51:289.

10. *Constitutional Government*, 135–36.

11. *Constitutional Government*, 139–41.

12. *Constitutional Government*, 102.

13. *Constitutional Government*, 91–95.

14. I am indebted to Joseph M. Bessette for this observation.

15. *Constitutional Government*, 109.

16. *Constitutional Government*, 66–67.

17. *Constitutional Government*, 59. Contrast this view to Jeffrey K. Tulis's argument that almost all nineteenth-century presidents were similar in terms of how they understood the constitutional order and their place in it. See *The Rhetorical Presidency* (Princeton: Princeton University Press, 1987), 61–93.

18. *Constitutional Government*, 67–68.

19. *Constitutional Government*, 54.

20. *Constitutional Government*, 65.

21. *Constitutional Government*, 57.

22. *Constitutional Government*, 59–60.

23. Wilson, *The State* (Boston: D. C. Heath, 1889), 566.

24. "Mr. Cleveland as President," in *PWW* 10:103–4.

25. "Mr. Cleveland as President," in *PWW* 10:113.

26. "A Campaign Address" (lecture, Trenton, NJ, October 3, 1910), in *PWW* 21:229–30. See also the account of this in Arthur S. Link, *Wilson: The Road to the White House* (Princeton: Princeton University Press, 1947), 181.

27. "Interview," May 9, 1911, in *PWW* 23:26.

28. "An Address in Jersey City on Behalf of Commission Government" (lecture, Jersey City, NJ, July 14, 1911), in *PWW* 23:201.

29. "A Statement on the Senatorship," December 8, 1910, in *PWW* 22:153.

30. For examples of this strategy, see To Wilson from Joseph Patrick Tumulty, December 15, 1910, in *PWW* 22:200; Wilson to Mary Allen Hulbert Peck, December 17, 1910, in *PWW* 22:210.

31. Link, *Road to the White House*, 253–55.

32. Wilson to Mary Allen Hulbert Peck, March 13, 1911, in *PWW* 22:501.

33. Editorial remarks, *PWW* 23:vii.

34. Link, *The New Freedom*, 152.

35. Link, *The New Freedom*, 153.

36. Paul Eidelberg, *A Discourse on Statesmanship: The Design and Transformation of the American Polity* (Urbana: University of Illinois Press, 1974), 4, 279, 286.

37. Henry A. Turner, "Woodrow Wilson: Exponent of Executive Leadership," *The Western Political Quarterly* 4 (1951): 97–115; see esp. 97–98, 103–6, 109, 112. For some other early accounts of Wilson that forward certain elements of the "modern presidency" thesis, see Elmer E. Cornwell Jr., *Presidential Leadership and Public Opinion* (Bloomington: Indiana University Press, 1965), 3–6, 32, 42–54; Richard P. Longaker, "Woodrow Wilson and the Presidency," in *The Philosophy and Policies of Woodrow Wilson*, ed. Earl Latham (Chicago: University of Chicago Press, 1958), 67.

38. James W. Ceaser, Glen E. Thurow, Jeffrey K. Tulis, Joseph M. Bessette, "The Rise of the Rhetorical Presidency," *Presidential Studies Quarterly* 11 (Spring 1981): 159. See also 161, 163, 166.

39. Tulis, *The Rhetorical Presidency*, 132–44. In a more recent article, Tulis suggests that the "rhetorical presidency" may have subsided with George H. W. Bush and Bill Clinton. See "Revising the Rhetorical Presidency," in *Beyond the Rhetorical Presidency*, ed. Martin J. Medhurst (College Station: Texas A&M University Press, 1996), 3–14.

40. See Charles R. Kesler, "Separation of Powers and the Administrative State," in *The Imperial Congress*, ed. Gordon S. Jones and John A. Marini (New York: Pharos Books, 1988), 20–40; Kesler, "The Public Philosophy of the New Freedom and the New Deal," in *The New Deal and Its Legacy*, ed. Robert Eden (New York: Greenwood Press, 1989), 155–66; and Kesler, "Woodrow Wilson and the Statesmanship of Progress," in *Natural Right and Political Right*, ed. Thomas B. Silver and Peter W. Schramm (Durham, NC: Carolina Academic Press, 1984), 103–27.

41. Robert Eden, "Opinion Leadership and the Problem of Executive Power: Woodrow Wilson's Original Position," *Review of Politics* 57 (Summer 1995): 483–503; Eden, "The Rhetorical Presidency and the Eclipse of Executive Power: Woodrow Wilson's *Constitutional Government in the United States*," *Polity* (Spring 1996): 357–78.

42. Eden, "Opinion Leadership," 500–503; Eden, "Eclipse of Executive Power," 366–73.

43. Eden, "Eclipse of Executive Power," 376.

44. Stid, *President as Statesman*, 53, 59. Stid does concede that Wilson employed a much more aggressive leadership model in the realm of foreign affairs. See 61–62.

45. David K. Nichols, *The Myth of the Modern Presidency* (University Park: Pennsylvania State University Press, 1994), esp. 13–20.

46. Wilson, *Division and Reunion: 1829–1889* (1893; repr., New York: Longmans, Green, 1901); Wilson, *A History of the American People*, 5 vols. (New York: Harper & Brothers Publishers, 1902).

47. Terri Bimes and Stephen Skowronek, "Woodrow Wilson's Critique of Popular Leadership: Reassessing the Modern-Traditional Divide in Presidential History," *Polity* 29 (Fall 1996): 28–39, 41, 42, 44.

48. *Division and Reunion*, 73.

49. "Government by Debate," December 1882, in *PWW* 2:182.

50. Wilson specifically attacked Stickney's essay "Parliamentary Government in America," published in the October 1879 edition of the *Fortnightly Review*. Stid has an elaboration of Wilson's critique of Stickney, referring also to Stickney's 1879 book, *A True Republic*, where Stickney argued not only for an end to parties but for an end to regular elections. Stickney simultaneously argued for the establishment of a professional administration controlled by the president. Stid, *President as Statesman*, 17–19. Stid also provides an account of the criticism made by antiparty reformers of *Congressional Government*, which journals such as *The Nation* denounced for maintaining a role for parties.

51. "Congressional Government," October 1879, in *PWW* 1:554–55. See also "Government by Debate," in *PWW* 2:210–15.

52. See two entries from Wilson's "Shorthand Diary": November 6, 1876 (in *PWW* 1:221) and November 10, 1876 (in *PWW* 1:224).

53. "Government by Debate," in *PWW* 2:184–85.

54. "Wanted—A Party," September 1, 1886, in *PWW* 5:342.

55. "Edmund Burke: The Man and His Times," August 31, 1893, in *PWW* 8:332–33.

56. "Government by Debate," in *PWW* 2:164–65.

57. "Politics: 1857–1907," July 31, 1907, in *PWW* 17:322.

58. "Leaderless Government," August 5, 1897, in *PWW* 10:302; "Independent Conviction," July 16, 1877, in *PWW* 1:280.

59. "Cabinet Government in the United States," August 1879, in *PWW* 1:507.

60. "Some Thoughts on the Present State of Public Affairs," January 30, 1878, in *PWW* 1:348–49, 353–54.

61. Stid points to an important difference between Wilson's and Burke's view of parties. He explains that, for Burke, parties served as a check on the dangers posed by the independence of statesmen. For Wilson, parties were designed to encourage statesmanship—to offer men the opportunity to lead under a responsible party model. Stid, *President as Statesman*, 18. Austin Ranney also connects the vision of a responsible party system to Wilson's call for new leadership. Ranney, *The Doctrine of Responsible Party Government: Its Origins and Present State* (Urbana: University of Illinois Press, 1954), 30, 32, 38.

62. Ranney makes this point as well, contending that the changes in Wilson's views of the structure of government do not substantially affect how he sees political parties. Responsible parties are, Ranney explains, central to the various institutional proposals that

Wilson made. Ranney, *Responsible Party Government*, 42. See also Zentner's illuminating article, "President and Party." In it, Zentner counters those who see a tension between presidential government and responsible party government. He explains that Wilson's theory of responsible parties is perfectly consistent with the development of centralized executive leadership: "Wilson's aim was to locate leadership of the centralized administrative state in the presidency. His vehicle for bringing about this centralized state structure was a reformed party system. He intended the party to be merely an instrument for presidential leadership." Zentner, "President and Party," 666.

63. *Constitutional Government*, 221–22.

64. *Constitutional Government*, 218.

65. *Constitutional Government*, 204, 207.

66. *Constitutional Government*, 221. As Zentner reasons, the new circumstances brought about by history meant that parties were no longer to be concerned with helping a particular faction secure political victory, but rather to give expression to the unified will of the nation and to facilitate the leadership of that will: "Democracy has now reached the age of maturity. Distinctions of class, race, wealth and, most important, party are now resolved in the common thought and single personality of the nation. The progressive argument presumes that there are no important differences of opinion that must be muted through respect for the constitutional order. For the progressives, the main object of political parties, then, is not to gain public office in order to further a set of political opinions, but to provide the platform from which presidential leaders may interpret the will of the people so that all political differences may be resolved." Zentner, "Caesarism and the American Presidency," *Southeastern Political Science Review* 24:4 (December 1996): 636.

67. *Constitutional Government*, 217.

68. *Constitutional Government*, 207.

69. *Constitutional Government*, 208–9.

70. *Constitutional Government*, 213–14.

71. See, for example, Wilson, *The New Freedom* (New York: Doubleday, Page, 1913), 230.

72. James W. Ceaser, *Presidential Selection: Theory and Development* (Princeton: Princeton University Press, 1979). For Ceaser, even though political parties were not part of the founding design, they served the ends of the founders' constitutionalism. The founders had sought to reduce the risk of demagoguery by instituting the electoral college system. While this system did not operate for long under the founders' original understanding, the party system that eventually took its place served many of the same functions. See, especially, 173–74, where Ceaser explains the evolution of Wilson's views on presidential selection and his intention to discover a way around the inertia that the founders had intentionally built into the system. See also 199, where Ceaser argues that Wilson's new kind of party is a "temporary organization"—one that has no permanent principles to which it makes the candidate conform. Rather, candidates get elected on the basis of the popularity of their personal program, then the party puts itself at the service of that particular program and that particular leader. When a different candidate emerges and garners popular support for a different kind of personal program, the party shifts accordingly.

73. "An Address" (lecture, Jersey City, NJ, January 5, 1911), in *PWW* 22:297.

74. *The New Freedom*, 27.

75. *Constitutional Government*, 211–12.

76. *Constitutional Government*, 221.

77. "A Statement on the Geran Election Reform Bill," February 15, 1911, in *PWW* 22:430; "A Statement about an Altercation with James Richard Nugent," March 20, 1911, in *PWW* 22:512.

78. Arthur S. Link, "Woodrow Wilson and the Democratic Party," *Review of Politics* 18 (April 1956): 146–56; repr. in Link, *The Higher Realism of Woodrow Wilson and Other Essays* (Nashville, TN: Vanderbilt University Press, 1971), 60, 62–68. See also Stephen Skowronek, *Building a New American State: The Expansion of National Administrative Capacities, 1877–1920* (Cambridge: Cambridge University Press, 1982), 175, 211. Here Skowronek explains that early in the Wilson presidency, party and administrative development went hand in hand—that is, partnership with his party helped Wilson to enact the legislation that expanded national administration. Later, however, the bureaucracy and the party became competitors.

79. *Constitutional Government*, 220.

80. Harry V. Jaffa, "The Nature and Origin of the American Party System," in *Political Parties U.S.A.*, ed. Robert A. Goldwin (Chicago: Rand McNally, 1961), 67–68.

81. Jaffa, 71–72.

82. William J. Crotty traces contemporary developments in the party system to their roots in the American tradition. He distinguishes between the "nihilists"—like those in the progressive movement who wanted to eliminate parties—and the "idealists." Idealists like Wilson (along with Henry Jones Ford, Stephen Bailey, and E. E. Schattschneider) saw parties as perfectible, with the potential to play a key role in political reform. Crotty explains that the idealist position culminated in 1950 with the report by the Committee on Political Parties of the American Political Science Association, under the direction of Schattschneider, which proposed various ways of effecting a more responsible two-party system. Crotty, "The Philosophies of Party Reform," in *Party Renewal in America: Theory and Practice*, ed. Gerald M. Pomper (New York: Praeger Publishers, 1980), 32–35. For another assessment of the impact of progressivism on political parties, see Wilson Carey MacWilliams, "Parties as Civic Associations," in Pomper, ed., *Party Renewal in America*, 62.

83. 1912 Progressive Party Platform, in *National Party Platforms, 1840–1972*, ed. Donald Bruce Johnson and Kirk H. Porter (Urbana: University of Illinois Press, 1973), 175–76.

84. See, for example, Karl Marx, *On the Jewish Question*, in *Karl Marx: Selected Writings*, ed. Lawrence H. Simon (Indianapolis: Hackett Publishing Company, Inc., 1994), 16. See also Marx and Friedrich Engels, *The Communist Manifesto*, in *Marx: Selected Writings*, 170–73.

85. Herbert Croly, *Progressive Democracy*, ed. Sidney A. Pearson, Jr. (1914; repr., New Brunswick, NJ: Transaction Publishers, 1998), 341. Sidney M. Milkis discusses the distinction between Wilson's partisanship and Croly's antipartisan crusade. Milkis focuses on Croly's critique of parties as a means of showing how Franklin Roosevelt governed differently from Wilson. Franklin Roosevelt, Milkis explains, essentially shared Wilson's aims, but seems to have reached Croly's conclusion that such progressive aims could not be accomplished by depending principally on the party system. In other words, Franklin Roosevelt, like Croly, saw a fundamental tension between partisanship and effective national administration. Wilson, by contrast, espoused a "false hope for partisanship." Milkis, *The President and the Parties: The Transformation of the American Party System*

Since the New Deal (New York: Oxford University Press, 1993), 32–34. More recently, Milkis explains how Wilson differed from other progressives on the party question: "Progressives such as Woodrow Wilson, hoping to combine progressive reform and grassroots democracy, looked to the transformation rather than the demise of the party system. He called for the creation of a more national and programmatic party system capable of carrying out platforms and proposals presented to the people during the course of an election." For Theodore Roosevelt and Croly, by contrast, "public opinion would reach fulfillment with the formation of an independent executive power, freed from the provincial, special, and corrupt influence of political parties and commercial interests." Milkis, *Political Parties and Constitutional Government* (Baltimore: The Johns Hopkins University Press, 1999), 8–9, 43.

86. Ranney, *Responsible Party Government*, 47.

87. For example: "Marginal Notes on *The Federalist on the New Constitution*," February 1880, in *PWW* 1:601.

88. Kent A. Kirwan, "Historicism and Statesmanship in the Reform Argument of Woodrow Wilson," *Interpretation* (September 1981): 346.

89. *Constitutional Government*, 142–43.

90. *Constitutional Government*, 157.

91. *Constitutional Government*, 157–88.

92. *Constitutional Government*, 167.

93. *Constitutional Government*, 167–68. For a similar conception of the judiciary, see "Notes for Lectures in a Course on Constitutional Government," September 19, 1898, in *PWW* 11:26. Wilson contended there that "the object of constituting men judges is . . . to make the interpretation of the law adjust itself to the major purposes of government."

94. *Constitutional Government*, 159, 168.

95. *Constitutional Government*, 160.

Chapter Six

Who Governs? Wilson's Leadership Doctrine and the Question of Democracy

The preceding chapters have discussed Wilson's plan for the rearrangement of American political institutions. Operating under the general framework of separating politics and administration, Wilson envisioned a weakened Congress, more energy and power for the president, and greater freedom of movement for the bureaucracy. The presidency is brought closer to popular opinion, while the bureaucracy is insulated from it. So who is it that governs? Is it the people, whom a strong president dependent upon their will would seem to empower, or is it the bureaucratic experts, who are shielded from the meddling of politics and public opinion as they carry out the business of administration? The answer seems to lie in an important characteristic of Wilson's thought and in much of progressivism: the rhetoric is intensely popular and democratic, yet the reality of the argument is to put political power in the hands of governing elites who possess advanced knowledge of the spirit of the age and the course of history. This model applies to both sides of the politics-administration dichotomy, although most obviously to administration. Wilson reasoned that government can be administered in a businesslike or professional manner only if it is largely removed from politics and public opinion. But it is also the case, on the politics side of the politics-administration divide, that Wilson's strong presidency does not allow for as much popular connection to actual governing as might first be believed. Each of these sides will be treated in the next two chapters: chapter 7 will address the extent to which the influence of public opinion is weakened by the ceding of significant governing authority to an unelected bureaucracy; the current chapter will address the politics side of the divide, posing the question of how democratic Wilson's political vision actually is. To answer this question, we must address Wilson's estimation of the people, and how this estimation fits into his doctrine of political leadership.

It is certainly true that Wilson's famous chapter on the presidency in *Constitutional Government* emphasizes the president's connection to the people. Yet Wilson's president seems to serve not merely as a follower of the public's will but as its potential shaper and leader. The president, who is to lead the political arm of government, is a force that will see to it that the government adapts to the spirit of the times and the interests of the current age. The president must interpret the spirit of the age, and in so doing must bring along not only the other institutions of government but also the people themselves. Wilson wrote that the president will be "a man who understands his own day and the needs of the country, and who has the personality and the initiative to enforce his views both upon the people and upon Congress." The president, if he is to be a true national leader, perceives the contemporary spirit (and what it requires of government) more clearly than do the people themselves. The public trusts the vision of the president to be the best interpretation of the contemporary spirit; the president will have a "knowledge of [the public's] needs" and a "perception of the best means by which those needs may be met." The president's position of leadership gives him the "capacity to prevail" over the public who "believes in a man." So the president is not simply a means for raw popular opinion to gain more of an active voice in governing; as Wilson wrote, "A president whom [the country] trusts can not only lead it, but form it to his own views." Such a president leads by "giving direction to opinion."[1] When Wilson writes at the beginning of *Constitutional Government* that a constitutional government is "one whose powers have been adapted to the interests of its people,"[2] it turns out that the president will be responsible for putting forth a strong and independent vision of what those interests are. Such a role for the president is the institutional manifestation of Wilson's long-held doctrine of leadership.

THE ROLE OF PUBLIC OPINION

To say that Wilson's doctrine of leadership is "popular" is hardly groundbreaking, but what is the nature of this popular leadership? Is the purpose of encouraging a more direct connection between the leader and public opinion merely to enable the people to have a stronger voice in governance? While this is so on one level, it is not accurate to say that Wilson simply trusted raw public opinion and, accordingly, encouraged popular leadership as a means of giving public opinion pride of place in the American system. It is more accurate to say that Wilson's leader was to govern in accord with his "interpretation" of the public will. Yet Wilson clearly believed that the public, most often, did not understand what its true will or spirit actually was. It was the job of political leadership to discern it, and to educate, form, and guide public opinion in accord with the leadership's own vision of the public's true will. This is a central irony in Wilson's political thinking: while his rhetoric pushed for a popularization of the American system of governance, Wilson did not maintain a terribly high opinion of the people themselves. Hence, his calls for popularizing the "politics" half of the politics-administration dichotomy rely heavily on the ability of leadership to educate and move the public through political rhetoric. The public will is to govern, but only insofar as it is led by educated elites who see more clearly than anybody else where that will is actually going.

Universal Suffrage

Wilson's treatment of universal suffrage illustrates that his doctrine of popular leadership is not necessarily democratic. The young Wilson, in particular, complained bitterly about the ills of universal suffrage. In one note, he remarked that the practice seemed contrary to wise tradition:

> Is the principle of universal suffrage for instance consistent with those principles of government which bear the sanction of the wisest Englishmen of eight centuries and which have secured personal freedom and political liberty to a great nation for more than eight hundred years? Is it necessary or even compatible with the healthy operation of a free government?[3]

He went on to reason that the public might be made capable of practicing the universal franchise if it could be educated and led by properly trained orators, and the existence of such orators is one of the many features he admired about the British system: "The English people were then educated in their political rights and in principles of state-craft much as were the Athenian people—by direct instruction from popular orators."[4] In his reflections on the public's inability to know its own true mind, and in his corresponding critique of universal suffrage, Wilson mirrored arguments offered in Walter Bagehot's book on the English constitution. Bagehot explains that for popular government to be good government, the people must at least have enough sense to recognize that that they should be ruled by someone wiser than they are, and to consent to such rule. He elaborates upon this point by contending that the best popular governments need to be "deferential"—that is, the people must freely consent to the rule of educated elites.[5]

The young Wilson went so far as to remark in one note that "universal suffrage is at the foundation of every evil in this country."[6] But when addressing the question for his essay "Cabinet Government in the United States," Wilson was more measured. He acknowledged again the great weakness of universal suffrage, but also suggested that it was only part of a systemic problem in American government:

> While it is indisputably true that universal suffrage is a constant element of weakness, and exposes us to many dangers which we might otherwise escape, its operation does not suffice alone to explain existing evils. Those who make this the scapegoat of all our national grievances have made too superficial an analysis of the abuses about which they so loudly complain.[7]

And, to be sure, Wilson dropped his overt opposition to universal suffrage as he matured. His faith in the progress of history led him to believe that the public was capable of governing, if only it could be properly prepared and led. Educating the public is, therefore, an essential part of leadership. This is at the root of Wilson's frequent despair over his native South. As long as southern leaders failed to properly educate the people, there would be no progress in the South, and universal suffrage would continue to be a great evil.[8] His critique of universal suffrage is also important to understanding his hostility to populism. The populist movement, as Wilson understood it, was a movement of mass public opinion, but lacked the necessary education by and guidance of elite leadership.

Direct Democracy

The notion that the people need to be educated and guided by elite leadership is also relevant to understanding Wilson's view of direct democracy, which became a significant issue in the latter stages of his career. It was a hallmark of certain parts of the progressive movement to push for such measures as the ballot initiative, the referendum, and the recall—particularly at the state and local levels. Wilson himself was lukewarm toward such proposals, although he expressed more support for them as he grew older. Wilson's criticism of the referendum, which he puts forth in *The State*, typifies his early view of direct democracy. He worried that the people were not sufficiently educated to make policy decisions directly, without the guidance of leadership, and he commented that direct democracy "assumes a discriminating judgment and a fullness of information on the part of the people touching questions of public policy which they do not often possess."[9] In 1895, Wilson seemed even more emphatic that the people were not fit to govern directly: "The people should not govern; they should elect the governors: and these governors should be elected for periods long enough to give time for policies not too heedful of transient breezes of public opinion. The power of the people ought to be the power of *criticism* and of choice upon *broad* questions."[10]

When he entered into the national spotlight, Wilson eased his criticisms of direct democracy, although he never suggested that the mechanisms of direct democracy should be adopted as the norm. During the New Freedom campaign, Wilson expressed support for the direct primary and the direct election of U.S. senators. He was less supportive of the ballot initiative, the referendum, and the recall, and he was opposed unequivocally to the recall of judges.

Wilson's advocacy of the direct primary is a logical corollary to his plan for reforming political parties. If parties and party leaders were to be put at the service of candidates as opposed to exercising mastery over them, then the choice of party nominees had to be taken away from the party leadership and placed in the hands of the rank-and-file members. Such a reform would also make the connection between the people and the candidates direct, and this connection would enable a potential leader to employ the rhetorical arts as a means of garnering public support during a primary campaign.[11] The direct election of senators would also place potential leaders in direct contact with public opinion. Wilson mocked the opposition to this proposed change, characterizing it as an antiquated and blind reverence for outdated constitutional forms. "I have seen some thoughtful men discuss [direct election] with a sort of shiver," Wilson said, "as if to disturb the original constitution of the United States Senate was to do something touched with impiety, touched with irreverence for the Constitution itself." He went on to attack the state legislatures as corrupt and, therefore, incapable of implementing the will of the people with regard to the selection of senators.[12]

When discussing the ballot initiative, the referendum, and the recall, the closest Wilson came to expressing outright support for them was to note their usefulness as *temporary* measures, designed to remedy the problems created by unrepresentative and unresponsive institutions. Wilson made clear that the purpose of governing institutions is not to serve as a kind of filter for public opinion, and that the goal is to bring the people in much closer connection to their political leadership. When "something intervenes between the people and the government," Wilson contended, "there must be some arm direct enough and strong enough to thrust aside the something that comes in the way."[13] It is in such cases that the mechanisms of direct democracy might be useful as temporary remedies:

> Let no man be deceived by the cry that somebody is proposing to substitute direct legislation by the people, or the direct reference of laws passed in the legislature, to the vote of the people, for representative government. The advocates of these reforms have always declared, and declared in unmistakable terms, that they were intending to recover representative government, not supersede it; that the initiative and referendum would find no use in places where legislatures were really representative of the people whom they were elected to serve. The initiative is a means of seeing to it that measures which the people want shall be passed—when legislatures deny or ignore public opinion.[14]

Wilson explained that direct-democracy measures are also a good means of circumventing the problem of fixed terms. He had always sympathized with the ability of parliamentary systems to change political leadership at the point when the leadership had lost the support of public opinion. The fixed terms of American officials thwart this kind of flexibility; direct-democracy mechanisms open up possibilities for the public to see its will manifested even in those cases where the traditional institutions are no longer representative of the public mind.[15]

THE ROOTS OF WILSON'S LEADERSHIP DOCTRINE

Wilson's emphasis on the need for public opinion to be educated, guided, and led is consistent throughout all of his scholarship.[16] As early as 1890, when he wrote his essay "Leaders of Men," Wilson called for a popular leader who could succeed on the basis of his ability to move the masses. This doctrine of leadership was carried through to Wilson's later writings emphasizing the presidency as the focal point of American government. Yet the roots of Wilson's thinking on leadership reach deeper than "Leaders of Men." Even the young Wilson, who was interested more in the leaders who would emerge in congressional debate than he was in the presidency, emphasized the need for leaders who could sway public opinion through rhetorical skill. To be sure, the young Wilson looked more to the leadership of so-called literary men— intellectuals who would elevate the public through their grand rhetorical skill. But the fundamental characteristic of leadership was essentially the same to the young Wilson as it was to the author of *Constitutional Government*: a leader must have a vision of where history is moving the public spirit, and he must use the power of his rhetoric to convince the people to follow that vision.

In the earliest records we have of Wilson's writings—those from his days as a college student at Princeton—Wilson was focused on the importance of rhetoric and rhetorical training. Wilson wrote at that time that the aim of rhetoric was "persuasion and conviction—the control of other minds by a strange personal influence and power." He complained that Princeton did not adequately teach rhetoric, and that when rhetoric was taught, it was taught improperly. Rhetoric, Wilson argued, must be seen as a tool—as a means to the practical end of influencing other men's minds. He cited Demosthenes as an example of a figure who should serve as a model for rhetorical study, because Demosthenes, "more than any other orator of ancient or modern times, knew how to sway the human mind."[17] To Demosthenes Wilson added several of the great English orators, particularly William Pitt, the earl of Chatham. Indeed, Wilson offered a clear connection between Pitt and Demosthenes: "Athens had at times responded as one man to the rapid, vehement, cogent sentences of Demosthenes; the British Parliament, the English nation, harkened with glad eagerness to the organ tones of Pitt's eloquence, and dared not disobey."[18]

As Wilson demonstrated with these ancient and modern examples, the ability to motivate men is the central characteristic of leadership. And if America's leaders were to acquire this skill, training in the art of rhetoric needed to be an integral part of university education. Wilson frequently wrote editorials to the Princeton newspaper calling for the establishment of true rhetorical training at the university.[19] Wilson believed that a good portion of the public was ignorant, so leaders hoping to move the people in any particular direction would have to educate the people. In order to educate the people, the future leaders of America had to be properly educated themselves. But this was emphatically not the case with the leaders in Congress as Wilson saw them; he complained of the lack of education among members of Congress, and "the absence from Congress of any considerable body of the country's most promising young men."[20] America was in no position to progress as a nation as long as its leaders had no training or skill in the rhetorical techniques that would be required to move the people down the path that history had laid out.

The examples of leaders the young Wilson cited form a consistent theme: leadership and rhetorical skill are intimately linked. To lead means to move men, and to move men requires rhetoric. In praising William Gladstone, for instance, Wilson contended that he is a model leader precisely because of his abilities as an orator. "It is as an orator," Wilson wrote, "that Mr. Gladstone more forcibly appeals to our imaginations."[21] Wilson's biographical sketch of Gladstone, like several such sketches, emphasized the personality of the leader. Wilson seemed much less interested in the ideas or principles espoused by leaders than he was in their spirit or personality. This is just as true of Wilson's sketches of American leaders as it is of his writings on the British. When Wilson wrote about early Americans, he normally wrote about their personality traits, not their ideas (which, in general, he found outdated). In his early sketches of men who he considered to be great leaders, Wilson also gave special praise to those who could alter their style of rhetoric to fit a particular audience. Gladstone had this ability to play to his audience; he could use grand oratory in parliamentary debate, and he could speak the language of the common man when out on a campaign. As Wilson explained:

> His genius as an orator most conspicuously manifests itself in his power of adapting his style to the audience he is addressing. One day he is speaking to a meeting of the most intelligent and learned members of his constituency, and his style is one of measured calmness, his treatment following the leadings of a

strict, though eloquent, logic. The next day, perhaps, he meets the farmers of the country side upon the hustings, and the style is changed. It is aflame with earnest persuasion and glowing with passionate sentiment. He is speaking like an Englishman to Englishmen, with eager patriotism and a fire of high resolve.[22]

The key is for the leader to know what he must do in order to move whatever audience it is that he happens to be addressing.

In 1890, when Wilson turned to putting his thoughts on leadership into more coherent and sustained form in the essay "Leaders of Men," he emphasized less the parliamentary oratory of the "literary man" and devoted great energy to the "man of action"—to the popular leader who could move the great masses. He feared that the intellectual men might look down upon democracy and upon doing what is necessary to move the average man:

> The true leader of men, it is plain, is equipped by lacking such sensibilities, which the literary man, when analyzed, is found to possess as a chief part of his make-up. He lacks that subtle power of sympathy which enables the men who write the great works of the imagination to put their minds under the spell of a thousand individual motives not their own but the living force in the several characters they interpret.[23]

While Wilson's connection between leadership and rhetoric remained steadfast throughout his writings, his treatment of the topic in "Leaders of Men" and subsequent works placed greater and greater hope in the ability of an individual leader to connect to the public directly. He worried less about improving the quality of rhetoric in Congress, focusing instead on the popular rhetoric of the president.

THE LEADER AS INTERPRETER AND MOVER OF MEN

The basic ideas that constitute Wilson's model of presidential leadership are evident in "Leaders of Men," one of his most important early works.[24] It is in this essay that Wilson explicated that "leadership, for the statesman, is *interpretation*."[25] By emphasizing "interpretation," Wilson distinguished his doctrine of leadership from the classical understanding of statesmanship. Traditionally speaking, the art of statesmanship revolves around practical wisdom, or prudence.[26] A classical statesman combines a knowledge of the right ends with a sober understanding of the conventional circumstances, and the result is the best approximation of the good that can be achieved under those circumstances. The statesman's understanding of right ends does not come from the circumstances or people themselves but from some standard of right that transcends a particular time and place. Wilson's leader, by contrast, takes his direction from the evolving spirit of the people. He therefore "reads up" from the people their will, their spirit. But the leader is not merely an empty vessel, responding to whatever direction the public will happens to give him. This is because the leader often reads the implicit will of the public better than the public itself does. The leader also stands ahead of the people. He "interprets" not only their spirit but the historical direction in which that spirit is moving. The leader, therefore, has a vision of the people's future. As an interpreter, he sees that future more clearly than the people themselves do. The task of Wilson's leader is to formulate a vision of the people's future and to illuminate for them the path to it.[27]

Wilson explained in "Leaders of Men" that the leader sees more clearly than others the "road" that society, as an organism, is traveling on as it develops. He referred to a leader who sees the "direction" of society and who "must discern and strengthen the tendencies that make for development"; he must "perceive the direction of the nation's permanent forces."[28] As Wilson wrote in another essay, a leader must be of the people; he must embody the spirit of the people. But he is also ahead of the people on the path toward progress. "He must," Wilson urged, "come out from among the people and go ahead of them."[29]

Jeffrey Tulis's book, *The Rhetorical Presidency*, devotes an entire chapter to the impact of Wilson's leadership doctrine on the development of the presidency. In explaining Wilson's concept of leadership as "interpretation," Tulis argues that it has two elements. First, the leader must be able to discern the true spirit of the people. The surface of politics is often contentious, with one faction vying against another. Yet Wilson's assumption is that there is a genuine, cohesive public will that lies beneath that surface, and so it is the task of the leader to "interpret" or read that genuine public will. Second, the leader's job entails education—instructing the public, in simple terms, of what it is that it truly desires.[30]

While the primary characteristic for leadership is the talent for "interpretation" of the spirit and future of the people, the leader must also have the ability to persuade the people that his vision of their future is, in fact, their future, and he must be able to mobilize them in that direction. Wilson wrote that, in interpreting, the leader reads the true spirit of the age and then engages in "*preparation* of the nation for the next move in the progress of politics." Society must be made to progress, Wilson explained, because it is organic "and, like every organism, it must grow as a whole or else be deformed."[31] The leader is someone who can articulate his vision of society's direction and move the people accordingly. This is why Wilson's desire to democratize the presidency is an important manifestation of his leadership doctrine. A more democratized presidency is one that is more amenable to the tools of popular rhetoric; it is one where the leader can use his mastery of popular rhetoric to mold public opinion. "The leader of men," Wilson explained, "must have such sympathetic and penetrative insight as shall enable him to discern quite unerringly the motives which move other men *in the mass*."[32] He elaborated that *it is the will of the leader, not the opinion of the masses, that governs*:

> His will seeks the lines of least resistance; but the whole question with him is a question of *the application of force*. There are men to be moved: how shall he move them? He supplies the power; others supply only the materials upon which that power operates. . . . It is the *power* which dictates, dominates: the materials yield. Men are as clay in the hands of the consummate leader.[33]

In order to move men in the mass, the leader does not raise the masses to his level, but rather appeals to what is common to them. Wilson explained that a leader moves men through sympathy—through a demonstration that he shares their sentiments. A leader achieves this sense of sympathy with the people through "simplicity and directness." Leaders, Wilson continued, "give you the fine gold of truth in the nugget, not cunningly beaten into elaborate shapes and chased with intricate patterns." They speak the language of the dominant spirit in a manner that strikes a chord with the masses. "The morality which they seek to enforce," Wilson concluded, "is large and obvious."[34] Ultimately, men in mass behave differently than those same men might behave as individuals. The American founders saw this tendency of human nature as one of the great dangers in democratic government, since a mass could easily be led to act irrationally by "the artful misrepresentations of interested men."[35] Wilson, instead, saw it as an opportunity. Wilson's leader must understand how men behave in mass and use that knowledge to propel them in the direction required by history.

While Wilson's leader moves men by appealing to what is common among them, by sympathizing with them, he himself is not necessarily common. Rather, the leader is more fit to govern than the people themselves; he is distinguished by the vision he has of the future. It is important to keep in mind that it is the *leader's* vision that governs; he must simply convince the people that his vision embodies their future. In his lecture on "Liberty and Government," Wilson defined democracy to include strong, visionary leadership by the few men who have the capacity for it.[36] He elaborated in "The Modern Democratic State":

> Where all minds are awake some minds will be wide awake. And such are the conditions of common counsel: a few minds to originate and suggest, many minds to weigh and appreciate; some to draw up resolutions, many to consider

them. The limitations of the public meeting are the limitations of the nation's deliberations. Not everybody can lead: but everybody can have a voice in deciding results.[37]

It is the role of the leaders to educate the public, so that the public will be more capable of understanding the vision laid out for it. Education must prepare the people for accepting leadership, making it possible for them to consider leadership suggestions.

As an example, Wilson most frequently named Lincoln as the kind of rhetorical leader that he had in mind—at least among American presidents. He contrasted Lincoln to several earlier presidents, especially Jefferson, whom he believed did not sufficiently seek out a close connection to public opinion.[38] Wilson praised Lincoln, by contrast, for serving as a man of the people, for embodying the spirit of the masses. Yet he also praised Lincoln for standing out in front of the masses, for seeing their own will more clearly than they were able to see it themselves:

> A great nation is not led by a man who simply repeats the talk of the street-corners or the opinions of the newspapers. A nation is led by a man who hears more than those things; or who, rather, hearing those things, understands them better, unites them, puts them into a common meaning; speaks, not the rumors of the street, but a new principle for a new age; a man in whose ears the voices of the nation do not sound like the accidental and discordant notes that come from the voice of a mob, but concurrent and concordant like the united voices of a chorus, whose many meanings, spoken by melodious tongues, unite in his understanding in a single meaning and reveal to him a single vision, so that he can speak what no man else knows, the common meaning of the common voice. Such is the man who leads a great, free, democratic nation.[39]

Wilson described Lincoln as the perfect American. Like Jackson, he was a man of the people, and came from the frontier. But unlike Jackson, Lincoln was able to interpret the true spirit of the American people and to understand that the American future was one of nationalization. In this respect, Lincoln was the leader for whom the time was ripe. He was the agent of change the progress of history required: "To the Eastern politicians he seemed like an accident; but to history he must seem like a providence."[40] Displaying the qualities necessary for any modern leader, Lincoln used popular rhetoric to affect the people, to pull them in the direction of his vision for their future. "He was vastly above [the people] in intellectual and moral stature," Wilson wrote of Lincoln. "He gained an easy mastery over them, too, by cultivating, as he did, the directer [*sic*] and more potent forms of speech."[41] In this assessment, it is important to keep in mind (as explained in chapter 1) Wilson's apparent misreading of Lincoln—Lincoln did not promote "a new principle for a new age" but promoted instead a return in his own age to the principles of the founding. Nonetheless, Wilson's commentary on Lincoln is useful in what it reveals about Wilson's own understanding of leadership.[42]

The Problem of Demagoguery

Wilson's leader employs popular rhetoric to move the masses. This approach requires a direct relationship between the leader and the people, one that contradicts a key tenet of the constitutionalism of the American founders. At the constitutional convention of 1787, the delegates considered two options for presidential selection: election by the national legislature, or direct election by the people. They rejected the first option on separation-of-powers grounds, but this did not lead them to adopt the second option. While the argument was not made in direct terms at the convention itself, *The Federalist* explains that direct election was avoided because of the fear that the closer the connection between the people and their leader, the greater the danger of demagoguery. If the founders believed that the greatest threat to self-government was the danger of faction, which was "sown in the nature of man," then they also understood that the manner in which faction was most likely to arise was through the catalyst of demagoguery. The founders well understood the threat posed to a democracy by "the arts of men, who flatter [the people's] prejudices to betray their interests." While insisting that the president must remain faithful to the rational, "deliberate sense of the community," *The Federalist* also urged caution: "It is a just observation that the people commonly *intend* the PUBLIC GOOD. This often applies to their very errors. But their good sense would despise the adulator who should pretend that they always *reason right* about the *means* of promoting it." Such an "adulator"—a flatterer of the people—was precisely the figure the founders had in mind when they feared the havoc a demagogue could wreak on the American experiment with self-government. Accordingly, by establishing such mechanisms as the electoral college and a four-year term of office, the founders sought to create some degree of distance between the president and the immediate pressures of public opinion. Such institutional arrangements would help the president in his ability to avoid "an unqualified complaisance to every sudden breeze of passion, or to every transient impulse that the people may receive" from demagogic leaders who are skilled in the art of rhetoric.[43] Wilson's doctrine of leadership does not seek merely to remove this distance between the president and the people; indeed, it relies for its success upon a direct relationship with the people, and the skillful use of rhetoric to move the people in a particular direction.

Part of the reason that Wilson does not appear to share the founders' fear of demagoguery is that he did not share their permanent or ahistorical understanding of human nature. As explained in the first three chapters, Wilson asserted that human nature improves through the progress of history, and so the threat of faction recedes as time marches on. Demagoguery, then, which feeds on the irrational passions of the people, becomes less of a concern as modern democracy comes into its own. Such reasoning is an important component of Wilson's essay "The Modern Democratic State," in which he explains why modern democracy, unlike classical democracy, is permanent. Demagoguery was a genuine threat to classical attempts at democracy, because the public spirit was not yet historically prepared for genuine self-government. Hence, demagoguery could easily help to establish a tyranny, and this is why the Aristotelian cycle of regimes was an apt framework for analyzing ancient democracy. But modern democracy is different; it is here to stay because it is the ultimate end of history and history has prepared the way for it. The kind of demagoguery about which Wilson was concerned in modern times was the demagoguery that might allow a minority to rule over a majority. There was no concern for what the founders would have called "majority faction"—for the public will being misled by artful men. The kind of demagoguery that Wilson feared might be called "hard demagoguery," leading to what the founders would have called a "minority faction." This is the danger of extreme minority views impeding the progress of genuine democracy.[44] The best way to prevent this phenomenon is, of course, to make the government as popular as possible, and this is a core characteristic of Wilson's modern democratic state. But in spite of the argument that history dissolves the threat of demagoguery in modern democracy, Wilson also understood that he still had to distinguish his own doctrine of leadership from demagoguery, and in "Leaders of Men" he attempted to draw such a distinction.

Wilson conceded in "Leaders of Men" that the difference between his leader and the demagogue is not a difference in the tools that each employs. Both rely upon artful rhetoric, addressed directly to the people, and both seek to move the people through these direct rhetorical appeals. The difference, Wilson explained, is the end for which the popular arts are employed. The demagogue has only his own private gain in mind, whereas Wilson's leader truly discerns the implicit will of the people. The leader's vision is a genuine vision of the people's future, and the leader employs the popular arts both to read the public's will and to convince the people to follow his vision.[45] Wilson also commented that demagoguery proposes ideas that are fleeting, and frequently urges new and perhaps contradictory directions. The people will recognize the genuine vision of a leader because they will see a vision that is durable and lasting.[46]

Wilson's Own Political Rhetoric

The difficulty in discerning the difference between demagoguery and Wilson's doctrine of leadership is illustrated by Wilson's own political rhetoric.[47] His appeals in the New Freedom campaign often bordered on soft demagoguery—

particularly in their flattery of the people. In his speech "Freemen Need No Guardians," Wilson contrasted government by "trustees" or "guardians"—government by those who claim to act *for* the people but act only in their own interest—to his own vision of government, where he would merely be the servant of the people. Wilson came close to denying that he actually had views of his own, emphasizing that the people were his boss and he would simply carry out whatever their instructions happened to be:

> I have listened to some very honest and eloquent orators whose sentiments were noteworthy for this: that when they spoke of the people, they were not thinking of themselves; they were thinking of somebody whom they were commissioned to take care of. They were always planning to do things *for* the American people, and I have seen them visibly shiver when it was suggested that they arrange to have something done by the people for themselves. They said, "What do they know about it?" I always feel like replying, "What do *you* know about it? You know your own interest, but who has told you our interests, and what do you know about them?" For the business of every leader of government is to hear what the nation is saying and to know what the nation is enduring. It is not his business to judge *for* the nation, but to judge *through* the nation as its spokesman and voice.[48]

Wilson's rhetoric here seems in tension with his many statements that the people are not capable of knowing their own mind—that they need education and leadership. Furthermore, as will be explained in the following chapter, much of Wilson's vision of modern administration is predicated on the assumption that there is a certain class of experts who need to be free from political pressure in order to administer progress on behalf of the people. Indeed, in the midst of engaging here in a lengthy criticism of those who purport to act "*for* the American people," Wilson also claimed that the people need someone like him to act on their behalf: "We need some man who has not been associated with the governing classes and the governing influences of this country to stand up and speak for us." The speech sounded so much like demagoguery that Wilson himself found it necessary to deny that quality: "I do not mean anything demagogic."[49]

Other campaign speeches similarly raise the issue of demagoguery. In "Life Comes from the Soil," Wilson again engaged in flattery of the people: "I have found audiences made up of the 'common people' quicker to take a point, quicker to understand an argument, quicker to discern a tendency and to comprehend a principle, than many a college class that I have lectured to."[50] And in "Parliament of the People," Wilson vented that "when I hear a popular vote spoken of as mob government, I feel like telling the man who dares so to speak that he has no right to call himself an American."[51] This Wilson is a far cry from the apparently "un-American" Wilson, who had strong criticism for universal suffrage and proclaimed repeatedly that the people were not capable of governing themselves without extensive guidance.

Leadership and Historicism

For Wilson, the distinction between leadership and demagoguery ultimately comes down to this: the leader reads the true spirit of his age and has a genuine vision of where history is going. As previously explained, the leader sees the people's future more clearly than the people themselves do. This is why the leader may often seem to be isolated; he is out ahead of the people, and must persuade them to follow because there can be no compromise by one who genuinely sees where history is going. In this respect, "Leaders of Men" presents a remarkable foreshadowing of Wilson's own future isolation as a leader:

> Leadership does not always wear the harness of compromise. Once and again one of those great influences which we call a *cause* arises in the midst of a nation. Men of strenuous minds and high ideals come forward, with a sort of gentle majesty, as champions of a political or moral principle. . . . The attacks they sustain are more cruel than the collisions of arms. Their souls are pierced with a thousand keen arrows of obloquy. Friends desert and despise them. They stand alone: and oftentimes are made bitter by their isolation. They are doing nothing less than defy public opinion, and shall they convert it by blows? Yes. Presently, the forces of the popular thought hesitate, waver, seem to doubt their power to subdue a half score stubborn minds. Again a little while and those forces have actually yielded. Masses come over to the side of the reform. Resistance is left to the minority, and such as will not be convinced are crushed.[52]

This account of how a leader moves the public is also remarkably similar to Hegel's account of historical progress in *The Philosophy of History*. While Wilson's leader does not "wear the harness of compromise," Hegel's agent of historical change, the World-Historical Individual, "is not so unwise as to indulge in a variety of wishes to divide his regards. He is devoted to the One Aim, regardless of all else." Under Wilson's leader, "Masses come over to the side of the reform. Resistance is left to the minority, and such as will not be convinced are crushed." Hegel writes of his leader: "So mighty a form" must "crush to pieces many an object in its path."[53] For both Wilson and Hegel, leadership is intimately connected to history, which is an irresistible force of progress. The one crucial difference, of course, is that Wilson's leader has to some degree a vision of where history is going, while Hegel's World-Historical Individual is more of an unconscious tool of world history.

Several of Wilson's early essays reveal this theme of the leader who knows where history is going and who, accordingly, can accept no compromise in bringing the people along toward that end. In one such essay, Wilson explained that a "Christian statesman" is one who sees the true end and fights for it incessantly. The people who follow must either accept his vision of the truth or be considered enemies. "When he does not actively advocate truth," Wilson wrote, "he advocates error. Those who are not for truth are against it. There is here no neutrality."[54] Wilson presses this argument in his essay on John Bright, where he makes clear that prudence is not among the vital qualities of leadership. Instead, politics is all about knowing what history demands and making it happen by maintaining unbending devotion to that true aim. As Wilson remarked, "Tolerance is an admirable intellectual gift: but it is little worth in politics. Politics is a war of *causes*: a joust of principles." Not prudence, but a pure commitment to the cause is the vital characteristic: "Absolute identity with one's cause is the first and great condition of successful leadership."[55]

While there are important differences between Wilson's leader and Hegel's World-Historical Individual, both Wilson and Hegel assert that history itself produces agents of change when the time is ripe, and the historical spirit works through these leaders in order to bring about the next stage in the progress of politics. "Leaders of Men" gives an account of history's "great reformers," explaining that they are "*produced* by occasions. They are early vehicles of the Spirit of the Age." In discussing how history progresses from one epoch to the next, Wilson offered an example that Hegel also used, the Reformation in Germany. Naming this and other examples, Wilson remarked:

> Take what example you please, and in every case what took place was the destruction of an anomaly, the wiping out of an anachronism. Does not every historian of insight perceive the *timeliness* of these reforms? Is it not the judgment of history that they were the products of a period, that there was laid upon their originators, not the gift of creation, but in a superior degree the gift of insight, the spirit of the age? It was theirs to hear the inarticulate voices that stir in the night-watches, apprising the lonely sentinel of what the day will bring forth.[56]

When the time is ripe for change, history produces a swell in public sentiment, and this public sentiment becomes embodied in some clear leader. The leader rides (and perhaps stimulates) this swell in public feeling as a means of effecting the change that the times demand. As Wilson remarked, "Such awakenings of the minds and hearts of whole peoples produced leaders as of course. Great passions, when they run through a whole population, inevitably find a great spokesman. A people cannot remain dumb which is moved by profound impulses of conviction; and when spokesmen and leaders are found, effective concert of action seems to follow as naturally."[57] Changes in history happen for a reason, as part of a plan, and the leaders of change act in accord with that plan. Therefore, a leader's claim to legitimacy is the fact that his vision coincides with the spirit of history.

Wilson referred to his leader as "educated" and "knowledgeable." The leader knows the right principles for which he must strive. Wilson also made clear that the leader's knowledge comes not from some transhistorical or rational comprehension of principle but instead is derived from his ability to see the future:

Across the mind of the statesman flash ever and anon brilliant, though partial, intimations of future events. His prophetic finger points out the true way and he does the deeds of the present in the declining light of the past not only but in the rising dawn of the future as well. That something which is more than fore-sight and less than prophetic knowledge marks the statesman a peculiar being among his contemporaries.[58]

It is precisely because of this vision of the future that the leader can rise above the pull of self-interest. Unlike *The Federalist*, which argues that leaders (like all men) will act, at least to some degree, in accord with their own interest, Wilson's leader is selflessly devoted to the true end. And while *The Federalist* attempts to institutionalize leadership such that duty and interest "coincide,"[59] Wilson saw such a plan as both untenable and unnecessary: "That all the acts of a statesman should be performed without a view to self-interest needs no proof. We have only to look at the results of selfishness to conclude that self-interest and the interest of the state must often clash with and counteract each other when brought in contact."[60]

Wilson's confidence that a leader can rise above the contending forces of self-interest rests on a key assumption: that history gives to the nation a fundamental unity of will. While this unity may not be obvious, lying as it does beneath the clashing of opposing political forces, the true leader can discern or "interpret" the implicit will of the public in spite of the often confusing and contradictory sentiments of public opinion. Wilson showed that this "interpretation" could be formed by turning to the Hegelian model of the executive leader. Wilson even pointed to Frederick the Great of Prussia, who understood the monarchy as the embodiment of the unified public will.[61] Monarchy thus understood serves as a starting point for the ideal executive leader, to which Wilson added the mechanism of election by the people. Wilson's vision of the reformed presidency is grounded in a democratized monarch, whose indivisible will is ideal for representing the unified will of the people. The need for an indivisible leader stems from the reality that public opinion is often fragmented, and therefore requires a leader who can identify the genuine unity of public will that is implicit beneath the contentions on the surface. The public needs to have its own will indicated to it by this indivisible leader: "The many, the people, who are sovereign have no single ear which one can approach, and are selfish, ignorant, timid, stubborn, or foolish with the selfishnesses, the ignorances, the stubbornnesses, the timidities, or the follies of several thousand persons—albeit there are hundreds who are wise."[62] The task of democratic leadership, then, is to show the people that the single will of the ruler is, in fact, their own implicit will:

Whoever would effect a change in modern constitutional government must first educate his fellow-citizens to want *some* change. That done, he must persuade them to want the particular change he wants. He must first make public opinion willing to listen and then see to it that it listen to the right things. He must stir it up to search for an opinion, and then manage to put the right opinion in its way.[63]

Zentner elaborates on the notion of grounding leadership in the single will of the monarch, contending that "Wilson's president is a certain admixture of Hegel's executive and monarch." The key difference between Hegel and Wilson is, of course, that Wilson's leader is popularly elected, whereas Hegel relied upon the monarch's connection to tradition or custom as a means of representing the wholeness or unity of the people's spirit.[64]

There is no question that Wilson's vision for American institutions is popular in character, and that it seeks to reduce drastically the distance between the people and their political leadership that the American founders had built into the system. But while politics becomes more popular, this popularization seems to be accomplished in such a way that the people become more open to government by political elites.[65] In the present chapter, I have endeavored to make this argument by pointing out that the most important political institution to Wilson—the presidency—is made more democratic precisely so that its latent rhetorical power can be employed to move the masses more efficiently in the direction that the leader believes history is traveling. Politics remains important, but not in day-to-day governing. Instead, a more democratized politics becomes important because it facilitates the popular arts and serves as the means whereby a strong presidential leader can persuade the people that his vision of the future corresponds to their implicit will. In the next chapter, I discuss the other important way in which Wilson's institutional vision opens the door for elite governance: his theory of administration. In examining this second part of the "politics-administration" dichotomy, we will see Wilson's argument that many substantial policy decisions should be made not by the political branches representing the people but rather by administrative agencies on the basis of nonpartisan, scientific expertise.

NOTES

1. Wilson, *Constitutional Government in the United States* (New York: Columbia University Press, 1908), 65, 66, 68. Even in his earlier writings, where Wilson had looked to Congress to play the primary leadership role, there is some ambiguity as to whether the leaders simply follow public opinion or instead guide and shape it. In *Congressional Government*, for example, Wilson proclaimed that "an effective representative body, gifted with the power to rule, ought, it would seem, not only to speak the will of the nation . . . but also lead it to its conclusions." Wilson, *Congressional Government* (1885; repr., New York: Meridian Books, 1956), 195.

2. *Constitutional Government*, 2.

3. "Marginal Notes on John Richard Green," July 27, 1878, in Arthur S. Link, ed., *The Papers of Woodrow Wilson* (hereafter cited as *PWW*), 69 vols. (Princeton: Princeton University Press, 1966–1993), 1:388. Quotations from Wilson's writings will be modernized as necessary for grammar and spelling. Emphasis will be in the original unless otherwise specified.

4. "Marginal Notes on John Richard Green," in *PWW* 1:389.

5. Walter Bagehot, *The English Constitution* (1867; repr., Ithaca, NY: Cornell University Press, 1981), 171, 241, 247. David Easton believes that Bagehot's elitism is more prevalent in *Physics and Politics*, and that the elitism of that work is in tension with *The English Constitution*: "While, on the one hand, [Bagehot] did elevate the rational political class to a fundamental determining force in history, on the other, he did not feel it contradictory to find that the masses, when imbued with a certain kind of national character, might themselves seize destiny in their grasp. . . . In this way Bagehot automatically implies that in certain times and places classes other than an elite might shape the character of history. This is a dualistic element in Bagehot's thought." Easton, "Walter Bagehot and Liberal Realism," *American Political Science Review* 43 (1949): 28–29.

6. "Shorthand Diary," June 19, 1876, in *PWW* 1:143.

7. "Cabinet Government in the United States," August 1879, in *PWW* 1:494.

8. See, for example, "The Education of the People," August 20, 1880, in *PWW* 1:668; "Culture and Education in the South," March 29, 1883, in *PWW* 2:327. Wilson was also somewhat reluctant on the question of women's suffrage. See Arthur S. Link, *Wilson: The New Freedom* (Princeton: Princeton University Press, 1956), 257–59.

9. Wilson, *The State* (Boston: D. C. Heath, 1889), 490.

10. "Random Notes for 'The Philosophy of Politics,'" January 26, 1895, in *PWW* 9:132.

11. Wilson, *The New Freedom* (New York: Doubleday, Page, 1913), 229–30.

12. *The New Freedom*, 231, 233.

13. *The New Freedom*, 236.

14. *The New Freedom*, 237.

15. *The New Freedom*, 238.

16. Raymond Seidelmann and Edward J. Harpham point to a role for the discipline of political science in educating public opinion. They contend that Wilson saw the need for political reform but believed that public opinion would not call for the enactment of reforms if left on its own. Wilson, they argue, saw political science as a potentially useful means of leading public opinion toward the right course of action. Seidelmann and Harpham, *Disenchanted Realists: Political Science and the American Crisis, 1884–1984* (Albany: State University of New York Press, 1985), 51–52.

17. "Editorial, *The Princetonian*," June 7, 1877, in *PWW* 1:274–75.

18. "William Earl Chatham," October 1878, in *PWW* 1:409, 411.

19. See, for example: "Editorial, *The Princetonian*," October 4, 1877, in *PWW* 1:294–96; "Editorial, *The Princetonian*," January 24, 1878, in *PWW* 1:343–44.

20. "Some Thoughts on the Present State of Public Affairs," January 30, 1878, in *PWW* 1:352.

21. "Mr. Gladstone, a Character Sketch," April 1880, in *PWW* 1:637.

22. "Mr. Gladstone," in *PWW* 1:638.

23. "Leaders of Men," June 17, 1890, in *PWW* 6:648.

24. Wilson seems to have presented some version of "Leaders of Men" at several different occasions. The version of it contained in Wilson's papers was given as the commencement address at the University of Tennessee on June 17, 1890. A similar version had previously been delivered in Middletown, Connecticut, on December 3, 1889. See "Two News Items," December 9, 1889, in *PWW* 6:451.

25. "Leaders of Men," in *PWW* 6:659.

26. See, for example, the account of prudence, or *phronesis*, in Aristotle's *Nicomachean Ethics*, 1140a25–1140b30.

27. For my understanding of Wilson's claim that leadership is "interpretation," I am indebted to Charles R. Kesler. His account puts it this way: "As compared to the masses, leaders were more closely attuned to the spirit of the age; they were able to distinguish the faint but swelling notes of progress from the background noise of history. . . . The leaders' function was to mediate between the people and the future, not to educate or elevate the people's will to a rational or trans-historical, much less a constitutional, standard." Kesler, "Separation of Powers and the Administrative State," in *The Imperial Congress*, ed. Gordon S. Jones and John A. Marini (New York: Pharos Books, 1988), 33–34.

28. "Leaders of Men," in *PWW* 6:660.

29. "The True American Spirit," October 27, 1892, in *PWW* 8:39.

30. Jeffrey K. Tulis, *The Rhetorical Presidency* (Princeton: Princeton University Press, 1987), 129.

31. "Leaders of Men," in *PWW* 6:659.

32. "Leaders of Men," in *PWW* 6:649.

33. "Leaders of Men," in *PWW* 6:650.

34. "Leaders of Men," in *PWW* 6:652, 654.

35. Publius, *The Federalist Papers*, ed. Charles R. Kesler and Clinton Rossiter (New York: Mentor, 1999), 63:352.

36. "Liberty and Government," December 20, 1894, in *PWW* 9:107.

37. "The Modern Democratic State," December 1885, in *PWW* 5:91.

38. "An Address on Thomas Jefferson" (lecture, April 16, 1906), in *PWW* 16:363. Paul Eidelberg also treats Wilson's connection to earlier American leaders. In his groundbreaking and otherwise excellent account of Wilson's leadership doctrine, one that sees clearly the dangers of Wilson's departure from the founders' conception of statesmanship, Eidelberg pairs Wilson with Jefferson. Eidelberg comments that "it was Jefferson . . . who combined Wilson's basic notions on the Constitution and on the presidency." He comments further: "Not the *office*, but the *man*—the personal power of the man magnified by the power conferred upon him by the 'people'—this was the Jeffersonian practice that Wilson wished to establish as the political theory of his second founding." As my treatment of Jefferson and Wilson in chapter 1 would indicate, such an argument seems to miss the fundamental distinction between the natural rights liberalism of Jefferson and the historicist liberalism of Wilson. Eidelberg, *A Discourse on Statesmanship: The Design and Transformation of the American Polity* (Urbana: University of Illinois Press, 1974), 360–61. Wilson also deviated from Hamilton on the question of leadership; for an account of how this is so, see James W. Ceaser, *Presidential Selection: Theory and Development* (Princeton: Princeton University Press, 1979), 207.

39. "Abraham Lincoln: A Man of the People," February 12, 1909, in *PWW* 19:42.

40. "A Calendar of Great Americans," September 15, 1893, in *PWW* 8:378–79.

41. Wilson, *Division and Reunion, 1829–1889* (1893; repr., New York: Longmans, Green, 1901), 216.

42. While I lay out my own substantial objections to Wilson's understanding of Lincoln in chapter 1, I will refer here to Zentner's contrast between Wilson and Lincoln, which justly takes its cue from Lincoln's Lyceum Address—an address that points to the dangers of the very kind of Caesarism that Wilson himself seems to advocate. As Zentner writes, "The similarity between Lincoln and the progressives is attended by a fundamental difference: Lin-

coln appeals to the ancient faith of the American people, the faith in 'the Laws of Nature and Nature's God' espoused in the Declaration of Independence. Progressives, on the other hand, seek the charms of a would-be savior to cure the nation's ills, i.e., to overcome its ancient faith." Zentner, "Caesarism and the American Presidency," *Southeastern Political Science Review* 24:4 (December 1996): 637. Eidelberg was perhaps the first to identify Wilson's doctrine of leadership as "nothing less than Caesarism." But, Eidelberg contends, it was "Caesarism of the profoundest kind. Wilson virtually deifies the people on the one hand, and their chosen leader, the President, on the other. The people and their leader are joined in what might almost be termed a gnostic union." Eidelberg, *Discourse on Statesmanship*, 358.

43. *Federalist* 71:400.

44. "Modern Democratic State," in *PWW* 5:86–87. For the term *hard demagoguery*, I am indebted to Ceaser, *Presidential Selection*, 318–27.

45. "Leaders of Men," in *PWW* 6:659.

46. "Leaders of Men," in *PWW* 6:661. Wilson's distinction between leadership and demagoguery is a topic of extended discussion by both Ceaser and Tulis. For Ceaser's argument, see *Presidential Selection*, 193. For Tulis's argument, see *The Rhetorical Presidency*, 130–32. Tulis contends there that Wilson's distinction is problematic for several reasons. First, he asks, how does one distinguish between momentary passions and the durable will of the people, without the institutional deliberation that the founders intended? Second, once the founders' restraints on the presidency are abandoned, how can we be sure of electing only a leader and not a demagogue? Ultimately, Tulis argues that Wilson was not terribly concerned with demagoguery—he was willing to incur the risk of it for the sake of facilitating the popular leadership that he believed essential to reforming American government: "Wilson's doctrine stands on the premise that the need for more energy in the political system is greater than the risk incurred through the possibility of demagoguery. This represents a major shift, indeed a reversal, of the founding perspective." See also Daniel D. Stid, *The President as Statesman: Woodrow Wilson and the Constitution* (Lawrence: University Press of Kansas, 1998), 32.

47. Historians differ on the question of how much popular rhetoric Wilson employed during his own presidency. Link contends that Wilson did not really practice popular leadership during his presidency because he did not have the need: Wilson so thoroughly controlled the Democrats in Congress that there was little necessity to go over their heads with a direct appeal to the people. Link claims that Wilson's method of leadership was much like that of a prime minister—he was engaged in the various details of legislation and exercised full control of the party rank and file in the legislature. Link, *The New Freedom*, 151–52. Clements disagrees, arguing that it was precisely because of Wilson's popular leadership that he was able to wield so much influence over Democratic legislators. Clements cites Wilson's personal addresses to Congress as evidence that he frequently brought public opinion to bear on congressional deliberations. Kendrick A. Clements, *The Presidency of Woodrow Wilson* (Lawrence: University Press of Kansas, 1992), 35.

48. *The New Freedom*, 72–73.

49. *The New Freedom*, 67–68, 76.

50. *The New Freedom*, 84–85.

51. *The New Freedom*, 108.

52. "Leaders of Men," in *PWW* 6:663.

53. G. W. F. Hegel, *The Philosophy of History*, trans. J. Sibree (New York: Dover, 1956), 32.

54. "A Christian Statesman," September 1, 1876, in *PWW* 1:188.

55. "John Bright," March 6, 1880, in *PWW* 1:617.

56. "Leaders of Men," in *PWW* 6:664.

57. *Constitutional Government*, 36–37.

58. "The Ideal Statesman," January 30, 1877, in *PWW* 1:244.

59. *Federalist* 72:405.

60. "The Ideal Statesman," in *PWW* 1:243–44.

61. "The Study of Administration," November 1886, in *PWW* 5:365.

62. "Study of Administration," in *PWW* 5:368.

63. "Study of Administration," in *PWW* 5:369.

64. Scot J. Zentner, "President and Party in the Thought of Woodrow Wilson," *Presidential Studies Quarterly* 26:3 (Summer 1996): 667–68. The way Niels Aage Thorsen puts it, Wilson's leadership doctrine focuses on giving concreteness to mass opinion. His emphasis on "interpretation" suggests that leadership "is not intended to upset political reality but to disclose it." Thorsen, *The Political Thought of Woodrow Wilson 1875–1910* (Princeton: Princeton University Press, 1988), 62.

65. Most of the scholarship on this question contains a more democratic interpretation of Wilson's leadership doctrine than the one I present here. Thorsen downplays any potentially radical implications of the doctrine by suggesting that Wilson wanted to limit the political leader by granting a significant role to administration. Thorsen, *Political Thought of Woodrow Wilson*, 232. For Stid, Wilson's desire to connect closely the people and the leader serves as a means of restraining the latter. Stid, *President as Statesman*, 52. Zentner contends that "popular leadership is less the formation of public opinion and more the active response to demands for the support of individuality by institutions of the state." Zentner, "Liberalism and Executive Power: Woodrow Wilson and the American Founders," *Polity* 26:4 (Summer 1994): 591. Both Ceaser and Harry Clor argue that popular leadership for Wilson goes in both directions—that is, as Ceaser puts it, "Wilson's concept of interpretation seems intended to suggest a kind of middle ground between following or 'truckling' to public opinion and commanding or shaping it." Ceaser, *Presidential Selection*, 190. See also Clor, "Woodrow Wilson," in *American Political Thought: The Philosophic Dimension of American Statesmanship*, ed. Morton J. Frisch and Richard G. Stevens (1971; repr., Dubuque, IA: Kendall/Hunt, 1976), 193. Interestingly, while it may not necessarily represent his view of Wilson's entire corpus of work, Link's interpretation of Wilson's early writings was that they were decidedly elitist; he accuses Wilson of "a strong bias against popular democracy and [of] favor[ing] government by an aristocracy of intelligence and merit." Link has the same view of Wilson's contempt for the populist movement. Link, *Wilson: The Road to the White House* (Princeton: Princeton University Press, 1947), 15, 25.

Chapter Seven

Wilson's Science of Administration

Under Wilson's politics-administration dichotomy, politics is made more popular by eliminating the distance that had been designed into the system by the founders between raw public opinion and the institutions of national governance. In the preceding chapters I have argued that this decreased distance between the government and the people had at least as much to do with facilitating elite leadership via the popular arts as it did with actually granting the people greater control of their government. And while Wilson made politics more popular, he also shifted much responsibility for governing out of politics and into the realm of administration; administration is made more responsible for governing precisely because it is insulated from political influence. Put another way, in spite of the democratic rhetoric, it seems necessary to question how genuinely democratic Wilson's reforms were if they proposed to grant significant governing responsibility to institutions that were to be shielded from traditional political accountability.[1] From Wilson's point of view, shielding administration from political control was a means of purifying government—of keeping policy decisions above the fray of traditional political machinations. But can a system delegate governing authority to apolitical administrative experts and, at the same time, maintain its democratic character? That Wilson wanted to delegate some degree of governing authority to administration, and to shield this administration from politics, is undeniable. The questions of just *how much* authority he wanted to shift away from politics and into administration, and of *how strict* the separation between politics and administration was to be, are matters of significant debate that will be taken up in this chapter. The chapter will also ask how compatible Wilson's science of administration is with the traditional republican framework of American constitutionalism.

In order to grasp the new role that Wilson envisioned for administration, it is important to recall his critique of Congress. While it is the case that Wilson changed his mind on the question of which institution—Congress or the presidency—was to serve as the focus of national political leadership, Wilson consistently maintained that Congress had to abandon its traditional legislative functions. As chapter 4 explained, Wilson thought it a great problem that Congress stubbornly insisted on its constitutionally defined duty to legislate. Given the increased complexity of matters that deserved federal attention, Wilson urged Congress to abandon the business of legislating on the details of policy, leaving that responsibility to the experts in the bureaucracy who were best suited for it. Congress was too much dominated by the conflicts of interest that are common in politics, and did not, therefore, possess the requisite independence for making detailed policy decisions on the basis of expertise. This shift in responsibility for policymaking from a political institution to an administrative one is fundamental to Wilson's writings on the science of administration.

THE ROOTS OF WILSON'S VISION FOR ADMINISTRATION

Wilson's vision of a greatly enlarged role for administration in national governance is based on his belief that politics had become almost hopelessly corrupt and impure. As a young man, Wilson was disgusted with what he perceived to be the dominance of politics by narrow, special interests, and he repeatedly said that a career in politics was no longer a worthy goal for an educated young man who was interested in public service. Niels Thorsen suggests that, in this respect, the controversy over the Tilden-Hayes election in 1876 strongly influenced Wilson. Wilson was excited that a Democrat (Tilden) won the popular vote, but was simultaneously disgusted and disillusioned with the "deal" that gave the election to Hayes in return for a promise to remove federal troops from South Carolina and Louisiana. To Wilson, this episode perfectly illustrated the dirtiness of American politics.[2] Wilson seems to have been so disillusioned with national politics that he held out little hope that it could be reformed even if the Democrats were returned to national power. Commenting on the nomination of Hayes at the Republican national convention, Wilson speculated that the nomination might offer the Democrats the prospect of winning the White House, but even this gave him little enthusiasm. "The Democrats," Wilson wrote, "will be very likely to abuse power if they get it."[3]

Wilson blamed the spoils system for a large measure of the corruption in national politics. This was a system that subjected policymaking to narrow political interests, impeding the implementation of policy designed to engender progress for the nation as a whole.[4] It was for the purpose of reducing the control of corrupt politics over administration that Wilson attacked the practice of senatorial courtesy in executive appointments. It is a "very sorry, unseemly thing," Wilson wrote, to give individual senators the authority to reward political supporters through the de facto appointment power that senatorial courtesy provides them. In particular, the practice is anathema to the idea of civil service reform, and Wilson recognized that, if civil service reform is to advance, the constitutional prerogative of the Senate to confirm appointments must recede in significance. "By common consent," he reasoned, "civil-service reform must grow, and stretch its branches far and wide, even though its roots do spread themselves in such a way as inconveniently to encroach upon and cramp certain constitutional principles." Wilson's solution to the conflict between civil service reform and the "advice and consent" power of the Senate was to place the appointment power exclusively in the hands of a single executive. In this way, corruption could not be hidden among a group of relatively obscure individuals in the legislature, and it would be more difficult for politics to taint the vital mission of administration.[5]

Wilson's early desire to reduce the influence of corrupt political concerns on the mission of administration naturally raises the question of his connection both to the civil service reform movement and to the early agitators for civil service, the mugwumps. As Daniel Stid explains, Wilson's early writings reflect a debate of sorts that Wilson was having with certain mugwump agitators. Wilson thought that mugwumps like E. L. Godkin and Carl Schurz had their priorities wrong, because Wilson believed that reforming government to make it more responsible ought to be the first priority, followed by the implementation of civil service. Stid points to *Congressional Government*, where Wilson referenced Dorman Eaton's *Civil Service in Great Britain*—a key work for the American civil service reform movement. Wilson argued that Eaton's book supported his own order of priorities.[6] Herbert Storing also considers Wilson a civil service reformer but places him in what he calls the "second phase" of the movement. The first phase consisted largely of politicians and activists, whereas the second phase originated in the universities and sought civil service reform as part of a broader program for reform of American institutions.[7]

The university was critical, for in his earliest writings Wilson sounded the call for a class of educated experts who could rise above the corruption and narrowness of politics. Wilson saw a political system mired in special interest conflict, and he concluded that a young, apolitical class was what the country needed in order to right itself. Wilson wrote that "it would not be the part either of wisdom or of good will to encourage young men to do service in the partisan contentions of politics."[8] Instead, Wilson contended that this

young, educated, apolitical class must focus its energies on "national administration." He elaborated:

> The greatest issue of the time seems an issue of life and death. If the national
> administration can be reformed it can endure; if it cannot be, it must end. Ro-
> bust as its constitution has proved to be, the federal government cannot long
> continue to live in the poisonous atmosphere of fraud and malfeasance. If the
> civil service cannot by gentle means be purged of the vicious diseases which
> fifty years of the partisan spoils system have fixed upon it, heroic remedies must
> be resorted to.

The focus of the newly educated nonpartisan class must be to bring "a new
spirit"—"not a new party"—to "the present treatment and future settlement
of this and others of the pressing questions of public administration." Wilson
reiterated the theme that modern education is integral to training this new
class of apolitical experts. In particular, the elite universities should take it as
their primary mission to train those who will objectively administer the state.
"An intelligent nation cannot be led or ruled save by thoroughly-trained and
completely-educated men," Wilson explained. "Only comprehensive information and entire mastery of principles and details can qualify for command."
Wilson trumpets the power of expertise—of "special knowledge, and its importance to those who would lead."[9]

This envisioned role for education as central to the development of expertise led Wilson to characterize education in vocational terms. This does not
mean that education should be strictly technical—indeed, Wilson's reflections on curricula indicate quite the opposite (see chapter 2). However, education should be undertaken with an understanding that it is not an end in itself but a means of preparing and developing expertise for the end of public
service.[10] Wilson's teacher at Johns Hopkins, Herbert Baxter Adams, certainly shared this understanding of education and even planned for training
future bureaucrats on the basis of Wilson's work. Arthur Link notes that
Adams was so impressed with Wilson's administrative writings that he initiated planning for a "civil academy" in Washington, D.C. The academy was to
be affiliated with Johns Hopkins, and Adams wanted Wilson to serve as one
of its directors. Daniel C. Gilman, president of Johns Hopkins, actually asked
Wilson to draw up plans for the academy—plans that were never realized, at
least in Wilson's day.[11] All of these stratagems were consistent with what Wilson had for years been writing on the relationship between education and national administration. The young Wilson contended—in an editorial directed
against the "college loafer"—that the purpose of a university education is to
"furnish young men with a solid foundation . . . to send forth, in all directions,
men who can raise the people to the level of right and truth."[12] Wilson's plans

for the various reforms of American institutions, and for the development of a pure administration, required that education be understood in this light. He explained that "administration is something that men must learn, not something to skill in which they are born [*sic*]."[13] The requirement that education develop in young men the necessary skills for the success of national administration is, of course, where Wilson's own vocation comes in. As a young academic, Wilson frequently voiced his philosophical argument on education as he sought a university position. This was certainly true in his campaign to land a professorship at Princeton, during which he addressed fellow Princeton alumni about the need for a professor of politics at their alma mater.[14] Wilson also wrote his famous essay, "The Study of Administration," around this time, and the essay can, in some measure, be understood as his vision of how future administrators should be educated.

"THE STUDY OF ADMINISTRATION"

In one sense, Wilson's "Study of Administration" may be the most influential of his numerous academic writings. It is, arguably, responsible for launching the entire discipline of public administration, and public administration journals to this day continue to publish articles on Wilson's essay. The essay marks a focus in Wilson's work of this period on the need to empower national administration with the means of regulating progress, and on the need to staff administrative agencies with those who most clearly understand what particular means are required for national progress.[15] The general connection to Hegel's vision for the bureaucracy is difficult to ignore. Wilson's essay certainly seems to have been influenced by his reading of German authors who belonged to the Hegelian tradition, specifically Johann Bluntschli. The catalyst for Wilson's focus, around 1885, on the science of administration seems to have been his reading of Bluntschli's *Politik als Wissenschaft*, which was the third volume in his *Lehre vom Modernen Stat*. Bluntschli's papers were housed at the Johns Hopkins seminar room where Wilson studied, and Wilson's teacher Richard T. Ely had himself studied under Bluntschli at Heidelberg. In his own administrative writings, Wilson frequently consulted his bibliographical notes from Ely's lectures, almost all of which point to European sources on European administrative systems.[16] Ely's course on administration, which Wilson took in 1884 and 1885, was the only course of its kind anywhere in the country when Ely instituted it in 1882. Wilson completed his first sustained work on administration in November 1885 in an unpublished essay entitled "The Art of Governing." The following year, Wilson was invited to Cornell to deliver a lecture on his administrative work; he called the lecture "The Study of Administration" and subsequently published it as an essay.[17]

In "The Study of Administration," Wilson explicated in detail what had become his overarching prescription for governmental reform: that administration can and should be separated, at least to some significant degree, from politics. Wilson's plan for governmental reform had argued that the details of policymaking needed to be removed from the corrupt realm of politics and placed under the control of enlightened administrators. But in order for this to take place, Wilson needed to show that administration could separate itself from politics, and he needed to show why administration should not be subject to political control. His argument rested on the assertion, made in the "Study," that "administration lies outside the proper sphere of *politics*. Administrative questions," Wilson explained, "are not political questions." The exercise of administrative power, therefore, unlike the exercise of power by the traditional political branches, cannot be defined constitutionally. Wilson argued that "the field of administration is a field of business. It is removed from the hurry and strife of politics; it at most points stands apart even from the debatable ground of constitutional study."[18] In making this case, Wilson was merely extending his argument from "Government by Debate" to its logical conclusion. He argued there that administration needed to separate itself from political influence, and that large parts of national administration could be made permanent precisely because they were apolitical and therefore not subject to the changing fortunes of politics. The administrative departments, Wilson wrote, "should be organized in strict accordance with recognized business principles. The greater part of their affairs is altogether outside of politics."[19]

Even Wilson conceded that there are certain circumstances under which politics and administration cannot be strictly separated. But in cases where the two must overlap, Wilson was also clear that administration must have the upper hand.[20] As an illustration, he pointed to the fact that administration must have some bearing on the traditionally constitutional question of how the departments of government ought to be organized. Constitutionally, too much emphasis had been placed on organizing powers in such a way that government would act slowly and inefficiently. Wilson criticized this structure, arguing that the administrative principle of efficiency should govern the organization of departments. He elaborated:

> There is, indeed, one point at which administrative studies trench on constitutional ground—or at least upon what seems constitutional ground. The study of administration, philosophically viewed, is closely connected with the study of the proper distribution of constitutional authority. To be efficient it must discover the simplest arrangements by which responsibility can be unmistakably

fixed upon officials. . . . If administrative study can discover the best principles upon which to base such distribution, it will have done constitutional study an invaluable service. Montesquieu did not, I am convinced, say the last word on this head.[21]

This administrative perspective on the distribution of powers is essential to understanding Wilson's criticism of the separation of powers. The separation of powers does not, for Wilson, rest on political principle—on the idea that the departments ought to check one another for the purpose of controlling majority faction and protecting individual natural rights. The separation of powers is not, therefore, foundational in the American system; viewed from the perspective of administration, it is simply an ill-conceived arrangement of means. This is why the inefficient separation-of-powers system should be replaced with the more efficient separation of politics and administration, which will enable the bureaucracy to tend to the details of administering progress without being encumbered by the inefficiencies of politics.

Wilson's "Study" admits that there is nothing new about administration itself—administration is as old as government. But administration, Wilson pointed out, had not been appreciated as an object of study separate from politics. Therefore, the *science* of administrative methods had been neglected, and Wilson's work was an attempt to remedy that neglect.[22] The focus of earlier periods of government had been on the *theory* of politics—the ideas about what a government ought to do. But with the irreversible arrival of modern democracy, those theoretical questions had been settled by history. It was now time to turn our attention to the administrative methods that would lead to the achievement of those ends about which history had brought the public mind to essential consensus.

Historicism and Wilson's Theory of Administration

For Wilson, both the means and ends of government are contingent upon history. The American founders had designed a government that was appropriate for the historical spirit in which they lived—one where national power, especially executive power, was to be feared and severely circumscribed. Since the matters for which the founding-era government was responsible were relatively few, the strict, constitutional limitation of national power did not present much of a problem. But by bringing about new, complex conditions with which modern democracy had to contend, history was demanding an end to limited, constitutional government, and a reorientation to greater administrative discretion at the national level. It is in this way that Wilson's administrative theory is intimately connected with his historicism—indeed, the entire first part of the "Study" is dedicated to the argument that the age of constitutionalism was over and an age of administration was upon us. "It is," Wilson proclaimed, "getting to be harder to *run* a constitution than to frame one."[23] Our energies must, therefore, be directed to the particular administrative means necessary to achieve the political ends that have now been settled by history.

In the "Study," Wilson elaborated upon the connection between his progressive vision of history and his theory of administration. He contended that historical progress is inevitable for all nations, and while some nations are far ahead of others, each will ultimately progress in three stages. The first stage is that of "absolute rulers," which has an "administrative system adapted to absolute rule." In the second stage, which is based upon a reaction to unchecked administrative power, "constitutions are framed to do away with absolute rulers." Administration necessarily suffers during this stage, as it is "neglected for these higher concerns." The third and final stage is one where the people abandon their fear of unchecked administrative power. In direct opposition to the political theory of the founding generation, Wilson contended that state power does not remain a permanent threat, and therefore constitutional limitations on administrative discretion can be abandoned once the people have fully attained their sovereignty in modern democracy. In principle, the administrative power that existed during the first stage of absolute rule is the same as that which exists in the final stage of the people's sovereignty. The only difference is that history has, by the final stage, established the proper conditions for administrative rule: the people are confident in their sovereignty, so they no longer feel the need to reign in the power of the state. Wilson's example of Hegel's Prussia as an advanced state helps to illustrate this point. In Prussia, administration was not neglected. While there might have been a monarch, the Prussian monarch was a just one who considered himself the servant of the people's will. The people felt that their own will was manifested in the person of the monarch, and, accordingly, they were willing to grant broad discretion to national administration.[24] We see in the Prussian system—a system held up by Hegel in *The Philosophy of Right* as the most rational state at the end of history—the manifestation of Wilson's vision for the American executive and administration: a singular executive who embodies the will of the people, combined with broad administrative discretion carried out by bureaucrats who have advanced knowledge of the means necessary to manage progress. It is in this way that Wilson's administrative writings partner perfectly with his work on politics, each forming a vital part of the politics-administration dichotomy that makes up Wilson's vision for governmental reform.

Because history had engendered the complex conditions of the modern democratic state, Wilson argued that it was time for America to advance beyond the second stage of development—that of limited constitutionalism—

and on to the final stage of administrative government under the sovereignty of the people. This required that government no longer be based upon the principle of checks and balances, but instead upon the business-like principle of efficiency. As Wilson made clear in the "Study," the politics-administration distinction allows the increasingly complex "business" of governing a modern state to be handled by a professional class of experts instead of by a multiplicity of politicians with narrow, competing, and subjective interests. He praised the civil service reform movement because it sought to professionalize government, making it more efficient in terms of both personnel and organization. The new personnel would be more efficient administrators because they would be divorced from the realm of politics. Wilson emphasized that the *idea* of civil service reform is what really matters because it embodies the principle of separating administrative decision making from political influence. As Wilson explained, "Civil service reform is thus but a moral preparation for what is to follow. It is clearing the moral atmosphere of official life by establishing the sanctity of public office as public trust, and, by making the service unpartisan, it is opening the way for making it businesslike."[25]

Perhaps most important, a civil service appointment, with its secure tenure and independence from politics, would allow a bureaucrat to disregard special interests and act on behalf of the general interest. The civil servant would be beholden to no particular interest other than the public good. Here Wilson assumed—precisely as Hegel had in *The Philosophy of Right*—that a secure position in the bureaucracy would somehow eliminate the natural self-interestedness of the civil servant, and that an administrative appointment (with a good salary and life tenure) would somehow free the official of his particularity so that he could focus solely on the objective will.[26] Several commentators have noted this assumption of Wilson, and have deemed it a significant problem. Even Storing, who is generally sympathetic to civil service reform, is dubious of this notion that bureaucrats would somehow be above the self-interestedness of ordinary citizens. He worries that the civil service reformers "underestimated the enduring force of selfish interests, and consequently they failed to recognize sufficiently the permanent need to take account of such interests.[27] Robert D. Miewald offers a similar criticism, directly linking Wilson's "Study" to Hegel's state theory: "The bureaucracy becomes, in Hegel's theory of the state, the carrier and guardian of the general interest of all against the structured clash of particular interests within 'civil society.'" Miewald notes that it is precisely this problematic assumption that the bureaucracy would represent the "general interest" that was imported into America by the likes of Wilson. Hegel was appealing to Americans at this time, Miewald explains, because American critics of a corrupt bureaucracy saw in Hegel's system a bureaucracy above corruption, above self-interest, and focused only on the general good.[28]

The Role of Public Opinion

If bureaucracy, as it administers progress, is to act on behalf of the general interest, what is the role for public opinion? Wilson, after all, seems a consistent advocate of connecting politics much more directly with popular opinion. Yet his writings on the separation of politics and administration show that public opinion is not to be brought more directly into the realm of administrative decision making. "The problem," Wilson explained, "is to make public opinion efficient without suffering it to be meddlesome." Public opinion is a "clumsy nuisance" when it comes to the "oversight of the daily details and in the choice of the daily means of government." So while public opinion ought to be introduced more directly into politics, politics must confine itself to general superintendence—to the role of setting only the broad goals of the nation. "Let administrative study find the best means for giving public criticism this control and for shutting it out from all other interference," Wilson wrote.[29]

Wilson's separation of politics and administration becomes, then, a means for maintaining the democratic veneer of popular government while giving to unelected administrators the wide berth they need to manage the complex business of national progress. History requires that administration be efficient and powerful. Wilson is quite candid in the "Study" about what the greatest obstacle to this end will be. We must, he urged, "discover what there may be to hinder or delay us in naturalizing this much-to-be-desired science of administration. What, then, is there to prevent? Well, principally, popular sovereignty. It is harder for democracy to organize administration than for monarchy."[30] This argument helps to explain Wilson's admiration for the Prussian state, where the monarch embodies the public will and the system does not suffer from the inconvenience of democratic elections. Under such an arrangement, bureaucratic experts can operate the administration unhindered. In the American system, Wilson wanted to find an arrangement that would allow public opinion to have its say in the realm of politics but would keep it out of administration.

To be sure, in spite of his admiration for the Prussian monarchy, Wilson made clear that democracy is the superior system because it is the system brought about by history. In response to the accusation that his administrative vision would lead to the creation in America of something like an "official class" of elite administrators, Wilson contended that administration is always to be superintended—at least at a broad level—by public opinion. "To fear the creation of a domineering, illiberal officialism as a result of the studies I am here proposing," Wilson explained, "is to miss altogether the principle upon which I wish most to insist. That principle is, that administration in the United States must be at all points sensitive to public opinion."[31] Yet the superintendence by public opinion must not be too onerous, as this would undermine the apolitical nature of the bureaucracy and interfere with its efficiency. As he explained the problem,

> The very completeness of our most cherished political successes in the past embarrasses us. We have enthroned public opinion. . . . The very fact that we have realized popular rule in its fullness has made the task of *organizing* that rule just so much the more difficult. In order to make any advance at all we must instruct and persuade a multitudinous monarch called public opinion—a much less feasible undertaking than to influence a single monarch called a king.[32]

The key to governmental reform is to figure out how to reconcile the sovereignty of the people with efficient administration. This is where elite leadership becomes so important. Those who lead must have the keenest insight into what progress requires. They must also be able to convince the people that the leaders' vision of what is required for progress conforms to the public's own implicit will. Political leadership consequently must practice the popular arts, using its close connection to the people as a means of moving them in accord with the leaders' own vision of where history is going. On the administrative side, administrative study must teach "the people what sort of administration to desire and demand."[33]

The Novelty of Wilson's Administrative Theory

Whereas in his political rhetoric Wilson frequently placed himself in the tradition of prominent Americans who had preceded him, his academic writings are much more candid about the novelty of his ideas. This is particularly true of Wilson's administrative writings, in which he conceded that his vision for administration diverged sharply from the American constitutional tradition.[34] In the "Study," Wilson frankly acknowledged the foreign origin of his ideas on the science of administration:

> But where has this science grown up? Surely not on this side the sea. . . . American writers have hitherto taken no very important part in the advancement of this science. It has found its doctors in Europe. It is not of our making; it is a foreign science, speaking very little of the language of English or American principle. . . . It has been developed by French and German professors.[35]

Wilson virtually admitted deriving from German state theory, and Bluntschli in particular, the key principle whereby administration was to be freed from the corrupting machinations of politics—Wilson's bedrock separation of powers and administration: "This . . . distinction [between politics and administration is] of high authority; eminent German writers insist upon it as of course. Bluntschli, for instance, bids us separate administration alike from politics and from law."[36] It was not administration itself that was novel to the American tradition, but rather the consideration of administration as an authority distinct from politics and outside of political control. In this respect, the American tradition had to be corrected by German state theory, and this is exactly where Wilson looked for the sources of his administrative writings. In the bibliographic information that one finds throughout Wilson's writings during this period, the sources on administration are almost entirely foreign. In one such account of "the literature of the science," Wilson listed under modern sources sixteen German titles, twelve French, and one English. Wilson explained that the single English-language source—Frank J. Goodnow's *Comparative Administrative Law*—was "the only systematic work in English devoted distinctively to Administration as a separate 'discipline.'"[37]

The foreign methods of administration that Wilson wanted to import were, of course, parts of political systems that were quite different from the republican political system in America. His admiration for the Prussian bureaucracy—part of a monarchic system—is but one obvious example. So how could Wilson advocate adopting in America an administrative system that a monarchy inspired? The very principle that politics and administration are distinct allows such an adoption. Since administrative principles are clearly distinguishable from political principles, we can import a Prussian administrative structure while still maintaining the American political system of republicanism. Administration, because of its insulation from politics, is politically neutral—it can be plugged in to a variety of political systems. As Wilson explained famously in the "Study":

> It is the distinction, already drawn, between administration and politics which makes the comparative method so safe in the field of administration. When we study the administrative systems of France and Germany, knowing that we are not in search of *political* principles, we need not care a peppercorn for the constitutional or political reasons which Frenchmen or Germans give for their practices when explaining them to us. If I see a murderous fellow sharpening a knife cleverly, I can borrow his way of sharpening the knife without borrowing his probable intention to commit murder with it; and so, if I see a monarchist dyed in the wool managing a public bureau well, I can learn his business methods without changing one of my republican spots.

Or, as Wilson asked with regard to his "plug-and-play" notion of administration, "Why should we not use such parts of foreign contrivances as we want, if they be in any way serviceable? We are in no danger of using them in a foreign way. We borrowed rice, but we do not eat it with chopsticks."[38] In a note written around this time, Wilson was equally blunt: "Now the purpose of [administration] has been the execution of the will of a tyrant, again the execution of the will of the governed. But the organization for the one purpose may, if effective, serve—at least as a model—for the other."[39]

Such optimism for the importation of novel administrative systems is strange in light of what appears to be Wilson's conservative critique of social compact theory. As explained in the first part of this book, Wilson thought social compact theory dangerous because it encouraged the inorganic establishment of new political systems. Such was the basis of his critique of the French Revolution, which from Wilson's perspective turned into a disaster precisely because it attempted to import into an organic order or tradition something wholly new and foreign. Yet Wilson seems perfectly willing to import into the American political tradition a science of administration that, by his own admission, is entirely novel to it. The answer to this contradiction is that Wilson's apparent conservative organicism is not nearly as important as his progressive idealism. Or, put another way, his affinity for Burke gives way to his devotion to Hegelian political philosophy.

Wilson's emphasis on an administrative science novel to the republican tradition in America also explains why he turned, in the final part of the "Study," to comparative government. His contention—that the various administrative means of government are interchangeable, even among regimes with vastly different foundational principles and ends—is the fundamental premise of comparative government. In this regard, Wilson's work on administration can be said to have aided not only in the foundation of the public administration discipline in America but also in the foundation of comparative government. It is no coincidence that these disciplines are relatively new in America; they rely on political premises that were novel to the American tradition and were ushered in by Wilson and his contemporaries. Wilson himself explained the essential relationship between administration and comparative government, arguing that "without comparative studies in government we cannot rid ourselves of the misconception that administration stands upon an essentially different basis in a democratic state from that on which it stands in a nondemocratic state."[40] Importing monarchic administrative science into American democracy relies on the premise that administrative principles are strictly separate from political principles.

In one way, Wilson seems to have misunderstood his European sources on this very separation between politics and administration. Even Bluntschli himself did not actually place the separation in terms nearly so strict as those Wilson employs in the "Study." Several scholars mention Wilson's various misinterpretations and mistranslations of the Europeans on this question. In particular, Miewald makes the important point that, for the Germans, the independence of the bureaucracy was critical precisely so that it could serve as a check against the monarch. He contends that such independence for the bureaucracy was never intended, therefore, to be translated to a republican system.[41] This critique of Wilson is true as far as it goes. But it does not fully appreciate Hegel's principal reason for granting to the bureaucracy independent governing authority: the educated experts in the bureaucracy, insulated from the pressures of narrow self-interest, were to see more clearly than the people themselves the objective public will, and were to know best the administrative means necessary to achieve it. This is exactly the quality that Wilson himself ascribed to the bureaucracy, and it is the main reason why the administrative apparatus was to be so strictly separated from politics. In this respect, therefore, Wilson seems to have understood quite correctly the most important German of them all.

Wilson's vision for an independent bureaucracy does not require only that administration be separated from politics; it requires, more fundamentally, that administrative power be considered separately from constitutional power. We cannot, in other words, try to find the powers of administration under those that the Constitution grants to the political institutions. Wilson understood that the attempt to bring administration within the constitutional order—to look for administrative authority to rest on more fundamental constitutional authority—would create a significant obstacle to granting administrators the discretion necessary to administer progress. He reasoned that our comprehension of the clear distinction between politics and administration, or between constitutional law and regulation "might deliver us from the too great detail of legislative enactment; give us administrative elasticity and discretion; free us from the idea that checks and balances are to be carried down through all stages of organization."[42] As Wilson explained in his lecture notes on administration, the question of how far the law circumscribes the scope of administrative discretion was unsettled in America, and he urged that administration be properly understood and given as wide a sphere as possible. This wide sphere meant that administration would have to cross over the traditional separation-of-powers boundaries; indeed, Wilson contrasted the theory of separation of powers to what he called the "actual division of powers," where there are many "legislative and judicial acts of the administration."[43]

Wilson explained in the "Study" that administration and constitutional politics could not be combined even at a conceptual level. Administration "stands apart even from the debatable ground of constitutional study," he contended, because administrative power and the political powers ordained in the Constitution are different by nature. This is why he admitted that it is difficult even to place administration within the institutional order established by the Constitution:

> One cannot easily make clear to every one just where administration resides in the various departments of any practicable government without entering upon particulars so numerous as to confuse and distinctions so minute as to distract. No lines of demarcation, setting apart administrative from non-administrative functions, can be run between this and that department of government without being run up hill and down dale, over dizzy heights of distinction and through dense jungles of statutory enactment, hither and thither around "ifs" and "buts," "whens" and "howevers," until they become altogether lost to the common eye not accustomed to this sort of surveying.[44]

Wilson recognized that his proposed system was predicated on a novelty in American constitutionalism: namely, that there are legitimate state powers beyond those granted by the Constitution to the political branches of government. These powers are administrative, and their exercise independent from politics requires a transformation in the traditional understanding of American institutions.

In spite of Wilson's own insistence on the novelty of his administrative science, several scholars have argued that there is a fundamental continuity between the founders' constitutionalism and the administrative state that Wilson helped to usher in. John A. Rohr, for example, cites Wilson's politics-administration dichotomy as evidence that Wilson shared the founders' conservative concern about the potential excesses of democracy. Just as the founders created a distance between the people and the governing institutions, Rohr reasons, Wilson saw the independent bureaucracy as a means of checking democratic excess. Rohr equates, in other words, the founders' concern about majority faction with Wilson's model of governance by visionary elites.[45] That the former relies on carefully checking the centralized power of the state while the latter seeks to empower politically unaccountable bureaucrats to wield significant discretionary authority seems to be lost in this analysis. In another article, Rohr seeks to show that the administrative state is compatible with traditional American constitutionalism. But in this case, he blames Wilson (along with Goodnow and the civil service reformers) for giving administration a bad name. Here Rohr concedes that Wilson's particular form of administration "was at odds with the Constitution," but he maintains that, considered generally, "the administrative state is consistent with the Constitution, fulfills its design, and heals a longstanding, major defect." The defect is a lack of energy in the central government, so if the modern administrative state is not explicitly endorsed by the founders' Constitution, it is at least within the spirit of their intentions for the new government.[46] Rohr even goes on to suggest that the modern bureaucracy fulfills the role originally intended for the House of Representatives. Given the sharp increase in the nation's population, and the inability of the House to increase its size accordingly, the House can no longer be said to have the intimate sympathy with the people that the founders had intended. But the bureaucracy, because its members come from all facets of society, is truly "representative" in a sense that the House is not.[47] In echoing the sentiment of *Federalist* 52 that the founders looked to the House for an "intimate sympathy" with the people, Rohr of course forgets the very next sentence of that paper—that "frequent elections are unquestionably the only policy by which this dependence and sympathy can be effectually secured."[48] Here Rohr makes precisely the same error as Wilson, in spite of his attempt to distance Wilson's defense of administration from his own; that is, both Rohr and Wilson assume that an unelected and therefore politically unaccountable bureaucracy can somehow represent the public's true will.

Although more cautious and more appreciative of the differences between Wilson and the founders, Rohr's teacher Storing also asserts some important continuities. Storing contends that the founders were primarily concerned with administrative questions—that the 1787 Constitution reflected the desire of its framers to find a means for the national government to fulfill its ends more energetically and capably. In this respect, Storing argues, the founders and Wilson both assumed that the big questions in government had been settled; both, then, were concerned with the specific means necessary to achieve those political ends on which there was fundamental consensus. This argument is connected to Storing's assertion that the founders did not envision the need for any future acts of great statesmanship; since the primary constitutional questions had been settled, their focus was on a prudent means of administration. "There is never needed," Storing continues, "that kind of statesmanship which had formerly been regarded as its essence: great, 'way of life'-setting, character forming political leadership." Instead, only a narrow kind of leadership would be necessary, a kind of prudent administration. Storing concludes that Wilson's views on administration, although more radicalized, were simply the logical extension of this administrative focus of the founding: "The founders' maxims of administrative statesmanship became Woodrow Wilson's 'one rule of good administration for all governments alike.'"[49] Like Storing, Paul P. Van Riper sees in the founders' concern for effective administration a forerunner to Wilson's theory of administration. He applies this idea, in particular, to Hamilton, who Van Riper claims served as a model for a future energetic and independent bureaucracy. "If anyone deserves a title as *the* founder of the American administrative state," Van Riper asserts, "in terms of both theory and practice, it is not Wilson, Eaton, or Ely but Alexander Hamilton."[50]

These arguments seem to miss the fundamental innovation in Wilson's administrative theory. Wilson placed administrative power on an entirely different plane from constitutional power, and it is this sharp distinction between constitutional politics and administrative discretion that separates Wilson from those earlier American thinkers—particularly Hamilton—who had also placed great importance on national administration. It is common for scholars to refer to different positions in the progressive-era debates as "Hamiltonian" or "Jeffersonian"—indeed, Wilson was more often labeled as the latter, a characterization that is inaccurate for reasons that will be discussed in the conclusion. Wilson himself found it convenient, depending upon the circumstances, to claim the mantle of either Hamilton or Jefferson. Certainly it is not uncommon for Wilson's administrative writings to earn him a comparison with Hamilton.

Yet it is essential to remember that Wilson saw his argument on administration as something almost completely foreign precisely because the American tradition had failed to perceive the sharp contrast between constitutional and administrative power. This is why Wilson had to admit that it was difficult to conceive how one might place administrative discretion of the sort he had in mind within the traditional constitutional order. The key feature of Hamilton's argument for national administration, by contrast, was its placing of administrative authority (as broad as Hamilton surely envisioned it) in a subordinate position within the constitutional order. While Hamilton advocated an energetic national administration, his vision differed from Wilson's insofar as administrative power was always understood to be an instrument of an energetic executive and therefore accountable to the constitutional authority granted to the executive by the people. It is true that in *Federalist* 68, Hamilton writes that "the true test of a good government is its aptitude and tendency to produce good administration"; but he makes this statement only after clarifying that it would be a "heresy" to agree with the poet who says: "For forms of government let fools contest—that which is best administered is best."[51] One cannot consider the quality of administration, in other words, as a question that is unaffected by regime type. And this is why Hamilton and Wilson really mean different things when they use the term *administration*. Hamilton conceives of it as part of the republican executive, accountable to the reason of the people through the forms of the Constitution. Wilson makes a great effort to explain that his vision of administration is much different, because he believes that the quality of administration has been degraded by those (like Hamilton) who have conceived of it too narrowly—that is, conceived of it within the confines of the constitutional executive. Wilson's entire claim to charting new territory in the "Study" rests on this difference with the traditional understanding of administration. The problem with the old understanding, from a Wilsonian

perspective, is that it cannot conceive of administrative powers that are somehow bestowed upon the state outside of the formal granting of power to the political branches by the Constitution.

The other, even more fundamental, difference between Hamilton and Wilson,
which helps to demonstrate the sharp contrast between Wilson and the founders'
constitutionalism in general, is their understanding of the ends of government.
For Hamilton, an increasingly energetic national administration was important
as an improved means to the permanent and limited ends of government. In other
words, Hamilton saw the increased administrative power of the national government as a way to better secure the natural rights of individuals—the timeless
goals of any just government. From the perspective of Hamilton and many of the
founders, the practice of government in most states during the 1780s constituted
a grave failure to fulfill the fundamental obligation of government to secure
rights (the paper-money rage is a primary example); a newly energized national
government was seen as a potential solution to that problem. In this respect,
while Hamilton and Jefferson differed markedly on the question of means, they
were agreed on the essential purpose and role of government, with which the historicist state theory of Wilson is directly at odds.

The use of the labels "Hamiltonian" and "Jeffersonian"—both by the progressives themselves and by those who have written about the progressive
era—to distinguish between various elements of the movement is, therefore,
misleading. While Hamilton and Jefferson disagreed passionately about the
means of government, they were far more akin to each other on the fundamental principles of government than either of them was to Wilson. In the literature on the American political tradition, some historians and political scientists prefer to use the "Hamiltonian versus Jeffersonian" dichotomy to
characterize the differences between progressive figures like Herbert Croly or
Theodore Roosevelt, on the one hand, and Wilson, on the other. As useful as
such a distinction might be in analyzing the diversity within the progressive
movement, it also poses the danger of hiding the far more fundamental difference between progressive liberalism, which is grounded in historicism, and
founding-era liberalism, which is grounded in transhistorical natural-rights
theory and to which Hamilton and Jefferson were both primary adherents.

THE LECTURES ON ADMINISTRATION

In addition to the "Study," Wilson's other substantial body of work on administration was in the form of the extensive notes he prepared for his annual
five-week lectureship at Johns Hopkins. Beginning in 1888 and concluding in
1897, Wilson conducted the lectureship in which he not only built upon the

themes of the "Study" but also extended his administrative arguments into areas that had not previously been addressed. He gave the lectures in three cycles, each consisting of three years (1888–1890, 1891–1893, 1894–1896), with each year organized around approximately twenty-five lectures. In the first year of the cycle, Wilson's focus was the function of government and a comparison between the American central government and those of France, Prussia, Britain, and Switzerland. In the second year, the focus was on the operation of local government in Prussia, France, Britain, and the United States. In the final year of the cycle, Wilson focused on the role of municipal government in administration.[52]

Given the nature and detail of the lecture notes, in contradistinction to the "Study," it is even easier to see that Wilson's thinking on administration was entirely foreign to the American political tradition. Notes from the early years of the lectures point to Wilson's having read several of the Heinrich Marquardsen series in preparation, especially Otto von Sarwey's *Allgemeines Verwaltungsrecht* and Carl Gareis's *Allgemeines Staatsrecht*, in addition to Georg Jellinek's *Gesetz und Verordnung*, on which Wilson relied heavily for his discussion of the historical evolution of administration.[53] An extensive working bibliography that Wilson put together around this time is also revealing. Under the general category of "administration," there are fourteen entries: six are German, five are French, and the remainder are English-language translations of works by the German Rudolph Gneist. There is only one entry under the category of "modern constitutions"—the Marquardsen series *Handbuch des Oeffentlichen Rechts der Gegenwart*. There are several entries from Bluntschli, and both Hegel's *The Philosophy of History* and *The Philosophy of Right* are included.[54] In the margins of the actual lecture notes, next to several of his main points Wilson cited Bluntschli as a source.[55]

Relying on Sarwey, Wilson's notes define administration as a question of "adjustment," and this question is said to take two forms. The first regards the "adjustment of means to ends," and the second is the adjustment of "governmental function to historical conditions." Administrators are responsible for discerning what the historical spirit demands and for moving government accordingly. As in the "Study," Wilson's understanding of administration in his lecture notes is grounded in historicism. In discussing administration as "adjustment," Wilson noted that in order to keep administration up to date, bureaucrats must take into account the evolving and prevailing understanding of liberty.[56] He made clear that there is no transhistorical basis for law or regulation. The tasks of the state, which are carried out by administration, come from history. These tasks, Wilson explained, "the State has had laid upon it by reason of its history, through Law, which is the product of history."[57] This adjustment of administration to the evolving historical spirit makes administration organic. Administration is not, Wilson said, "a mere study of forms, but a study of the intimate principles of state life, of the minute tissue, the muscular and nervous system, of gov[ernmen]t."[58]

The connection between Wilson's administrative theory and historicism requires some further explanation, because some identify the theory not with historicism but with scientific positivism. Paul Eidelberg, for example, contends that Wilson's separation of politics and administration displays a neutrality toward the ends of government, thus making the whole scheme positivistic and morally relativistic.[59] Yet while Eidelberg properly demonstrates the departure in this approach from the political theory of the American founding, Wilson was no positivist, as Charles Kesler helps to explain. While it is the case that the science of administration was to be imported without regard to the regime form of its source, Wilson's argument for administration does not have the "value-free" quality of positivism. Rather, Wilson had great faith in history, and he believed that history had brought — or was bringing — the American nation to a definite ethical endpoint. The purpose of administration for Wilson is not to administer *any* political goal, but *the* political goal as he saw it (and self-defined it) at the end of history. As Kesler elaborates:

> Underlying and bridging the dichotomy [between politics and administration] was his faith that history was progressive, was good. Both politics and administration served the cause of progress — the one through leadership, sounding the trumpet of advance; the other through pacifying and reorganizing the newly won territory. For that reason, administration was not as "value-free" or "value-neutral" as Wilson and the reformers let on. In truth, the administrative class was intrinsically hostile to anyone who did not accept the rationale of its own existence, namely, the progressive theory of history.[60]

Werner J. Dannhauser's discussion of the differences between the bureaucratic theories of Hegel and Max Weber is useful in understanding the historicism of Wilson's administrative vision. For Hegel and historicism, bureaucracy is rational; it is part of history's rational end, which is what makes it legitimate. For Weber and positivism, the connection between bureaucracy and some higher notion of reason is not made. "The Hegelian state is part of an even grander rationality, a cosmos," Dannhauser explains. "Where Hegel finds rational order, Weber discerns only chaos."[61] In almost every instance where Wilson wrote about administration, he was careful to connect it to the demands of history and to argue that administration would understand itself only in light of the ethical content of the historical spirit.

This duty of administration to discern the historical spirit requires certain expert qualities, and it is here that Wilson repeated and confirmed an important theme from his "Study." Those who are to be charged with "adjusting" government to the evolving demands of history must be sufficiently educated and expert both to see what history demands and to know the proper means for adjusting the government accordingly. This is why Wilson said that the professional civil service must have three qualities: technical training, competitive examinations, and life tenure. As to the first, Wilson explained that modern government is complex; finding the specific means to adjust government to prevailing historical conditions therefore requires expertise. And without life tenure, the civil service will lack the job security that will be required to attract the most qualified professionals. Even more important, bureaucrats need to be free from self-interested considerations about their job security so that they can focus on the general interest. In this respect, Wilson attacked the writing of Gneist for suggesting that the bureaucracy ought to be accountable to party politics.[62] Wilson defended the insulation of the bureaucracy from political accountability with precisely the same kind of argument that Rohr employs in defense of the modern American administrative state. The bureaucracy, Wilson contended, is genuinely representative of the people—not because it subjects itself to popular election but because its membership is open to all classes of society. "Unquestionably," Wilson claimed, "the only sure and safe way to bring [accountability] is to draw the administrative personnel of the government by some free and open process from out of the general body of the nation, without preferring in the selection one class or order of society or blood or condition to another." Yet in spite of this openness to all classes of society, Wilson conceded that those awarded bureaucratic positions would naturally be those with an elite education. This system remains fundamentally "popular" as long as the competition for administrative positions remains, de jure, open to all.[63]

Wilson also repeated and confirmed the main principle of the "Study"— that administrative power exists independently of the Constitution. The Constitution, Wilson explained in his lecture notes, neither creates nor empowers administration. Rather, administration is a legitimate power that exists in any state. A constitution may limit or define the administrative sphere, but it does not originate or legitimize it. He elaborated:

> "Constitutionality" does not alter the nature of the (historical) State . . . the scope of Administration is, in every case, all the necessary and characteristic functions of the State, largely defined and regulated and always limited, as a matter of fact, by the laws, to which it is of course subject; but serving the State, not the law-making body in the State, and possessing a life not resident in the statutes.[64]

Wilson's notes made clear that the state creates the constitution, not vice versa. Therefore, administration does not answer to a specific, formal institution, but to the state itself, of which it is an essential part. Administration and the constitution are on a separate but equal footing with regard to the state.

Administration as Public Law

Wilson's lecture notes demonstrate that he did not view the separation of politics and administration in terms nearly so strict as those he had employed in the "Study." Several scholars note this difference,[65] which leads many of them to argue that it shows Wilson to be less radical than the "Study" makes him appear. But there is another way to think about this difference. Wilson did not see the separation between politics and administration so strictly precisely because he envisioned an enlarged orbit for administrative activity—one where administration would become responsible for several functions that had traditionally come within the sphere of politics. In particular, as his lecture notes indicate, Wilson understood that administration would—de facto if not de jure—come to take over the formerly political function of making law. As Kesler explains, the nature of law itself changes as history guides the nation from its constitutional stage into its administrative stage. In prior stages of development, lawmaking was based on political choices made between competing opinions or interests. But because history had since settled the question of political justice, the new task for law was to determine the particular means required to achieve the ends that were now determined. This historical development made law primarily administrative in character, not political.[66] As Wilson envisioned it, administration was to do what legislation had formerly done. This is why the key development of Wilson's lecture notes is that they put administration in terms of *public law*—the exact terms used in the modern administrative state to describe administrative policymaking.

Wilson's lecture notes emphasize that administration results from key historical developments—developments that had led administration to cross over into what had formerly been the exclusive province of politics. He mentions ways in which modern administration makes what had traditionally been legislative or judicial decisions. Administration, he says, makes law in an "essential" way, even if it does not have the constitutional sanction to do so in a "formal" way. Therefore, Wilson concludes, "Administration is indirectly a constant source of public law."[67] He lists "administrative law" as one of the principal sources of "public law," on an equal footing with international law, constitutional law, and civil and criminal law.[68] At one point, Wilson seems to confine administration, saying that it is "limited on many sides by Constitutional law." But as he proceeds to define administrative law, it becomes clear that its scope is strikingly broad:

The Question of the Functions of Government: Upon this ground constitutional and administrative theory meet, and enjoy possession in common. In a sense legislation and constituent law must determine the functions of government; and yet, looked at from another point of view, the functions of government are in a very real sense *independent of legislation, and even of constitutions*, because [they are] as old as government and inherent in its very nature. The bulk and complex minuteness of our positive law, which covers almost every case that can arise in Administration, obscures for us the fact that *Administration cannot wait upon legislation, but must be given leave, or take it, to proceed without specific warrant in giving effect to the characteristic life of the state*.[69]

This construction leads to several relevant conclusions. First, Wilson did not believe that constitutions or forms tell us much about government. Since administration is defined as adjustment to changing historical conditions, and since government must take its cue from the evolution of these conditions, it was only natural for Wilson to say that administration must in some ways define the function of government independent of constitutions. Second, administration takes its cue not only from formal law but also from its interpretation of custom. Custom is an expression of the organic spirit of the nation, and this spirit guides the bureaucracy's administration of progress. Finally, the latter part of the quotation certainly sounds the traditional language of prerogative (as Locke defines it, "doing public good without a rule"[70]), but in this case it is prerogative not for an elected executive but for an unelected bureaucracy. Indeed, Wilson conceded this point subsequently in the notes, when he addressed the "relation of the question to Prerogative." Wilson expanded upon this idea by making clear that administration need not rely for its jurisdiction upon a specific constitutional or statutory grant of authority. Instead of this traditional framework of republicanism, where the state may exercise only those powers granted to it by the people through the constitution, here Wilson explained the radically distinct doctrine that administration may do anything that is not expressly forbidden by the law. While he conceded that American government, unfortunately. had not yet adopted his understanding of the administrative sphere, "In the case of the Historically Normal Government, we may say that, in the absence of specific legal developments to the contrary, the presumption is in favor of the principle, that the sphere of administrative authority is as wide as the sphere in which it may move without infringing the laws."[71]

Ultimately, to the question of whether or not Wilson backed away from his claim in the "Study" that politics and administration are to be strictly separate, the answer is both yes and no. It is "yes" insofar as Wilson clearly envisioned administration's taking responsibility for many functions that had formerly been considered the exclusive province of politics. That is, the separation of politics and administration is muddied somewhat for the purpose of enlarging the orbit of administrative responsibility. The answer to the question is "no" insofar as Wilson did not negate his desire to grant independence and discretion to administrative officers.[72] In other words, to the extent that Wilson saw overlap between administration and politics, the overlap was not for the purpose of giving politics more control over the bureaucracy. Wilson remained, instead, consistent in his contention that administrators must be insulated from political influence in order to make decisions that reflect the general interest.

WILSON AS FOUNDER OF PUBLIC ADMINISTRATION?

Because Wilson's administrative writings were among the first in America to emphasize the distinction between politics and administration, Wilson is a central figure in the development of the discipline of public administration. Indeed, no one denies that Wilson's work makes him a seminal figure in the understanding of public administration as a separate and distinct discipline of study. But there is a debate over Wilson's place in the discipline. Some consider him its founder; this claim would be supported by the fact that Wilson's "Study" seems to have been the first American work to advocate the study of administration as a separate discipline. Others argue that he is not the founder of public administration, either because they see contemporary public administration as so divergent from Wilson's understanding that he cannot be considered part of the same movement[73] or because the discipline's roots reach back much earlier.[74] It is certainly not within the scope of this book to analyze in substance the various sides of this lively debate in the public administration literature—in one sense, we learn enough about the seriousness of Wilson's separation between politics and administration by the very fact that he is considered so important a figure in the public administration discipline. The chapter will conclude, however, with a brief consideration of some of the points in this debate to the extent that they help to further illuminate the main principles of Wilson's administrative theory.

   The doctrine of separation between politics and administration, emphasized in Wilson's "Study," was developed soon thereafter by Goodnow in his book *Politics and Administration*. It was subsequently carried on by the likes of Leonard D. White and W. F. Willoughby.[75] Goodnow taught municipal government and administrative law at Columbia while Wilson was teaching at Bryn Mawr, Wesleyan, and Princeton. In addition to *Politics and Administration* (1900), Goodnow published *Comparative Administrative Law* (1893) and *The Principles of Administrative Law in the United States* (1905), all works that were heavily influenced by Goodnow's study in Germany. A student of Goodnow's at Columbia, Ernest Freund, also studied in Germany and went on to publish one of the first administrative law casebooks.[76]

Wilson's politics-administration dichotomy is cited by those, like Link, who consider Wilson to be the founder of public administration in the United States. Wilson, remarks Link, "is rightfully to be regarded as the pioneer in and father of the study of administration in the United States."[77] White, himself a seminal figure in public administration, agrees that Wilson initiated the American version of the discipline. Indeed, one can see in White's understanding of the nature and origin of public administration the Wilsonian concept that administration does not fit well within the constitutional separation-of-powers arrangement. One also sees Wilson in White's assertion that history had brought the nation to an age of administration: "Students of public affairs are gradually discerning, in fact, that administration has become the heart of the modern problem of government." This is contrasted with "an earlier age," when legislatures had the time to manage the relatively small amount of problems that demanded their attention. "The role of administration in the modern state," White continues, "is profoundly affected by the general political and cultural environment of the age." And he credits Wilson with being the first to discern that administration was the defining characteristic of modern government.[78] Even in a much later publication, White maintains Wilson's status as the originator of the discipline in America: Wilson's study, White writes, was "the first recognition of the field of public administration as an object of study."[79]

However, there are scholars, like Lynton K. Caldwell, who are more cautious. Caldwell contends that "the actual influence of [Wilson's] essay is hard to assess." He points out that the "Study" is not tightly reasoned and that it fails to make specific suggestions as to how its principles might be implemented institutionally. This characteristic makes connecting the essay to subsequent, more concrete developments in public administration somewhat difficult, although Caldwell concedes that the essay "contained the seeds of almost every issue that has arisen regarding academic organization for the study of public administration. In it argument can be found for almost every intellectual position that has grown out of the ensuing debates."[80] Daniel W. Martin admits that Wilson's "Study" certainly influenced the development of public administration, but he contends that this influence did not come until at least the 1930s. Around the turn of the century, Martin claims, Americans who worked on public administration went directly to the European sources from which Wilson himself had drawn. Since Wilson's interpretations of these Europeans are often unreliable, Martin is cautious about crediting Wilson with too much influence on the origins of the discipline in America. He does agree, however, that Wilson became important to public administration practitioners in the 1930s because he offered them an attractive ideal: isolation or independence from politics.[81] Van Riper concurs with Martin that administrative works around the turn of the century do not cite Wilson, but from this omission draws the sharper conclusion that "any connection between Wilson's essay and the later development of the discipline is pure fantasy!"[82]

Whatever the truth is about the extent of Wilson's role in founding the public administration discipline, it is clear that in the post–World War II era the discipline did depart from some key Wilsonian tenets. Led by Herbert A. Simon, public administration scholars criticized Wilson's politics-administration dichotomy from the perspective of positivism, claiming that the distinction did not allow administration to be sufficiently scientific or "value-free."[83] This critique can be understood in light of my earlier point that Wilson's conception of administration, while distinct from politics, is not "value-free." That is, it is informed by historicism, not positivism, and therefore conceives of administration as carrying out the ethical mandates of history. The post–World War II critics discern this feature as well, and it is for this reason that they critique Wilson's dichotomy as insufficiently scientific. It is at this point, under Simon and his disciples, that public administration (and with it much of the study of politics in America) takes a decidedly positivistic and Weberian turn.[84] Wilson, of course, is not entirely blameless for this turn; he is responsible both for suggesting that politics and administration can somehow be separated, and for cutting politics and administration off from any transhistorical idea of ethics. Once this is done, it is not a huge conceptual leap for Simon to cut administration off from ethics altogether and to be left with an essentially pointless administrative science.[85] This is why the "turn" taken by the post–World War II criticism of Wilson can easily be overblown, and the wrong lessons can be drawn from it. While arguing about the finer points of distinction with regard to Wilson's politics-administration dichotomy may be of a certain scholarly value in the field of public administration, those of us interested in the development of American political thought cannot be distracted from the basic point that such argumentation poses the danger of obscuring. That basic point is that Wilson's distinction between politics and administration played a critical role in the development of the modern administrative state and, consequently, in the transformation of traditional American thinking about the means and ends of republican government.

NOTES

1. Kent A. Kirwan addresses the tension between Wilson's drive to make government more popular and his desire to see the best rule through administration. See Kirwan, "Historicism and Statesmanship in the Reform Argument of Woodrow Wilson," *Interpretation* (September 1981): 343, 346–48.

2. Niels Aage Thorsen, *The Political Thought of Woodrow Wilson 1875–1910* (Princeton: Princeton University Press, 1988), 11.

3. "Shorthand Diary," June 16, 1876, in Arthur S. Link, ed., *The Papers of Woodrow Wilson* (hereafter cited as *PWW*), 69 vols. (Princeton: Princeton University Press, 1966–1993), 1:142. Quotations from Wilson's writings will be modernized as necessary for grammar and spelling. Emphasis will be in the original unless otherwise specified. See also William Diamond, *The Economic Thought of Woodrow Wilson* (Baltimore: The Johns Hopkins University Press, 1943), 16–17, where Diamond connects Wilson's disgust over the impurity of politics to his religious background.

4. Wilson, *The State* (Boston: D. C. Heath, 1889), 564.

5. "The 'Courtesy of the Senate,'" November 15, 1885, in *PWW* 5:44–45, 48. Wilson also connected this problem to the municipal appointment power of mayors and the corruption that results from the involvement of city council members. As Stephen Skowronek explains, one of the reasons why President Wilson vetoed the Budget Act was that it gave Congress too much control over appointments. See Skowronek, *Building a New American State: The Expansion of National Administrative Capacities, 1877–1920* (Cambridge: Cambridge University Press, 1982), 207.

6. Daniel D. Stid, *The President as Statesman: Woodrow Wilson and the Constitution* (Lawrence: University Press of Kansas, 1998), 16.

7. Herbert J. Storing, "Political Parties and the Bureaucracy," in *Toward a More Perfect Union: Writings of Herbert J. Storing*, ed. Joseph M. Bessette (Washington, DC: AEI Press, 1995), 312–13. Originally published 1964.

8. "What Can Be Done for Constitutional Liberty: Letters from a Southern Young Man to Southern Young Men," March 21, 1881, in *PWW* 2:33.

9. "What Can Be Done for Constitutional Liberty," in *PWW* 2:34–36.

10. "Editorial, *The Princetonian*," May 24, 1877, in *PWW* 1:267. See also "True Scholarship," May 24, 1877, in *PWW* 1:269. Thorsen has a somewhat different view; he contends that Wilson—unlike the Germans—did not want to train technicians for the bureaucracy. See Thorsen, *Political Thought of Woodrow Wilson*, 187. I do not assert that Wilson advocated a narrowly technical university training—at least not at the undergraduate level. But I do assert that Wilson saw as the purpose of university education the training of young men for service in national administration. While he was clear at several points that undergraduate education needed to be broad and "literary," it is also the case that he believed that graduate education required greater specialization. For another account of the place Wilson gave to the university in his theory of administration, see Lynton K. Caldwell, "Public Administration and the Universities: A Half-Century of Development," *Public Administration Review* 25:1 (1965): 53.

11. Arthur S. Link, "Woodrow Wilson and the Study of Administration," in *The Higher Realism of Woodrow Wilson and Other Essays* (Nashville, TN: Vanderbilt University Press, 1971), 40.

12. "Editorial, *The Princetonian*," January 10, 1878, in *PWW* 1:336.

13. Wilson, *Congressional Government* (1885; repr., New York: Meridian Books, 1956), 170.

14. "An Address to the Princeton Alumni of New York" (lecture, New York, NY, March 23, 1886), in *PWW* 5:137–41.

15. Wilson was also spotlighting municipal reform, and at least part of that focus sprang from his work on administration. Wilson believed that a key historical development was

that cities were now understood to be administrative organs of the centralized state. City government was appealing to Wilson because he was interested in administration—and the primary purpose of cities in modern democracy is to administer. See, for example, "Systems of Municipal Organization," March 2, 1888, in *PWW* 5:697–705; "Report of a Commencement Address," June 27, 1890, in *PWW* 6:677–78.

16. Link, "Wilson and the Study of Administration," 39. Link, editorial note, in *PWW* 5:43. Both Thorsen and Henry A. Turner contend that Bagehot cannot be discounted as an important influence on Wilson's administrative writings. Thorsen points to Wilson's long quotation from Bagehot at the beginning of the "Study" (a quotation that Wilson attributes to Bagehot's "Essay on Sir William Pitt," when its true source is Bagehot's "The Character of Sir Robert Peel") as evidence of Bagehot's importance to the essay. Thorsen, *Political Thought of Woodrow Wilson*, 122. Turner connects Wilson's earlier writings on Congress, which were obviously influenced by Bagehot, to his subsequent writings on administration. Turner rightly notes that Wilson's vision for reforming Congress anticipates the enlarged role for administration that he outlines in "The Study." Turner, "Woodrow Wilson as Administrator," *Public Administration Review* 16:4 (1956): 249–50.

17. Link, "Wilson and the Study of Administration," 38–39. See also Daniel W. Martin, "The Fading Legacy of Woodrow Wilson," *Public Administration Review* 48 (March/April 1988): 633. Wilson's essay originally appeared in *Political Science Quarterly* 2 (June 1887): 197–222; it was later reprinted in the same journal, vol. 55 (December 1941): 481–506. Richard J. Stillman notes that the "Study" first appeared in print in 1887, six years prior to the first American textbook on administration—Frank Goodnow's *Comparative Administrative Law* (1893). See Stillman, "Woodrow Wilson and the Study of Administration: A New Look at an Old Essay," *American Political Science Review* 67 (June 1973): 585–86 (see note 23).

18. "The Study of Administration," November 1886, in *PWW* 5:370–71.

19. "Government by Debate," December 1882, in *PWW* 2:224.

20. Jameson W. Doig's interpretation of the "Study" contends that the essay envisions "large powers" for administration. Doig, "'If I See a Murderous Fellow Sharpening a Knife Cleverly . . .': The Wilsonian Dichotomy and the Public Authority Tradition," *Public Administration Review* 43 (July/August 1983): 292–304, esp. 294.

21. "Study of Administration," in *PWW* 5:372–73.

22. "Study of Administration," in *PWW* 5:360.

23. "Study of Administration," in *PWW* 5:361–62.

24. "Study of Administration," in *PWW* 5:365.

25. "Study of Administration," in *PWW* 5:370.

26. See G. W. F. Hegel, *Philosophy of Right*, trans. T. M. Knox (Oxford: Oxford University Press, 1967), 191–92.

27. Storing, "Political Parties and the Bureaucracy," 312.

28. Robert D. Miewald, "The Origins of Wilson's Thought: The German Tradition and the Organic State," in *Politics and Administration: Woodrow Wilson and American Public Administration*, ed. Jack Rabin and James S. Bowman (New York: Marcel Dekker, 1984), 18–19, 27. On the connection between German state theory and the immunity of Wilson's administrators from self-interest, see also Deil S. Wright, "A Century of the Intergovernmental Administrative State: Wilson's Federalism, New Deal Intergovernmental Relations, and Contemporary Intergovernmental Management," in *A Centennial History of the American Administrative State*, ed. Ralph Clark Chandler (New York: The Free Press, 1987), 224.

29. "Study of Administration," in *PWW* 5:374–75.

30. "Study of Administration," in *PWW* 5:368.

31. "Study of Administration," in *PWW* 5:376.

32. "Study of Administration," in *PWW* 5:368.

33. "Study of Administration," in *PWW* 5:375.

34. Paul Eidelberg also notes that Wilson's political science teachings are "markedly different" from those he espoused as a public figure, particularly with regard to administration. Eidelberg, *A Discourse on Statesmanship: The Design and Transformation of the American Polity* (Urbana: University of Illinois Press, 1974), 291.

35. "Study of Administration," in *PWW* 5:363.

36. "Study of Administration," in *PWW* 5:371.

37. "Notes for Lectures at the Johns Hopkins," January 26, 1891, in *PWW* 7:118–20.

38. "Study of Administration," in *PWW* 5:378.

39. "Notes on Administration," November 15, 1885, in *PWW* 5:50. Thorsen takes a much more benign view of Wilson's "Study" than the one I present here, but even he is critical of Wilson's assertion that foreign administrative systems can be adopted seamlessly into a republican political order. What Wilson asks, Thorsen reasons, is for citizens to suppress their political judgment of foreign administrative systems—they "must suppress knowledge about the ends of the action that is being observed." Thorsen, *Political Thought of Woodrow Wilson*, 130. Kent A. Kirwan is even more direct: "The tendency of his reform, grounded on the separation of administration from politics, is irresponsibility. . . . Is it not true that to separate administration from the liberal principles of American government is identical with resting it on what in practice are illiberal principles of government? Wilson's reformed civil service is but a thinly veiled replica of the Prussian civil service under Baron Stein, which he holds up for emulation. Proceeding on the assumption that administration is separable from politics, Wilson ends up with the practical result of an administrative system antithetical to the dominant principles of American politics." Kirwan, "The Crisis of Identity in the Study of Public Administration: Woodrow Wilson," *Polity* 9 (Spring 1977): 335–36.

40. "Study of Administration," in *PWW* 5:377.

41. Miewald, "Origins of Wilson's Thought," 21–22. See also Martin, "Fading Legacy of Woodrow Wilson," esp. 633; Kirwan, "Crisis of Identity," 331.

42. "Notes for Lectures," in *PWW* 7:122.

43. "Notes for Lectures," in *PWW* 7:134–38.

44. "Study of Administration," in *PWW* 5:371.

45. John A. Rohr, "The Constitutional World of Woodrow Wilson," in Rabin and Bowman, eds., *Politics and Administration*, 43–44.

46. John A. Rohr, "The Administrative State and Constitutional Principle," in Chandler, ed., *A Centennial History*, 116–20, 124.

47. Rohr, "The Administrative State and Constitutional Principle," 143–49.

48. Publius, *The Federalist Papers*, ed. Charles R. Kesler and Clinton Rossiter (New York: Mentor, 1999), 52:295.

49. Herbert J. Storing, "American Statesmanship: Old and New," in *Toward a More Perfect Union*, 412–14. In another article, Storing connects the founders with the modern administrative state by noting that an antipartisan spirit animated both the founders and the civil service reformers. The implication is that the insulation of administration from politics, at least in certain respects, helps to fulfill an intention of the founding generation.

"While the [civil service] reformers did not seek to eradicate parties," Storing writes, "they were, like the American founders, keenly aware that 'party spirit, from the first, has been the terror of republics.'" Storing, "Political Parties and the Bureaucracy," 308–9. Werner J. Dannhauser, crediting Storing, makes a similar argument, suggesting that the party system and the bureaucracy check each other, and that this checking is consistent with the founders' intent. Dannhauser, "Reflections on Statesmanship and Bureaucracy," in *Bureaucrats, Policy Analysts, Statesmen: Who Leads?* ed. Robert A. Goldwin (Washington, DC: AEI Press, 1980), 122.

50. Paul P. Van Riper, "The American Administrative State: Wilson and the Founders—An Unorthodox View," *Public Administration Review* 43 (November/December 1983): 479–80.

51. *Federalist* 68:382. For further explanation on the differences between Wilson and Hamilton, see Sidney M. Milkis, *The President and the Parties: The Transformation of the American Party System Since the New Deal* (New York: Oxford University Press, 1993), 25; David E. Marion, "Alexander Hamilton and Woodrow Wilson on the Spirit and Form of a Responsible Republican Government," *Review of Politics* 42:3 (July 1980): 309–27; Scot J. Zentner, "Liberalism and Executive Power: Woodrow Wilson and the American Founders," *Polity* 26:4 (Summer 1994): 593.

52. Link, "Wilson and the Study of Administration," 41. See also Stillman, "Wilson and the Study of Administration," 587 (note 27).

53. "Marginal Notes on Otto von Sarwey," December 1, 1889, in *PWW* 6:432–50, 464–66, 469–70.

54. "A Working Bibliography," March 27, 1890, in *PWW* 6:563–64, 568, 572–74, 586.

55. See, for example, "Notes for Lectures on Public Law," September 22, 1894, in *PWW* 9:28–39.

56. "Notes for Lectures," in *PWW* 7:116. See also "Notes for Lectures at the Johns Hopkins," February 1, 1892, in *PWW* 7:383.

57. "Notes for Lectures," in *PWW* 7:382.

58. "Notes for Lectures," in *PWW* 7:394.

59. Eidelberg, *Discourse on Statesmanship*, 300–302. For a further discussion of the positivistic and historicist elements of Wilson's administrative theory, see Kirwan, "Crisis of Identity," esp. 326, 330.

60. Charles R. Kesler, "Separation of Powers and the Administrative State," in *The Imperial Congress*, ed. Gordon S. Jones and John A. Marini (New York: Pharos Books, 1988), 36–37.

61. Dannhauser, "Statesmanship and Bureaucracy," 124. For a further discussion of Wilson's connection to Weber, as well as the important distinctions between the two, see Robert D. Cuff, "Wilson and Weber: Bourgeois Critics in an Organized Age," *Public Administration Review* 38 (May/June 1978): 241–42.

62. "Notes for Lectures," in *PWW* 7:391–93.

63. "Notes for Lectures in a Course on Constitutional Government," September 19, 1998, in *PWW* 11:21–24.

64. "Notes for Lectures," in *PWW* 7:128–29. This is repeated, nearly verbatim, in the second series of lectures: *PWW* 7:382.

65. Kirwan, "Crisis of Identity," 332; Larry Walker, "Woodrow Wilson, Progressive Reform, and Public Administration," *Political Science Quarterly* 104:3 (1989): 511; John M. Mulder, *Woodrow Wilson: The Years of Preparation* (Princeton: Princeton University

Press, 1978), 118; Phillip J. Cooper, "The Wilsonian Dichotomy in Administrative Law," in Rabin and Bowman, eds., *Politics and Administration*, 79–94; Kendrick A. Clements, "Woodrow Wilson and Administrative Reform," *Presidential Studies Quarterly* 28:2 (Spring 1998): 320–36. Clements even suggests that Wilson's previous assertion of a strict separation between politics and administration "was not really what he meant to say" (322).

66. Kesler, "Separation of Powers," 35. For Thorsen's interpretation of Wilson on this point, see Thorsen, *Political Thought of Woodrow Wilson*, 134–35.

67. "Notes for Lectures," in *PWW* 7:136–38. See also "Notes for Lectures on Administration," February 3, 1890, in *PWW* 6:485, where Wilson relied on Jellinek's *Gesetz und Verordnung* in asserting that "Administration is *itself a source of law* (Ordinance) i.e. of the *detail* of law." See also "Notes for Lectures," in *PWW* 7:114–15.

68. "Notes for Lectures," in *PWW* 7:120.

69. "Notes for Lectures," 7:121. Emphasis added. Wilson repeats this, nearly verbatim, in his notes for the second series of lectures: *PWW* 7:382.

70. John Locke, *Second Treatise of Government*, sec. 166.

71. "Notes for Lectures," in *PWW* 7:147–50. This construction is repeated in "Notes for Lectures on Public Law," September 22, 1894, in *PWW* 9:40. Several scholars see in Wilson's administrative thinking a development favoring the enlargement of the discretionary powers of the bureaucracy: Doig, "Wilsonian Dichotomy," 294–301; Miewald, "Origins of Wilson's Thought," 23–25. Clements also seems to fall into this category, although he suggests that an expansion of administrative discretion was not what Wilson really intended. Wilson, according to Clements, had reservations about granting so much independence to administrators, but he was ultimately not able to find a method to rein it in. Even Clements recognizes that Wilson's administrative principles—whether Wilson liked it or not—greatly broadened the scope of administrative discretion. See Clements, "Wilson and Administrative Reform," 321; Clements, *The Presidency of Woodrow Wilson* (Lawrence: University Press of Kansas, 1992), 6–7.

72. Some scholars have argued that once Wilson became president, he resisted granting significant new powers to national administration. See, for example, Cuff, "Wilson and Weber," 243. My own view is that the evidence from Wilson's presidency indicates otherwise, as I will argue in the book's conclusion.

73. Clements traces the different pieces of scholarship on Wilson's place in the public administration discipline. See Clements, "Wilson and Administrative Reform," 333–34 (note 1).

74. See, for example, Mark R. Rutgers, "Beyond Woodrow Wilson: The Identity of the Study of Public Administration in Historical Perspective," *Administration and Society* 29:3 (July 1997): 276–300.

75. Kirwan, "Crisis of Identity," 322; Frederick C. Mosher, *Democracy and the Public Service* (New York: Oxford University Press, 1968), 69.

76. Cooper, "The Wilsonian Dichotomy," 87–89. Wilson's role in the genesis of this movement is laid out by Nicholas Henry, who points to five paradigms in the intellectual development of public administration. Wilson is identified with the first paradigm, the politics-administration dichotomy. Nicholas Henry, "The Emergence of Public Administration as a Field of Study," in Chandler, ed., *A Centennial History*, 37–85.

77. Link, "Wilson and the Study of Administration," 44.

78. Leonard D. White, *Introduction to the Study of Administration* (New York: Macmillan, 1929), 5–9.

79. Leonard D. White, *The Republican Era: 1869–1901* (New York: Macmillan, 1958), 319, 396. Other scholars identifying Wilson as the founder—or at least the launching point—of public administration in America are Larry Walker and Vincent Ostrom. See Walker, "Progressive Reform and Public Administration," esp. 512, 518–20, 524–25; Ostrom, *The Intellectual Crisis in American Public Administration* (University: University of Alabama Press, 1973), 23–26, 30–33. See also Turner, "Wilson as Administrator," 251; Louis Brownlow, "Woodrow Wilson and Public Administration," *Public Administration Review* 16 (1956): 81; Wallace S. Sayre, "Premises of Public Administration: Past and Emerging," *Public Administration Review* 18:2 (1958): 102; Raymond Seidelmann and Edward J. Harpham, *Disenchanted Realists: Political Science and the American Crisis, 1884–1984* (Albany: State University of New York Press, 1985), 55. In addition to these sources on Wilson's role as the founder of American public administration, Ferrel Heady points to Wilson's pioneering role in the field of comparative public administration. Ferrel Heady, "Comparative Public Administration in the United States," in Chandler, ed., *A Centennial History*, 487.

80. Caldwell, "Public Administration and the Universities," 53. See also 54–58.

81. Martin, "Fading Legacy of Woodrow Wilson," 632–35.

82. Van Riper, "American Administrative State," 479.

83. See, for example, Herbert A. Simon, *Administrative Behavior*, 2nd ed. (New York: Macmillan, 1958), 52, 56–58. For scholarly treatments of Simon's departure, see Kirwan, "Crisis of Identity," 323–25, 341–42; Dwight Waldo, "Public Administration," *The Journal of Politics* 30:2 (May 1968): 443, 447, 449–50.

84. Ostrom connects Simon's critique to Weber's value-free positivism. Ostrom, *Intellectual Crisis*, 8.

85. Storing has a very useful critique of the fact-value distinction as it comes to be applied to public administration. See Storing, "The Science of Administration: Herbert A. Simon," in *Essays on the Scientific Study of Politics*, ed. Storing (New York: Holt, Rinehart and Winston, 1962), 149–50.

Conclusion

1912 and Beyond

The thesis of this book has been that Wilson was a central figure in progressivism's fundamental rethinking of traditional American constitutionalism. This argument runs contrary to that portion of the historical scholarship on Wilson that characterizes him as a constitutional conservative. The view that Wilson was a defender of traditional constitutionalism, one who resisted the expansion of national power that other prominent progressives advocated, takes two distinct forms in the scholarly literature. The first of these arguments is made by those who see Wilson as a fairly consistent conservative throughout his life; these interpreters often cast him as a Jeffersonian defender of his native South and the prerogatives of the states against the federal government.[1] The second of these arguments is made by those who concede that Wilson, as president, embarked upon a marked expansion of federal power; yet it is contended that this turn toward statism represents a major departure from the previous constitutionalism of Wilson's political thought.[2] There are also some important exceptions to the scholarly interpretation of Wilson as a defender of traditional constitutionalism.[3] Several of these, although not all, have come in the field of political theory;[4] most of them have profited from Arthur Link's publication of Wilson's papers, which give a much more complete picture of Wilson's academic thinking than was previously available. Indeed, Link's own interpretation of Wilson seems to have undergone significant development as a consequence of his work on the papers.[5]

My own work has endeavored to uncover Wilson's sharp critique of traditional American constitutionalism. As the first two chapters illustrated, Wilson was an early critic of the political theory on which the American Constitution was built and he sought to replace the founders' understanding of government with one much more in line with German state theory—particularly that of Hegel. Chapters 4 through 6 detailed Wilson's comprehensive critique of the Constitution itself—his plan for fundamentally altering the institutional design of 1787. And chapter 7 explained Wilson's desire to import a foreign administrative science into America, one that Wilson himself admitted did not fall within the sphere of traditional American constitutional thinking. Wilson, in fact, believed that history had brought America to a point where administration would come to the fore, and he knew that the exercise of administrative powers as he envisioned them did not derive from the Constitution's granting of power to the national government.

As for the claim that Wilson—either early on or throughout his career—was a defender of states' prerogatives and a proponent of federalism,[6] the examination of his understanding of American history in chapter 3 shows just the opposite to be true. While some have argued that Wilson's historical writings reveal a defense of traditional constitutionalism, those writings actually comport with Wilson's progressive statism. He wrote that American history had been a process of moving away from the original condition of states' rights and federalism, and toward our coming together as a single nation. Accordingly, progress had overcome the defenders of limited government and the defenders of states' rights. Wilson's histories are replete with criticisms of those who attempted to prevent progress and rein in the growing power of the central government.

In addition to the arguments that have been made in the book thus far, the question of Wilson's constitutionalism requires at least some consideration of 1912 and beyond. The New Freedom campaign is especially critical, because Wilson's program is often cast as a defense of limited government against the more overtly paternalistic New Nationalism program of Theodore Roosevelt, especially with regard to the question of expanding national administrative power. In the eyes of those who concede that Wilson's presidency embraced such an expansion of national administrative power, the Wilson of 1913 underwent a remarkable transformation from the Wilson of 1912, and some suggest that the conversion was undertaken only with great reluctance. The book will conclude by returning to the observation made in the introduction that what united Wilson and Roosevelt was far more substantial than what divided them, and that what united them has much to teach us about Wilson's thought and the thought of his day.

THE NEW FREEDOM

During the 1912 New Freedom campaign, Wilson was critical of the discretionary administrative power that Roosevelt proposed to grant to independent regulatory agencies. Wilson also delivered an oft-cited address to the New

York Press Club, where he proclaimed that "the history of liberty is the history of the limitation of governmental power."[7] Statements such as this lead many historians to see a genuine and principled difference in the 1912 campaign between Wilson's "conservative" New Freedom program and the New Nationalism program espoused by his rival Roosevelt, even while some allow that—once elected—President Wilson governed very much like a New Nationalist.[8]

Wilson's rhetoric on liberty, however, needs to be placed in the context of the political principles that he consistently espoused in his large corpus of work. As this book has endeavored to demonstrate, Wilson's call to unfetter the national government was not a philosophy to which he turned after 1912, but was in fact the premise of many of his most important writings at every stage of his career. Even Wilson's statement that "the history of liberty is the history of the limitation of governmental power" is not inconsistent with the overall theme of his thought. He continually took an historicist's view of liberty, where liberty has different meanings in different epochs. This outlook becomes clear, as previously indicated, in his interpretation of the Declaration of Independence, which suggests to Wilson that each generation is to determine the current form of liberty. Liberty has no permanent nature; instead, it has a history of evolving meaning. It was certainly the case, as Wilson said often about the American founding, that the history of liberty *had been* one of limiting the power of government. It was also the case that Wilson devoted substantial portions of his writing to urging an abandonment of this older, narrower understanding and an adoption of one more in keeping with the needs of modern society. As he made clear in *The State*, concern for individual liberty can never permanently limit or define the role of government: "*Government does now whatever experience permits or the times demand.*"[9] That Wilson would, in his presidency, embrace an expansion of national administrative power should not be seen as a sudden change; he wrote *The State* in 1889, and even then that work was built upon principles that Wilson had formed in earlier works. Furthermore, as John Wells Davidson points out, Wilson quickly made sure to qualify what he meant by his "history of liberty" remarks. Wilson sought, in particular, to counter the Roosevelt campaign's attempt to paint him as a Jeffersonian on the basis of those remarks.[10] Two weeks after his famous New York Press Club address, Wilson clarified his discussion of the scope of government:

> While we are followers of Jefferson, there is one principle of Jefferson's which no longer can obtain in the practical politics of America. You know that it was Jefferson who said that the best government is that which does as little governing as possible. . . . But that time is passed. America is not now and cannot in the future be a place for unrestricted individual enterprise.[11]

And Wilson made clear in *The New Freedom* that "freedom today is some-thing more than being let alone. The program of a government of freedom must in these days be positive, not negative merely."[12] Jeffersonian limited government may have constituted the *history* of liberty in America, but it played no part in Wilson's vision of America's future.

In general, Wilson's remarks on Jefferson and Jeffersonianism follow the same pattern as his remarks on the principles of the Declaration of Independence: that is, the principles ought to be followed, insofar as we are able to adjust them to accord with new historical conditions. The New Freedom campaign, in particular, often referred to Jefferson in the context of "updating" his ideas to fit modern times, and frequently noted that conditions in the early twentieth century were not what they were during Jefferson's own age. Wilson stated, for example, that

> we used to say that the ideal of government was for every man to be left alone
> and not interfered with, except when he interfered with somebody else; and that
> the best government was the government that did as little governing as possible.
> That was the idea that obtained in Jefferson's time. But we are coming now to
> realize that life is so complicated that we are not dealing with the old condi-
> tions.[13]

America could not, for instance, treat the labor question from the original Jeffersonian perspective of limited government. "The treatment of labor by the great corporations," Wilson explained, "is not what it was in Jefferson's time."[14]

We must also recall that Wilson had the same fundamental objection to Jefferson as he did to the natural-rights theory that Jefferson employed in the Declaration. Jefferson, after all, subscribed to the very social compact doctrine that Wilson considered to be the antithesis of the proper, historically contingent understanding of the scope and ends of government. Jefferson drew his understanding of the ends of government from the transhistorical "laws of nature and nature's God."[15] Wilson said at one point that such thinking was "un-American," and he defined the essence of Americanism as a willingness to adjust political principles to correspond with the evolving spirit of history. As Wilson elaborated in a passage I cited in chapter 1: "It is [Jefferson's] speculative philosophy that is exotic, and that runs like a false and artificial note through all his thought. It was un-American in being abstract, sentimental, and rationalistic, rather than practical. That he held it sincerely need not be doubted; but the more sincerely he accepted it so much the more thoroughly was he un-American."[16] When Wilson referred to Jefferson's "speculative philosophy," he meant, in particular, the natural-rights theory of the Declaration of Independence, and he implied that the Declaration itself was "un-American."

What, then, did Wilson mean in 1912 when he sought to employ a "Jeffersonian" solution to the problem of trusts? Wilson used Jeffersonianism to criticize both socialism and corporations in America. He argued that under both socialism and American corporate structure, the individual could hide within a larger organization. Regarding trust policy, this meant that U.S. law allowed individuals to escape legal responsibility for their own misdeeds, and he advocated changing the law to hold specific corporate officers responsible for specific illegal acts. This is what Wilson called Jeffersonian individualism: not a fixed understanding of the scope of government, but rather holding individuals directly accountable for unfair business practices.[17] Wilson also employed the term *Jeffersonian* as an alternative to Roosevelt's call for regulating business with administrative commissions. Wilson's "Jeffersonian" solution was instead to prosecute individually those who were identified as engaging in unfair practices.[18] Finally, Wilson did fashion himself as a Jeffersonian of sorts in his criticism of Roosevelt's plan for "big government."[19] But this criticism was short-lived, and clearly did not involve a restoration of the original Jeffersonian idea of individual liberty achieved by way of strict, constitutional limitations on the power of the state.

As to the 1912 campaign and Wilson's apparent opposition to the expansion of national administrative power, it was not as if Wilson had long opposed empowering regulatory agencies. First, Wilson was on record as a supporter of the Interstate Commerce Commission. We see this support in *Division and Reunion*, where Wilson argues that new conditions in the latter part of the nineteenth century justified the expansion of federal power into the economy. He remarks that "this Interstate Commerce Commission speedily became one of the most important tribunals of the country, administering the provisions of the law with both firmness and discretion, to the fortunate correction of many abuses."[20]

Second, and more important, Wilson's record as governor of New Jersey reveals his explicit endorsement of granting significant, independent power to regulatory agencies. Link's history shows that Wilson's 1911 legislative program was revolutionary in its regulatory apparatus and the discretionary power that it gave to regulators.[21] In particular, the public-utilities regulation (or Osborne-Egan Bill), which was one of Wilson's major legislative objectives, contained all of the provisions desired by the most aggressive progressives and was "one of the most thoroughgoing public utilities statutes in the country at the time." The law created a regulatory board empowered with broad discretion to fix rates. As Link describes it,

> the act created a board of three public utility commissioners, to be appointed by the governor with the consent of the Senate. . . . A "public utility" was defined by the statute as any individual, partnership, association, or joint-stock corporation that owned or operated in New Jersey any steam railroad, street railway, traction railway, canal, express company, subway system, pipe line, gas, electric light, heat, power, water, oil, sewer, telephone, or telegraph system, plant, or equipment for public use.

The powers of this commission were to "fix just and reasonable rates," to "set standards of service for electric companies," and to "order suspension of announced increases in rates." As Link summarizes: "A series of prohibitions against the activities of public utilities virtually gave the commission control over the financial transactions of all companies."[22] And Wilson was not merely a passive agent in signing this and other important pieces of legislation into law; quite to the contrary, Wilson was an active participant and in firm control of the Democratic majority in the legislature and the agenda enacted by it.

Wilson's New Jersey program was a model for progressives around the country—a program Wilson implemented just before his "conservative" campaign of 1912 and his subsequent "conversion" to the progressive policies of the New Nationalists upon assuming the presidency. As Kendrick Clements observes, the New Jersey program was itself modeled after Robert LaFollette's famous progressive agenda in Wisconsin.[23] Wilson himself made clear that he considered his New Jersey program to be a sharp departure from the traditionally conservative policies of the Democratic Party, and it was designed to appeal just as much to progressive Republicans as to progressive elements within his own party.[24] As he explained in reference to his election as governor, "It was no Democratic victory. It was a victory of the 'progressives' of both parties, who are determined to live no longer under either of the political organizations that have controlled the two parties of the State."[25] Wilson championed New Jersey's Geran Bill to establish direct primaries, and he repeatedly urged the legislature to ratify the Sixteenth Amendment to the U.S. Constitution. Of the latter, Wilson admitted that the states would be ceding power to the federal government but concluded that "it is clearly in the interest of the national life that the power should be conceded. It will free the government of the United States to put its fiscal policy upon a much more enlightened, a much more modern, a much more elastic basis than it now rests upon."[26]

Regarding the 1912 campaign itself, where Wilson criticized Roosevelt's New Nationalism and its call for expanding national administrative power, several practical matters merit consideration. Wilson's aim, naturally, was to win the election. And as the evidence from his 1910 gubernatorial race amply shows, in order to win office he was willing to use means that might contradict his own political principles; once elected, he would be in a position to put those principles into practice. Consider the point made by Clements, who reminds us that in spite of his general calls for businessmen to be held more individually accountable for their misdeeds, Wilson had developed no specific policy on the trust question prior to his nomination. Instead, Wilson designed his antitrust program in 1912 with the aim of distinguishing himself as clearly as possible from his main opponent.[27] And Wilson was effectively silent on the trust question prior to 1907 and 1908, which is when he began to seriously contemplate a future in politics and the corresponding need to carve out a unique position for himself in the national political debate. Consider also Wilson's clear dependence in 1912 on the Bryan wing of the Democratic Party. It took forty-six ballots for Wilson to win the party's nomination, and that occurred only after the intervention of Bryan in his favor.[28] Central to Bryan's populism was a fear of national executive power and a deep distrust of business interests in the Northeast. By campaigning against Roosevelt's plan to maintain the business trusts by bringing them into a regulatory relationship with the national government, Wilson certainly solidified his position with the Bryan Democrats who were essential to his victory. Once elected, Wilson lost little time in backtracking from those expedient campaign positions that had not been grounded in his own, long-held political principles. Wilson quickly disowned, for example, a plank of the Democratic platform—inserted under the influence of Bryan—that called for a single, six-year presidential term.[29] Certainly such a proposal was inconsistent with Wilson's advocacy of strong presidential leadership—a position that had been well established since the 1908 publication of *Constitutional Government*. And Wilson's early legislative program ended up embracing and putting into practice much of the New Nationalist agenda, including the very expansion of national administrative power that he had criticized in the campaign.[30]

WILSON'S PRESIDENCY

Advocates of national administration did indeed have much to be pleased about during Wilson's presidency. His record, as George E. Mowry writes, was "worthy of any reformer and . . . exceedingly embarrassing to the Progressive Party. Wilson had stolen its thunder and much of its excuse for being."[31] In a detailed account of President Wilson's legislative agenda, Larry Walker and Jeremy F. Plant conclude that "the domestic role of the national government was greatly enlarged, several new national administrative agencies were created, and the number of administrative personnel engaged in domestic programs of the national government was increased greatly." All of these conditions came about because "Wilson shared the Progressive conviction that the national government should be used as an active instrument of social progress through the exercise of regulatory powers." This conviction manifested itself in several key pieces of regulatory legislation: the Federal Reserve Act (1913), Federal Trade Commission Act (1914), Clayton Antitrust Act (1914), Shipping Act (1916), Keating-Owens Act (1916), Child Labor

Tax Act (1919), Transportation Act (1920), and Federal Water Power Act (1920).[32]

Much of this increased national regulatory power came at the expense of the states. Particularly revealing is the manner in which several major grants-in-aid programs from the national government to the states were administered. The grant programs had the effect of removing power from state legislatures and governors, and transferring that power to independent administrative boards or agencies. With the road-construction assistance laws of 1916, for example, recipient states were for the first time in history required by the federal government to establish a separate agency (a highway department or commission) to receive and administer the funds. Federal law stipulated that these administrative commissions—not the governor or the legislature—were to be empowered to select specific projects for funding. In another example, the Smith-Hughes Act of 1917 created the Federal Board for Vocational Education, which was given broad power to establish uniform national standards for vocational education, and to enforce those standards by withholding grant funds from noncomplying states. States were also required to establish their own administrative commissions in order to remove the fund-distribution power from the legislature or governor. As Walker and Plant summarize, the Wilson agenda initiated "close national supervision of program implementation at the state level . . . which concomitantly reduced the scope of the policy discretion enjoyed by state officials."[33]

Perhaps the most significant instance of Wilson's empowerment of the federal government was his successful campaign for passage of the Underwood Tariff Bill—a bill that enacted the first national income tax. Interestingly, many historical treatments of the tariff bill place relatively little emphasis on its income tax provision.[34] The income tax did, after all, establish for the first time that the federal government was to direct income redistribution around the country.[35] The overall logic of the Underwood legislation was to reduce protective tariffs and make up for the lost revenue with the income tax. Wilson had long opposed protective tariffs, at least partly because they favored the business interests of the Northeast over the agricultural interests of the South. Wilson had no problem with tariffs as a tool for raising revenue; he simply opposed them to the extent that the revenue-raising mechanism favored certain pet industries.[36] Wilson's opposition to the tariffs of the federal government has often been pointed to as an example of his prosouthern, anti–big government Jeffersonianism. He had at one point even characterized the federal government's tax power as a threat to the liberties of the people.[37] But this did not mean that Wilson was opposed to the tax power of the federal government. Rather, Wilson criticized the tariff because it was largely a secret tax—the people would not pay it directly but only indirectly through the increased prices of consumer goods. So Wilson's critique of the tariff was grounded in his call for "openness" in government—this is why he had no difficulty embracing the federal income tax.[38]

While acknowledging the marked increase in the scope of the federal government under Wilson, and especially the increase in national administrative power, some scholars contend that Wilson consented reluctantly to these measures. According to this argument, circumstances made unavoidable Wilson's expansion of national administration—an expansion that otherwise undercut Wilson's New Freedom platform. Clements, for example, concedes that "virtually all of the major reforms of Wilson's period relied on professional administrators for their implementation." Yet he maintains that this was "less deliberate choice than an admission that since it was impossible to specify in legislation all the practices that were to be regulated or banned, there was no alternative to trusting administrators." Clements also points to wartime mobilization as an extraordinary circumstance that pushed Wilson into a further expansion of national administration.[39] This is an argument echoed by Daniel Stid, who also contends that in 1916 Wilson embraced much of the New Nationalism out of political expedience (the Democrats had fared badly in the 1914 midterm elections).[40] With regard to the argument on wartime mobilization, Robert H. Wiebe makes the important point that national administrative power had already been expanded quite significantly prior to the onset of war; war preparation simply had the effect of revealing just how bureaucratized American national government had already become.[41] Furthermore, the contention that deference to national administration was something that Wilson reluctantly accepted in the face of certain circumstances during his presidency does not seem to hold up in light of what Wilson had been writing as far back as the 1880s. It was in *Congressional Government* (1885), after all, that Wilson noted the complexity of modern government and urged Congress to abandon its legislative function in deference to the expertise of modern administration. And it was in "The Study of Administration" (1886) that Wilson called for the empowerment of national administration and the insulation of that administration from the political sphere. So President Wilson's turn to discretionary national administration did not represent a radical break from a vision of government to which he had long subscribed.

This point helps to show why the debate over Wilson's presidency has often been cast in the wrong terms. Wilson's inauguration is frequently seen as the "turning point" that marked Wilson's move from conservatism to progressivism. Wilson did, after all, employ Jeffersonian rhetoric in critiquing Roosevelt's New Nationalism in the 1912 campaign, and then turned around as president and embraced the very policies for which he had attacked Roosevelt. But given Wilson's lifelong embrace of progressive principles, it seems more accurate to understand the 1912 New Freedom campaign as an anomaly.[42] Wilson did indeed act in the face of political expediency, but the political expediency was the need, in 1912, to downplay the progressivism to which he had long subscribed. Once elected and freed of this necessity, Wilson reverted to and pursued policies that flowed quite logically from the large corpus of work on the principles of government that he had developed over the course of thirty years.[43]

WILSON'S SELF-UNDERSTANDING

In favoring an expansion of national power and in questioning the traditional, limited government constitutionalism of the founding, Wilson was by no means a conservative. It is important to note, however, that he did reflect on the meaning of "conservatism," and that he did, with some justification, fancy himself a conservative in the Burkean sense. That is, Wilson shared Burke's antipathy toward the place of abstract theory in politics. It was a form of organicist conservatism that led Wilson to reject the founding-era proposition that individual natural rights can somehow permanently define or limit the ends of government. For Wilson, any reference to abstract political ideas was fundamentally dangerous and revolutionary. This is why Wilson often equated the American Revolution with the French Revolution, and it is why he consistently expressed a preference for British government, which had gradually developed out of an organic constitutional tradition. The purpose and scope of government, Wilson believed, could be defined only by the demands of the time, and thus were subject to evolve along with the march of history. So for Wilson, conservatism meant embracing continuous change in the political order—but it was to be gradual, evolutionary change.[44]

It is ironic that today many conservatives, like Wilson, look to Burke as a guiding figure in their political thinking. Unlike those modern conservatives who rely on Burke, however, Wilson saw no conflict between the organic, Burkean conservatism he claimed to admire, and the advocacy of a wholesale departure from traditional American constitutionalism. This perspective helps to explain why Wilson owed less to Burke[45] and others in the generally conservative English Historical School and more to the idealistic and utopian brand of historicism in the Hegelian tradition.

POSTSCRIPT ON WILSON'S INTERNATIONALISM

In the book as a whole, and in chapter 2 in particular, I have characterized Wilson's political science as a product of "realism"—a doctrine, grounded in historical thinking, that eschews universal ideals and contends instead that politics must be guided by the evolving and concrete realities pertaining to particular peoples or nations. Such is the basis for Wilson's discomfort with the abstract theory of the Declaration of Independence or, indeed, with any set of principles that claims to transcend the particulars of historical development.

Yet a big part of the story for Wilson in the years beyond 1912 was his leadership in America's involvement in World War I and his championing the cause of internationalism at the conclusion of the war. Wilson's leadership here is commonly understood to be antithetical to realism, embracing instead a universal vision of democratic government for all nations and peoples. There is no doubt that it is this principle for which Wilson is most well known today, and a good argument can be made that American foreign policy is still very much driven by these Wilsonian ideas. While Wilson's writings on the theory of the state and on the principles of constitutionalism are often not well known outside of certain scholarly circles, his "Fourteen Points," or the precepts of his war message to Congress, are widely circulated and studied. In 1917, he famously called upon Congress to declare war because "the world must be made safe for democracy." In pursuing this aim, America was not a self-interested actor but was instead "one of the champions of the rights of mankind." Wilson explained that "we have no selfish ends to serve. We desire no conquest, no dominion. We seek no indemnities for ourselves, no material compensation for the sacrifices we shall freely make."[46] Wilson repeated this thinking when he outlined the road map for peace in a program of fourteen points, which called for "a general association of nations" founded on the "principle of justice" for "all peoples and nationalities, and their right to live on equal terms of liberty and safety with one another."[47] Such statements lend themselves to the assumption that Wilson owed less to Hegel and more to the idealism of Immanuel Kant, who seemed to call for just such a universal order.[48]

Since this book focuses on Wilson's political and constitutional thinking, which he developed long before he entered into public life, it is well beyond its scope to treat the question of Wilson's internationalism with any depth. Indeed, while relatively few works have been written on Wilson's political thought, a great many works have been written on Wilson's leadership in the international arena. But since Wilson's internationalism is certainly relevant to my argument that Wilson was a Hegelian, it is possible to say at least something about the connection between the two topics and to make some suggestions for further reflection.

The most important point is that there was not as sharp a discontinuity between Wilson's historical thinking and his foreign policy as might initially seem to be the case. Some of Wilson's earliest reflections upon American foreign policy were, in fact, grounded in concepts of historicity and realism. The best example of this is probably Wilson's set of observations on the conclusion of the Spanish-American War: in 1901 he used a speech entitled "The Ideals of America" to comment on American policy toward Cuba and the Philippines. Taking the opportunity presented by the 125th anniversary of the Battle of Trenton, Wilson began his foreign policy remarks by first reminding Americans of how it was that they came to acquire the practice of self-government. He argued that they had not acquired democratic government by simply declaring their independence and establishing a legal framework in the Constitution of 1787. Real democratic government in America had, instead, developed gradually over the course of more than 100 years; democratic government had become perfected in America not by the imposition of a form or idea, but by the gradual process of historical development. This is what distinguished democracy in America from attempts at democracy in France, and he used this contrast to warn those who were too ready to impose the American model on the Philippines:

> Have they, then, forgot that tragic contrast upon which the world gazed in the days when our Washington was President: on the one side of the sea, in America, peace [and] ordered government . . . on the other, in France, a nation frenzied, distempered, seeking it knew not what . . . .[49]

The historical conditions in America were such that the people were prepared for self-government, Wilson contended. He cited Burke's defense of the colonies to this effect, and used Burke's words to make his general point that "the general character and situation of a people must determine what sort of government is fit for them"[50]—a point perfectly consistent with Wilson's historical understanding of government as it has been laid out in this book.

Insofar as self-government was not something for which the American people grasped but was, instead, something for which history prepared them, the American Revolution was not, strictly speaking, a revolution at all. The English Crown was denying to the Americans that for which the time was ripe, so the founders, Wilson explained, were "a generation, not of revolutionists, but of statesmen. They fought, not to pull down, but to preserve,—not for some fair and far-off thing they wished for, but for a familiar thing they had and meant to keep."[51] In colonial practice the Americans had gradually established a tradition of self-governing institutions, and the British Crown sought to turn back the clock and deny Americans the self-government that was historically inevitable. Just as America would soon become the beacon for democracy around the world, Wilson explained, revolutionary America was really a beacon for democratic development in all of England. "It turned out," he reasoned, "that the long struggle in America had been the first act in the drama whose end and culmination should be the final establishment of constitutional government for England and for English communities everywhere."[52] The English people as a whole—including the Americans—had been prepared by history for self-government. America was simply leading the way for all of England toward that for which the time was ripe. So here, as later, Wilson sees America as a beacon for democracy, but only insofar as history has brought about the proper conditions for democratic government.

This understanding of the origins of American democracy served as the foundation for the policy Wilson advocated with respect to Cuba and the Philippines. Both nations, he explained, deserved America's assistance in developing self-government, when "they are ready."[53] The Filipinos had to undertake the slow process of historical development before America could grant self-government—"they can have liberty no cheaper than we got it," as Wilson put it. "They are children and we are men in these deep matters of government and justice." Being further along in the process of democracy's development, America would be wise to wait for the proper historical conditions in the Philippines. Wilson warned against any policy that would attempt to impose democracy too soon:

> There are, unhappily, some indications that we have ourselves yet to learn the things we would teach. You have but to think of the large number of persons of your own kith and acquaintance who have for the past two years been demanding . . . that we give the Philippines independence and self-government now, at once, out of hand. It were easy enough to give them independence, if by independence you mean only disconnection with any government outside the islands, the independence of a rudderless boat adrift. But self-government? How is that "given"? *Can* it be given? Is it not gained, earned, graduated into from the hard school of life?[54]

And so if America were to serve as a beacon of democracy for other nations, it must be as an example of the kind of historical conditions that must be in place in order for self-government to function properly and permanently.

There are certain elements of this more concrete approach in Wilson's later foreign policy as president. As Wilson had explained in his theory of the state, government must reflect the historically conditioned will of the people. When in his 1917 war speech to Congress he railed against autocracy, Wilson employed the same approach: "The menace to peace and freedom," he explained, "lies in the existence of autocratic governments backed by organized force which is controlled wholly by their will, not by the will of their people."[55] Russia served as Wilson's example here. As strange as it may seem in hindsight, he rejoiced at developments in Russia because he saw in them democracy coming to a people who had been historically prepared for it:

> Russia was known by those who knew it best to have been always in fact democratic at heart, in all the vital habits of her thought, in all the intimate relationships of her people that spoke their mutual instinct, their habitual attitude towards life. The autocracy that crowned the summit of her political structure, long as it had stood and terrible as was the reality of its power, was not in fact Russian in origin, character, or purpose.[56]

As was the case with his 1901 remarks on the history of colonial America, Wilson here endorsed democratic "revolution" as the arrival of something for which the time was ripe—as history matching up democratic government with the right set of conditions.

That Wilson also took leave of this more concrete approach to foreign policy as he led America through war and peace is undeniable. This may be because Wilson was quite inexperienced in foreign affairs and, as someone who had spent his life thinking and writing about American domestic politics, was unprepared for the role in which world events would thrust him. Indeed, this departure from the very consistent historicity and realism of his political thinking may have much to do with explaining the tragic nature of Wilson's last years in office.

But it is also important, finally, to be clear about what Wilson did and did not have in mind when he conceived of the League of Nations. The idealistic rhetoric notwithstanding, Wilson did not contemplate a form of world government along the lines of the United Nations. In particular, he was not ready to turn over American foreign policy—or the direction of international affairs generally—to some assemblage of nations that would not be dominated by American or at least Western leadership. And herein lies the potential connection of even Wilson's postwar diplomacy to his long-held historicism. As Wilson explained in his writings on state theory, there are advanced peoples and there are those who are further behind in the march of progress. And as he explained in his commentary on Cuba and the Philippines, the American people—and the English race generally—were on the forefront of historical development. Just as America had once served as a beacon for the English race in the march toward the ultimate democracy, so too would the peoples of the West, who were out in front on the path of historical development, lead the postwar international order.

NOTES

1. See, for example, E. David Cronon's introduction to *The Political Thought of Woodrow Wilson*, ed. Cronon (Indianapolis: The Bobbs-Merrill Company, Inc., 1965), xlv. Cronon writes there that "in politics Wilson was by inheritance and inclination a Jeffersonian states'-rights Democrat. He feared the concentration of power, whether in private or government hands, and preferred to leave authority widely dispersed among local and state governments." George E. Mowry also characterizes Wilson as "espousing the tenets of Jeffersonian liberalism." See Mowry's *Theodore Roosevelt and the Progressive Movement* (New York: Hill and Wang, 1960), 277. And Eldon J. Eisenach blames Wilson for derailing the progressive movement. Wilson, according to Eisenach, was a conservative who opposed the expansion of national power, particularly in his unwillingness to read liberally the Constitution's commerce clause—this was a "reactionary" stance that countered "more than two decades of economic teaching in America exposing the moral bankruptcy and intellectual absurdity of laissez faire as a national economic policy." See Eisenach's *The Lost Promise of Progressivism* (Lawrence: University Press of Kansas, 1994), 125. See also Charles Noble, "The Political Origins of the Modern American State," *Comparative Politics* 17 (April 1985): 313–36, esp. 325.

2. See, for example, George W. Ruiz, "The Ideological Convergence of Theodore Roosevelt and Woodrow Wilson," *Presidential Studies Quarterly* 19 (Winter 1989): 159–77; David Steigerwald, "The Synthetic Politics of Woodrow Wilson," *Journal of the History of Ideas* 50 (July/September 1989): 465–84; William Diamond, *The Economic Thought of Woodrow Wilson* (Baltimore: The Johns Hopkins University Press, 1943), 87; John J. Broesamle, "The Democrats from Bryan to Wilson," in *The Progressive Era*, ed. Lewis L. Gould (Syracuse, NY: Syracuse University Press, 1974), 105; Harry Clor, "Woodrow Wilson," in *American Political Thought: The Philosophic Dimensions of American Statesmanship*, ed. Morton J. Frisch and Richard G. Stevens (1971; repr., Dubuque, IA: Kendall/Hunt, 1976), 206–8.

3. See Kendrick A. Clements, *The Presidency of Woodrow Wilson* (Lawrence: University Press of Kansas, 1992), 2–3, who suggests that those seeing Wilson as an advocate of limited government "have missed his stress upon progress." See also Niels Aage Thorsen, who writes: "Historians who see Wilson as a nostalgic man who longed for the return of a political state of innocence or an economic state of Jeffersonian yeomanry have missed the point that it was the overcoming of the past, not its repetition, which made *progress* such a prominent term in his historical writing" (emphasis in original). Thorsen, *The Political Thought of Woodrow Wilson 1875–1910* (Princeton: Princeton University Press, 1988), 219. See Henry Wilkinson Bragdon, *Woodrow Wilson: The Academic Years* (Cambridge, MA: Belknap Press, 1967), 197: Wilson's "later alleged 'conversion' to progressivism did not mark an unprecedented shift to the left but continued a point of view he had earlier expressed." See also Larry Walker, "Woodrow Wilson, Progressive Reform, and Public Administration," *Political Science Quarterly* 104:3 (1989): 509–25; Martin J. Sklar, *The United States as a Developing Country* (Cambridge: Cambridge University Press, 1992), 111–12.

4. See James W. Ceaser, Glen E. Thurow, Jeffrey Tulis, and Joseph M. Bessette, "The Rise of the Rhetorical Presidency," *Presidential Studies Quarterly* 11 (Spring 1981): 158–71; Ceaser, *Presidential Selection: Theory and Development* (Princeton: Princeton University Press, 1979), esp. 170–212; Tulis, *The Rhetorical Presidency* (Princeton:

Princeton University Press, 1987), esp. 118–32; Paul Eidelberg, *A Discourse on States-manship* (Urbana: University of Illinois Press, 1974), esp. 279–362; Robert Eden, *Political Leadership and Nihilism* (Tampa: University of South Florida Press, 1983); Eden, "Opinion Leadership and the Problem of Executive Power: Woodrow Wilson's Original Position," *Review of Politics* 57 (Summer 1995): 483–503; Eden, "The Rhetorical Presidency and the Eclipse of Executive Power: Woodrow Wilson's *Constitutional Government in the United States*," *Polity* 18:3 (Spring 1996): 357–78; Charles R. Kesler, "Separation of Politics and the Administrative State," in *The Imperial Congress*, ed. Gordon S. Jones and John A. Marini (New York: Pharos Books, 1988), 20–40; and Kesler, "The Public Philosophy of the New Freedom and the New Deal," in *The New Deal and Its Legacy*, ed. Eden (New York: Greenwood Press, 1989), 155–66.

5. In an early history, Arthur S. Link contrasts Wilson's defense of laissez faire to the more aggressive elements of the progressive movement, and characterizes Wilson as a states'-rights conservative in *Wilson: The Road to the White House* (Princeton: Princeton University Press, 1947), 241. Wilson's later embrace of strong national government leads Link to conclude that "Wilson's political thought simply cannot be studied as a whole. There are too many incongruities, too many contradictions" (31). In a more recent essay, however, Link appears to reject his earlier characterization of Wilson as a supporter of states' rights; see Link, "Woodrow Wilson: The American as Southerner," *The Journal of Southern History* 36:1 (February 1970): 3–17.

6. For an account of the scholarly literature on the question of Wilson and federalism, see chapter 3, note 45. On this question, see also Anthony Gaughan, "Woodrow Wilson and the Legacy of the Civil War," *Civil War History* 43:3 (1977): 225–42.

7. "Address to the New York Press Club" (lecture, September 9, 1912), in Arthur S. Link, ed., *The Papers of Woodrow Wilson* (hereafter cited as *PWW*), 69 vols. (Princeton: Princeton University Press, 1966–1993), 25:124. Quotations from Wilson's writings will be modernized as necessary for grammar and spelling. Emphasis will be in the original unless otherwise specified.

8. Sidney M. Milkis, in a recent essay, points to the emphasis on the local community as a distinguishing characteristic of the New Freedom's brand of progressivism: "Progressivism, Then and Now," introduction to *Progressivism and the New Democracy*, ed. Milkis and Jerome M. Mileur (Amherst: University of Massachusetts Press, 1999), 1–39, esp. 10. In his book *Political Parties and Constitutional Government* (Baltimore: The Johns Hopkins University Press, 1999), Milkis places Wilson among those "many reformers [who] were profoundly uneasy about the prospect of expanding national administrative power" (47). But this seems somewhat of a change from Milkis's earlier work in *The President and the Parties* (New York: Oxford University Press, 1993), where he acknowledges that the real differences between Roosevelt and Wilson were not terribly significant. He writes that the differences in 1912 "were more a matter of emphasis than fundamental philosophical dispute. Wilson's political writings and his two terms as president reveal that he shared the view of 'new nationalists' that Jefferson's commitment to limited government was no longer compatible with individual liberty" (22).

9, Wilson, *The State* (Boston: D. C. Heath, 1889), 651.

10. John Wells Davidson, "Wilson in the Campaign of 1912," in *The Philosophy and Policies of Woodrow Wilson*, ed. Earl Latham (Chicago: University of Chicago Press, 1958), 88–91.

11. "A Campaign Address in Scranton, Pennsylvania" (lecture, Scranton, PA, September 23, 1912), in *PWW* 25:222.

12. Wilson, *The New Freedom* (New York: Doubleday, Page, 1913), 284.

13. *The New Freedom*, 20.

14. *The New Freedom*, 22–23.

15. Declaration of Independence, par. 1.

16. "A Calendar of Great Americans," September 15, 1893, in *PWW* 8:374.

17. "An Address on Thomas Jefferson" (lecture, April 16, 1906), in *PWW* 16:365–66.

18. "Law or Personal Power," April 13, 1908, in *PWW* 18:263–69.

19. See, for example, "The Authors and Signers of the Declaration of Independence," July 4, 1907, in *PWW* 17:248–59.

20. Wilson, *Division and Reunion: 1829–1889* (1893; repr., New York: Longmans, Green, 1901), 296.

21. Link, *Road to the White House*, 239–67.

22. Link, *Road to the White House*, 262. Link references here the *Laws of New Jersey*, 1911, chap. 195, 374–89. See also "A Statement on the Work of the New Jersey Legislative Session of 1911," April 22, 1911, in *PWW* 22:579.

23. Clements, *Presidency of Woodrow Wilson*, 23.

24. See, for example, Wilson to George Lawrence Record, October 24, 1910, in *PWW* 21:406–11.

25. Wilson to George Brinton McClellan Harvey, November 15, 1910, in *PWW* 22:47.

26. "To the Legislature of New Jersey," March 20, 1911, in *PWW* 22:511–12. See also "To the Senate of New Jersey," April 4, 1911, in *PWW* 22:534; "To the Legislature of New Jersey," February 26, 1912, in *PWW* 24:216–17.

27. Clements, *Presidency of Woodrow Wilson*, 27–28. Clements goes on to note that Wilson's alternative to regulating trusts, which was essentially to pass new antitrust legislation and engage in vigorous prosecution of particular violators, turned out to be quite vague. Wilson adviser Louis D. Brandeis found it difficult to draw up a specific list of business practices that would be defined as illegal, so the Wilson campaign fell back on general promises to punish businesses engaging in unfair activities. "The difference between that and Roosevelt's alleged paternalism," comments Clements, "was difficult to discern" (28).

28. For an argument on the role of the Bryan faction in Wilson's nomination, see Link, *Road to the White House*, 463–64. Link questions the assumption that Bryan's intervention was decisive in securing the nomination, nevertheless acknowledging the overall importance of Bryan to Wilson's 1912 campaign.

29. Wilson to Alexander Mitchell Palmer, February 5, 1913, in *PWW* 27:98–101. That Wilson distanced himself from this and other measures favored by populists should not be surprising. While New Freedom progressives are occasionally said to have populist roots, this was not the case, at least, for Wilson. From his earliest writings, Wilson expressed something approaching hatred and fear of populists, sentiments that were closely connected to his criticism of universal suffrage. See chapter 6.

30. For an overview of this program, and the delight it gave to New Nationalists, see Link, *Wilson: The New Freedom* (Princeton: Princeton University Press, 1956), 152–223, and Clements, *Presidency of Woodrow Wilson*, x.

31. Mowry, *Theodore Roosevelt and the Progressive Movement*, 287. See also Link, *The New Freedom*, 223.

32. Larry Walker and Jeremy F. Plant, "Woodrow Wilson and the Federal System," in *Politics and Administration: Woodrow Wilson and American Public Administration*, ed. Jack Rabin and James S. Bowman (New York: Marcel Dekker, 1984), 123–24.

33. Walker and Plant, "Woodrow Wilson and the Federal System," 125.

34. See, for example, Link, *The New Freedom*, 182–93. Of an entire chapter on the tariff legislation, Link devotes just a few pages to its income tax provisions. Clements's account is an exception, with Clements contending that the newly instituted income tax was clearly the most significant aspect of the law. Clements, *Presidency of Woodrow Wilson*, 39.

35. The Underwood legislation established a 1 percent "normal tax" on income, with the following surtaxes: 1 percent on $20,000 to $50,000, 2 percent on $50,000 to $75,000, 3 percent on $75,000 to $100,00, 4 percent on $100,000 to $250,000, 5 percent on $250,000 to $500,000, and 6 percent on incomes higher than $500,000. See Link, *The New Freedom*, 191–93.

36. See, for example, "Testimony before the Tariff Commission" (Atlanta, GA, September 23, 1882), in *PWW* 2:140–43.

37. "Government by Debate," December 1882, in *PWW* 2:188–89.

38. For additional examples of Wilson's critique of the tariff, see "Taxation and Appropriation," January 12, 1888, in *PWW* 5:653–55; "The Democratic Opportunity," November 1, 1909, in *PWW* 19:467.

39. Clements, "Woodrow Wilson and Administrative Reform," *Presidential Studies Quarterly* 28:2 (Spring 1998): 330–32.

40. Daniel D. Stid, *The President as Statesman: Woodrow Wilson and the Constitution* (Lawrence: University Press of Kansas, 1998), 109.

41. Robert H. Wiebe, *The Search for Order: 1877–1920* (New York: Hill and Wang, 1967), 293.

42. In *The Warrior and the Priest: Woodrow Wilson and Theodore Roosevelt* (Cambridge, MA: Belknap Press, 1983), John Milton Cooper Jr. implies that Wilson's "Jeffersonianism" of 1912 was somewhat of an anomaly. See 219.

43. Several pieces of scholarship support the argument that Wilson's expansion of national administrative power was not a radical departure from, but rather a natural continuation of, the corpus of political thought developed throughout his academic and political career. Thorsen, *Political Thought of Woodrow Wilson*, 195–97; Sklar, *The United States as a Developing Country*, 111–12; Wiebe, *The Search for Order*, 218–21; Donald R. Brand, *Corporatism and the Rule of Law: A Study of the National Recovery Administration* (Ithaca, NY: Cornell University Press, 1988), 66–67.

44. For Wilson's reflections on conservatism as evolutionary change, see, for example, Wilson, *Constitutional Government in the United States* (New York: Columbia University Press, 1908), 193–94; and "A Speech in St. Peter's Hall in Jersey City Opening the Campaign" (lecture, Jersey City, NJ, September 28, 1910), in *PWW* 21:191.

45. It should be noted that Wilson employed a somewhat selective interpretation of Burke. Wilson emphasized those writings of Burke that attack the role of abstract theory in politics, like *Reflections on the Revolution in France*, yet he ignored those occasions where Burke employed the argument of natural rights, as he did when he defended the American colonists as a member of Parliament.

46. "An Address to a Joint Session of Congress" (lecture, Washington, DC, April 2, 1917), in *PWW* 41:525.

47. "An Address to a Joint Session of Congress" (lecture, Washington, DC, January 8, 1918), in *PWW* 45:538–39.

48. Too much can be made of Wilson's alleged departure into Kantian idealism, since in principled terms Kantian and Hegelian thinking are related in important ways. Both

modes of thinking focus on willing the universal. For Kant, as demonstrated by the categorical imperative, the universal was to be willed not with reference to a particular political state but instead from the subjective principle of volition—the individual maxim. See Immanuel Kant, *Groundwork of the Metaphysic of Morals*, trans. H. J. Paton (New York: Harper & Row, 1964), 65–71. Hegel, too, focused on willing the universal, but did not believe that this could take place outside of the laws of his rational end-state. He therefore critiqued Kant's categorical imperative as excessively idealistic and unrealistic. Hegel wrote: "Such an abstraction as 'good for its own sake,' has no place in living reality. If men are to act, they must not only intend the Good, but must have decided for themselves whether this or that particular thing is a Good. What special course of action, however, is good or not, is determined, as regards the ordinary contingencies of private life, by the laws and customs of a State." G. W. F. Hegel, *The Philosophy of History*, trans. J. Sibree (New York: Dover, 1956), 28–29. Hegel put forth a doctrine that explained how history would bring about the ideal end through the concrete development of the state. The theme of this book has been that Wilson adopted this mode of thinking. Wilson's foreign policy seems to have been predicated on the assumption that America was at the forefront of history, and that, accordingly, it could serve as a beacon for those nations that were attempting to progress, on America's path, to the ultimate stage of democracy.

49. "The Ideals of America" (lecture, Trenton, NJ, December 26, 1901), in *PWW* 12:217. I am indebted to John W. Grant for suggesting this address to me.

50. "Ideals of America," in *PWW* 12:211–12.

51. "Ideals of America," in *PWW* 12:218.

52. "Ideals of America," in *PWW* 12:212.

53. "Ideals of America," in *PWW* 12:217.

54. "Ideals of America," in *PWW* 12:222–23.

55. "Address to Congress" (lecture, Washington, DC, April 2, 1917), in *PWW* 41:523.

56. "Address to Congress," April 2, 1917, in *PWW* 41:524.

Index

About the Author

Ronald J. Pestritto, Ph.D., is associate professor of politics at the University of Dallas, where he teaches graduate and undergraduate courses in political philosophy, American politics, and American political thought. He is also a research fellow of the Claremont Institute for the Study of Statesmanship and Political Philosophy. His previous books include *Founding the Criminal Law: Punishment and Political Thought in the Origins of America*.